Julius Bien & Co Lith. N.Y.

JAVANESE ILLUMINATED MANUSCRIPT.

The origin of the Oceanic dialects, and of those of India beyond the Ganges, more especially the civilized idioms of the Indian Archipelago, is referred to a language which was that of an unknown people inhabiting the island of Java. From this primitive language the modern Javanese is supposed to be immediately derived. Javanese literature consists of poems, dramas, songs, and historical and religious writings. The accompanying facsimile is from a mythological-religious tract written upon a vegetable paper of native manufacture, and ornamented with grotesque drawings.

LIBRARY OF THE

WORLD'S BEST LITERATURE

ANCIENT AND MODERN

CHARLES DUDLEY WARNER

EDITOR

HAMILTON WRIGHT MABIE   LUCIA GILBERT RUNKLE

GEORGE HENRY WARNER

ASSOCIATE EDITORS

Connoisseur Edition

VOL. XII.

NEW YORK

THE INTERNATIONAL SOCIETY

Connoisseur Edition

LIMITED TO FIVE HUNDRED COPIES IN BUCKRAM

No. 169

THE ADVISORY COUNCIL

TABLE OF CONTENTS

VOL. XII

FULL-PAGE ILLUSTRATIONS

VOLUME XII

VIGNETTE PORTRAITS

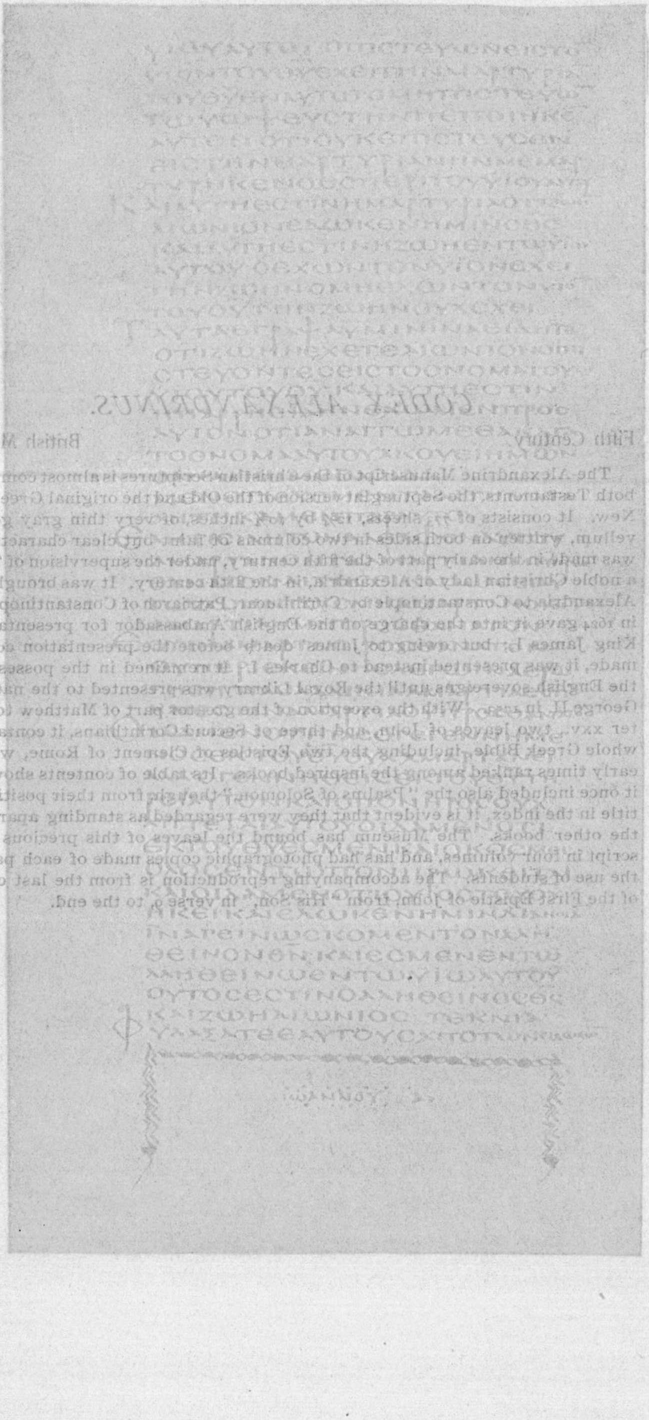

DENIS DIDEROT

(1713–1784)

Among the French Encyclopædists of the eighteenth century Denis Diderot holds the place of leader. There were intellects of broader scope and of much surer balance in that famous group, but none of such versatility, brilliancy, and outbursting force. To his associates he was a marvel and an inspiration.

He was born in October 1713, in Langres, Haute-Marne, France; and died in Paris July 31st, 1784. After a classical education in Jesuit schools, he utterly disgusted his father by turning to the Bohemian life of a littérateur in Paris. Although very poor, he married at the age of thirty. The whole story of his married life — the common Parisian story in those days — reflects no credit on him; though his *liaison* with Mademoiselle Voland presents the aspects of a friendship abiding through life. Poverty spurred him to exertion. Four days of work in 1746 are said to have produced 'Pensées Philosophiques' (Philosophic Thoughts). This book, with a little essay following it, 'Interprétation de la Nature,' was his first open attack on revealed religion. Its argument, though only negative, and keeping within the bounds of theism, foretokened a class of utterances which were frequent in Diderot's later years, and whose assurance of his materialistic atheism would be complete had they not been too exclamatory for settled conviction. He contents himself with glorifying the passions, to the annulling of all ethical standards. On this point at least his convictions were stable, for long afterward he writes thus to Mademoiselle Voland:—"The man of mediocre passion lives and dies like the brute. . . . If we were bound to choose between Racine, a bad husband, a bad father, a false friend, and a sublime poet, and Racine, good father, good husband, good friend, and dull worthy man, I hold to the first. Of Racine the bad man, what remains? Nothing. Of Racine the man of genius? The work is eternal."

Denis Diderot

About 1747 he produced an allegory, 'Promenade du Sceptique.' This French 'Pilgrim's Progress' scoffs at the Church of Rome for denying pleasure, then decries the pleasures of the world, and ends by asserting the hopeless uncertainty of the philosophy which both scoffs at the Church and decries worldly pleasure. At this period he was evidently inclined to an irregular attack on the only forms of Christianity familiar to him, asceticism and pietism.

In 1749 Diderot first showed himself a thinker of original power, in his Letter on the Blind. This work, 'Lettre sur les Aveugles à l'Usage de Ceux qui Voient' (Letter on the Blind for the Use of Those who See) opened the eyes of the public to Diderot's peculiar genius, and the eyes of the authorities to the menace in his principles. The result was his imprisonment, and from that the spread of his views. His offense was, that through his ingenious supposition of the mind deprived of its use of one or more of the bodily senses, he had shown the relativity of all man's conceptions, and had thence deduced the relativity, the lack of absoluteness, of all man's ethical standards — thus invalidating the foundations of civil and social order. The broad assertion that Diderot and his philosophic group caused the French Revolution has only this basis, that these men were among the omens of its advance, feeling its stir afar but not recognizing the coming earthquake. Yet it may be conceded that Diderot anticipated things great and strange; for his mind, although neither precise nor capable of sustained and systematic thought, was amazingly original in conception and powerful in grasp. The mist, blank to his brethren, seems to have wreathed itself into wonderful shapes to his eye; he was the seer whose wild enthusiasm caught the oracles from an inner shrine. A predictive power appears in his Letter on the Blind, where he imagines the blind taught to read by touch; and nineteenth-century hypotheses gleam dimly in his random guess at variability in organisms, and at survival of those best adapted to their environment.

Diderot's monumental work, 'L'Encyclopédie,' dates from the middle of the century. It was his own vast enlargement of Ephraim Chambers's Cyclopædia of 1727, of which a bookseller had demanded a revision in French. D'Alembert was secured as his colleague, and in 1751 the first volume appeared. The list of contributors includes most of the great contemporary names in French literature. From these, Diderot and D'Alembert gathered the inner group known as the French Encyclopædists, to whose writings has been ascribed a general tendency to destroy religion and to reconstitute society. The authorities interfered repeatedly, with threats and prohibitions of the publication; but the science of government included the science of connivance for an adequate consideration, and the great work went forward. Its danger lurked in its principles; for Diderot dealt but little in the cheap flattery which the modern demagogue addresses to the populace. D'Alembert, wearied by ten years of persecution, retired in 1759, leaving the indefatigable Diderot to struggle alone through seven years, composing and revising hundreds of articles, correcting proofs, supervising the unrivaled illustrations of the mechanic arts, while quieting the opposition of the authorities.

The Encyclopædia under Diderot followed no one philosophic path. Indeed, there are no signs that he ever gave any consideration to either the intellectual or the ethical force of consistency. His writing indicates his utter carelessness both as to the direction and as to the pace of his thought. He had an abiding conviction that Christianity was partly delusion and largely priestcraft, and was maintained chiefly for upholding iniquitous privilege. His antagonism was developed primarily from his emotions and sympathies rather than from his intellect; hence it sometimes swerved, drawing perilously near to formal orthodoxy. Moreover, this vivacious philosopher sometimes rambled into practical advice, and easily effervesced into fervid moralizings of the sentimental and almost tearful sort. His immense natural capacity for sentiment appears in his own account of his meeting with Grimm after a few months' absence. His sentimentalism, however, had its remarkable counterpoise in a most practical tendency of mind. In the Encyclopædia the interests of agriculture and of all branches of manufacture were treated with great fullness; and the reform of feudal abuses lingering in the laws of France was vigorously urged in a style more practical than cyclopædic.

Diderot gave much attention to the drama, and his 'Paradoxe sur le Comédien' (Paradox on the Actor) is a valuable discussion. He is the father of the modern domestic drama. His influence upon the dramatic literature of Germany was direct and immediate; it appeared in the plays of Lessing and Schiller, and much of Lessing's criticism was inspired by Diderot. His 'Père de Famille' (Family-Father) and 'Le Fils Naturel' (The Natural Son) marked the beginning of a new era in the history of the stage, in the midst of which we are now living. Breaking with the old traditions, Diderot abandoned the lofty themes of classic tragedy and portrayed the life of the *bourgeoisie.* The influence of England, frequently manifest in the work of the Encyclopædists, is evident also here. Richardson was then the chief force in fiction, and the sentimental element so characteristic in him reappears in the dramas of Diderot.

Goethe was strongly attracted by the genius of Diderot, and thought it worth his while not only to translate but to supply with a long and luminous commentary the latter's 'Essay on Painting.' It was by a singular trick of fortune, too, that one of Diderot's most powerful works should first have appeared in German garb, and not in the original French until after the author's death. A manuscript copy of the book chanced to fall into the hands of Goethe, who so greatly admired it that he at once translated, annotated, and published it. This was the famous dialogue 'Le Neveu de Rameau' (Rameau's Nephew), a work which only Diderot's peculiar genius could have produced. Depicting the typical parasite, shameless, quick-witted for every species of villainy, at home in every possible meanness, the dialogue is a probably unequaled compound of satire, high æsthetics, gleaming humor, sentimental moralizing, fine musical criticism, and scientific character analysis, with passages of brutal indecency.

Among literary critics of painting, Diderot has his place in the highest rank. His nine 'Salons'—criticisms which in his good-nature he wrote for the use of his friend Grimm, on the annual exhibitions in the Paris Salon from 1759 onward—have never been surpassed among non-technical criticisms for brilliancy, freshness, and philosophic suggestiveness. They reveal the man's elemental strength; which was not in his knowledge, for he was without technical training in art and had seen scarcely any of the world's masterpieces, but in his sensuously sympathetic nature, which gave him quickness of insight and delicacy in interpretation.

He had the faculty of making and keeping friends, being unaffected, genial, amiable, enthusiastically generous and helpful to his friends, and without vindictiveness to his foes. He needed these qualities to counteract his almost utter lack of conscientiousness, his gush of sentiment, his unregulated morals, his undisciplined genius, his unbalanced thought. His style of writing, often vivid and strong, is as often awkward and dull, and is frequently lacking in finish. As a philosophic author and thinker his voluminous work is of little enduring worth, for though plentiful in original power it totally lacks organic unity; his thought rambles carelessly, his method is confused. It has been said of him that he was a master who produced no masterpiece. But as a talker, a converser, all witnesses testify that he was wondrously inspiring and suggestive, speaking sometimes as from mysterious heights of vision or out of unsearchable deeps of thought.

FROM ‹RAMEAU'S NEPHEW›

Be the weather fair or foul, it is my custom in any case at five o'clock in the afternoon to stroll in the Palais Royal. I am always to be seen alone and meditative, on the bench D'Argenson. I hold converse with myself on politics or love, on taste or philosophy, and yield up my soul entirely to its own frivolity. It may follow the first idea that presents itself, be the idea wise or foolish. In the Allée de Foi one sees our young rakes following upon the heels of some courtesan who passes on with shameless mien, laughing face, animated glance, and a pug nose; but they soon leave her to follow another, teasing them all, joining none of them. My thoughts are my courtesans.

When it is really too cold or rainy, I take refuge in the Café de la Régence and amuse myself by watching the chess-players. Paris is the place of the world and the Café de la Régence the place of Paris where the best chess is played. There one witnesses the most carefully calculated moves; there one hears the most vulgar conversation; for since it is possible to be at once a man of intellect and a great chess-player, like Légal, so also one may be at once a great chess-player and a very silly person, like Foubert or Mayot.

One afternoon I was there, observing much, speaking rarely, and hearing as little as possible, when one of the most singular personages came up to me that ever was produced by this land of ours, where surely God has never caused a dearth of singular characters. He is a combination of high-mindedness and baseness, of sound understanding and folly; in his head the conceptions of honor and dishonor must be strangely tangled, for the good qualities with which nature has endowed him he displays without boastfulness, and the bad qualities without shame. For the rest, he is firmly built, has an extraordinary power of imagination, and possesses an uncommonly strong pair of lungs. Should you ever meet him and succeed in escaping from the charm of his originality, it must be by stopping both ears with your fingers or by precipitate flight. Heavens, what terrible lungs!

And nothing is less like him than he himself. Sometimes he is thin and wasted, like a man in the last stages of consumption; you could count his teeth through his cheeks; you would think he had not tasted food for several days, or had come from La Trappe.

A month later he is fattened and filled out as if he had never left the banquets of the rich or had been fed among the Bernardines. To-day, with soiled linen, torn trousers, clad in rags, and almost barefoot, he passes with bowed head, avoids those whom he meets, till one is tempted to call him and bestow upon him an alms. To-morrow, powdered, well groomed, well dressed, and well shod, he carries his head high, lets himself be seen, and you would take him almost for a respectable man.

So he lives from day to day, sad or merry, according to the circumstances. His first care, when he rises in the morning, is to take thought where he is to dine. After dinner he bethinks himself of some opportunity to procure supper, and with the night come new cares. Sometimes he goes on foot to his little attic, which is his home if the landlady, impatient at long arrears of rent, has not taken the key away from him. Sometimes he goes to one of the taverns in the suburbs, and there, between a bit of bread and a mug of beer, awaits the day. If he lacks the six sous necessary to procure him quarters for the night, which is occasionally the case, he applies to some cabman among his friends or to the coachman of some great lord, and a place on the straw beside the horses is vouchsafed him. In the morning he carries a part of his mattress in his hair. If the season is mild, he spends the whole night strolling back and forth on the Cours or in the Champs Élysées. With the day he appears again in the city, dressed yesterday for to-day and to-day often for the rest of the week.

For such originals I cannot feel much esteem, but there are others who make close acquaintances and even friends of them. Once in the year perhaps they are able to put their spell upon me, when I meet them, because their character is in such strong contrast to that of every-day humanity, and they break the oppressive monotony which our education, our social conventions, our traditional proprieties have produced. When such a man enters a company, he acts like a cake of yeast that raises the whole, and restores to each a part of his natural individuality. He shakes them up, brings things into motion, elicits praise or censure, drives truth into the open, makes upright men recognizable, unmasks the rogues, and there the wise man sits and listens and is enabled to distinguish one class from another.

This particular specimen I had long known; he frequented a house into which his talents had secured him the entrée. These people had an only daughter. He swore to the parents that he would marry their daughter. They only shrugged their shoulders, laughed in his face, and assured him that he was a fool. But I saw the day come when the thing was accomplished. He asked me for some money, which I gave him. He had, I know not how, squirmed his way into a few houses, where a *couvert* stood always ready for him, but it had been stipulated that he should never speak without the consent of his hosts. So there he sat and ate, filled the while with malice; it was fun to see him under this restraint. The moment he ventured to break the treaty and open his mouth, at the very first word the guests all shouted « O Rameau! » Then his eyes flashed wrathfully, and he fell upon his food again with renewed energy.

You were curious to know the man's name; there it is. He is the nephew of the famous composer who has saved us from the church music of Lulli which we have been chanting for a hundred years, . . . and who, having buried the Florentine, will himself be buried by Italian virtuosi; he dimly feels this, and so has become morose and irritable, for no one can be in a worse humor — not even a beautiful woman who in the morning finds a pimple on her nose — than an author who sees himself threatened with the fate of outliving his reputation, as Marivaux and Crébillon *fils* prove.

Rameau's nephew came up to me. « Ah, my philosopher, do I meet you once again? What are you doing here among the good-for-nothings? Are you wasting your time pushing bits of wood about? »

I — No; but when I have nothing better to do, I take a passing pleasure in watching those who push them about with skill.

He — A rare pleasure, surely. Excepting Légal and Philidor, there is no one here that understands it. . . .

I — You are hard to please. I see that only the best finds favor with you.

He — Yes, in chess, checkers, poetry, oratory, music, and such other trumpery. Of what possible use is mediocrity in these things?

I — I am almost ready to agree with you. . . .

He—You have always shown some interest in me, because I'm a poor devil whom you really despise, but who after all amuses you.

I—That is true.

He—Then let me tell you. (Before beginning, he drew a deep sigh, covered his forehead with both hands, then with calm countenance continued:—) You know I am ignorant, foolish, silly, shameless, rascally, gluttonous.

I—What a panegyric!

He—It is entirely true. Not a word to be abated; no contradiction, I pray you. No one knows me better than I know myself, and I don't tell all.

I—Rather than anger you, I will assent.

He—Now, just think, I lived with people who valued me precisely because all these qualities were mine in a high degree.

I—That is most remarkable. I have hitherto believed that people concealed these qualities even from themselves, or excused them, but always despised them in others.

He—Conceal them? Is that possible? You may be sure that when Palissot is alone and contemplates himself, he tells quite a different story. You may be sure that he and his companion make open confession to each other that they are a pair of arrant rogues. Despise these qualities in others? My people were much more reasonable, and I fared excellently well among them. I was cock of the walk. When absent, I was instantly missed. I was pampered. I was their little Rameau, their good Rameau, the shameless, ignorant, lazy Rameau, the fool, the clown, the gourmand. Each of these epithets was to me a smile, a caress, a slap on the back, a box on the ears, a kick, a dainty morsel thrown upon my plate at dinner, a liberty permitted me after dinner as if it were of no account; for I am of no account. People make of me and do before me and with me whatever they please, and I never give it a thought. . . .

I—You have been giving lessons, I understand, in accompaniment and composition?

He—Yes.

I—And you knew absolutely nothing about it?

He—No, by Heaven; and for that very reason I was a much better teacher than those who imagine they know something about it. At all events, I didn't spoil the taste nor ruin the hands of my young pupils. If when they left me they went to a competent master, they had nothing to unlearn, for they had learned nothing, and that was just so much time and money saved.

I — But how did you do it?

He — The way they all do it. I came, threw myself into a chair: — « How bad the weather is! How tired the pavement makes one! » Then some scraps of town gossip: . . . « At the last Amateur Concert there was an Italian woman who sang like an angel. . . . Poor Dumênil doesn't know what to say or do, » etc., etc. . . . « Come, mademoiselle, where is your music-book? » And as mademoiselle displays no great haste, searches every nook and corner for the book, which she has mislaid, and finally calls the maid to help her, I continue: — « Little Clairon is an enigma. There is talk of a perfectly absurd marriage of — what is her name? » — « Nonsense, Rameau, it isn't possible. » — « They say the affair is all settled. » . . . « There is a rumor that Voltaire is dead. » — « All the better. » — « Why all the better? » — « Then he is sure to treat us to some droll skit. That's a way he has, a fortnight before his death. » What more should I say? I told a few scandals about the families in the houses where I am received, for we are all great scandal-mongers. In short, I played the fool; they listened and laughed, and exclaimed, « He is really too droll, isn't he? » Meanwhile the music-book had been found under a chair, where a little dog or a little cat had worried it, chewed it, and torn it. Then the pretty child sat down at the piano and began to make a frightful noise upon it. I went up to her, secretly making a sign of approbation to her mother. « Well, now, that isn't so bad, » said the mother; « one needs only to make up one's mind to a thing; but the trouble is, one will not make up one's mind; one would rather kill time by chattering, trifling, running about, and God knows what. Scarcely do you turn your back but the book is closed, and not until you are at her side again is it opened. Besides, I have never heard you reprimand her. » In the mean time, since something had to be done, I took her hands and placed them differently. I pretended to lose my patience; I shouted, — « Sol, sol, sol, mademoiselle, it's a *sol*. » The mother: « Mademoiselle, have you no ears? I'm not at the piano, I'm not looking at your notes, but my own feeling tells me that it ought to be a *sol*. You give the gentleman infinite trouble. You remember nothing, and make no progress. » To break the force of this reproof a little, I tossed my head and said: « Pardon me, madame, pardon me. It would be better if mademoiselle would only practice a little, but after all it is not so bad.»—« In your place I would keep her a whole year at one piece.»—« Rest assured, I shall not let her off until she has mastered every difficulty; and that will not take so long, perhaps, as mademoiselle thinks.» — « Monsieur Rameau, you flatter her; you are too good.» And that is the only thing they would remember of the whole lesson, and would upon occasion repeat to me. So the lesson came to an end. My pupil handed me the fee, with a graceful gesture and a courtesy which her dancing-master had taught her. I put the money into my pocket, and the mother said, « That's very nice, mademoiselle. If Favillier were here, he would praise you.» For appearance's sake I chattered for a minute or two more; then I vanished; and that is what they called in those days a lesson in accompaniment.

I—And is the case different now?

He—Heavens! I should think so. I come in, I am serious, throw my muff aside, open the piano, try the keys, show signs of great impatience, and if I am kept a moment waiting I shout as if my purse had been stolen. In an hour I must be there or there; in two hours with the Duchess So-and-so; at noon I must go to the fair Marquise; and then there is to be a concert at Baron de Bagge's, Rue Neuve des Petits Champs.

I—And meanwhile no one expects you at all.

He—Certainly not. . . . And precisely because I can further my fortune through vices which come natural to me, which I acquired without labor and practice without effort, which are in harmony with the customs of my countrymen, which are quite to the taste of my patrons, and better adapted to their special needs than inconvenient virtues would be, which from morning to night would be standing accusations against them, it would be strange indeed if I should torture myself like one of the damned to twist and turn and make of myself something which I am not, and hide myself beneath a character foreign to me, and assume the most estimable qualities, whose worth I will not dispute, but which I could acquire and live up to only by great exertions, and which after all would lead to nothing,—perhaps to worse than nothing. Moreover, ought a beggar like me, who lives upon the wealthy, constantly to hold up to his patrons a mirror of good conduct? People praise virtue but hate it; they fly from it, let it freeze; and in this world a man has to keep his feet warm. Besides, I should always be in the sourest humor: for why is it that the pious and the devotional are so hard, so repellent, so unsociable? It is because they have imposed upon themselves a task contrary to their nature. They suffer, and when a man suffers he makes others suffer. Now, that is no affair of mine or of my patrons'. I must be in good spirits, easy, affable, full of sallies, drollery, and folly. Virtue demands reverence, and reverence is inconvenient; virtue challenges admiration, and admiration is not entertaining. I have to do with people whose time hangs heavy on their hands; they want to laugh. Now consider the folly: the ludicrous makes people laugh, and I therefore must be a fool; I must be amusing, and if nature had not made me so, then by hook or by crook I should have made myself seem so. Fortunately I have no need to play the hypocrite. There are hypocrites enough of all colors without me, and not counting those who deceive themselves. . . . Should it ever occur to friend Rameau to play Cato, to despise fortune, women, good living, idleness, what would he be? A hypocrite. Let Rameau remain what he is, a happy robber among wealthy robbers, and a man without either real or boasted virtue. In short, your idea of happiness, the happiness of a few enthusiastic dreamers like you, has no charm for me. . . .

I—He earns his bread dearly, who in order to live must assail virtue and knowledge.

He—I have already told you that we are of no consequence. We slander all men and grieve none.

[The dialogue reverts to music.]

I—Every imitation has its original in nature. What is the musician's model when he breaks into song?

He—Why do you not grasp the subject higher up? What is song?

I—That, I confess, is a question beyond my powers. That's the way with us all. The memory is stored with words only, which we think we understand because we often use them and even apply them correctly, but in the mind we have only indefinite conceptions. When I use the word "song," I have no more definite idea of it than you and the majority of your kind have when you say reputation, disgrace, honor, vice, virtue, shame, propriety, mortification, ridicule.

He—Song is an imitation in tones, produced either by the voice or by instruments, of a scale invented by art, or if you will, established by nature; an imitation of physical sounds or passionate utterances; and you see, with proper alterations this definition could be made to fit painting, oratory, sculpture, and poetry. Now to come to your question, What is the model of the musician or of song? It is the declamation, when the model is alive or sensate; it is the tone, when the model is insensate. The declamation must be regarded as a line, and the music as another line which twines about it. The stronger and the more genuine is this declamation, this model of song, the more numerous the points at which the accompanying music intersects it, the more beautiful will it be. And this our younger composers have clearly perceived. When one hears «Je suis un pauvre diable,» one feels that it is a miser's complaint. If he didn't sing, he would address the earth in the very same tones when he intrusts to its keeping his gold: «O terre, reçois mon trésor.» . . . In such works with the greatest variety of characters, there is a convincing truth of declamation that is unsurpassed. I tell you, go, go, and hear the aria where the young man who feels that he is dying, cries out, «Mon cœur s'en va.» Listen to the air, listen to the accompaniment, and then tell me what difference there is between the true tones of a dying man and the handling of this music. You will see that the line of the melody exactly coincides with the line of declamation. I say nothing of the time, which is one of the conditions of song; I confine myself to the expression, and there is nothing truer than the statement which I have somewhere read, «Musices seminarium accentus,»—the accent is the seed-plot of the melody. And for that reason, consider how difficult and important a matter it is to be able to write a good recitative. There is no beautiful aria out of which a beautiful recitative could not be made; no beautiful recitative out of which a clever man could not produce a beautiful aria. I will not assert that one who recites well will also be able to sing well, but I should be much surprised if a good singer could not recite well. And you may believe all that I tell you now, for it is true.

(And then he walked up and down and began to hum a few arias from the 'Île des Fous,' etc., exclaiming from time to time, with upturned eyes and hands upraised:—) «Isn't that beautiful, great heavens! isn't that beautiful? Is it possible to have a pair of ears on one's head and question its beauty?" Then as his enthusiasm rose he sang quite softly, then more loudly as he became more impassioned, then with gestures, grimaces, contortions of body. "Well," said I, "he is losing his mind, and I may expect a new scene." And in fact, all at once he burst out singing. . . . He passed from one aria to another, fully thirty of them,— Italian, French, tragic, comic, of every sort. Now with a deep bass he descended into hell; then, contracting his throat, he split the upper air with a falsetto, and in gait, mien, and action he imitated the different singers, by turns raving, commanding, mollified, scoffing. There was a little girl that wept, and he hit off all her pretty little ways. Then he was a priest, a king, a tyrant; he threatened, commanded, stormed; then he was a slave and submissive. He despaired, he grew tender, he lamented, he laughed, always in the tone, the time, the sense of the words, of the character, of the situation.

All the chess-players had left their boards and were gathered around him; the windows of the café were crowded with passers-by, attracted by the noise. There was laughter enough to bring down the ceiling. He noticed nothing, but went on in such a rapt state of mind, in an enthusiasm so close to madness, that I was uncertain whether he would recover, or if he would be thrown into a cab and taken straight to the mad-house; the while he sang the Lamentations of Jomelli.

With precision, fidelity, and incredible warmth, he rendered one of the finest passages, the superb obligato recitative in which the prophet paints the destruction of Jerusalem; he wept himself, and the eyes of the listeners were moist. More could not be desired in delicacy of vocalization, nor in the expression of overwhelming grief. He dwelt especially on those parts in which the great composer has shown his greatness most clearly. When he was not singing, he took the part of the instruments; these he quickly dropped again, to return to the vocal part, weaving one into the other so perfectly that the connection, the unity of the whole, was preserved. He took possession of our souls and held them in the strangest suspense I have ever experienced. Did I admire him? Yes, I admired him. Was I moved and melted? I was moved and melted, and yet something of the ludicrous mingled itself with these feelings and modified their nature.

But you would have burst out laughing at the way he imitated the different instruments. With a rough muffled tone and puffed-out cheeks he represented horns and bassoon; for the oboe he assumed a rasping nasal tone; with incredible rapidity he made his voice run over the string instruments, whose tones he endeavored to reproduce with the greatest accuracy; the flute passages he whistled; he rumbled out the sounds of the German flute; he shouted and sang with the gestures of a madman, and so alone and unaided he impersonated the entire ballet corps, the singers, the whole orchestra,—in short, a complete performance,—dividing himself into twenty different characters, running, stopping, with the mien of one entranced, with glittering eyes and foaming mouth. . . . He was quite beside himself. Exhausted by his exertions, like a man awakening from a deep sleep or emerging from a long period of abstraction, he remained motionless, stupefied, astonished. He looked about him in bewilderment, like one trying to recognize the place in which he finds himself. He awaited the return of his strength, of his consciousness; he dried his face mechanically. Like one who upon awaking finds his bed surrounded by groups of people, in complete oblivion and profound unconsciousness of what he had been doing, he cried, «Well, gentlemen, what's the matter? What are you laughing at? What are you wondering about? What's the matter?»

I—My dear Rameau, let us talk again of music. Tell me how it comes that with the facility you display for appreciating the finest passages of the great masters, for retaining them in your memory, and for rendering them to the delight of others with all the enthusiasm with which the music inspires you,—how comes it that you have produced nothing of value yourself?

(Instead of answering me, he tossed his head, and raising his finger towards heaven, cried:—)

The stars, the stars! When nature made Leo, Vinci, Pergolese, Duni, she wore a smile; her face was solemn and commanding when she created my dear uncle Rameau, who for ten years has been called the great Rameau, and who will soon be named no more. But when she scraped his nephew together, she made a face and a face and a face.—(And as he spoke he made grimaces, one of contempt, one of irony, one of scorn. He went through the motions of kneading dough, and smiled at the ludicrous forms he gave it. Then he threw the strange pagoda from him.) So she made me and threw me down among other pagodas, some with portly well-filled paunches, short necks, protruding goggle eyes, and an apoplectic appearance; others with lank and crooked necks and emaciated forms, with animated eyes and hawks' noses. These all felt like laughing themselves to death when they saw me, and when I saw them I set my arms akimbo and felt like laughing myself to death, for fools and clowns take pleasure in one another; seek one another out, attract one another. Had I not found upon my arrival in this world the proverb ready-made, that the money of fools is the inheritance of the clever, the world would have owed it to me. I felt that nature had put my inheritance into the purse of the pagodas, and I tried in a thousand ways to recover it.

I—I know these ways. You have told me of them. I have admired them. But with so many capabilities, why do you not try to accomplish something great?

He—That is exactly what a man of the world said to the Abbé Le Blanc. The abbé replied:—«The Marquise de Pompadour takes me in hand and brings me to the door of the Academy; then she withdraws her hand; I fall and break both legs.»—«You ought to pull yourself together,» rejoined the man of the world, «and break the door in with your head.»—«I have just tried that,» answered the abbé, «and do you know what I got for it? A bump on the head.» . . . (Then he drank a swallow from what remained in the bottle and turned to his neighbor.) Sir, I beg you for a pinch of snuff. That's a fine snuff-box you have there. You are a musician? No! All the better for you. They are a lot of poor deplorable wretches. Fate made me one of them, me! Meanwhile at Montmartre there is a mill, and in the mill there is perhaps a miller or a miller's lad, who will never hear anything but the roaring of the mill, and who might have composed the most beautiful of songs. Rameau, get you to the mill, to the mill; it's there you belong. . . . But it is half-past five. I hear the vesper bell which summons me too. Farewell. It's true, is it not, philosopher, I am always the same Rameau?

I—Yes, indeed. Unfortunately.

He—Let me enjoy my misfortune forty years longer. He laughs best who laughs last.

Translated for ‹A Library of the World's Best Literature.›

FRANZ VON DINGELSTEDT

(1814–1881)

Franz von Dingelstedt was born at Halsdorf, Hessen, Germany, June 30th, 1814. He attained eminence as a poet and dramatist, but his best powers were devoted to his principal calling as theatre director.

His boyhood's education was received at Rinteln. At the University of Marburg he applied himself to theology and philology, but more especially to modern languages and literature. After leaving the university he became instructor at Ricklingen, near Hanover. He was characterized, even as a young man, by his political freedom and independence of thought; and at Cassel, where in 1836 he was teacher in the Lyceum, he was on this account looked upon so much askance that it was found expedient to transfer him to the gymnasium at Fulda (1838). He resigned this position, however, in order to devote himself to writing. A collection of his poems appeared in 1838–45, and of these, 'Lieder eines Kosmopolitischen Nachtwächters' (Songs of a Cosmopolitan Night-Watchman: 1841) may be said to have produced a genuine agitation. These were not only important as literature, but as political promulgations, boldly embodying the radical sentiments of freethinking Germany.

Dingelstedt

In 1841 he went to Augsburg, connected himself with the Allgemeine Zeitung, and traveled as newspaper correspondent in France, Holland, Belgium, and England. 'Das Wanderbuch' (The Wander-Book), and 'Jusqu' à la Mer — Erinnerungen aus Holland' (As Far as the Sea — Remembrances of Holland: 1847), were the fruits of these journeys. He had in contemplation a voyage to the Orient, and preparatory to this he settled for a short time in Vienna; but the journey was not undertaken, for just at this time he was appointed librarian of the Royal Library of Stuttgart, and reader to the king, with the title of Court Councilor. Here in 1844 he married the celebrated singer Jenny Lutzer. He returned to Vienna, where in 1850 his drama 'Das Haus der Barneveldt' (The House of the Barneveldts) was produced with such brilliant success that he was thereupon appointed stage manager of the National Theatre at Munich. To this for six years he devoted his best efforts, presenting in the most admirable manner the finest of the German classics. The merit of his work was recognized by the king, who ennobled him in 1857. He was pre-eminently a theatrical manager, and served successively at Weimar (1857) and at Vienna, where he was appointed director of the Court Opera House in 1867, and of the Burg Theatre in 1870. He brought the classic plays of other lands upon the stage, and his revivals of Shakespeare's historical plays and the 'Winter's Tale,' and of Molière's 'L'Avare' (The Miser), were brilliant events in the theatrical annals of Vienna. He was made Imperial Councilor by the Emperor, and raised in 1876 to the rank of baron. In 1875 he took the position of general director of both court theatres of Vienna. He died at Vienna, May 15th, 1881.

The novels 'Licht und Schatten der Liebe' (The Light and Shadow of Love: 1838); 'Heptameron,' 1841; and 'Novellenbuch,' 1855, were not wholly successful; but in contrast to these, 'Unter der Erde' (Under the Earth: 1840); 'Sieben Friedliche Erzählungen' (Seven Peaceful Tales: 1844), and 'Die Amazone' (The Amazon: 1868), are admirable.

Regarded purely as literature, Dingelstedt's best productions are his early poems, although his commentaries upon Shakespeare and Goethe are wholly praiseworthy. He was successful chiefly as a political poet, but his muse sings also the joys of domestic life. 'Hauslieder' (Household Songs: 1844), and his poems upon Chamisso and Uhland, are among the most beautiful personal poems in German literature.

A MAN OF BUSINESS

From 'The Amazon': copyrighted by G. P. Putnam's Sons

Herr Krafft was about to reply, but was prevented by the hasty appearance of Herr Heyboldt, the first procurist, who entered the apartment; not an antiquated comedy figure in shoe-buckles, coarse woolen socks, velvet pantaloons, and a long-tailed coat, his vest full of tobacco, and a goose-quill back of his comically flexible ear; no, but a fine-looking man, dressed in the latest style and in black, with a medal in his button-hole, and having an earnest, expressive countenance. He was householder, member of the City Council, and militia captain; the gold medal and colored ribbon on his left breast told of his having saved, at the risk of his own life, a Leander who had been carried away by the current in the swimming-baths.

His announcement, urgent as it was, was made without haste, deliberate and cool, somewhat as the mate informs the captain that an ugly wind has sprung up. « Herr Principal, » he said, « the crowd has broken in the barriers and one wing of the gateway; they are attacking the counting-house. » « Who breaks, pays, » said Krafft, with a joke; « we will charge the sport to their account. » — « The police are not strong enough; they have sent to the Royal Watch for military. » — « That is right, Heyboldt. No accident, no arms or legs broken? » — « Not that I know of. » — « Pity for Meyer Hirsch; he would have thundered magnificently in the official Morning News against the excesses of the rage for speculation. Nor any one wounded by the police? » — « Not any, so far. » — « Pity for Hirsch Meyer. The oppositional Evening Journal has missed a capital opportunity of weeping over the barbarity of the soldateska. At all events, the two papers must continue to write — one for, the other against us. Keep Hirsch Meyer and Meyer Hirsch going. » — « All right, Herr Principal. » — « Send each of them a polite line, to the effect that we have taken the liberty of keeping a few shares for him, to sell them at the most favorable moment, and pay him over the difference. » — « It shall be attended to, Herr Principal. » — « So our Southwestern Railway goes well, Heyboldt? » — « By steam, Herr Principal. » The sober man smiled at his daring joke, and Herr Krafft smiled affably with him. « The amount that we have left to furnish will be exhausted before one has time to turn around. The people throw money, bank-notes, government bonds, at our cashiers, who cannot fill up the receipts fast enough. On the Bourse they fought for the blanks. » — « For the next four weeks we will run the stock up, Heyboldt; after that it can fall, but slowly, with decorum. » — « I understand, Herr Principal. »

A cashier came rushing in without knocking. « Herr Principal, » he stammered in his panic, « we have not another blank, and the people are pouring in upon us more and more violently. Wild shouts call for you. » « To your place, sir, » thundered Krafft at him. « I shall come when I think it time. In no case, » he added more quietly, « before the military arrive. We need an interference, for the sake of the market. » The messenger disappeared; but pale, bewildered countenances were to be seen in the doorways of the comptoir; the house called for its master: the trembling daughter sent again and again for her father.

«Let us bring the play to a close,» said Herr Krafft, after brief deliberation; he stepped into the middle office, flung open a window, and raising his harsh voice to its loudest tones, cried to the throng below, «You are looking for me, folks. Here I am. What do you want of me?» «Shares, subscriptions,» was the noisy answer.—«You claim without any right or any manners. This is my house, a peaceable citizen's house. You are breaking in as though it were a dungeon, an arsenal, a tax-office,—as though we were in the midst of a revolution. Are you not ashamed of yourselves?» A confused murmur rang through the astonished ranks. «If you wish to do business with me,» continued the merchant, «you must first learn manners and discipline. Have I invited your visit? Do I need your money, or do you need my shares? Send up some deputies to convey your requests. I shall have nothing to do with a turbulent mob.» So saying, he closed the window with such violence that the panes cracked, and the fragments fell down on the heads of the assailants.

«The Principal knows how to talk to the people,» said Heyboldt with pride to Roland, the mute witness of this strange scene. «He speaks their own language. He replies to a broken door with a broken window.»

Meantime a company of soldiers had arrived on double-quick, with a flourish of drums. The officer's word of command rang through the crowd, now grown suddenly quiet: «Fix bayonets! form line! march!» Yard and passages were cleared, the doors guarded; in the street the low muttering tide, forced back, made a sort of dam. Three deputies, abashed and confused, appeared at Krafft's door and craved audience. The merchant received them like a prince surrounded by his court, in the midst of his clerks, in the large counting-room. The spokesman commenced: «We ask your pardon, Herr Krafft, for what has happened.»—«For shame, that you should drag in soldiers as witnesses and peacemakers in a quiet little business affair among order-loving citizens.»—«It was reported that we had been fooled with these subscriptions, and that the entire sum had been already disposed of on the Bourse.»—«And even if that were so, am I to be blamed for it? The Southwestern Railway must raise thirty millions. Double, treble that amount is offered it. Can I prevent the necessity of reducing the subscriptions?»—«No; but they say that we poor folks shall not get a cent's worth; the big men of the Bourse have gobbled up the best bits right before our noses.»—«They say so? Who says so? Court Cooper Täubert, I ask you who says so?»—«Gracious Herr Court Banker—» «Don't Court or Gracious me. My name is Krafft, Herr Hans Heinrich Krafft. I think we know each other, Master Täubert. It is not the first time that we have done business together. You have a very snug little share in my workingmen's bank. Grain-broker Wüst, you have bought one of the houses in my street. Do I ever dun you for the installments of purchase money?» «No indeed, Herr Krafft; you are a good man, a public-spirited man, no money-maker, no leech, no Jew!» cried the triumvirate of deputies in chorus.—«I am nothing more than you are: a man of business, who works for his living, the son of a peasant, a plain simple citizen. I began in a smaller way than any of you; but I shall never forget that I am flesh of your flesh, blood of your blood. Facts have proved it. I will give you a fresh proof to-day. Go home and tell the people who have sent you, Hans Heinrich Krafft will give up the share which his house has subscribed to the Southwestern Railway, in favor of the less wealthy citizens of this city. This sum of five hundred thousand thalers shall be divided up *pro rata* among the subscriptions under five hundred dollars.»

«Heaven bless you, Herr Krafft!» stammered out the court cooper, and the grain-broker essayed to shed a tear of gratitude; the confidential clerk Herr Lange, the third of the group, caught at the hand of the patron to kiss it, with emotion. Krafft drew it back angrily. «No self-abasement, Herr Lange,» he said. «We are men of the people; let us behave as such. God bless you, gentlemen. You know my purpose. Make it known to the good people waiting outside, and see that I am rid of my billeting. Let the subscriptions be conducted quietly and in good order. Adieu, children!» The deputation withdrew. A few minutes afterwards there was heard a thundering hurrah:—«Hurrah for Herr Krafft! Three cheers for Father Krafft!» He showed himself at the window, nodded quickly and soberly, and motioned to them to disperse.

While the tumult was subsiding, Krafft and Roland retired into the private counting-room. «You have,» the latter said, «spoken nobly, acted nobly.»—«I have made a bargain, nothing more, nothing less; moreover, not a bad one." — "How so?" — "In three months I shall buy at 70, perhaps still lower, what I am now to give up to them at 90." — "You know that beforehand?" — "With mathematical certainty. The public expects an El Dorado in the Southwestern Railway, as it does in every new enterprise. The undertaking is a good one, it is true, or I should not have ventured upon it. But one must be able to wait until the fruit is ripe. The small holders cannot do that; they sow to-day, and to-morrow they wish to reap. At the first payment their heart and their purse are all right. At the second or third, both are gone. Upon the least rise they will throw the paper, for which they were ready to break each other's necks, upon the market, and so depreciate their property. But if some fortuitous circumstance should cause a pressure upon the money market, then they drop all that they have, in a perfect panic, for any price. I shall watch this moment, and buy. In a year or so, when the road is finished and its communications complete, the shares that were subscribed for at 90, and which I shall have bought at 60 to 70, will touch 100, or higher."

"That is to say," said Roland, thoughtfully, "you will gain at the expense of those people whose confidence you have aroused, then satisfied with objects of artificial value, and finally drained for yourself." "Business is business," replied the familiar harsh voice. "Unless I become a counterfeiter or a forger I can do nothing more than to convert other persons' money into my own; of course, in an honest way." — "And you do this, without fearing lest one day some one mightier and luckier than you should do the same to you?" — "I must be prepared for that; I am prepared." — "Also for the storm,— not one of your own creating, but one sent by the wrath of God, that shall scatter all this paper splendor of our times, and reduce this appalling social inequality of ours to a universal zero?" "Let us quietly abide this Last Day," laughed the banker, taking the artist by the arm.

THE WATCHMAN

THE last faint twinkle now goes out
Up in the poet's attic;
And the roisterers, in merry rout,
Speed home with steps erratic.

Soft from the house-roofs showers the snow,
The vane creaks on the steeple,
The lanterns wag and glimmer low
In the storm by the hurrying people.

The houses all stand black and still,
The churches and taverns deserted,
And a body may now wend at his will,
With his own fancies diverted.

Not a squinting eye now looks this way,
Not a slanderous mouth is dissembling,
And a heart that has slept the livelong day
May now love and hope with trembling.

Dear Night! thou foe to each base end,
While the good still a blessing prove thee,
They say that thou art no man's friend,—
Sweet Night! how I therefore love thee!

DIOGENES LAERTIUS

(200–250 A. D. ?)

It is curious how often we are dependent, for our knowledge of some larger subject, upon a single ancient author, who would be hardly worthy of notice but for the accidental loss of the books composed by fitter and abler men. Thus, our only general description of Greece at the close of the classical period is written by a man who describes many objects that he certainly did not see, who leaves unmentioned numberless things we wish explained, and who has a genius for so misplacing an adverb as to bring confusion into the most commonplace statement. But not even to Pausanias do we proffer such grudging gratitude and such ungrateful objurgations as to Diogenes Laertius, our chief — often our sole — authority for the 'Lives and Sayings of the Philosophers.' His book is a fascinating one, and even amusing,— if we can forget what we so much wanted in its stead. At second or third hand, from the compendiums of the schools rather than from the original works of the great masters themselves, Diogenes does give us a fairly intelligible sketch, as a rule, of the outward life lived by each sage. This slight frame is crammed with anecdotes, evidently culled with most eager and uncritical hand from miscellaneous collections. Many of these stories are so fragmentary as to be pointless. Others are unquestionably attached to the wrong person. This method is at its maddest in the author's sketch of his namesake, the Recluse of the Tub. (One of Ali Baba's *jars*, by the way, would give a better notion of the real hermitage.) Since this «philosopher» had himself little character and no doctrines, the loose string of anecdotes, puns, and saucy answers suits all our needs. Throughout the work are scattered apocryphal letters, and feeble poetic epigrams composed by the compiler himself. The leaning of our most unphilosophic author was apparently toward Epicurus. The loss of that teacher's own works causes us to prize doubly the extensive fragments of them preserved in this relatively copious and serious study. The lover of the great Epicurean poem of Lucretius on the 'Nature of Things' will often be surprised to find here the source of many among the Roman poet's most striking doctrines and images. The sketch of Zeno is also an important authority on Stoicism. Instruction in these particular chapters, then, and rich diversion elsewhere, await the reader of this most gossipy, formless, and uncritical volume. The English reader, by the way, ought to be provided with something better than the «Bohn» version. This adds a goodly harvest of ludicrous misprints and other errors of every kind to Diogenes's own mixture of borrowed wisdom and native silliness. The classical student will prefer the *Didot* edition by Cobet, with the Latin version in parallel columns.

It has been thought desirable to offer here a version, slightly abridged, of Diogenes's chapter on Socrates. The original sources, in Plato's and Xenophon's extant works, will almost always explain, or correct, the statements of Diogenes. Such wild shots as the assertion that the plague repeatedly visited Athens, striking down *every inhabitant* save the temperate Socrates, hardly need a serious rejoinder. Diogenes cannot even speak with approximate accuracy of Socrates's famous Dæmon or Inward Monitor. We know, on the best authority, that it prophesied nothing, even proposed nothing, but only vetoed the rasher impulses of its human companion. But to apply the tests of mere accuracy to Diogenes would be like criticizing Uncle Remus for his sins against English syntax.

Of the author's life we know nothing. Our assignment of him to the third century is based merely on the fact that he quotes writers of the second, and is himself in turn cited by somewhat later authors.

LIFE OF SOCRATES

From the ‹Lives and Sayings of the Philosophers›

Socrates was the son of Sophroniscus, a sculptor and Phænarete a midwife [as Plato also states in the ‹Theætetus›], and an Athenian, of the deme Alopeke. He was believed to aid Euripides in composing his dramas. Hence Mnesimachus speaks thus:—

> «This is Euripides's new play, the ‹Phrygians›:
> And Socrates has furnished him the sticks.»

And again:—

> «Euripides, Socratically patched.»

Callias also, in his ‹Captives,› says:—

> *A*—«Why art so solemn, putting on such airs?
> *B*— Indeed I may; the cause is Socrates.»

Aristophanes, in the ‹Clouds,› again, remarks:—

> «And this is he who for Euripides
> Composed the talkative wise tragedies.»

He was a pupil of Anaxagoras, according to some authorities, but also of Damon, as Alexander states in his 'Successions.' After the former's condemnation he became a disciple of Archelaus the natural philosopher. But Douris says he was a slave, and carried stones. Some say, too, that the Graces on the Acropolis are his; they are clothed figures. Hence, they say, Timon in his 'Silli' declares:—

> "From them proceeded the stone-polisher,
> Prater on law, enchanter of the Greeks,
> Who taught the art of subtle argument,
> The nose-in-air, mocker of orators,
> Half Attic, the adept in irony."

For he was also clever in discussion. But the Thirty Tyrants, as Xenophon tells us, forbade him to teach the art of arguing. Aristophanes also brings him on in comedy, making the Worse Argument seem the better. He was moreover the first, with his pupil Æschines, to teach oratory. He was likewise the first who conversed about life, and the first of the philosophers who came to his end by being condemned to death. We are also told that he lent out money. At least, investing it, he would collect what was due, and then after spending it invest again. But Demetrius the Byzantine says it was Crito who, struck by the charm of his character, took him out of the workshop and educated him.

Realizing that natural philosophy was of no interest to men, it is said, he discussed ethics, in the workshops and in the agora, and used to say he was seeking

> "Whatsoever is good in human dwellings, or evil."

And very often, we are told, when in these discussions he conversed too violently, he was beaten or had his hair pulled out, and was usually laughed to scorn. So once when he was kicked, and bore it patiently, some one expressed surprise; but he said, "If an ass had kicked me, would I bring an action against him?"

Foreign travel he did not require, as most men do, except when he had to serve in the army. At other times, remaining in Athens, he disputed in argumentative fashion with those who conversed with him, not so as to deprive them of their belief, but to strive for the ascertainment of truth. They say Euripides gave him the work of Heraclitus, and asked him, "What do you think of it?" And he said, "What I understood is fine; I suppose what I did not understand is, too; only it needs a Delian diver!» He attended also to physical training, and was in excellent condition. Moreover, he went on the expedition to Amphipolis, and when Xenophon had fallen from his horse in the battle of Delium he picked him up and saved him. Indeed, when all the other Athenians were fleeing he retreated slowly, turning about calmly, and on the lookout to defend himself if attacked. He also joined the expedition to Potidæa — by sea, for the war prevented a march by land; and it was there he was said once to have remained standing in one position all night. There too, it is said, he was pre-eminent in valor, but gave up the prize to Alcibiades, of whom he is stated to have been very fond. Ion of Chios says moreover that when young he visited Samos with Archelaus, and Aristotle states that he went to Delphi. Favorinus again, in the first book of his 'Commentaries,' says he went to the Isthmus.

He was also very firm in his convictions and devoted to the democracy, as was evident from his not yielding to Critias and his associates when they bade him bring Leon of Salamis, a wealthy man, to them to be put to death. He was also the only one who opposed the condemnation of the ten generals. When he could have escaped from prison, too, he would not. The friends who wept at his fate he reproved, and while in prison he composed those beautiful discourses.

He was also temperate and austere. Once, as Pamphila tells us in the seventh book of her 'Commentaries,' Alcibiades offered him a great estate, on which to build a house; and he said, «If I needed sandals, and you offered me a hide from which to make them for myself, I should be laughed at if I took it.» Often, too, beholding the multitude of things for sale, he would say to himself, «How many things I do not need!» He used constantly to repeat aloud these iambic verses:—

> «But silver plate and garb of purple dye
> To actors are of use,— but not in life.»

He disdained the tyrants,— Archelaus of Macedon, Scopas of Crannon, Eurylochus of Melissa,— not accepting gifts from them nor visiting them. He was so regular in his way of living that he was frequently the only one not ill when Athens was attacked by the plague.

Aristotle says he wedded two wives, the first Xanthippe, who bore him Lamprocles, and the second Myrto, daughter of

Aristides the Just, whom he received without dowry and by whom he had Sophroniscus and Menexenus. Some however say he married Myrto first; and some again that he had them both at once, as the Athenians on account of scarcity of men passed a law to increase the population, permitting any one to marry one Athenian woman and have children by another; so Socrates did this.

He was a man also able to disdain those who mocked him. He prided himself on his simple manner of living, and never exacted any pay. He used to say he who ate with best appetite had least need of delicacies, and he who drank with best appetite had least need to seek a draught not at hand; and that he who had fewest needs was nearest the gods. This indeed we may learn from the comic poets, who in their very ridicule covertly praise him. Thus Aristophanes says:—

«O thou who hast righteously set thy heart on attaining to noble wisdom,
How happy the life thou wilt lead among the Athenians and the Hellenes!
Shrewdness and memory both are thine, and energy unwearied
Of mind; and never art thou tired from standing or from walking.
By cold thou art not vexed at all, nor dost thou long for breakfast.
Wine thou dost shun, and gluttony, and every other folly.»

Ameipsias also, bringing him upon the stage in the philosopher's cloak, says:—

«O Socrates, best among few men, most foolish of many, thou also
Art come unto us; thou'rt a patient soul; but where didst get that doublet?
That wretched thing in mockery was presented by the cobblers!
Yet though so hungry, he never however has stooped to flatter a mortal.»

This disdain and arrogance in Socrates has also been exposed by Aristophanes, who says:—

«Along the streets you haughtily strut; your eyes roll hither and thither:
Barefooted, enduring discomforts, you go with countenance solemn among us.»

And yet sometimes, suiting himself to the occasion, he dressed finely; as when for instance in Plato's 'Symposium' he goes to Agathon's.

He was a man able both to urge others to action, and to dissuade them. Thus, when he conversed with Theætetus on Knowledge, he sent him away inspired, as Plato says. Again, when Euthyphron had indicted his own father for manslaughter, by conversing with him on piety Socrates turned him from his purpose. Lysis also by his exhortations he rendered a most moral man. He was moreover skillful in fitting his arguments to the circumstances. He changed the feeling of his son Lamprocles when he was enraged with his mother, as Xenophon somewhere relates. Plato's brother Glaucon, who wished to be active in politics, he dissuaded because of his inexperience, as Xenophon states; but Charmides on the other hand, who was well fitted, he urged on. He roused the spirit of Iphicrates the general also, pointing out to him the cocks of Midias the barber fighting those of Callias. He said it was strange that every man could tell easily how many sheep he had, but could not call by name the friends whom he had acquired, so negligent were men in that regard. Once seeing Euclid devoting great pains to captious arguments, he said, «O Euclid, you will be able to manage sophists — but men, never!» For he thought hair-splitting on such matters useless, as Plato also says in his 'Euthydemus.'

When Glaucon offered him some slaves, so that he might make a profit on them, he did not take them.

He praised leisure as the best of possessions, as Xenophon also says in his 'Symposium.' He used to say, too, that there was but one good — knowledge; and one evil — ignorance. Wealth and birth, he said, had no value, but were on the contrary wholly an evil. So when some one told him Antisthenes's mother was a Thracian, «Did you think,» quoth he, «so fine a man must be the child of two Athenians?» When Phædo had been captured in war and shamefully enslaved, Socrates bade Crito ransom him, and made him a philosopher.

He also learned, when already an old man, to play the lyre, saying there was no absurdity in learning what one did not know. He used to dance frequently, too, thinking this exercise helpful to health. This Xenophon tells us in the 'Symposium.'

He used to say that his Dæmon foretold future events: and that he knew nothing, except that very fact that he did know nothing. Those who bought at a great price what was out of season, he said, had no hope of living till the season came around. Once being asked what was virtue in a young man, he said,

"To avoid excess in all things." He used to say one should study geometry (surveying) just enough to be able to measure land in buying and selling it.

When Euripides in the 'Auge' said of virtue:—

"These things were better left to lie untouched,"

he rose up and left the theatre, saying it was absurd to think it proper to seek for a slave if he was not to be found, but to let virtue perish unregarded. When his advice was asked whether to marry or not, he said, "Whichever you do, you will regret it!" He used to say that he marveled that those who made stone statues took pains to make the stone as like the man as possible, but took none with themselves, that they might not be like the stone. He thought it proper for the young to look constantly in the mirror, so that if they had beauty they might prove themselves worthy of it, and if they were ugly, that they might conceal their ugliness by their accomplishments.

When he had invited rich friends to dinner, and Xanthippe was ashamed, he said, "Do not be troubled. If they are sensible, they will bear with us. If not, we shall care nothing for them." Most men, he said, lived to eat; but he ate to live. As to those who showed regard for the opinions of the ignoble multitude, he said it was as if a man should reject one tetradrachm [coin] as worthless, but accept a heap of such coins as good. When Æschines said, "I am poor and have nothing else, but I give you myself," he said, "Do you then not realize you are offering me the greatest of gifts?" To him who said, "The Athenians have condemned you to death," he responded, "And nature has condemned them also thereto:" though some ascribe this to Anaxagoras. When his wife exclaimed, "You die innocent!" he answered, "Do you wish I were guilty?"

When a vision in sleep seemed to say:—

"Three days hence thou'lt come to the fertile region of Phthia,"

he said to Æschines, "On the third day I shall die." When he was to drink the hemlock, Apollodorus gave him a fine garment to die in: "But why," quoth he, "is this garment of mine good enough to live in, but not to perish in?" To him who said, "So-and-so speaks ill of you," he answered, "Yes, he has not learned to speak well." When Antisthenes turned the ragged side of his cloak to the light, he remarked, "I see your vanity through your cloak.» He declared we ought to put ourselves expressly at the service of the comedy writers: «For if they say anything about us that is true, they will correct us; and if what they say be untrue, it does not concern us at all.»

When Xanthippe had first reviled him, then drenched him with water, «Didn't I tell you,» said he, «it was thundering and would soon rain?» To Alcibiades, who said Xanthippe's scolding was unbearable, he replied, «I am accustomed to it, as to a constantly creaking pulley. And you,» he added, «endure the cackling of geese.» Alcibiades said, «Yes, for they bring me eggs and goslings.» «And Xanthippe,» retorted Socrates, «bears me children.» Once when she pulled off his cloak in the agora, his friends advised him to defend himself with force. «Yes,» said he, «by Jove, so that as we fight, each of you may cry, 'Well done, Socrates!' 'Good for you, Xanthippe!'» He used to say he practiced on Xanthippe just as trainers do with spirited horses. «Just as they if they master them are able to control any other horse, so I who am accustomed to Xanthippe shall get on easily with any one else.»

It was for such words and acts as this that the Delphic priestess bore witness in his honor, giving to Chairephon that famous response:—

«Wisest of all mankind is Socrates.»

He became extremely unpopular on account of this oracle; but also because he convicted of ignorance those who had a great opinion of themselves, particularly Anytus, as Plato also says in the 'Meno.' For Anytus, enraged at the ridicule Socrates brought upon him, first urged Aristophanes and the rest on to attack him, and then induced Meletus to join in indicting him for impiety and for corrupting the young men. Plato in the 'Apology' says there were three accusers,—Anytus, Lycon, and Meletus: Anytus being incensed at him in behalf of the artisans and politicians, Lycon for the orators, and Meletus for the poets, all of whom Socrates pulled to pieces. The sworn statement of the plaintiffs ran as follows; for it is still recorded, Favorinus says, in the State archives:—«Socrates is guilty, not honoring the gods whom the State honors, but introducing other strange divinities; and he is further guilty of corrupting the young. Penalty, death.»

When Lysias wrote a speech for his defense, he read it, and said, «A fine speech, Lysias, but not suited to me;» for indeed it was rather a lawyer's plea than a philosopher's. Lysias said, «But why, if the speech is a fine one, should it not be suitable for you?» Socrates replied, «Would not fine robes, then, and sandals, be unfitting for me?»

While he was on trial, it is stated that Plato ascended the *bema* and began, «Being the youngest, O men of Athens, of all who ever came upon the bema» — but at this point the judges cried out, «Come down! come down!» So he was convicted by two hundred and eighty-one votes more than were cast for his acquittal. And when the judges considered what penalty or fine he should receive, he said he would pay five-and-twenty drachmæ. Euboulides says he agreed to pay a hundred, but when the judges expressed their indignation aloud, he said, «For what I have done, I consider the proper return to be support at the public expense in the town hall.» But they condemned him to death, the vote being larger than before by eighty.

Not many days later he drank the hemlock in the prison, after uttering many noble words, recorded by Plato in the 'Phædo.' According to some, he wrote a poem beginning —

«Greeting, Apollo of Delos, and Artemis, youthful and famous.»

He also versified, not very successfully, a fable of Æsop's which began —

«Æsop once to the people who dwell in the city of Corinth
Said, 'Let virtue be judged not by the popular voice.'»

So he passed from among men; but straightway the Athenians repented of their action, so that they closed the gymnasia, and exiling the other accusers, put Meletus to death. Socrates they honored with a statue of bronze, the work of Lysippus, which was set up in the Pompeion. Anytus in exile, entering Heraclea, was warned out of town that very day.

The Athenians have had the same experience not only in Socrates's case, but with many others. Indeed, it is stated that they fined Homer as a madman, and adjudged Tyrtæus to be crazy. Euripides reproves them in the 'Palamedes,' saying: —

«Ye have slain, ye have slain the all-wise, the harmless nightingale of the Muses.»

That is so. But Philochorus says Euripides died before Socrates.

Socrates and Euripides were both disciples of Anaxagoras. It appears to me, too, that Socrates did talk on natural philosophy. In fact, Xenophon says so, though he states that Socrates held discourse only upon moral questions. Plato indeed, in the 'Apology,' mentioning Anaxagoras and other natural philosophers, himself says of them things whereof Socrates denies any knowledge; yet it is all ascribed to Socrates.

Aristotle states that a certain mage from Syria came to Athens, and among other prophecies concerning Socrates foretold that his death would be a violent one.

The following verses upon him are our own:—

Drink, in the palace of Zeus, O Socrates, seeing that truly
Thou by a god wert called wise, who is wisdom itself.
Foolish Athenians, who to thee offered the potion of hemlock,
Through thy lips themselves draining the cup to the dregs!

Translated for 'A Library of the World's Best Literature,' by William C. Lawton.

EXAMPLES OF GREEK WIT AND WISDOM

Bias

Once he was on a voyage with some impious men. The vessel was overtaken by a storm, and they began to call upon the gods for aid. But Bias said, «Be silent, so they may not discover that you are aboard our ship!»

He declared it was pleasanter to decide a dispute between his enemies than between friends. «For of two friends,» he explained, «one is sure to become my enemy; but of two enemies I make one friend.»

Plato

It is said Socrates, in a dream, seemed to be holding on his knees a cygnet, which suddenly grew wings and flew aloft, singing sweetly. Next day Plato came to him; and Socrates said he was the bird.

It is told that Plato, once seeing a man playing at dice, reproved him. «The stake is but a trifle,» said the other. «Yes, but,» responded Plato, «the habit is no trifle.»

Once when Xenocrates came into Plato's house, the latter bade him scourge his slave for him, explaining that he could not do it himself, because he was angry. Again, he said to one of his slaves, «You would have had a beating if I were not angry.»

Aristippus

Dionysius once asked him why it is that the philosophers are seen at rich men's doors, not the rich men at the doors of the sages. Aristippus replied, «Because the wise realize what they lack, but the rich do not.» On a repetition of the taunt on another occasion he retorted, «Yes, and physicians are seen at sick men's doors; yet none would choose to be the patient rather than the leech!»

Once when overtaken by a storm on a voyage to Corinth, he was badly frightened. Somebody said to him, «We ordinary folk are not afraid, but you philosophers play the coward.» «Yes,» was his reply, «we are not risking the loss of any such wretched life as yours.»

Some one reproached him for his extravagance in food. He answered, «If you could buy these same things for threepence, wouldn't you do it?»—«Oh yes.»—«Why then, 'tis not I who am too fond of the luxurious food, but you that are over-fond of your money!»

Aristotle

When asked, «What is Hope?» he answered, «The dream of a man awake.» Asked what grows old quickest, he replied, «Gratitude.» When told that some one had slandered him in his absence, he said, «He may beat me too—in my absence!» Being asked how much advantage the educated have over the ignorant, he replied, «As much as the living over the dead.»

Some one asked him why we spend much time in the society of the beautiful. «That,» he said, «is a proper question for a blind man!» [*Cf.* Emerson's 'Rhodora.']

Once being asked how we should treat our friends, he said, «As we would wish them to treat us.» Asked what a friend is, he answered, «One soul abiding in two bodies.»

Theophrastus

To a man who at a feast was persistently silent, he remarked, « If you are ignorant, you are acting wisely; if you are intelligent, you are behaving foolishly. »

Demetrius

It was a saying of his that to friends in prosperity we should go when invited, but to those in misfortune unbidden.

When told that the Athenians had thrown down his statues, he answered, « But not my character, for which they erected them. »

Antisthenes

Some one asked him what he gained from philosophy. He replied, « The power to converse with myself. »

He advised the Athenians to pass a vote that asses were horses. When they thought that irrational, he said, « But certainly, your generals are not such because they have learned anything, but simply because you have elected them! »

Diogenes

He used to say that when in the course of his life he saw pilots, and physicians, and philosophers, he thought man the most sensible of animals; but when he saw interpreters of dreams, and soothsayers, and those who paid attention to them, and those puffed up by fame or wealth, he believed no creature was sillier than man.

Some said to him, « You are an old man. Take life easy now. » He replied, « And if I were running the long-distance race, should I when nearing the goal slacken, and not rather exert myself? »

When he saw a child drink out of his hands, he took the cup out of his wallet and flung it away, saying, « A child has beaten me in simplicity. »

He used to argue thus, « All things belong to the gods. The wise are the friends of the gods. The goods of friends are common property. Therefore all things belong to the wise. »

To one who argued that *motion* was impossible, he made no answer, but rose and walked away.

When the Athenians urged him to be initiated into the Mysteries, assuring him that in Hades those who were initiated have the front seats, he replied, «It is ludicrous, if Agesilaus and Epaminondas are to abide in the mud, and some ignoble wretches who are initiated are to dwell in the Isles of the Blest!»

Plato made the definition «Man is a two-footed featherless animal,» and was much praised for it. Diogenes plucked a fowl and brought it into his school, saying «This is Plato's man!» So the addition was made to the definition, «with broad nails.»

When a man asked him what was the proper hour for lunch, he said, «If you are rich, when you please; if you are poor, when you can get it.»

He used often to shout aloud that an easy life had been given by the gods to men, but they had covered it from sight in their search for honey-cakes and perfumes and such things.

The musician who was always left alone by his hearers he greeted with «Good morning, cock!» When the other asked him the reason, he said, «Because your music starts everybody up.»

When an exceedingly superstitious man said to him, «With one blow I will break your head!» he retorted, «And with a sneeze at your left side I will make you tremble.»

When asked what animal had the worst bite, he said, «Of wild beasts, the sycophant; and of tame creatures, the flatterer.»

Being asked when was the proper time to marry, he responded, «For young men, not yet; and for old men, not at all.»

When he was asked what sort of wine he enjoyed drinking, he answered, «Another man's.» [Of a different temper was Dante, who knew too well «how salt the bread of others tastes!»]

Some one advised him to hunt up his runaway slave. But he replied, «It is ridiculous if Manes lives without Diogenes, but Diogenes cannot without Manes.»

When asked why men give to beggars, but not to philosophers, he said, «Because they expect themselves to become lame and blind; but philosophers, never!»

Cleanthes

When a comic actor apologized for having ridiculed him from the stage, he answered gently, «It would be preposterous, when

Bacchus and Hercules bear the raillery of the poets without showing any anger, if I should be indignant when I chance to be attacked."

PYTHAGORAS

Precepts

Do NOT stir the fire with a sword.

Do not devour your heart.

Always have your bed packed up.

Do not walk in the main street.

Do not cherish birds with crooked talons.

Avoid a sharp sword.

When you travel abroad, look not back at your own borders.

[Diogenes explains this: be resigned to death.]

Consider nothing exclusively your own.

Destroy no cultivated tree, or harmless animal.

Modesty and decorum consist in never yielding to laughter, and yet not looking stern. [*Cf.* Emerson on Manners.]

Translated for 'A Library of the World's Best Literature,' by William C. Lawton.

ISAAC D'ISRAELI

(1766–1848)

Among the writers whose education and whose tastes were the outcome of the classicism of the eighteenth century, yet whose literary life lapped over into the Victorian epoch, was Isaac D'Israeli, born at Enfield in May 1766. D'Israeli was of Jewish origin, his ancestors having fled from the Spanish persecutions of the fifteenth century to find a home in Venice, whence a younger branch migrated to England.

At the time of his birth his family had stood for generations among the foremost English Jews, his father having been made a citizen by special legislation. The boy, however, did not inherit the commercial spirit which had established his house. He was a lover of books and a dreamer of dreams, and so early developed literary tendencies that his frightened father sent him off to Amsterdam to school, in the hope of curing proclivities so dangerous. Here he became familiar with the works of the Encyclopædists, and adopted the theories of Rousseau. On returning to England in his nineteenth year, he replied to his father's proposition that he should enter a commercial house at Bordeaux, by a long poem in which he passionately inveighed against the commercial spirit, and avowed himself a student of philosophy and letters. His father's reluctant acquiescence was obtained at last through the good offices of the laureate Pye, to whom the youth had already dedicated his first book, 'A Defence of Poetry.'

Isaac D'Israeli

At the outset of his career he found himself received with consideration by the men whose acquaintance he most desired. Following the fashion of the day, and inspired by the books of anecdotes so successfully published by his friend Douce, D'Israeli in 1791 produced anonymously a small volume entitled 'Curiosities of Literature,' the copyright of which he magnanimously presented to his publisher. The extraordinary success of this book can be accounted for only by the curious taste of the time, which still reflected the more unworthy traditions of the Addisonian era. It was an age of clubs and tea-tables, of society scandal-mongering and fireside gossip;

and the reading public welcomed a contribution whose refined dilettantism so well matched its own. The mysteries of Eleusis and the origin of wigs received the same grave attention. This popularity induced D'Israeli to buy back the copyright at a generous valuation; he enlarged the work to five volumes, which passed through twelve in his own lifetime, and still serves to illustrate a curious literary phase.

Other compilations of similar nature met the same success: 'The Calamities of Authors,' 'Quarrels of Authors,' and 'Literary Recollections'; but the 'Amenities of Literature,' his last work, is the most purely literary in form, and affords perhaps the best index to D'Israeli's abilities as a writer. The reader of to-day, however, is struck by the ephemeral nature of this criticism, which yet by a curious literary experience is keeping a place among the permanent productions of its age. The reader is everywhere impressed by the human sympathy, by the wide if rather superficial knowledge, and by innumerable felicities of expression and style, which betray the cultivated mind. To lovers of the curious the books still appeal, and they will continue to hold an honorable place among the bric-a-brac of literature.

The spirit of curiosity which characterized the mind of D'Israeli assumed its most dignified concrete form in the 'Commentaries on the Reign of Charles I.' D'Israeli had an artistic sense of the values in a historical picture, with a keen perception of the importance of side lights; and although the book is not a great contribution to the literature of history, yet it became popular, and in July 1832 earned for its author the degree of D. C. L. from Oxford.

D'Israeli's romances were tedious tales, but his hold upon the public was secure, and the vast amount of miscellaneous matter which he published always found a delighted audience. 'The Genius of Judaism,' a philosophical inquiry into the historical significance of the permanence of the Jewish race, showed the author's psychic limitations. He designed a history of English literature, for which he had gathered much material, but increasing blindness forced him to abandon it. Much of D'Israeli's popularity was unquestionably due to his qualities of heart. His nature was fine; he was an affectionate and devoted friend, and held an enviable position in the literary circles of the day. Campbell, Byron, Rogers, and Scott alike admired and loved him, while a host of lesser men eagerly sought his friendship.

Although brought up in the Jewish faith, D'Israeli affiliated early in life with the Church of England, in which his three sons and one daughter were baptized. He died in 1848, and was buried at Brandenham. Twenty years later his daughter-in-law, the Countess of Beaconsfield, erected at Hughenden a monument to his memory.

OLD BLACK-LETTER QUARTO.

Slightly reduced facsimile of title-page of first edition of

"THE POSIES."

London, about 1572. Original, 4⅛ x 6⅜ inches.

An example of title-page, typography, and spelling a hundred years after the introduction of printing into England. The Old English, Gothic, or Black-letter type was being superseded by the modern "Roman;" and on this title page both forms were used.

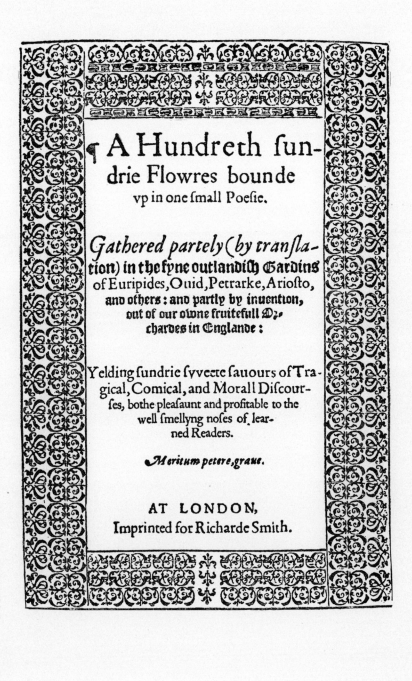

¶ A Hundreth sundrie Flowres bounde vp in one small Poesie.

Gathered partely (by translation) in the fyne outlandish Gardins of Euripides, Ouid, Petrarke, Ariosto, and others: and partly by inuention, out of our owne fruitefull Orchardes in Englande:

Yelding sundrie svveete sauours of Tragical, Comical, and Morall Discourses, bothe pleasaunt and profitable to the well smellyng noses of learned Readers.

Meritum petere, graue.

AT LONDON,
Imprinted for Richarde Smith.

POETS, PHILOSOPHERS, AND ARTISTS MADE BY ACCIDENT

From 'Curiosities of Literature'

Accident has frequently occasioned the most eminent geniuses to display their powers. It was at Rome, says Gibbon, on the fifteenth of October, 1764, as I sat musing amidst the ruins of the Capitol, while the barefooted friars were singing vespers in the Temple of Jupiter, that the idea of writing the decline and fall of the city first started to my mind.

Father Malebranche, having completed his studies in philosophy and theology without any other intention than devoting himself to some religious order, little expected the celebrity his works acquired for him. Loitering in an idle hour in the shop of a bookseller, and turning over a parcel of books, 'L'Homme de Descartes' fell into his hands. Having dipt into some parts, he read with such delight that the palpitations of his heart compelled him to lay the volume down. It was this circumstance that produced those profound contemplations which made him the Plato of his age.

Cowley became a poet by accident. In his mother's apartment he found, when very young, Spenser's 'Fairy Queen,' and by a continual study of poetry he became so enchanted of the Muse that he grew irrecoverably a poet.

Dr. Johnson informs us that Sir Joshua Reynolds had the first fondness of his art excited by the perusal of Richardson's Treatise.

Vaucanson displayed an uncommon genius for mechanics. His taste was first determined by an accident: when young, he frequently attended his mother to the residence of her confessor; and while she wept with repentance, he wept with weariness! In this state of disagreeable vacation, says Helvetius, he was struck with the uniform motion of the pendulum of the clock in the hall. His curiosity was roused; he approached the clock-case, and studied its mechanism; what he could not discover he guessed at. He then projected a similar machine, and gradually his genius produced a clock. Encouraged by this first success, he proceeded in his various attempts; and the genius which thus could form a clock, in time formed a fluting automaton.

If Shakespeare's imprudence had not obliged him to quit his wool trade and his town; if he had not engaged with a company of actors, and at length, disgusted with being an indifferent performer, he had not turned author, the prudent wool-seller had never been the celebrated poet.

Accident determined the taste of Molière for the stage. His grandfather loved the theatre, and frequently carried him there. The young man lived in dissipation; the father, observing it, asked in anger if his son was to be made an actor. "Would to God," replied the grandfather, "he was as good an actor as Montrose." The words struck young Molière; he took a disgust to his tapestry trade; and it is to this circumstance France owes her greatest comic writer.

Corneille loved; he made verses for his mistress, became a poet, composed 'Mélite,' and afterwards his other celebrated works. The discreet Corneille had remained a lawyer.

Thus it is that the devotion of a mother, the death of Cromwell, deer-stealing, the exclamation of an old man, and the beauty of a woman, have given five illustrious characters to Europe.

We owe the great discovery of Newton to a very trivial accident. When a student at Cambridge, he had retired during the time of the plague into the country. As he was reading under an apple-tree, one of the fruit fell, and struck him a smart blow on the head. When he observed the smallness of the apple, he was surprised at the force of the stroke. This led him to consider the accelerating motion of falling bodies; from whence he deduced the principle of gravity, and laid the foundation of his philosophy.

Ignatius Loyola was a Spanish gentleman who was dangerously wounded at the siege of Pampeluna. Having heated his imagination by reading the Lives of the Saints, which were brought to him in his illness instead of a romance, he conceived a strong ambition to be the founder of a religious order; whence originated the celebrated society of the Jesuits.

Rousseau found his eccentric powers first awakened by the advertisement of the singular annual subject which the Academy of Dijon proposed for that year, in which he wrote his celebrated Declamation against the arts and sciences; a circumstance which determined his future literary efforts.

La Fontaine, at the age of twenty-two, had not taken any profession or devoted himself to any pursuit. Having accidentally heard some verses of Malherbe, he felt a sudden impulse, which directed his future life. He immediately bought a Malherbe, and was so exquisitely delighted with this poet that after passing the nights in treasuring his verses in his memory, he would run in the daytime to the woods, where, concealing himself, he would recite his verses to the surrounding dryads.

Flamsteed was an astronomer by accident. He was taken from school on account of his illness, when Sacrobosco's book 'De Sphæra' having been lent to him, he was so pleased with it that he immediately began a course of astronomic studies. Pennant's first propensity to natural history was the pleasure he received from an accidental perusal of Willoughby's work on birds; the same accident, of finding on the table of his professor Reaumur's 'History of Insects,'—of which he read more than he attended to the lecture,—and having been refused the loan, gave such an instant turn to the mind of Bonnet that he hastened to obtain a copy, but found many difficulties in procuring this costly work. Its possession gave an unalterable direction to his future life: this naturalist indeed lost the use of his sight by his devotion to the microscope.

Dr. Franklin attributes the cast of his genius to a similar accident. "I found a work of Defoe's, entitled an 'Essay on Projects,' from which perhaps I derived impressions that have since influenced some of the principal events of my life."

I shall add the incident which occasioned Roger Ascham to write his 'Schoolmaster,' one of the most curious and useful treatises among our elder writers.

At a dinner given by Sir William Cecil during the plague in 1563, at his apartments at Windsor, where the Queen had taken refuge, a number of ingenious men were invited. Secretary Cecil communicated the news of the morning, that several scholars at Eton had run away on account of their master's severity, which he condemned as a great error in the education of youth. Sir William Petre maintained the contrary; severe in his own temper, he pleaded warmly in defense of hard flogging. Dr. Wootton, in softer tones, sided with the Secretary. Sir John Mason, adopting no side, bantered both. Mr. Haddon seconded the hard-hearted Sir William Petre, and adduced as an evidence that the best schoolmaster then in England was the hardest flogger. Then was it that Roger Ascham indignantly exclaimed that if such a master had an able scholar it was owing to the boy's genius and not the preceptor's rod. Secretary Cecil and others were pleased with Ascham's notions. Sir Richard Sackville was silent; but when Ascham after dinner went to the Queen to read one of the orations of Demosthenes, he took him aside, and frankly told him that though he had taken no part in the debate he would not have been absent from that conversation for a great deal; that he knew to his cost the truth Ascham had supported, for it was the perpetual flogging of such a schoolmaster that had given him an unconquerable aversion to study. And as he wished to remedy this defect in his own children, he earnestly exhorted Ascham to write his observations on so interesting a topic. Such was the circumstance which produced the admirable treatise of Roger Ascham.

THE MARTYRDOM OF CHARLES THE FIRST

From the 'Commentaries on the Reign of Charles the First'

At Whitehall a repast had been prepared. The religious emotions of Charles had consecrated the sacrament, which he refused to mingle with human food. The Bishop, whose mind was unequal to conceive the intrepid spirit of the King, dreading lest the magnanimous monarch, overcome by the severity of the cold, might faint on the scaffold, prevailed on him to eat half a manchet of bread and taste some claret. But the more consolatory refreshment of Charles had been just imparted to him in that singular testimony from his son, who had sent a *carte blanche* to save the life of his father at any price. This was a thought on which his affections could dwell in face of the scaffold which he was now to ascend.

Charles had arrived at Whitehall about ten o'clock, and was not led to the scaffold till past one. It was said that the scaffold was not completed; it might have been more truly said that the conspirators were not ready. There was a mystery in this delay. The fate of Charles the First to the very last moment was in suspense. Fairfax, though at the time in the palace, inquired of Herbert how the King was, when the King was no more! and expressed his astonishment on hearing that the execution had just taken place. This extraordinary simplicity and abstraction from the present scene of affairs has been imputed to the General as an act of refined dissimulation, yet this seems uncertain. The Prince's *carte blanche* had been that morning confided to his

CHARLES I. GOING TO EXECUTION.

Photogravure from a painting by E. Crofts.

hands, and he surely must have laid it before the «Grandees of the Army,» as this new order of the rulers of England was called. Fairfax, whose personal feelings respecting the King were congenial with those his lady had so memorably evinced, labored to defer for a few days the terrible catastrophe; not without the hope of being able, by his own regiment and others in the army, to prevent the deed altogether. It is probable — inexplicable as it may seem to us — that the execution of Charles the First really took place unknown to the General. Fairfax was not unaccustomed to discover that his colleagues first acted, and afterwards trusted to his own discernment.

Secret history has not revealed all that passed in those three awful hours. We know, however, that the warrant for the execution was not signed till within a few minutes before the King was led to the scaffold. In an apartment in the Palace, Ireton and Harrison were in bed together, and Cromwell, with four colonels, assembled in it. Colonel Huncks refused to sign the warrant. Cromwell would have no further delay, reproaching the Colonel as «a peevish, cowardly fellow,» and Colonel Axtell declared that he was ashamed for his friend Huncks, remonstrating with him, that «the ship is coming into the harbor, and now would he strike sail before we come to anchor?» Cromwell stepped to a table, and wrote what he had proposed to Huncks; Colonel Hacker, supplying his place, signed it, and with the ink hardly dry, carried the warrant in his hand and called for the King.

At the fatal summons Charles rose with alacrity. The King passed through the long gallery by a line of soldiers. Awe and sorrow seem now to have mingled in their countenances. Their barbarous commanders were intent on their own triumph, and no farther required the forced cry of «Justice and Execution.» Charles stepped out of an enlarged window of the Banqueting House, where a new opening leveled it with the scaffold. Charles came forward with the same indifference as «he would have entered Whitehall on a masque night,» as an intelligent observer described. The King looked towards St. James's and smiled. Curious eyes were watchful of his slightest motions; and the Commonwealth papers of the day express their surprise, perhaps their vexation, at the unaltered aspect and the firm step of the Monarch. These mean spirits had flattered themselves that he who had been cradled in royalty, who had lived years in the fields of honor, and was now, they presumed, a recreant in imprisonment,—"the grand Delinquent of England,"—as they called him, would start in horror at the block.

This last triumph at least was not reserved for them,—it was for the King. Charles, dauntless, strode "the floor of Death," to use Fuller's peculiar but expressive phraseology. He looked on the block with the axe lying upon it, with attention; his only anxiety was that the block seemed not sufficiently raised, and that the edge of the axe might be turned by being swept by the flappings of cloaks, or blunted by the feet of some moving about the scaffold. "Take care they do not put me to pain!—Take heed of the axe! take heed of the axe!" exclaimed the King to a gentleman passing by. "Hurt not the axe; that may hurt me!" His continued anxiety concerning these *circumstances* proves that he felt not the terror of death, solely anxious to avoid the pain, for he had an idea of their cruelty. With that sedate thoughtfulness which was in all his actions, he only looked at the business of the hour. One circumstance Charles observed with a smile. They had a notion that the King would resist the executioner; on the suggestion of Hugh Peters, it is said, they had driven iron staples and ropes into the scaffold, that their victim, if necessary, might be bound down upon the block.

The King's speech has many remarkable points, but certainly nothing so remarkable as the place where it was delivered. This was the first "King's Speech" spoken from a scaffold. Time shall confirm, as history has demonstrated, his principle that "They mistook the nature of government; for people are free under a government, not by being sharers in it, but by the due administration of the laws." "It was for this," said Charles, "that now I am come here. If I could have given way to an arbitrary sway, for to have all laws changed according to the power of the sword, I need not have come here; and therefore I tell you that I am *the Martyr of the People!*"

SYDNEY DOBELL

(1824–1874)

Sydney Dobell, the son of a wine merchant, was born at Cranbrook in Kent. His parents, both persons of strong individuality, believed in home training, and not one of their eight children went either to school or to university. They belonged to the Broad Church Community founded by Sydney's maternal grandfather, Samuel Thompson; a church intended to recall in its principles the primitive Christian ages. The parents looked upon Sydney, their eldest-born, as destined to become the apostle of this creed. He grew up in a kind of religious fervor, with his precocious mind unnaturally stimulated; a course of conduct which materially weakened his constitution, and made him a chronic invalid at the early age of thirty-three. He read whatever books came to hand, many of them far beyond his years. At the age of eight he filled his diary with theological discussions.

Entering his father's counting-house as a mere lad, he remained to the end of his life a business man of great energy. Notwithstanding his rare poetic endowments, he never seems to have entertained a single-minded purpose to be a poet and nothing more. On the contrary, he thought the ideal and the practical life perfectly compatible, and he strove to unite in himself the poet and the man of affairs. He wrote habitually until 1856, when regular literary work was forbidden by his physicians. With characteristic energy he now turned his thoughts into other channels; identified himself with the affairs of Gloucester, where he was living, looked after his business, and was one of the first to adopt the system of industrial co-operation. The last four years of his life, a period of suffering and helplessness, he spent at Barton-End House, above the Stroud valley, where he died in the spring of 1874.

In the work of Dobell it is curious to find so few traces of the influences under which he grew up. He had every encouragement to become a writer of religious poetry; yet much of his work is philosophic and recondite. His delicate health is in a measure responsible for his failure to achieve the success which his natural endowments promised. All his literary work was done between the ages of twenty-three and thirty-three. 'The Roman,' his first long poem, appeared in 1850. Dedicated to the Italian struggle for liberty, it showed his breadth of sympathy. In 'Balder,' finished in 1853,

Dobell is at his best both as thinker and as poet. Yet its many fine passages, its wealth of metaphor, and the exquisite songs of Amy, hardly counterbalance the remoteness of its theme, and its over-subtle analysis of morbid psychic states. It is a poem to be read in fragments, and has aptly been called a mine for poets.

With Alexander Smith he published in 1855 a series of sonnets inspired by the Crimean War. This was followed in 1856 by 'England in War Time,' a collection of Dobell's lyrical and descriptive poems, which possess more general human interest than any other of his books.

After continuous work was interdicted, he still contributed verse and prose to the periodicals. His essays have been collected by Professor Nichol, under the title 'Thoughts on Art, Philosophy, and Religion.' As a poet Dobell belongs to the so-called "spasmodic school," a school "characterized by an undercurrent of discontent with the mystery of existence, by vain effort, unrewarded struggle, skeptical unrest, and an uneasy striving after some incomprehensible end. . . . Poetry of this kind is marked by an excess of metaphor which darkens rather than illustrates, and by a general extravagance of language. On the other hand, it manifests freshness and originality, and a rich natural beauty." Dobell's descriptions of scenery are among the finest in English literature. His senses were abnormally acute, like those of a savage, a condition which intensified his appreciation of natural beauty. Possessing a vivid imagination and wide sympathies, he was often over-subtle and obscure. He strove to realize in himself his ideal of a poet, and during his years of ill-health gave himself up to promoting the welfare of his fellow-men; but of his seventeen years of inactivity he says:—"The keen perception of all that should be done, and that so bitterly cries for doing, accompanies the consciousness of all that I might but cannot do."

EPIGRAM ON THE DEATH OF EDWARD FORBES

NATURE, a jealous mistress, laid him low.
He wooed and won her; and, by love made bold,
She showed him more than mortal man should know—
Then slew him lest her secret should be told.

HOW'S MY BOY?

«Ho, sailor of the sea!
How's my boy — my boy?» —
«What's your boy's name, good wife,
And in what good ship sailed he?»

«My boy John —
He that went to sea —
What care I for the ship, sailor?
My boy's my boy to me.

«You come back from the sea,
And not know my John?
I might as well have asked some landsman,
Yonder down in the town.
There's not an ass in all the parish
But knows my John.

«How's my boy — my boy?
And unless you let me know,
I'll swear you are no sailor,
Blue jacket or no —
Brass buttons or no, sailor,
Anchor and crown or no —

«Sure, his ship was the Jolly Briton —»
«Speak low, woman, speak low!»

«And why should I speak low, sailor,
About my own boy John?
If I was loud as I am proud
I'd sing him over the town!
Why should I speak low, sailor?» —
«That good ship went down.»

«How's my boy — my boy?
What care I for the ship, sailor?
I was never aboard her.
Be she afloat or be she aground,
Sinking or swimming, I'll be bound
Her owners can afford her!
I say, how's my John?» —
«Every man on board went down,
Every man aboard her.»

«How's my boy — my boy?
What care I for the men, sailor?
I'm not their mother.
How's my boy — my boy?
Tell me of him and no other!
How's my boy — my boy?»

THE SAILOR'S RETURN

This morn I lay a-dreaming,
This morn, this merry morn;
When the cock crew shrill from over the hill,
I heard a bugle horn.

And through the dream I was dreaming,
There sighed the sigh of the sea,
And through the dream I was dreaming,
This voice came singing to me: —

«High over the breakers,
Low under the lee,
Sing ho!
The billow,
And the lash of the rolling sea!

«Boat, boat, to the billow,
Boat, boat, to the lee!
Love, on thy pillow,
Art thou dreaming of me?

«Billow, billow, breaking,
Land us low on the lee!
For sleeping or waking,
Sweet love, I am coming to thee!

«High, high, o'er the breakers,
Low, low, on the lee,
Sing ho!
The billow
That brings me back to thee!»

AFLOAT AND ASHORE

«Tumble and rumble, and grumble and snort,
Like a whale to starboard, a whale to port;
Tumble and rumble, and grumble and snort,
And the steamer steams thro' the sea, love!»

«I see the ship on the sea, love;
I stand alone
On this rock;
The sea does not shock
The stone;
The waters around it are swirled,
But under my feet
I feel it go down
To where the hemispheres meet
At the adamant heart of the world.
Oh that the rock would move!
Oh that the rock would roll
To meet thee over the sea, love!
Surely my mighty love
Should fill it like a soul,
And it should bear me to thee, love;
Like a ship on the sea, love,
Bear me, bear me, to thee, love!»

«Guns are thundering, seas are sundering, crowds are wondering,
Low on our lee, love.
Over and over the cannon-clouds cover brother and lover, but over and over
The whirl-wheels trundle the sea, love;
And on through the loud pealing pomp of her cloud
The great ship is going to thee, love,
Blind to her mark, like a world through the dark,
Thundering, sundering, to the crowds wondering,
Thundering over to thee, love.»

«I have come down to thee coming to me, love;
I stand, I stand
On the solid sand;
I see thee coming to me, love;
The sea runs up to me on the sand:
I start—'tis as if thou hadst stretched thine hand
And touched me through the sea, love.
I feel as if I must die,
For there's something longs to fly,
Fly and fly, to thee, love.

As the blood of the flower ere she blows
Is beating up to the sun,
And her roots do hold her down,
And it blushes and breaks undone
In a rose,
So my blood is beating in me, love!
I see thee nigh and nigher;
And my soul leaps up like sudden fire,
My life's in the air
To meet thee there,
To meet thee coming to me, love!
Over the sea,
Coming to me,
Coming, and coming to me, love!»

«The boats are lowered: I leap in first,
Pull, boys, pull! or my heart will burst!
More! more!—lend me an oar!—
I'm thro' the breakers! I'm on the shore!
I see thee waiting for me, love!»

«A sudden storm
Of sighs and tears,
A clenching arm,
A look of years.
In my bosom a thousand cries,
A flash like light before my eyes,
And I am lost in thee, love!»

THE SOUL

From ‹Balder›

And as the mounting and descending bark,
Borne on exulting by the under deep,
Gains of the wild wave something not the wave,
Catches a joy of going and a will
Resistless, and upon the last lee foam
Leaps into air beyond it,—so the soul
Upon the Alpine ocean mountain-tossed,
Incessant carried up to heaven, and plunged
To darkness, and, still wet with drops of death,
Held into light eternal, and again
Cast down, to be again uplift in vast
And infinite succession, cannot stay
The mad momentum.

ENGLAND

From ‹Balder›

THIS dear English land!
This happy England, loud with brooks and birds,
Shining with harvests, cool with dewy trees,
And bloomed from hill to dell: but whose best flowers
Are daughters, and Ophelia still more fair
Than any rose she weaves; whose noblest floods
The pulsing torrent of a nation's heart;
Whose forests stronger than her native oaks
Are living men; and whose unfathomed lakes,
Forever calm, the unforgotten dead
In quiet grave-yards willowed seemly round,
O'er which To-day bends sad, and sees his face.
Whose rocks are rights, consolidate of old
Through unremembered years, around whose base
The ever-surging peoples roll and roar
Perpetual, as around her cliffs the seas
That only wash them whiter; and whose mountains,
Souls that from this mere footing of the earth
Lift their great virtues through all clouds of Fate
Up to the very heavens, and make them rise
To keep the gods above us!

AMERICA

NOR force nor fraud shall sunder us! O ye
Who north or south, or east or western land,
Native to noble sounds, say truth for truth,
Freedom for freedom, love for love, and God
For God; O ye who in eternal youth
Speak with a living and creative flood
This universal English, and do stand
Its breathing book; live worthy of that grand
Heroic utterance — parted, yet a whole,
Far, yet unsevered, — children brave and free
Of the great Mother tongue, and ye shall be
Lords of an empire wide as Shakespeare's soul,
Sublime as Milton's immemorial theme,
And rich as Chaucer's speech, and fair as Spenser's dream.

AMY'S SONG OF THE WILLOW

From 'Balder'

THE years they come, and the years they go,
Like winds that blow from sea to sea;
From dark to dark they come and go,
All in the dew-fall and the rain.
Down by the stream there be two sweet willows,
—Hush thee, babe, while the wild winds blow,—
One hale, one blighted, two wedded willows,
All in the dew-fall and the rain.

She is blighted, the fair young willow;
—Hush thee, babe, while the wild winds blow,—
She hears the spring-blood beat in the bark;
She hears the spring-leaf bud on the bough;
But she bends blighted, the wan weeping willow,
All in the dew-fall and the rain.

The stream runs sparkling under the willow,
—Hush thee, babe, while the wild winds blow,—
The summer rose-leaves drop in the stream;
The winter oak-leaves drop in the stream;
But she bends blighted, the wan weeping willow,
All in the dew-fall and the rain.

Sometimes the wind lifts the bright stream to her,
—Hush thee, babe, while the wild winds blow,—
The false stream sinks, and her tears fall faster;
Because she touched it her tears fall faster;
Over the stream her tears fall faster,
All in the sunshine or the rain.

The years they come, and the years they go;
Sing well-away, sing well-away!
And under mine eyes shines the bright life-river;
Sing well-away, sing well-away!
Sweet sounds the spring in the hale green willow,
The goodly green willow, the green waving willow,
Sweet in the willow, the wind-whispering willow;
Sing well-away, sing well-away!
But I bend blighted, the wan weeping willow,
All in the sun, and the dew, and the rain.

AUSTIN DOBSON

(1840–)

BY ESTHER SINGLETON

At first thought it seems difficult to consider Austin Dobson as belonging to the Victorian period, so entirely is he saturated with the spirit of the eighteenth century. A careful study of his verse reveals the fact that the Georgian era, seen through the vista of his poetic imagination, is divested of all that is coarse, dark, gross, and prosaic. The mental atmosphere and the types and characters that he gives, express only beauty and charm.

Austin Dobson

One approaches the poems of Austin Dobson as one stands before a rare collection of enamels, fan-mounts, jeweled snuff-boxes, and delicate carvings in ivory and silver; and after delighting in the beauty and finish of these graceful curios, passes into a gallery of paintings and water-colors, suggesting Watteau, Fragonard, Boucher, Meissonier, and Greuze. We also wander among trim box-hedges and quaint gardens of roses and bright hollyhocks; lean by sun-dials to watch the shadow of Time; and enjoy the sight of gay belles, patched and powdered and dressed in brocaded gowns and gypsy hats. Gallant beaux, such as are associated with Reynolds's portraits, appear, and hand them into sedan-chairs or lead them through stately minuets to the notes of Rameau, Couperin, and Arne.

Just as the scent of rose-leaves, lavender, and musk rises from antique Chinese jars, so Dobson's delicate verse reconstructs a life

«Of fashion gone, and half-forgotten ways.»

He is equally at home in France. Nothing could be more sympathetic and exquisite than 'A Revolutionary Relic,' 'The Curé's Progress,' 'Une Marquise,' and the 'Proverbs in Porcelain,' one of which is cited below.

In the 'Vers de Société,' as well as his other poetry, Dobson fulfills all the requirements of light verse — charm, mockery, pathos, banter, and, while apparently skimming the surface, often shows us the strange depths of the human heart. He blends so many qualities that he deserves the praise of T. B. Aldrich, who says, «Austin Dobson has the grace of Suckling and the finish of Herrick, and is easily master of both in metrical art.»

Henry Austin Dobson, the son of Mr. George Clarisse Dobson, a civil engineer, was born in Plymouth, England, January 18th 1840. His early years were spent in Anglesea, and after receiving his education in Beaumaris, Coventry, and Strasburg, he returned to England to become a civil engineer. In 1856 he entered the civil service of Great Britain, and ever since that date he has held offices in the Board of Trade. His leisure was devoted to literature, and when Anthony Trollope first issued his magazine St. Paul's in 1868, he introduced to the public the verse of Austin Dobson. In 1873 his fugitive poems were published in a small volume entitled 'Vignettes in Rhyme' and 'Vers de Société.' This was followed in 1877 by 'Proverbs in Porcelain,' and both books, with additional poems, were printed again in two volumes: 'Old World Idylls' (1883), and 'At the Sign of the Lyre' (1885). Mr. Dobson's original essays are contained in three volumes: 'Four Frenchwomen,' studies of Charlotte Corday, Madame Roland, the Princess de Lamballe, and Madame de Genlis (1890), and 'Eighteenth-Century Vignettes' (first series 1892, second series 1894), which touch upon a host of picturesque and fascinating themes. He has written also several biographies: of Hogarth, of Fielding, of Steele (1886), of Goldsmith (1888), and a 'Memoir of Horace Walpole' (1890). He has also written felicitous critical introductions to many new editions of the eighteenth-century classics.

Austin Dobson has been most happy in breathing English life into the old poems of French verse, such as ballades, villanelles, roundels, and rondeaux; and he has also written clever and satirical fables, cast in the form and temper of Gay and Prior, with quaint obsolete affectations, redolent of the classic age of Anne.

So serious is his attitude towards art, and so large his audience, that the hope expressed in the following rondeau will certainly be realized:—

In after days, when grasses high
O'er-top the stone where I shall lie,
  Though ill or well the world adjust
  My slender claim to honored dust,
I shall not question nor reply.

I shall not see the morning sky,
I shall not hear the night-wind sigh;
  I shall be mute, as all men must,
    In after days.

But yet, now living, fain were I
That some one then should testify,
    Saying—*He held his pen in trust*
    To Art, not serving shame or lust.
Will none?—Then let my memory die
        In after days!

Esther Singleton

ON A NANKIN PLATE

VILLANELLE

«Ah me, but it might have been!
Was there ever so dismal a fate?»
Quoth the little blue mandarin.

«Such a maid as was never seen:
She passed, tho' I cried to her, ‹Wait,›—
Ah me, but it might have been!

«I cried, ‹O my Flower, my Queen,
Be mine!›—'Twas precipitate,»
Quoth the little blue mandarin.

«But then . . . she was just sixteen,—
Long-eyed, as a lily straight,—
Ah me, but it might have been!

«As it was, from her palankeen
She laughed—‹You're a week too late!›»
(Quoth the little blue mandarin.)

«That is why, in a mist of spleen
I mourn on this Nankin Plate.
Ah me, but it might have been!»
Quoth the little blue mandarin.

THE OLD SEDAN-CHAIR

«What's not destroyed by Time's devouring Hand?
Where's Troy,— and where's the May-Pole in the Strand?»
—BRAMSTON'S ‹ART OF POLITICKS.›

IT STANDS in the stable-yard, under the eaves,
Propped up by a broomstick and covered with leaves;
It once was the pride of the gay and the fair,
But now 'tis a ruin,— that old Sedan-chair!

It is battered and tattered,— it little avails
That once it was lacquered, and glistened with nails;
For its leather is cracked into lozenge and square
Like a canvas by Wilkie,— that old Sedan-chair.

See, here come the bearing-straps; here were the holes
For the poles of the bearers— when once there were poles;
It was cushioned with silk, it was wadded with hair,
As the birds have discovered,— that old Sedan-chair.

«Where's Troy?» says the poet! Look; under the seat
Is a nest with four eggs; 'tis a favored retreat
Of the Muscovy hen, who has hatched, I dare swear,
Quite an army of chicks in that old Sedan-chair.

And yet— Can't you fancy a face in the frame
Of the window,— some high-headed damsel or dame,
Be-patched and be-powdered, just set by the stair,
While they raise up the lid of that old Sedan-chair?

Can't you fancy Sir Plume, as beside her he stands,
With his ruffles a-droop on his delicate hands,
With his cinnamon coat, with his laced solitaire,
As he lifts her out light from that old Sedan-chair?

Then it swings away slowly. Ah, many a league
It has trotted 'twixt sturdy-legged Terence and Teague;
Stout fellows!— but prone, on a question of fare,
To brandish the poles of that old Sedan-chair!

It has waited by portals where Garrick has played;
It has waited by Heidegger's «Grand Masquerade»;
For my Lady Codille, for my Lady Bellair,
It has waited— and waited, that old Sedan-chair!

Oh, the scandals it knows! Oh, the tales it could tell
Of Drum and Ridotto, of Rake and of Belle,—
Of Cock-fight and Levee, and (scarcely more rare!)
Of Fête-days at Tyburn, that old Sedan-chair!

«*Heu! quantum mutata,*» I say as I go.
It deserves better fate than a stable-yard, though!
We must furbish it up, and dispatch it,—«With Care,»—
To a Fine-Art Museum—that old Sedan-chair.

THE BALLAD OF PROSE AND RHYME

When the ways are heavy with mire and rut,
In November fogs, in December snows,
When the North Wind howls, and the doors are shut,—
There is place and enough for the pains of prose;
But whenever a scent from the whitethorn blows,
And the jasmine-stars at the casement climb,
And a Rosalind-face at the lattice shows,
Then hey! for the ripple of laughing rhyme!

When the brain gets dry as an empty nut,
When the reason stands on its squarest toes,
When the mind (like a beard) has a «formal cut,»—
There is place and enough for the pains of prose;
But whenever the May-blood stirs and glows,
And the young year draws to the «golden prime,»
And Sir Romeo sticks in his ear a rose,—
Then hey! for the ripple of laughing rhyme!

In a theme where the thoughts have a pedant-strut,
In a changing quarrel of «Ayes» and «Noes,»
In a starched procession of «If» and «But,»—
There is place and enough for the pains of prose;
But whenever a soft glance softer grows
And the light hours dance to the trysting-time,
And the secret is told «that no one knows,»—
Then hey! for the ripple of laughing rhyme!

ENVOY

In the work-a-day world,—for its needs and woes,
There is place and enough for the pains of prose;
But whenever the May-bells clash and chime,
Then hey! for the ripple of laughing rhyme!

THE CURÉ'S PROGRESS

Monsieur the Curé down the street
Comes with his kind old face,—
With his coat worn bare, and his straggling hair,
And his green umbrella-case.

You may see him pass by the little «*Grande Place,*»
And the tiny «*Hôtel-de-Ville*»;
He smiles as he goes, to the *fleuriste* Rose,
And the *pompier* Théophile.

He turns as a rule through the «*Marché*» cool,
Where the noisy fishwives call;
And his compliment pays to the «*belle Thérèse,*»
As she knits in her dusky stall.

There's a letter to drop at the locksmith's shop,
And Toto, the locksmith's niece,
Has jubilant hopes, for the Curé gropes
In his tails for a *pain d'épice.*

There's a little dispute with a merchant of fruit
Who is said to be heterodox,
That will ended be with a «*Ma foi, oui!*»
And a pinch from the Curé's box.

There is also a word that no one heard
To the furrier's daughter Lou;
And a pale cheek fed with a flickering red,
And a «*Bon Dieu garde M'sieu!*»

But a grander way for the *Sous-Préfet,*
And a bow for Ma'am'selle Anne;
And a mock «off-hat» to the Notary's cat,
And a nod to the Sacristan:—

For ever through life the Curé goes
With a smile on his kind old face—
With his coat worn bare, and his straggling hair,
And his green umbrella-case.

«GOOD-NIGHT, BABETTE»

«Si vieillesse pouvait!»

SCENE.—*A small neat room. In a high Voltaire chair sits a white-haired old gentleman.*

M. VIEUXBOIS [*turning querulously*]

Day of my life! Where *can* she get?
BABETTE! I say! BABETTE!—BABETTE!

BABETTE [*entering hurriedly*]

Coming, M'sieu'! If M'sieu' speaks
So loud, he won't be well for weeks!

M. VIEUXBOIS

Where have you been?

BABETTE

Why, M'sieu' knows:—
April! . . . Ville-d' Avray! . . . Ma'm'selle ROSE!

M. VIEUXBOIS

Ah! I am old,—and I forget.
Was the place growing green, BABETTE?

BABETTE

But of a greenness!—Yes, M'sieu'!
And then the sky so blue!—so blue!
And when I dropped my *immortelle*,
How the birds sang!

[*Lifting her apron to her eyes.*]

This poor Ma'm'selle!

M. VIEUXBOIS

You're a good girl, BABETTE, but she,—
She was an angel, verily.
Sometimes I think I see her yet
Stand smiling by the cabinet;
And once, I know, she peeped and laughed
Betwixt the curtains. . . .

Where's the draught?

[*She gives him a cup.*]

Now I shall sleep, I think, BABETTE;—
Sing me your Norman *chansonnette*.

BABETTE [*sings*]

« *Once at the Angelus*
(Ere I was dead),
Angels all glorious
Came to my bed;—
Angels in blue and white,
Crowned on the head.»

M. VIEUXBOIS [*drowsily*]

«She was an Angel» . . . «Once she laughed» . . .
What! was I dreaming?
Where's the draught?

BABETTE [*showing the empty cup*]

The draught, M'sieu'?

M. VIEUXBOIS

How I forget!
I am so old! But sing, BABETTE!

BABETTE [*sings*]

« *One was the Friend I left*
Stark in the Snow;
One was the Wife that died
Long,—long ago;
One was the Love I lost—
How could she know?»

M. VIEUXBOIS [*murmuring*]

Ah PAUL! . . . old PAUL! . . . EULALIE, too!
And ROSE . . . And O! «the sky so blue!»

BABETTE [*sings*]

« *One had my Mother's eyes,*
Wistful and mild;
One had my Father's face;
One was a Child:
All of them bent to me,—
Bent down and smiled!»

[He is asleep!]

M. VIEUXBOIS [*almost inaudibly*]

How I forget!
I am so old! . . . Good-night, BABETTE!

THE LADIES OF ST. JAMES'S

A Proper New Ballad of the Country and the Town

«Phyllida amo ante alias.»—Virgil.

The ladies of St. James's
Go swinging to the play;
Their footmen run before them
With a «Stand by! Clear the way!»
But Phyllida, my Phyllida!
She takes her buckled shoon,
When we go out a-courting
Beneath the harvest moon.

The ladies of St. James's
Wear satin on their backs;
They sit all night at *Ombre*,
With candles all of wax:
But Phyllida, my Phyllida!
She dons her russet gown,
And runs to gather May-dew
Before the world is down.

The ladies of St. James's!
They are so fine and fair,
You'd think a box of essences
Was broken in the air:
But Phyllida, my Phyllida!
The breath of heath and furze,
When breezes blow at morning,
Is not so fresh as hers.

The ladies of St. James's!
They're painted to the eyes;
Their white it stays forever,
Their red it never dies:
But Phyllida, my Phyllida!
Her color comes and goes;
It trembles to a lily,—
It wavers like a rose.

The ladies of St. James's!
You scarce can understand
The half of all their speeches,
Their phrases are so grand:

But Phyllida, my Phyllida!
Her shy and simple words
Are clear as after rain-drops
The music of the birds.

The ladies of St. James's!
They have their fits and freaks;
They smile on you — for seconds;
They frown on you — for weeks:
But Phyllida, my Phyllida!
Come either storm or shine,
From Shrove-tide unto Shrove-tide,
Is always true — and mine.

My Phyllida! my Phyllida!
I care not though they heap
The hearts of all St. James's,
And give me all to keep;
I care not whose the beauties
Of all the world may be,—
For Phyllida, my Phyllida,
Is all the world to me.

DORA *VERSUS* ROSE

«The Case is Proceeding»

From the tragic-est novels at Mudie's —
At least on a practical plan —
To the tales of mere Hodges and Judys,
One love is enough for a man.
But no case that I ever yet met is
Like mine: I am equally fond
Of Rose, who a charming brunette is,
And Dora, a blonde.

Each rivals the other in powers —
Each waltzes, each warbles, each paints —
Miss Rose, chiefly tumble-down towers;
Miss Do., perpendicular saints.
In short, to distinguish is folly;
'Twixt the pair I am come to the pass
Of Macheath, between Lucy and Polly,—
Or Buridan's ass.

If it happens that Rosa I've singled
  For a soft celebration in rhyme,
Then the ringlets of Dora get mingled
  Somehow with the tune and the time;
Or I painfully pen me a sonnet
  To an eyebrow intended for Do.'s,
And behold I am writing upon it
  The legend, «To Rose.»

Or I try to draw Dora (my blotter
  Is all over scrawled with her head),
If I fancy at last that I've got her,
  It turns to her rival instead;
Or I find myself placidly adding
  To the rapturous tresses of Rose
Miss Dora's bud-mouth, and her madding,
  Ineffable nose.

Was there ever so sad a dilemma?
  For Rose I would perish (*pro tem.*);
For Dora I'd willingly stem a—
  (Whatever might offer to stem);
But to make the invidious election,—
  To declare that on either one's side
I've a scruple,—a grain,—more affection,
  I *cannot* decide.

And as either so hopelessly nice is,
  My sole and my final resource
Is to wait some indefinite crisis,—
  Some feat of molecular force,
To solve me this riddle conducive
  By no means to peace or repose,
Since the issue can scarce be inclusive
  Of Dora *and* Rose.

(AFTER-THOUGHT)

But perhaps if a third (say, a Norah),
  Not quite so delightful as Rose,
Nor wholly so charming as Dora,
  Should appear, is it wrong to suppose,—
As the claims of the others are equal,—
  And flight—in the main—is the best,—
That I might . . . But no matter,—the sequel
  Is easily guessed.

UNE MARQUISE

A Rhymed Monologue in the Louvre

«Belle Marquise, vos beaux yeux me font mourir d'amour.»
—Molière.

I

As you sit there at your ease,
O Marquise!
And the men flock round your knees
Thick as bees,
Mute at every word you utter,
Servants to your least frill-flutter,
«*Belle Marquise!*»
As you sit there, growing prouder,
And your ringed hands glance and go,
And your fan's *frou-frou* sounds louder,
And your «*beaux yeux*» flash and glow;—
Ah, you used them on the Painter,
As you know,
For the Sieur Larose spoke fainter,
Bowing low,
Thanked Madame and Heaven for Mercy
That each sitter was not Circe,—
Or at least he told you so;—
Growing proud, I say, and prouder
To the crowd that come and go,
Dainty Deity of Powder,
Fickle Queen of Fop and Beau,
As you sit where lustres strike you,
Sure to please,
Do we love you most, or like you,
«*Belle Marquise!*»

II

You are fair; oh yes, we know it
Well, Marquise;
For he swore it, your last poet,
On his knees;
And he called all heaven to witness
Of his ballad and its fitness,
«*Belle Marquise!*»
You were everything in *ère*
(With exception of *sévère*),—

You were *cruelle* and *rebelle*,
With the rest of rhymes as well;
You were «*Reine*» and «*Mère d'Amour*»;
You were «*Vénus à Cythère*»;
«*Sappho mise en Pompadour*,»
And «*Minerve en Parabère*»;
You had every grace of heaven
In your most angelic face,
With the nameless finer leaven
Lent of blood and courtly race;
And he added, too, in duty,
Ninon's wit and Boufflers's beauty;
And La Vallière's *yeux veloutés*
Followed these;
And you liked it, when he said it
(On his knees),
And you kept it, and you read it,
«*Belle Marquise!*»

III

Yet with us your toilet graces
Fail to please,
And the last of your last faces,
And your *mise*;
For we hold you just as real,
«*Belle Marquise!*»
As your *Bergers* and *Bergères*,
Tes d'Amour and *Batelières*;
As your *parcs*, and your Versailles,
Gardens, grottoes, and *socailles*;
As your Naiads and your trees;—
Just as near the old ideal
Calm and ease,
As the Venus there by Coustou,
That a fan would make quite flighty,
Is to her the gods were used to,—
Is to grand Greek Aphroditè,
Sprung from seas.
You are just a porcelain trifle,
«*Belle Marquise!*»
Just a thing of puffs and patches
Made for madrigals and catches,
Not for heart-wounds, but for scratches,
O Marquise!

Just a pinky porcelain trifle,
«*Belle Marquise!*»
Wrought in rarest *rose-Dubarry*,
Quick at verbal point and parry,
Clever, doubtless; — but to marry,
No, Marquise!

IV

For your Cupid, you have clipped him,
Rouged and patched him, nipped and snipped him,
And with *chapeau-bras* equipped him,
«*Belle Marquise!*»
Just to arm you through your wife-time,
And the languors of your lifetime,
«*Belle Marquise!*»
Say, to trim your toilet tapers
Or — to twist your hair in papers,
Or — to wean you from the vapors; —
As for these,
You are worth the love they give you,
Till a fairer face outlive you,
Or a younger grace shall please;
Till the coming of the crows'-feet,
And the backward turn of beaux' feet,
«*Belle Marquise!*»
Till your frothed-out life's commotion
Settles down to Ennui's ocean,
Or a dainty sham devotion,
«*Belle Marquise!*»

V

No: we neither like nor love you,
«*Belle Marquise!*»
Lesser lights we place above you,—
Milder merits better please.
We have passed from *Philosophe*-dom
Into plainer modern days,—
Grown contented in our oafdom,
Giving grace not all the praise;
And, *en partant, Arsinoé*,—
Without malice whatsoever,—
We shall counsel to our Chloë
To be rather good than clever;

For we find it hard to smother
  Just one little thought, Marquise!
Wittier perhaps than any other,—
You were neither Wife nor Mother,
  «*Belle Marquise!*»

A BALLAD TO QUEEN ELIZABETH

OF THE SPANISH ARMADA

KING PHILIP had vaunted his claims;
  He had sworn for a year he would sack us;
With an army of heathenish names
  He was coming to fagot and stack us;
  Like the thieves of the sea he would track us,
And shatter our ships on the main;
  But we had bold Neptune to back us,—
And where are the galleons of Spain?

His caracks were christened of dames
  To the kirtles whereof he would tack us;
With his saints and his gilded stern-frames,
  He had thought like an egg-shell to crack us;
  Now Howard may get to his Flaccus,
And Drake to his Devon again,
  And Hawkins bowl rubbers to Bacchus,—
For where are the galleons of Spain?

Let his Majesty hang to St. James
  The axe that he whetted to hack us:
He must play at some lustier games.
  Or at sea he can hope to out-thwack us;
  To his mines of Peru he would pack us
To tug at his bullet and chain;
  Alas! that his Greatness should lack us!—
But where are the galleons of Spain?

ENVOY

GLORIANA!—the Don may attack us
Whenever his stomach be fain;
  He must reach us before he can rack us, . . .
And where are the galleons of Spain?

THE PRINCESS DE LAMBALLE

From ‹Four Frenchwomen›

A TENDER wife, a loving daughter, and a loyal friend,—shall we not here lay down upon the grave of Marie de Lamballe our reverential tribute, our little chaplet of *immortelles*, in the name of all good women, wives, and daughters?

«*Elle était mieux femme que les autres.*»* To us that apparently indefinite, exquisitely definite sentence most fitly marks the distinction between the subjects of the two preceding papers and the subject of the present. It is a transition from the stately figure of a marble Agrippina to the breathing, feeling woman at your side; it is the transition from the statuesque Rachelesque heroines of a David to the «small sweet idyl» of a Greuze. And, we confess it, we were not wholly at ease with those tragic, majestic figures. We shuddered at the dagger and the bowl which suited them so well. We marveled at their bloodless serenity, their superhuman self-sufficiency; inly we questioned if they breathed and felt. Or was their circulation a matter of machinery—a mere dead-beat escapement? We longed for the *sexe prononcé* of Rivarol—we longed for the showman's «female woman!» We respected and we studied, but we did not love them. With Madame de Lamballe the case is otherwise. Not grand like this one, not heroic like that one, «*elle est mieux femme que les autres.*»

She at least is woman—after a fairer fashion—after a truer type. Not intellectually strong like Manon Philipon, not Spartan-souled like Marie de Corday, she has still a rare intelligence, a courage of affection. She has that *clairvoyance* of the heart which supersedes all the stimulants of mottoes from Reynel or maxims from Rousseau; she has that «angel instinct» which is a juster lawgiver than Justinian. It was thought praise to say of the Girondist lady that she was a greater man than her husband; it is praise to say of this queen's friend that she was more woman than Madame Roland. Not so grand, not so great, we like the princess best. *Elle est mieux femme que les autres.*

* She was more woman than the others.

MARY MAPES DODGE

(1840?–)

To write a story which in thirty years should pass through more than a hundred editions, which should attain the apotheosis of an *edition de luxe*, which should be translated into at least four foreign languages, be allotted the Montyon prize of 1500 francs for moral as well as literary excellence, and be crowned by the French Academy — this is a piece of good fortune which falls to the lot of few story-tellers. The book which has deserved so well is 'Hans Brinker, or The Silver Skates,' a story of life in Holland. Its author, born in New York, is a daughter of Professor James Jay Mapes, an eminent chemist and inventor, an accomplished writer and brilliant talker.

MARY MAPES DODGE

In a household where music, art, and literature were cultivated, and where the most agreeable society came, talents were not likely to be overlooked. Mrs. Dodge, very early widowed, began writing before she was twenty, publishing short stories, sketches, and poems in various periodicals. 'Hans Brinker' appeared in 1864, — her delight in Motley's histories and their appeal to her own Dutch blood inspiring her to write it. Of this book Mr. Frank R. Stockton says: —

"There are strong reasons why the fairest orange groves, the loftiest mountain peaks, or the inspiriting waves of the rolling sea, could not tempt average boys and girls from the level stretches of the Dutch canals, until they had skated through the sparkling story, warmed with a healthy glow.

"This is not only a tale of vivid description, interesting and instructive; it is a romance. There are adventures, startling and surprising, there are mysteries of buried gold, there are the machinations of the wicked, there is the heroism of the good, and the gay humor of happy souls. More than these, there is love — that sentiment which glides into a good story as naturally as into a human life; and whether the story be for old or young, this element gives it an ever-welcome charm. Strange fortune and good fortune come to Hans and to Gretel, and to many other deserving characters in the tale, but there is nothing selfish about these heroes and heroines. As soon as a new generation of young people grows up to be old enough to enjoy this perennial story, all these characters return to the days of their youth, and are ready to act their parts again to the very end, and to feel in their own souls, as everybody else feels, that their story is just as new and interesting as when it was first told.»

Besides this book, Mrs. Dodge has published several volumes of juvenile verse, such as ‹Rhymes and Jingles,› and ‹When Life was Young›; a volume of serious verse, ‹Along the Way›; a volume of satirical and humorous sketches, ‹Theophilus and Others›; a second successful story for young people, ‹Donald and Dorothy,› and a number of other works. Her stories evince an unusual faculty of construction and marked inventiveness,—inherited perhaps from her father,—truthful characterization, literary feeling, a strong sense of humor, and a high ethical standard. Her whimsical character sketch, ‹Miss Maloney on the Chinese Question,› which has been reprinted thousands of times and repeated by every elocutionist in the land, is in its way as searching a satire as Bret Harte's ‹Heathen Chinee.›

Since its beginning in 1873, Mrs. Dodge has edited the St. Nicholas Magazine, whose pages bear witness to her enormous industry.

THE RACE

From ‹Hans Brinker, or The Silver Skates.› Copyright 1896, by Charles Scribner's Sons

THE 20th of December came at last, bringing with it the perfection of winter weather. All over the level landscape lay the warm sunlight. It tried its power on lake, canal, and river; but the ice flashed defiance, and showed no sign of melting. The very weathercocks stood still to enjoy the sight. This gave the windmills a holiday. Nearly all the past week they had been whirling briskly; now, being rather out of breath, they rocked lazily in the clear still air. Catch a windmill working when the weathercocks have nothing to do!

There was an end to grinding, crushing, and sawing for that day. It was a good thing for the millers near Broek. Long before noon, they concluded to take in their sails and go to the race. Everybody would be there. Already the north side of the frozen Y was bordered with eager spectators; the news of the great skating-match had traveled far and wide. Men, women, and children, in holiday attire, were flocking toward the spot. Some wore furs and wintry cloaks or shawls; but many,

THE SKATER OF THE ZUYDER ZEE.

Photogravure from a Painting by G. H. Boughton, A. R. A.

consulting their feelings rather than the almanac, were dressed as for an October day.

The site selected for the race was a faultless plain of ice near Amsterdam, on that great *arm* of the Zuyder Zee, which Dutchmen of course must call the Eye. The townspeople turned out in large numbers. Strangers in the city deemed it a fine chance to see what was to be seen. Many a peasant from the northward had wisely chosen the 20th as the day for the next city-trading. It seemed that everybody, young and old, who had wheels, skates, or feet at command, had hastened to the scene.

There were the gentry in their coaches, dressed like Parisians fresh from the Boulevards; Amsterdam children in charity uniforms; girls from the Roman Catholic Orphan House, in sable gowns and white head-bands; boys from the Burgher Asylum, with their black tights and short-skirted harlequin coats. There were old-fashioned gentlemen in cocked hats and velvet knee-breeches; old-fashioned ladies too, in stiff quilted skirts and bodices of dazzling brocade. These were accompanied by servants bearing foot-stoves and cloaks. There were the peasant folk, arrayed in every possible Dutch costume,— shy young rustics in brazen buckles; simple village maidens concealing their flaxen hair under fillets of gold; women whose long narrow aprons were stiff with embroidery; women with short corkscrew curls hanging over their foreheads; women with shaved heads and close-fitting caps, and women in striped skirts and windmill bonnets; men in leather, in homespun, in velvet and broadcloth; burghers in modern European attire, and burghers in short jackets, wide trousers, and steeple-crowned hats.

There were beautiful Friesland girls in wooden shoes and coarse petticoats, with solid gold crescents encircling their heads, finished at each temple with a golden rosette, and hung with lace a century old. Some wore necklaces, pendants, and earrings of the purest gold. Many were content with gilt, or even with brass; but it is not an uncommon thing for a Friesland woman to have all the family treasure in her headgear. More than one rustic lass displayed the value of two thousand guilders upon her head that day.

Scattered throughout the crowd were peasants from the Island of Marken, with sabots, black stockings, and the widest of breeches; also women from Marken, with short blue petticoats, and black jackets gayly figured in front. They wore red sleeves, white aprons, and a cap like a bishop's mitre over their golden hair.

The children often were as quaint and odd-looking as their elders. In short, one-third of the crowd seemed to have stepped bodily from a collection of Dutch paintings.

Everywhere could be seen tall women and stumpy men, lively-faced girls, and youths whose expressions never changed from sunrise to sunset.

There seemed to be at least one specimen from every known town in Holland. There were Utrecht water-bearers, Gouda cheese-makers, Delft pottery-men, Schiedam distillers, Amsterdam diamond-cutters, Rotterdam merchants, dried-up herring-packers, and two sleepy-eyed shepherds from Texel. Every man of them had his pipe and tobacco pouch. Some carried what might be called the smoker's complete outfit,—a pipe, tobacco, a pricker with which to clean the tube, a silver net for protecting the bowl, and a box of the strongest of brimstone matches.

A true Dutchman, you must remember, is rarely without his pipe on any possible occasion. He may for a moment neglect to breathe; but when the pipe is forgotten, he must be dying indeed. There were no such sad cases here. Wreaths of smoke were rising from every possible quarter. The more fantastic the smoke-wreath, the more placid and solemn the smoker.

Look at those boys and girls on stilts! That is a good idea. They can look over the heads of the tallest. It is strange to see those little bodies high in the air, carried about on mysterious legs. They have such a resolute look on their round faces, what wonder that nervous old gentlemen with tender feet wince and tremble while the long-legged little monsters stride past them!

You will read in certain books that the Dutch are a quiet people. So they are, generally. But listen! did you ever hear such a din? All made up of human voices—no, the horses are helping somewhat, and the fiddles are squeaking pitifully; (how it must pain fiddles to be tuned!) but the mass of the sound comes from the great *vox humana* that belongs to a crowd.

That queer little dwarf, going about with a heavy basket, winding in and out among the people, helps not a little. You can hear his shrill cry above all other sounds, «Pypen en tabac! Pypen en tabac!»

Another, his big brother, though evidently some years younger, is selling doughnuts and bonbons. He is calling on all pretty children, far and near, to come quickly or the cakes will be gone.

You know quite a number among the spectators. High up in yonder pavilion, erected upon the border of the ice, are some persons whom you have seen very lately. In the centre is Madame Van Gleck. It is her birthday, you remember; she has the post of honor. There is Mynheer Van Gleck, whose meerschaum has not really grown fast to his lips; it only appears so. There are Grandfather and Grandmother, whom you met at the St. Nicholas fête. All the children are with them. It is so mild, they have brought even the baby. The poor little creature is swaddled very much after the manner of an Egyptian mummy; but it can crow with delight, and when the band is playing, open and shut its animated mittens in perfect time to the music.

Grandfather, with his pipe and spectacles and fur cap, makes quite a picture as he holds Baby upon his knee. Perched high upon their canopied platforms, the party can see all that is going on. No wonder the ladies look complacently at the glassy ice; with a stove for a footstool, one might sit cosily beside the North Pole.

There is a gentleman with them, who somewhat resembles St. Nicholas as he appeared to the young Van Glecks on the fifth of December. But the Saint had a flowing white beard, and this face is as smooth as a pippin. His Saintship was larger round the body too, and (between ourselves) he had a pair of thimbles in his mouth, which this gentleman certainly has not. It cannot be St. Nicholas, after all.

Near by in the next pavilion sit the Van Holps, with their son and daughter (the Van Gends) from The Hague. Peter's sister is not one to forget her promises. She has brought bouquets of exquisite hot-house flowers for the winners.

These pavilions,—and there are others beside,—have all been erected since daylight. That semicircular one, containing Mynheer Korbes's family, is very pretty, and proves that the Hollanders are quite skilled at tent-making; but I like the Van Glecks' best,—the centre one, striped red and white, and hung with evergreens.

The one with the blue flags contains the musicians. Those pagoda-like affairs, decked with sea-shells and streamers of every possible hue, are the judges' stands; and those columns and flagstaffs upon the ice mark the limit of the race-course. The two white columns twined with green, connected at the top by that long floating strip of drapery, form the starting-point. Those flagstaffs, half a mile off, stand at each end of the boundary line, cut sufficiently deep to be distinct to the skaters, though not deep enough to trip them when they turn to come back to the starting-point.

The air is so clear, it seems scarcely possible that the columns and flagstaffs are so far apart. Of course the judges' stands are but little nearer together. Half a mile on the ice, when the atmosphere is like this, is but a short distance after all, especially when fenced with a living chain of spectators.

The music has commenced. How melody seems to enjoy itself in the open air! The fiddles have forgotten their agony, and everything is harmonious. Until you look at the blue tent, it seems that the music springs from the sunshine, it is so boundless, so joyous. Only the musicians are solemn.

Where are the racers? All assembled together near the white columns. It is a beautiful sight,—forty boys and girls in picturesque attire, darting with electric swiftness in and out among each other, or sailing in pairs and triplets, beckoning, chatting, whispering, in the fullness of youthful glee.

A few careful ones are soberly tightening their straps; others, halting on one leg, with flushed eager faces, suddenly cross the suspected skate over their knee, give it an examining shake, and dart off again. One and all are possessed with the spirit of motion. They cannot stand still. Their skates are a part of them, and every runner seems bewitched.

Holland is the place for skaters, after all. Where else can nearly every boy and girl perform feats on the ice that would attract a crowd if seen on Central Park? Look at Ben! I did not see him before. He is really astonishing the natives; no easy thing to do in the Netherlands. Save your strength, Ben; you will need it soon. Now other boys are trying! Ben is surpassed already. Such jumping, such poising, such spinning, such india-rubber exploits generally! That boy with a red cap is the lion now; his back is a watch-spring, his body is cork—no, it is iron, or it would snap at that. He is a bird, a top, a rabbit, a corkscrew, a sprite, a flesh-ball, all in an instant. When you think he is erect, he is down; and when you think he is down, he is up. He drops his glove on the ice, and turns a somerset as he picks it up. Without stopping, he snatches the cap from

Jacob Poot's astonished head, and claps it back again «hind side before.» Lookers-on hurrah and laugh. Foolish boy! It is arctic weather under your feet, but more than temperate overhead. Big drops already are rolling down your forehead. Superb skater as you are, you may lose the race.

A French traveler, standing with a notebook in his hand, sees our English friend Ben buy a doughnut of the dwarf's brother, and eat it. Thereupon he writes in his note-book that the Dutch take enormous mouthfuls, and universally are fond of potatoes boiled in molasses.

There are some familiar faces near the white columns. Lambert, Ludwig, Peter, and Carl are all there, cool, and in good skating order. Hans is not far off. Evidently he is going to join in the race, for his skates are on,—the very pair that he sold for seven guilders. He had soon suspected that his fairy godmother was the mysterious «friend» who bought them. This settled, he had boldly charged her with the deed; and she, knowing well that all her little savings had been spent in the purchase, had not had the face to deny it. Through the fairy god-mother, too, he had been rendered amply able to buy them back again. Therefore Hans is to be in the race. Carl is more indignant than ever about it; but as three other peasant boys have entered, Hans is not alone.

Twenty boys and twenty girls. The latter by this time are standing in front, braced for the start; for they are to have the first «run.» Hilda, Rychie, and Katrinka are among them. Two or three bend hastily to give a last pull at their skate-straps. It is pretty to see them stamp, to be sure that all is firm. Hilda is speaking pleasantly to a graceful little creature in a red jacket and a new brown petticoat. Why, it is Gretel! What a difference those pretty shoes make; and the skirt and the new cap! Annie Bouman is there too. Even Janzoon Kolp's sister has been admitted; but Janzoon himself has been voted out by the directors because he killed the stork, and only last summer was caught in the act of robbing a bird's nest,—a legal offense in Holland.

This Janzoon Kolp, you see, was— There, I cannot tell the story just now. The race is about to commence.

Twenty girls are formed in a line. The music has ceased.

A man whom we shall call the crier stands between the columns and the first judges' stand. He reads the rules in a loud voice:—

« *The girls and boys are to race in turn, until one girl and one boy have beaten twice. They are to start in a line from the united columns, skate to the flagstaff line, turn, and then come back to the starting-point; thus making a mile at each run.*»

A flag is waved from the judges' stand. Madame Van Gleck rises in her pavilion. She leans forward with a white handkerchief in her hand. When she drops it, a bugler is to give the signal for them to start.

The handkerchief is fluttering to the ground. Hark!

They are off!

No. Back again. Their line was not true in passing the judges' stand.

The signal is repeated.

Off again. No mistake this time. Whew! how fast they go!

The multitude is quiet for an instant, absorbed in eager, breathless watching.

Cheers spring up along the line of spectators. Huzza! five girls are ahead. Who comes flying back from the boundary mark? We cannot tell. Something red, that is all. There is a blue spot flitting near it, and a dash of yellow nearer still. Spectators at this end of the line strain their eyes, and wish they had taken their post nearer the flagstaff.

The wave of cheers is coming back again. Now we can see. Katrinka is ahead!

She passes the Van Holp pavilion. The next is Madame Van Gleck's. That leaning figure gazing from it is a magnet. Hilda shoots past Katrinka, waving her hand to her mother as she passes. Two others are close now, whizzing on like arrows. What is that flash of red and gray? Hurrah, it is Gretel! She too waves her hand, but toward no gay pavilion. The crowd is cheering; but she hears only her father's voice, «Well done, little Gretel!» Soon Katrinka, with a quick merry laugh, shoots past Hilda. The girl in yellow is gaining now. She passes them all,—all except Gretel. The judges lean forward without seeming to lift their eyes from their watches. Cheer after cheer fills the air; the very columns seem rocking. Gretel has passed them. She has won.

«GRETEL BRINKER, ONE MILE!» shouts the crier.

The judges nod. They write something upon a tablet which each holds in his hand.

While the girls are resting,—some crowding eagerly around our frightened little Gretel, some standing aside in high disdain,—the boys form in a line.

Mynheer Van Gleck drops the handkerchief this time. The buglers give a vigorous blast. Off start the boys!

Half-way already. Did ever you see the like!

Three hundred legs flashing by in an instant. But there are only twenty boys. No matter; there were hundreds of legs, I am sure. Where are they now? There is such a noise one gets bewildered. What are the people laughing at? Oh! at that fat boy in the rear. See him go! See him! He'll be down in an instant; no, he won't. I wonder if he knows he is all alone: the other boys are nearly at the boundary line. Yes, he knows it. He stops. He wipes his hot face. He takes off his cap, and looks about him. Better to give up with a good grace. He has made a hundred friends by that hearty, astonished laugh. Good Jacob Poot!

The fine fellow is already among the spectators, gazing as eagerly as the rest.

A cloud of feathery ice flies from the heels of the skaters as they «bring to,» and turn at the flagstaffs.

Something black is coming now,—one of the boys; it is all we know. He has touched the *vox humana* stop of the crowd; it fairly roars. Now they come nearer; we can see the red cap. There's Ben, there's Peter, there's Hans!

Hans is ahead. Young Madame Van Gend almost crushes the flowers in her hand: she had been quite sure that Peter would be first. Carl Schummel is next, then Ben, and the youth with the red cap. The others are pressing close. A tall figure darts from among them. He passes the red cap, he passes Ben, then Carl. Now it is an even race between him and Hans. Madame Van Gend catches her breath.

It is Peter! He is ahead! Hans shoots past him. Hilda's eyes fill with tears: Peter *must* beat. Annie's eyes flash proudly. Gretel gazes with clasped hands: four strokes more will take her brother to the columns.

He is there! Yes; but so was young Schummel just a second before. At the last instant, Carl, gathering his powers, had whizzed between them, and passed the goal.

«CARL SCHUMMEL, ONE MILE!» shouts the crier.

Soon Madame Van Gleck rises again. The falling handkerchief starts the bugle, and the bugle, using its voice as a bowstring, shoots off twenty girls like so many arrows.

It is a beautiful sight; but one has not long to look: before we can fairly distinguish them they are far in the distance. This time they are close upon one another. It is hard to say, as they come speeding back from the flagstaff, which will reach the columns first. There are new faces among the foremost,—eager glowing faces, unnoticed before. Katrinka is there, and Hilda; but Gretel and Rychie are in the rear. Gretel is wavering, but when Rychie passes her she starts forward afresh. Now they are nearly beside Katrinka. Hilda is still in advance: she is almost «home.» She has not faltered since that bugle note sent her flying: like an arrow, still she is speeding toward the goal. Cheer after cheer rises in the air. Peter is silent, but his eyes shine like stars. «Huzza! Huzza!»

The crier's voice is heard again.

«HILDA VAN GLECK, ONE MILE!»

A loud murmur of approval runs through the crowd, catching the music in its course, till all seems one sound, with a glad rhythmic throbbing in its depths. When the flag waves all is still.

Once more the bugle blows a terrific blast. It sends off the boys like chaff before the wind,—dark chaff, I admit, and in big pieces.

It is whisked around at the flagstaff, driven faster yet by the cheers and shouts along the line. We begin to see what is coming. There are three boys in advance this time, and all abreast, — Hans, Peter, and Lambert. Carl soon breaks the ranks, rushing through with a whiff. Fly, Hans; fly, Peter; don't let Carl beat again! — Carl the bitter, Carl the insolent. Van Mounen is flagging, but you are as strong as ever. Hans and Peter, Peter and Hans; which is foremost? We love them both. We scarcely care which is the fleeter.

Hilda, Annie, and Gretel, seated upon the long crimson bench, can remain quiet no longer. They spring to their feet, so different! and yet one in eagerness. Hilda instantly reseats herself: none shall know how interested she is; none shall know how anxious, how filled with one hope. Shut your eyes then, Hilda, hide your face rippling with joy. Peter has beaten.

"PETER VAN HOLP, ONE MILE!" calls the crier.

The same buzz of excitement as before, while the judges take notes, the same throbbing of music through the din; but something is different. A little crowd presses close about some object near the column. Carl has fallen. He is not hurt, though somewhat stunned. If he were less sullen, he would find more sympathy in these warm young hearts. As it is, they forget him as soon as he is fairly on his feet again.

The girls are to skate their third mile.

How resolute the little maidens look, as they stand in a line! Some are solemn with a sense of responsibility; some wear a smile, half bashful, half provoked; but one air of determination pervades them all.

This third mile may decide the race. Still, if neither Gretel nor Hilda win, there is yet a chance among the rest for the silver skates.

Each girl feels sure that this time she will accomplish the distance in one-half the time. How they stamp to try their runners! How nervously they examine each strap! How erect they stand at last, every eye upon Madame Van Gleck!

The bugle thrills through them again. With quivering eagerness they spring forward, bending, but in perfect balance. Each flashing stroke seems longer than the last.

Now they are skimming off in the distance.

Again the eager straining of eyes; again the shouts and cheering; again the thrill of excitement, as after a few moments, four or five in advance of the rest come speeding back, nearer, nearer to the white columns.

Who is first? Not Rychie, Katrinka, Annie, nor Hilda, nor the girl in yellow, but Gretel,—Gretel, the fleetest sprite of a girl that ever skated. She was but playing in the earlier race: *now* she is in earnest, or rather, something within her has determined to win. That blithe little form makes no effort; but it cannot stop,—not until the goal is passed!

In vain the crier lifts his voice: he cannot be heard. He has no news to tell: it is already ringing through the crowd,—*Gretel has won the silver skates!*

Like a bird she has flown over the ice; like a bird she looks about her in a timid, startled way. She longs to dart to the sheltered nook where her father and mother stand. But Hans is beside her; the girls are crowding round. Hilda's kind, joyous voice breathes in her ear. From that hour none will despise her. Goose-girl or not, Gretel stands acknowledged Queen of the Skaters.

With natural pride, Hans turns to see if Peter Van Holp is witnessing his sister's triumph. Peter is not looking toward them at all. He is kneeling, bending his troubled face low, and working hastily at his skate-strap. Hans is beside him at once.

«Are you in trouble, mynheer?»

«Ah, Hans! that you? Yes; my fun is over. I tried to tighten my strap to make a new hole, and this botheration of a knife has cut it nearly in two.»

«Mynheer,» said Hans, at the same time pulling off a skate, «you must use my strap!»

«Not I, indeed, Hans Brinker!» cried Peter, looking up; «though I thank you warmly. Go to your post, my friend: the bugle will sound in a minute.»

«Mynheer,» pleaded Hans in a husky voice, «you have called me your friend. Take this strap—quick! There is not an instant to lose. I shall not skate this time: indeed, I am out of practice. Mynheer, you *must* take it;» and Hans, blind and deaf to any remonstrance, slipped his strap into Peter's skate, and implored him to put it on.

«Come, Peter!» cried Lambert from the line: «we are waiting for you.»

«For Madame's sake,» pleaded Hans, «be quick! She is motioning to you to join the racers. There, the skate is almost on: quick, mynheer, fasten it. I could not possibly win. The race lies between Master Schummel and yourself.»

«You are a noble fellow, Hans!» cried Peter, yielding at last. He sprang to his post just as the handkerchief fell to the ground. The bugle sends forth its blast, loud, clear, and ringing.

Off go the boys!

«Mein Gott!» cries a tough old fellow from Delft. «They beat everything, these Amsterdam youngsters. See them!»

See them, indeed! They are winged Mercuries, every one of them. What mad errand are they on? Ah, I know; they are hunting Peter Van Holp. He is some fleet-footed runaway from Olympus. Mercury and his troop of winged cousins are in full chase. They will catch him! Now Carl is the runaway. The pursuit grows furious. Ben is foremost!

The chase turns in a cloud of mist. It is coming this way. Who is hunted now? Mercury himself. It is Peter, Peter Van Holp! Fly, Peter! Hans is watching you. He is sending all his fleetness, all his strength, into your feet. Your mother and sister are pale with eagerness. Hilda is trembling, and dare not look up. Fly, Peter! The crowd has not gone deranged; it is only cheering. The pursuers are close upon you. Touch the white column! It beckons; it is reeling before you—it—

«Huzza! Huzza! Peter has won the silver skates!»

«PETER VAN HOLP!» shouted the crier. But who heard him? «Peter Van Holp!» shouted a hundred voices; for he was the favorite boy of the place. «Huzza! Huzza!»

Now the music was resolved to be heard. It struck up a lively air, then a tremendous march. The spectators, thinking something new was about to happen, deigned to listen and to look.

The racers formed in single file. Peter, being tallest, stood first. Gretel, the smallest of all, took her place at the end. Hans, who had borrowed a strap from the cake-boy, was near the head.

Three gayly twined arches were placed at intervals upon the river, facing the Van Gleck pavilion.

Skating slowly, and in perfect time to the music, the boys and girls moved forward, led on by Peter. It was beautiful to see the bright procession glide along like a living creature. It curved and doubled, and drew its graceful length in and out among the arches; whichever way Peter, the head, went, the body was sure to follow. Sometimes it steered direct for the centre arch; then, as if seized with a new impulse, turned away and curled itself about the first one; then unwound slowly, and bending low, with quick snake-like curvings, crossed the river, passing at length through the farthest arch.

When the music was slow, the procession seemed to crawl like a thing afraid; it grew livelier, and the creature darted forward with a spring, gliding rapidly among the arches, in and out, curling, twisting, turning, never losing form, until at the shrill call of the bugle rising above the music it suddenly resolved itself into boys and girls, standing in double semicircle before Madame Van Gleck's pavilion.

Peter and Gretel stand in the centre, in advance of the others. Madame Van Gleck rises majestically. Gretel trembles, but feels that she must look at the beautiful lady. She cannot hear what is said, there is such a buzzing all around her. She is thinking that she ought to try and make a courtesy, such as her mother makes to the *meester*, when suddenly something so dazzling is placed in her hand that she gives a cry of joy.

Then she ventures to look about her. Peter too has something in his hands. «Oh, oh! how splendid!» she cries; and «Oh! how splendid!» is echoed as far as people can see.

Meantime the silver skates flash in the sunshine, throwing dashes of light upon those two happy faces.

«Mevrouw Van Gend sends a little messenger with her bouquets,—one for Hilda, one for Carl, and others for Peter and Gretel.»

At sight of the flowers, the Queen of the Skaters becomes uncontrollable. With a bright stare of gratitude, she gathers skates and bouquet in her apron, hugs them to her bosom, and darts off to search for her father and mother in the scattering crowd.

JOHN DONNE

(1573–1631)

"The memory of Dr. Donne must not, cannot die, as long as men speak English," wrote Izaak Walton, "whilst his conversation made him and others happy. His life ought to be the example of more than that age in which he died."

Born in 1573, all the influences of the age in which Donne lived nourished his large nature and genius. Shakespeare and Marlowe were nine years older than he; Chapman fourteen; Spenser, Lyly, and Richard Hooker each twenty; while Sir Philip Sidney counted one year less. Lodge and Puttenham were grown men, and Greene and Nash riotous boys. In the following year Ben Jonson "came forth to warm our ears," and soon after we have his future co-worker Inigo Jones. It was the time of a multitude of poets,—Drayton, the Fletchers, Beaumont, Wither, Herrick, Carew, Suckling, and others. Imagination was foremost, and was stimulated by vast discoveries. Debates upon ecclesiastical reform, led by Wyclif, Tyndal, Knox, Foxe, Sternhold, Hopkins, and others, had prepared the way; and the luminous literatures of Greece and Italy, but recently brought into England, had made men's spirits receptive and creative. It was a period of vast conceptions, when men discovered themselves and the world afresh.

John Donne

Under such outward conditions Donne was born, in London, "of good and virtuous parents," says Walton, being descended on his mother's side from no less distinguished a personage than Sir Thomas More. In 1584, when he was eleven years old, with a good command both of French and Latin, he passed from the hands of tutors at home to Hare Hall, a much frequented college at Oxford. Here he formed a friendship with Henry Wotton, who, after the poet's death, collected the material from which Walton wrote his tender and sincere 'Life of Donne.'

After leaving Oxford he traveled for three years on the Continent, and on his return in 1592 became a member of Lincoln's Inn, with intent to study law; but his law never, says Walton, "served him for other use than an ornament and self-satisfaction.» While a member of Lincoln's Inn he became one of the coterie of the poets of his youth. To this time are to be referred those of his ‹Divine Poems› which show him a sincere Catholic. Stirred by the increasing differences between the Romanist and the Anglican denominations, Donne turned toward theological questions, and finally cast his lot with the new doctrines. His large nature, impetuously reacting from the asceticism to which he had been bred, turned to excess and overboldness in action, and an occasional coarseness of phrasing in his poems.

The first of his famous ‹Satires› are dated 1593, and all were probably written before 1601. During this time also he squandered his father's legacy of £3000. In 1596, when the Earl of Essex defeated the Spanish navy and pillaged Cadiz, Donne, now one of the first poets of the time, was among his followers. «Not long after his return into England . . . the Lord Ellesmere, the Keeper of the Great Seal, . . . taking notice of his learning, languages, and other abilities, and much affecting his person and behavior, took him to be his chief secretary, supposing and intending it to be an introduction to some weighty employment in the State; . . . and did always use him with much courtesy, appointing him a place at his own table.» Here he met the niece of Lady Ellesmere, — the daughter of Sir George More, Lord Lieutenant of the Tower,— whom at Christmas, 1600, he married, despite the opposition of her father. Sir George, transported with wrath, obtained Donne's imprisonment; but the poet finally regained his liberty and his wife, Sir George in the end forgiving the young couple. «Mr. Donne's estate was the greatest part spent in many chargeable travels, books, and dear-bought experience; he [being] out of all employment that might yield a support for himself and wife.» The depth and intensity of Donne's feeling for this beautiful and accomplished woman are manifested, says Mr. Norton, in all the poems known to be addressed to her, such as ‹The Anniversary› and ‹The Token.›

Of ‹The Valediction Forbidding Mourning› Walton declares:—«I beg leave to tell that I have heard some critics, learned both in languages and poetry, say that none of the Greek or Latin poets did ever equal them;» while from Lowell's unpublished ‹Lecture on Poetic Diction› Professor Norton quotes the opinion that «This poem is a truly sacred one, and fuller of the soul of poetry than a whole Alexandrian Library of common love verses.»

During this period of writing for court favors, Donne wrote many of his sonnets and studied the civil and canon law. After the death of his patron Sir Francis in 1606, Donne divided his time between Mitcham, whither he had removed his family, and London, where he frequented distinguished and fashionable drawing-rooms. At this time he wrote his admirable epistles in verse, 'The Litany,' and funeral elegies on Lady Markham and Mistress Bulstrode; but those poems are merely «occasional,» as he was not a poet by profession. At the request of King James he wrote the 'Pseudo-Martyr,' published in 1610. In 1611 appeared his funeral elegy 'An Anatomy of the World,' and one year later another of like texture, 'On the Progress of the Soul,' both poems being exalted and elaborate in thought and fancy.

The King, desiring Donne to enter into the ministry, denied all requests for secular preferment, and the unwilling poet deferred his decision for almost three years. All that time he studied textual divinity, Greek, and Hebrew. He was ordained about the beginning of 1615. The King made him his chaplain in ordinary, and promised other preferments. «Now,» says Walton, «the English Church had gained a second St. Austin, for I think none was so like him before his conversion, none so like St. Ambrose after it; and if his youth had the infirmities of the one, his age had the excellences of the other, the learning and holiness of both.»

In 1621 the King made him Dean of St. Paul's, and vicar of St. Dunstan in the West. By these and other ecclesiastical emoluments «he was enabled to become charitable to the poor and kind to his friends, and to make such provision for his children that they were not left scandalous, as relating to their or his profession or quality.»

His first printed sermons appeared in 1622. The epigrammatic terseness and unexpected turns of imagination which characterize the poems, are found also in his discourses. Three years later, during a dangerous illness, he composed his 'Devotion.' He died on the 31st of March, 1631.

«Donne is full of salient verses,» says Lowell in his 'Shakespeare Once More,' «that would take the rudest March winds of criticism with their beauty; of thoughts that first tease us like charades, and then delight us with the felicity of their solution.» There are few in which an occasional loftiness is sustained throughout, but this occasional excellence is original, condensed, witty, showing a firm and strong mind, clear to a degree almost un-English. His poetry has somewhat of the stability of the Greeks, though it may lack their sweetness and art. His grossness was the heritage of his time. He is classed among the «metaphysical poets,» of whom Dr. Johnson wrote:—«They were of very little care to clothe their notions with elegance of dress, and therefore miss the notice and the praise which are often gained by those who think less, but are more diligent to adorn their thoughts.» It was in obedience to such a dictum, and to Dryden's suggestion, doubtless, that Pope and Parnell recast and re-versified the 'Satires.'

The first edition of Donne's poems appeared two years after his death. Several editions succeeded during the seventeenth century. In the more artificial eighteenth century his harsh and abrupt versification and remote theorems made him difficult to understand. The best editions are 'The Complete Poems of John Donne,' edited by Dr. Alexander Grosart (1872); and 'The Poems of John Donne,' from the text of the edition of 1633, edited by Charles Eliot Norton (1895), from whose work the citations in this volume are taken.

THE UNDERTAKING

I have done one braver thing
Than all the Worthies did,
And yet a braver thence doth spring,
Which is, to keep that hid.

It were but madness now t' impart
The skill of specular stone,
When he which can have learned the art
To cut it, can find none.

So, if I now should utter this,
Others (because no more
Such stuff to work upon there is)
Would love but as before:

But he who loveliness within
Hath found, all outward loathes;
For he who color loves, and skin,
Loves but their oldest clothes.

If, as I have, you also do
Virtue attired in women see,
And dare love that and say so too,
And forget the He and She;

And if this love, though placèd so,
From profane men you hide,
Which will no faith on this bestow,
Or, if they do, deride;

Then you have done a braver thing
Than all the Worthies did,
And a braver thence will spring,
Which is, to keep that hid.

A VALEDICTION FORBIDDING MOURNING

As virtuous men pass mildly away,
And whisper to their souls to go,
Whilst some of their sad friends do say,
«The breath goes now,» and some say «No»;

So let us melt and make no noise,
No tear-floods nor sigh-tempests move;
'Twere profanation of our joys
To tell the laity our love.

Moving of th' earth brings harms and fears;
Men reckon what it did and meant;
But trepidation of the spheres,
Though greater far, is innocent.

Dull sublunary lovers' love
(Whose soul is sense) cannot admit
Absence, because it doth remove
Those things which elemented it.

But we by a love so much refined
That ourselves know not what it is,
Inter-assurèd of the mind,
Care less eyes, lips, hands to miss.

Our two souls, therefore, which are one,
Though I must go, endure not yet
A breach, but an expansiòn,
Like gold to airy thinness beat.

If they be two, they are two so
As stiff twin compasses are two;
Thy soul, the fixt foot, makes no show
To move, but doth if the other do,

And though it in the centre sit,
Yet when the other far doth roam,
It leans and hearkens after it,
And grows erect as that comes home.

Such wilt thou be to me, who must,
Like th' other foot, obliquely run;
Thy firmness makes my circle just,
And makes me end where I begun.

SONG

GO AND catch a falling star,
    Get with child a mandrake root,
  Tell me where all past years are,
    Or who cleft the devil's foot,
Teach me to hear mermaids singing,
Or to keep off envy's stinging,
        And find
        What wind
Serves to advance an honest mind.

If thou be'st born to strange sights,
  Things invisible to see,
Ride ten thousand days and nights,
  Till age snow white hairs on thee,
Then, when thou return'st, wilt tell me
All strange wonders that befell thee,
        And swear,
        Nowhere
Lives a woman true and fair.

If thou find'st one, let me know;
  Such a pilgrimage were sweet;
Yet do not: I would not go,
  Though at next door we might meet;
Though she were true when you met her,
And last till you write your letter,
        Yet she
        Will be
False, ere I come, to two or three.

LOVE'S GROWTH

I SCARCE believe my love to be so pure
        As I had thought it was,
        Because it doth endure
Vicissitude and season as the grass;
Methinks I lied all winter, when I swore
My love was infinite, if spring make it more.
But if this medicine love, which cures all sorrow
  With more, not only be no quintessence
  But mixed of all stuffs paining soul or sense,
And of the sun his working vigor borrow,

Love's not so pure and abstract as they use
To say, which have no mistress but their muse,
But as all else, being elemented too,
Love sometimes would contemplate, sometimes do.

And yet no greater, but more eminent,
Love by the spring is grown;
As in the firmament
Stars by the sun are not enlarged, but shown,
Gentle love-deeds, as blossoms on a bough,
From love's awakened root do bud out now.
If, as in water stirred, more circles be
Produced by one, love such additions take,
Thou, like so many spheres, but one heaven make,
For they are all concentric unto thee;
And though each spring do add to love new heat,
As princes do in times of action get
New taxes and remit them not in peace,
No winter shall abate the spring's increase.

SONG

Sweetest Love, I do not go
For weariness of thee,
Nor in hope the world can show
A fitter Love for me:
But since that I
Must die at last, 'tis best
To use myself in jest
Thus by feigned deaths to die.

Yesternight the sun went hence,
And yet is here to-day;
He hath no desire nor sense,
Nor half so short a way.
Then fear not me,
But believe that I shall make
Speedier journeys, since I take
More wings and spurs than he.

Oh, how feeble is man's power,
That, if good fortune fall,
Cannot add another hour,
Nor a lost hour recall!

But come bad chance,
And we join to it our strength,
And we teach it art and length,
Itself o'er us to advance.

When thou sigh'st, thou sigh'st not wind,
But sigh'st my soul away;
When thou weep'st, unkindly kind,
My life's blood doth decay.
It cannot be
That thou lov'st me as thou say'st,
If in thine my life thou waste;
Thou art the best of me.

Let not thy divining heart
Forethink me any ill;
Destiny may take thy part,
And may thy fears fulfill:
But think that we
Are but turned aside to sleep:
They who one another keep
Alive, ne'er parted be.

FEODOR MIKHAILOVITCH DOSTOÉVSKY

(1821–1881)

BY ISABEL F. HAPGOOD

In certain respects Dostoévsky is the most characteristically national of Russian writers. Precisely for that reason, his work does not appeal to so wide a circle outside of his own country as does the work of Turgénieff and Count L. N. Tolstoy. This result flows not only from the natural bent of his mind and temperament, but also from the peculiar vicissitudes of his life as compared with the comparatively even tenor of their existence, and the circumstances of the time in which he lived. These circumstances, it is true, were felt by the writers mentioned; but practically they affected him far more deeply than they did the others, with their rather one-sided training; and his fellow-countrymen — especially the young of both sexes — were not slow to express their appreciation of the fact. His special domain was the one which Turgénieff and Tolstoy did not understand, and have touched not at all, or only incidentally, — the great middle class of society, or what corresponds thereto in Russia.

Feodor Dostoévsky

Through his father, Mikhail Andréevitch Dostoévsky, Feodor Mikhailovitch belonged to the class of «nobles,» — that is to say, to the gentry; through his mother, to the respectable, well-to-do merchant class, which is still distinct from the other, and was even more so during the first half of the present century; and in personal appearance he was a typical member of the peasant class. The father was resident physician in the Marie Hospital for the Poor in Moscow, having entered the civil service at the end of the war of 1812, during which he had served as a physician in the army. In the very contracted apartment which he occupied in the hospital, Feodor was born — one of a family of seven children, all of whom, with the exception of the eldest and the youngest, were born there — on October 30th (November 11th), 1821. The parents were very upright, well-educated, devoutly religious people; and as Feodor expressed it many years later to his elder brother, after their father died, « Do you know, our parents were very superior people, and they would have been superior even in these days.» The children were brought up at home as long as possible, and received their instruction from tutors and their father. Even after the necessity of preparing the two elder boys for a government institution forced the parents to send them to a boarding-school during the week, they continued their strict supervision over their associates, discouraged nearly all friendships with their comrades, and never allowed them to go into the street unaccompanied, after the national custom in good families, even at the age of seventeen or more.

Feodor, according to the account of his brothers and relatives, was always a quiet, studious lad, and he with his elder brother Mikhail spent their weekly holidays chiefly in reading, Walter Scott and James Fenimore Cooper being among their favorite authors; though Russian writers, especially Pushkin, were not neglected. During many of these years the mother and children passed the summers on a little estate in the country which the father bought, and it was there that Feodor Mikhailovitch first made acquaintance with the beauties of nature, to which he eloquently refers in after life, and especially with the peasants, their feelings and temper, which greatly helped him in his psychological studies and in his ability to endure certain trials which came upon him. There can be no doubt that his whole training contributed not only to the literary tastes which the famous author and his brother cherished throughout their lives, but to the formation of that friendship between them which was stronger than all others, and to the sincere belief in religion and the profound piety which permeated the spirit and the books of Feodor Mikhailovitch.

In 1837 the mother died, and the father took his two eldest sons to St. Petersburg to enter them in the government School of Engineers. But the healthy Mikhail was pronounced consumptive by the doctor, while the sickly Feodor was given a certificate of perfect health. Consequently Mikhail was rejected, and went to the Engineers' School in Revel, while Feodor, always quiet and reserved, was left lonely in the St. Petersburg school. Here he remained for three years, studying well, but devoting a great deal of time to his passionately beloved literary subjects, and developing a precocious and penetrating critical judgment on such matters. It is even affirmed that he began or wrote the first draft of his famous book 'Poor People,' by night, during this period; though in another account he places its composition later. After graduating well as ensign in 1841, he studied for another year, and became an officer with the rank of sub-lieutenant, and entered on active service, attached to the draughting department of the Engineers' School, in August 1843.

A little more than a year later he resigned from the service, in order that he might devote himself wholly to literature. His father had died in the mean time, and had he possessed any practical talent he might have lived in comfort on the sums which his guardian sent him. But throughout his life people seemed to fleece him at will; he lost large sums at billiards with strangers, and otherwise; he was generous and careless; in short, he was to the end nearly always in debt, anxiety, and difficulties. Then came the first important crisis in his life. He wrote (or re-wrote) 'Poor People'; and said of his state of mind, as he reckoned up the possible pecuniary results, that he could not sleep for nights together, and «If my undertaking does not succeed, perhaps I shall hang myself.» The history of that success is famous and stirring. His only acquaintance in literary circles was his old comrade D. V. Grigorovitch (also well known as a writer), and to him he committed the manuscript. His friend took it to the poet and editor Nekrásoff, in the hope that it might appear in the 'Collection' which the latter was intending to publish. Dostoévsky was especially afraid of the noted critic Byelinsky's judgment on it: «He will laugh at my 'Poor People,' said he; «but I wrote it with passion, almost with tears.»

He spent the evening with a friend, reading with him, as was the fashion of the time, Gogol's 'Dead Souls,' and returned home at four o'clock in the morning. It was one of the «white nights» of early summer, and he sat down by his window. Suddenly the door-bell rang, and in rushed Grigorovitch and Nekrásoff, who flung themselves upon his neck. They had begun to read his story in the evening, remarking that «ten pages would suffice to show its quality.» But they had gone on reading, relieving each other as their voices failed them with fatigue and emotion, until the whole was finished. At the point where Pokrovsky's old father runs after his coffin, Nekrásoff pounded the table with the manuscript, deeply affected, and exclaimed, «Deuce take him!» Then they decide to hasten to Dostoévsky: «No matter if he is asleep — we will wake him up. *This* is above sleep.»

This sort of glory and success was exactly of that pure, unmixed sort which Dostoévsky had longed for. When Nekrásoff went to Byelinsky with the manuscript of 'Poor People,' and announced, «A new Gogol has made his appearance!» the critic retorted with severity, «Gogols spring up like mushrooms among us.» But when he had read the story he said, «Bring him hither, bring him quickly;» and welcomed Dostoévsky when he came, with extreme dignity and reserve, but exclaimed in a moment, «Do you understand yourself what sort of a thing this is that you have written?» From that moment the young author's fame was assured, and he became known and popular even in advance of publication in a wide circle of literary and other people, as was the fashion of those days in Russia. When the story appeared, the public rapturously echoed the judgment of the critics.

The close friendship which sprang up between Byelinsky and Dostoévsky was destined, however, to exert an extraordinary influence upon Dostoévsky's career, quite apart from its critical aspect. Byelinsky was an atheist and a socialist, and Dostoévsky was brought into relations with persons who shared those views, although he himself never wavered, apparently, in his religious faith, and was never in harmony with any other aspirations of his associates except that of freeing the serfs. Notwithstanding this, he became involved in the catastrophe which overtook many visitors, occasional or constant, of the «circles» at whose head stood Petrashevsky. The whole affair is known as the Conspiracy of Petrashevsky. During the '40's the students at the St. Petersburg University formed small gatherings where sociological subjects were the objects of study, and read the works of Stein, Haxthausen, Louis Blanc, Fourier, Proudhon, and other similar writers. Gradually assemblies of this sort were formed outside of the University. Petrashevsky, an employee of the Department of Foreign Affairs, who had graduated from the Lyceum and the University, and who was ambitious of winning power and a reputation for eccentricity, learned of these little clubs and encouraged their growth. He did not however encourage their close association among themselves, but rather, entire dependence on himself, as the centre of authority, the guide; and urged them to inaugurate a sort of propaganda. Dostoévsky himself declared, about thirty years later, that «the socialists sprang from the followers of Petrashevsky; they sowed much seed.» He has dealt with them and their methods in his novel 'Demons'; though perhaps not with exact accuracy. But they helped him to an elucidation of the contemporary situation, which Turgénieff had treated in 'Virgin Soil.' The chief subject of their political discussions was the emancipation of the serfs, and many of Petrashevsky's followers reckoned upon a rising of the serfs themselves, though it was proved that Dostoévsky maintained the propriety and necessity of the reform proceeding from the government. This was no new topic; the Emperor Nicholas I. had already begun to plan the Emancipation, and it is probable that it would have taken place long before it did, had it not been for this very conspiracy. From the point of view of the government, the movement was naturally dangerous, especially in view of what was taking place in Europe at that epoch. Dostoévsky bore himself critically toward the socialistic writings and doctrines, maintaining that in their own Russian system of workingmen's guilds with reciprocal bonds there existed surer and more normal foundations than in all the dreams of Saint-Simon and all his school. He did not even visit very frequently the circle to which he particularly belonged, and was rarely at the house of Petrashevsky, whom many personally disliked.

But on one occasion, as he was a good reader, he was asked to read aloud Byelinsky's famous letter to Gogol, which was regarded as a victorious manifest of «Western» (*i. e.*, of socialistic) views. This, technically, was propagating revolution, and was the chief charge against him when the catastrophe happened, and he, together with over thirty other «Petrashevtzi,» was arrested on April 23d (May 5th), 1849. In the Peter-Paul Fortress prison, where he was kept for eight months pending trial, Dostoévsky wrote 'The Little Hero,' two or three unimportant works having appeared since 'Poor People.' At last he, with several others, was condemned to death and led out for execution. The history of that day, and the analysis of his sensations and emotions, are to be found in several of his books: 'Crime and Punishment,' 'The Idiot,' 'The Karamazoff Brothers.' At the last moment it was announced to them that the Emperor had commuted their sentence to exile in varying degrees, and they were taken to Siberia. Alexei Pleshtcheeff, then twenty-three years of age, the man who sent Byelinsky's letter to Dostoévsky, was banished for a short term of years to the disciplinary brigade in Orenburg; and when I saw him in St. Petersburg forty years later, I was able to form a faint idea of what Dostoévsky's popularity must have been, by the way in which he,—a man of much less talent, originality, and personal power,—was surrounded, even in church, by adoring throngs of young people. Dostoévsky's sentence was «four years at forced labor in prison; after that, to serve as a common soldier»; but he did not lose his nobility and his civil rights, being the first noble to retain them under such circumstances.

The story of what he did and suffered during his imprisonment is to be found in his 'Notes from the House of the Dead,' where, under the disguise of a man sentenced to ten years' labor for the murder of his wife, he gives us a startling, faithful, but in some respects a consoling picture of life in a Siberian prison. His own judgment as to his exile was, «The government only defended itself;» and when people said to him, «How unjust your exile was!» he replied, even with irritation, «No, it was just. The people themselves would have condemned us.» Moreover, he did not like to give benefit readings in later years from his 'Notes from the House of the Dead,' lest he might be thought to complain. Besides, this catastrophe was the making of him, by his own confession; he had become a confirmed hypochondriac, with a host of imaginary afflictions and ills, and had this affair not saved him from himself he said that he «should have gone mad.» It seems certain, from the testimony of his friend and physician, that he was already subject to the epileptic fits which he himself was wont to attribute to his imprisonment; and which certainly increased in severity as the years went on, until they occurred once a month or oftener, in consequence of overwork and excessive nervous strain. In his novel 'The Idiot,' whose hero is an epileptic, he has made a psychological study of his sensations before and after such fits, and elsewhere he makes allusions to them.

After serving in the ranks and being promoted officer when he had finished his term of imprisonment, he returned to Russia in 1859, and lived first at Tver; afterward, when permitted, in St. Petersburg. The history of his first marriage — which took place in Siberia, to the widow of a friend — is told with tolerable accuracy in his 'Humbled and Insulted,' which also contains a description of his early struggles and the composition of 'Poor People,' the hero who narrates the tale of his love and sacrifice being himself. Like that hero, he tried to facilitate his future wife's marriage to another man. He was married to his second wife, by whom he had four children, in 1867, and to her he owed much happiness and material comfort. It will be seen that much is to be learned concerning our author from his own novels, though it would hardly be safe to write a biography from them alone. Even in 'Crime and Punishment,' his greatest work in a general way, he reproduces events of his own life, meditations, wonderfully accurate descriptions of the third-rate quarter of the town in which he lived after his return from Siberia, while engaged on some of his numerous newspaper and magazine enterprises.

This journalistic turn of mind, combined in nearly equal measures with the literary talent, produced several singular effects. It rendered his periodical 'Diary of a Writer' the most enormously popular publication of the day, and a success when previous ventures had failed, though it consisted entirely of his own views on current topics of interest, literary questions, and whatever came into his head. On his novels it had a rather disintegrating effect. Most of them are of great length, are full of digressions from the point, and there is often a lack of finish about them which extends not only to the minor characters but to the style in general. In fact, his style is neither jewel-like in its brilliancy, as is Turgénieff's, nor has it the elegance, broken by carelessness, of Tolstoy's. But it was popular, remarkably well adapted to the class of society which it was his province to depict, and though diffuse, it is not possible to omit any of the long psychological analyses, or dreams, or series of ratiocinations, without injuring the web of the story and the moral, as chain armor is spoiled by the rupture of a link. This indeed is one of the great difficulties which the foreigner encounters in an attempt to study Dostoévsky: the translators have been daunted by his prolixity, and have often cut his works down to a mere skeleton of the original. Moreover, he deals with a sort of Russian society which it is hard for non-Russians to grasp, and he has no skill whatever in presenting aristocratic people or society, to which foreigners have become accustomed in the works of his great contemporaries Turgénieff and Tolstoy; while he never, despite all his genuine admiration for the peasants and keen sympathy with them, attempts any purely peasant tales like Turgénieff's 'Notes of a Sportsman' or Tolstoy's 'Tales for the People.' Naturally, this is but one reason the more why he should be studied. His types of hero, and of feminine character, are peculiar to himself. Perhaps the best way to arrive at his ideal—and at his own character, *plus* a certain irritability and tendency to suspicion of which his friends speak—is to scrutinize the pictures of Prince Myshkin ('The Idiot'), Ivan ('Humbled and Insulted'), and Alyosha ('The Karamazoff Brothers'). Pure, delicate both physically and morally, as Dostoévsky himself is described by those who knew him best; devout, gentle, intensely sympathetic, strongly masculine yet with a large admixture of the feminine element—such are these three; such is also, in his way, Raskolnikoff ('Crime and Punishment'). His feminine characters are the precise counterparts of these in many respects, but are often also quixotic even to boldness and wrong-headedness, like Aglaya ('The Idiot'), or to shame, like Sonia ('Crime and Punishment'), and the heroine of 'Humbled and Insulted.' But Dostoévsky could not sympathize with and consequently could not draw an aristocrat; his frequently recurring type of the dissolute petty noble or rich merchant is frequently brutal; and his unclassed women, though possibly quite as true to life as these men, are painful in their callousness and recklessness. His earliest work, 'Poor People,' written in the form of letters, is worthy of all the praises which have been bestowed upon it, simple as is the story of the poverty-stricken clerk who is almost too humble to draw his breath; who pleads that one must wear a coat and boots which do not show the bare feet, during the severe Russian winter, merely because public opinion forces one thereto; and who shares his rare pence with a distant but equally needy relative who is in a difficult position. As a compact, subtle psychological study, his 'Crime and Punishment' cannot be overrated, repulsive as it is in parts. The poor student who kills the aged usurer with intent to rob, after prolonged argument with himself that great geniuses, like Napoleon I. and the like, are justified in committing any crime, and that he has a right to relieve his poverty; and who eventually surrenders himself to the authorities and accepts his exile as moral salvation,—is one of the strongest in Russian literature, though wrong-headed and easily swayed, like all the author's characters.

In June 1880 Dostoévsky made a speech at the unveiling of Pushkin's monument in Moscow, which completely overshadowed the speeches of Turgénieff and Aksakoff, and gave rise to what was probably the most extraordinary literary ovation ever seen in Russia. By that time he had become the object of pilgrimages, on the part of the young especially, to a degree which no other Russian author has ever experienced, and the recipient of confidences, both personal and written, which pressed heavily on his time and strength. That ovation has never been surpassed, save by the astonishing cóncourse at his funeral. He died of a lesion of the brain on January 28th (February 8th), 1881. Thousands followed his coffin for miles, but there was no «demonstration,» as that word is understood in Russia. Nevertheless it was a demonstration in an unexpected way, since all classes of society, even those which had not seemed closely interested or sympathetic, now joined in the tribute of respect, which amounted to loving enthusiasm.

The works which I have mentioned are the most important, though he wrote also 'The Stripling' and numerous shorter stories. His own characterization of his work, when reproached with its occasional lack of continuity and finish, was that his aim was to make his point, and the exigencies of money and time under which he labored were to blame for the defects which, with his keen literary judgment, he perceived quite as clearly as did his critics. If that point be borne in mind, it will help the reader to appreciate his literary-journalistic style, and to pardon shortcomings for the sake of the pearls of principle and psychology which can be fished up from the profound depths of his voluminous tomes, and of his analysis. The gospel which Dostoévsky consistently preached, from the beginning of his career to the end, was love, self-sacrifice even to self-effacement. That was and is the secret of his power, even over those who did not follow his precepts.

Isabel F. Hapgood

FROM ‹POOR PEOPLE›

Letter from Varvara Dobrosyeloff to Makar Dyevushkin

Pokrovsky was a poor, very poor young man; his health did not permit of his attending regularly to his studies, and so it was only by way of custom that we called him a student. He lived modestly, peaceably, quietly, so that we could not even hear him from our room. He was very queer in appearance; he walked so awkwardly, bowed so uncouthly, spoke in such a peculiar manner, that at first I could not look at him without laughing. Moreover, he was of an irritable character, was constantly getting angry, flew into a rage at the slightest trifle, shouted at us, complained of us, and often went off to his own room in a fit of wrath without finishing our lesson. He had a great many books, all of them expensive, rare books. He gave lessons somewhere else also, received some remuneration, and just as soon as he had a little money, he went off and bought more books.

In time I learned to understand him better. He was the kindest, the most worthy man, the best man I ever met. My mother respected him highly. Later on, he became my best friend — after my mother, of course. . . .

From time to time a little old man made his appearance at our house — a dirty, badly dressed, small, gray-haired, sluggish, awkward old fellow; in short, he was peculiar to the last degree. At first sight one would have thought that he felt ashamed of something, that his conscience smote him for something. He writhed and twisted constantly; he had such tricks of manner and ways of shrugging his shoulders, that one would not have been far wrong in assuming that he was a little crazy. He would come and stand close to the glazed door in the vestibule, and not dare to enter. As soon as one of us, Sasha or I or one of the servants whom he knew to be kindly disposed toward him, passed that way, he would begin to wave his hands, and beckon us to him, and make signs; and only when we nodded to him or called to him, — the signal agreed upon, that there was no stranger in the house and that he might enter when he pleased, — only then would the old man softly open the door, with a joyous smile, rubbing his hands together with delight, and betake himself to Pokrovsky's room. He was his father.

Afterward I learned in detail the story of this poor old man. Once upon a time he had been in the government service somewhere or other, but he had not the slightest capacity, and his place in the service was the lowest and most insignificant of all. When his first wife died (the mother of the student Pokrovsky), he took it into his head to marry again, and wedded a woman from the petty-merchant class. Under the rule of this new wife, everything was at sixes and sevens in his house; there was no living with her; she drew a tight rein over everybody. Student Pokrovsky was a boy at that time, ten years of age. His stepmother hated him. But fate was kind to little Pokrovsky. Bykoff, a landed proprietor, who was acquainted with Pokrovsky the father and had formerly been his benefactor, took the child under his protection and placed him in a school. He took an interest in him because he had known his dead mother, whom Anna Feodorovna had befriended while she was still a girl, and who had married her off to Pokrovsky. From school young Pokrovsky entered a gymnasium, and then the University, but his impaired health prevented his continuing his studies there. Mr. Bykoff introduced him to Anna Feodorovna, recommended him to her, and in this way young Pokrovsky had been taken into the house as a boarder, on condition that he should teach Sasha all that was necessary.

But old Pokrovsky fell into the lowest dissipation through grief at his wife's harshness, and was almost always in a state of drunkenness. His wife beat him, drove him into the kitchen to live, and brought matters to such a point that at last he got used to being beaten and ill-treated, and made no complaint. He was still far from being an old man, but his evil habits had nearly destroyed his mind. The only sign in him of noble human sentiments was his boundless love for his son. It was said that young Pokrovsky was as like his dead mother as two drops of water to each other. The old man could talk of nothing but his son, and came to see him regularly twice a week. He dared not come more frequently, because young Pokrovsky could not endure his father's visits. Of all his failings, the first and greatest, without a doubt, was his lack of respect for his father. However, the old man certainly was at times the most intolerable creature in the world. In the first place he was dreadfully inquisitive; in the second, by his chatter and questions he interfered with his son's occupations; and lastly, he sometimes presented himself in a state of intoxication. The son broke the father, in a degree, of his faults,—of his inquisitiveness and his chattering; and ultimately brought about such a condition of affairs that the latter listened to all he said as to an oracle, and dared not open his mouth without his permission.

There were no bounds to the old man's admiration of and delight in his Petinka, as he called his son. When he came to visit him he almost always wore a rather anxious, timid expression, probably on account of his uncertainty as to how his son would receive him, and generally could not make up his mind for a long time to go in; and if I happened to be present, he would question me for twenty minutes: How was Petinka? Was he well? In what mood was he, and was not he occupied in something important? What, precisely, was he doing? Was he writing, or engaged in meditation? When I had sufficiently encouraged and soothed him, the old man would at last make up his mind to enter, and would open the door very, very softly, very, very cautiously, and stick his head in first; and if he saw that his son was not angry, and nodded to him, he would step gently into the room, take off his little coat, and his hat, which was always crumpled, full of holes and with broken rims, and hang them on a hook, doing everything very softly, and inaudibly. Then he would seat himself cautiously on a chair and never take his eyes from his son, but would watch his every movement in his desire to divine the state of his Petinka's temper. If the son was not exactly in the right mood, and the old man detected it, he instantly rose from his seat and explained, "I only ran in for a minute, Petinka. I have been walking a good ways, and happened to be passing by, so I came in to rest myself." And then silently he took his poor little coat and his wretched little hat, opened the door again very softly, and went away, forcing a smile in order to suppress the grief which was seething up in his soul, and not betray it to his son.

But when the son received his father well, the old man was beside himself with joy. His satisfaction shone forth in his face, in his gestures, in his movements. If his son addressed a remark to him, the old man always rose a little from his chair, and replied softly, cringingly, almost reverently, and always made an effort to employ the most select, that is to say, the most ridiculous expressions. But he had not the gift of language; he always became confused and frightened, so that he did not know what to do with his hands, or what to do with his person, and went on, for a long time afterward, whispering his answer to himself, as though desirous of recovering his composure. But if he succeeded in making a good answer, the old man gained courage, set his waistcoat to rights, and his cravat and his coat, and assumed an air of personal dignity. Sometimes his courage rose to such a point, his daring reached such a height, that he rose gently from his chair, went up to the shelf of books, took down a book. He did all this with an air of artificial indifference and coolness, as though he could always handle his son's books in this proprietary manner, as though his son's caresses were no rarity to him. But I once happened to witness the old man's fright when Pokrovsky asked him not to touch his books. He became confused, hurriedly replaced the book upside down, then tried to put it right, turned it round and set it wrong side to, leaves out, smiled, reddened, and did not know how to expiate his crime.

One day old Pokrovsky came in to see us. He chatted with us for a long time, was unusually cheerful, alert, talkative; he laughed and joked after his fashion, and at last revealed the secret of his raptures, and announced to us that his Petinka's birthday fell precisely a week later, and that it was his intention to call upon his son, without fail, on that day; that he would don a new waistcoat, and that his wife had promised to buy him some new boots. In short, the old man was perfectly happy, and chattered about everything that came into his head.

His birthday! That birthday gave me no peace, either day or night. I made up my mind faithfully to remind Pokrovsky of my friendship, and to make him a present. But what? At last I hit upon the idea of giving him some books. I knew that he wished to own the complete works of Pushkin, in the latest edition. I had thirty rubles of my own, earned by my handiwork. I had put this money aside for a new gown. I immediately sent old Matryona, our cook, to inquire the price of a complete set. Alas! The price of the eleven volumes, together with the expenses of binding, would be sixty rubles at the very least. I thought and thought, but could not tell what to do. I did not wish to ask my mother. Of course she would have helped me; but, in that case every one in the house would have known about our gift; moreover, the gift would have been converted into an expression of gratitude, a payment for Pokrovsky's labors for the whole year. My desire was to make the present privately, unknown to any one. And for his toilsome lessons to me I wished to remain forever indebted to him, without any payment whatever. At last I devised an escape from my predicament. I knew that one could often buy at half price from the old booksellers in the Gostinny Dvor, if one bargained well, little used and almost entirely new books. I made up my mind to go to the Gostinny Dvor myself. So it came about; the very next morning both Anna Feodorovna and we needed something. Mamma was not feeling well, and Anna Feodorovna, quite opportunely, had a fit of laziness, so all the errands were turned over to me, and I set out with Matryona.

To my delight I soon found a Pushkin, and in a very handsome binding. I began to bargain for it. How I enjoyed it! But alas! My entire capital consisted of thirty rubles in paper, and the merchant would not consent to accept less than ten rubles in silver. At last I began to entreat him, and I begged and begged, until eventually he yielded. But he only took off two rubles and a half, and swore that he had done so only for my sake, because I was such a nice young lady, and that he would not have come down in his price for any one else. Two rubles and a half were still lacking! I was ready to cry with vexation. But the most unexpected circumstance came to my rescue in my grief. Not far from me, at another stall, I caught sight of old Pokrovsky. Four or five old booksellers were clustered about him; he had completely lost his wits, and they had thoroughly bewildered him. Each one was offering him his wares, and what stuff they were offering, and what all was he not ready to buy! I stepped up to him and asked him what he was doing there? The old man was very glad to see me; he loved me unboundedly,—no less than his Petinka, perhaps. «Why, I am buying a few little books, Varvara Alexievna,» he replied; «I am buying some books for Petinka.» I asked him if he had much money? «See here,»—and the poor old man took out all his money, which was wrapped up in a dirty scrap of newspaper; «here's a half-ruble, and a twenty-kopek piece, and twenty kopeks in copper coins.» I immediately dragged him off to my bookseller. «Here are eleven books, which cost altogether thirty-two rubles and a half; I have thirty; put your two rubles and a half with mine, and we will buy all these books and give them to him in partnership.» The old man was quite beside himself with joy, and the bookseller loaded him down with our common library.

The next day the old man came to see his son, sat with him a little while, then came to us and sat down beside me with a very comical air of mystery. Every moment he grew more sad and uneasy; at last he could hold out no longer.

«Listen, Varvara Alexievna,» he began timidly, in a low voice: «do you know what, Varvara Alexievna?» The old man was dreadfully embarrassed. «You see, when his birthday comes, do you take ten of those little books and give them to him yourself, that is to say, from yourself, on your own behalf; then I will take the eleventh and give it from myself, for my share. So you see, you will have something to give, and I shall have something to give; we shall both have something to give.»

I was awfully sorry for the old man. I did not take long to think it over. The old man watched me anxiously. «Listen to me, Zakhar Petrovitch,» I said: «do you give him all.»—«How all? Do you mean all the books?»—«Yes, certainly, all the books.»—«And from myself?»—«From yourself.»—«From myself alone—that is, in my own name?»—«Yes, in your own name.» I thought I was expressing myself with sufficient clearness, but the old man could not understand me for a long time.

«You see,» he explained to me at last, «I sometimes indulge myself, Varvara Alexievna,—that is to say, I wish to state to you that I nearly always indulge myself,—I do that which is not right,—that is, you know, when it is cold out of doors, and when various unpleasant things happen at times, or when I feel sad for any reason, or something bad happens,—then sometimes, I do not restrain myself, and I drink too much. This is very disagreeable to Petrushka, you see, Varvara Alexievna; he gets angry, and he scolds me and reads me moral lectures. So now I should like to show him by my gift that I have reformed, and am beginning to conduct myself well; that I have been saving up my money to buy a book, saving for a long time, because I hardly ever have any money, except when it happens that Petrushka gives me some now and then. He knows that. Consequently, he will see what use I have made of my money, and he will know that I have done this for his sake alone.» . . .

«Well, yes,» he said, after thinking it over, «yes! That will be very fine, that would be very fine indeed,—only, what are you going to do, Varvara Alexievna?» — «Why, I shall not give anything.» — «What!» cried the old man almost in terror; «so you will not give Petinka anything, so you do not wish to give him anything?» He was alarmed. At that moment it seemed as though he were ready to relinquish his own suggestions, so that I might have something to give his son. He was a kind-hearted old man! I explained that I would be glad to give something, only I did not wish to deprive him of the pleasure.

. . . .

On the festive day he made his appearance at precisely eleven o'clock, straight from the mass, in his dress coat, decently patched, and actually in a new waistcoat and new boots. We were all sitting in the hall with Anna Feodorovna, and drinking coffee (it was Sunday). The old man began, I believe, by saying that Pushkin was a good poet; then he lost the thread of his discourse and got confused, and suddenly jumped to the assertion that a man must behave well, and that if he does not behave himself well, then it simply means that he indulges himself; he even cited several terrible examples of intemperance, and wound up by stating that for some time past he had been entirely a reformed character, and that he now behaved with perfect propriety. That even earlier he had recognized the justice of his son's exhortations, and had treasured them all in his heart, and had actually begun to be sober. In proof of which he now presented these books, which had been purchased with money which he had been hoarding up for a long time.

I could not refrain from tears and laughter, as I listened to the poor old fellow; he knew well how to lie when the occasion demanded! The books were taken to Pokrovsky's room and placed on the shelf. Pokrovsky immediately divined the truth.

. . . .

Pokrovsky fell ill, two months after the events which I have described above. During those two months he had striven incessantly for the means of existence, for up to that time he had never had a settled position. Like all consumptives, he bade farewell only with his last breath to the hope of a very long life. . . . Anna Feodorovna herself made all the arrangements about the funeral. She bought the very plainest sort of a coffin, and hired a truckman. In order to repay herself for her expenditure, Anna Feodorovna took possession of all the dead man's books and effects. The old man wrangled with her, raised an uproar, snatched from her as many books as possible, stuffed all his pockets with them, thrust them into his hat and wherever he could, carried them about with him all the three days which preceded the funeral, and did not even part with them when the time came to go to the church. During all those days he was like a man stunned, who has lost his memory, and he kept fussing about near the coffin with a certain strange anxiety; now he adjusted the paper band upon the dead man's brow, now he lighted and snuffed the candles. It was evident that he could not fix his thoughts in orderly manner on anything. Neither my mother nor Anna Feodorovna went to the funeral services in the church. My mother was ill, but Anna Feodorovna quarreled with old Pokrovsky just as she was all ready to start, and so stayed away. The old man and I were the only persons present. A sort of fear came over me during the services — like the presentiment of something which was about to happen. I could hardly stand out the ceremony in church. At last they put the lid on the coffin and nailed it down, placed it on the cart and drove away. I accompanied it only to the end of the street. The truckman drove at a trot. The old man ran after the cart, weeping aloud; the sound of his crying was broken and shaken by his running. The poor man lost his hat and did not stop to pick it up. His head was wet with the rain; the sleet lashed and cut his face. The old man did not appear to feel the bad weather, but ran weeping from one side of the cart to the other. The skirts of his shabby old coat waved in the wind like wings. Books protruded from every one of his pockets; in his hands was a huge book, which he held tightly clutched. The passers-by removed their hats and made the sign of the cross. Some halted and stared in amazement at the poor old man. Every moment the books kept falling out of his pockets into the mud. People stopped him, and pointed out his losses to him; he picked them up, and set out again in pursuit of the coffin. At the corner of the street an old beggar woman joined herself to him to escort the coffin. At last the cart turned the corner, and disappeared from my eyes. I went home. I flung myself, in dreadful grief, on my mother's bosom.

LETTER FROM MAKAR DYEVUSHKIN TO VARVARA ALEXIEVNA DOBROSYELOFF

SEPTEMBER 9TH.

My dear Varvara Alexievna!

I am quite beside myself as I write this. I am utterly upset by a most terrible occurrence. My head is whirling. I feel as though everything were turning in dizzy circles round about me. Ah, my dearest, what a thing I have to tell you now! We had not even a presentiment of such a thing. No, I don't believe that I did not have a presentiment — I foresaw it all. My heart forewarned me of this whole thing! I even dreamed of something like it not long ago.

This is what has happened! I will relate it to you without attempting fine style, and as the Lord shall put it into my soul. I went to the office to-day. When I arrived, I sat down and began to write. But you must know, my dear, that I wrote yesterday also. Well, yesterday Timofei Ivan'itch came to me, and was pleased to give me a personal order. «Here's a document that is much needed,» says he, «and we're in a hurry for it. Copy it, Makar Alexievitch,» says he, «as quickly and as neatly and carefully as possible: it must be handed in for signature to-day.» I must explain to you, my angel, that I was not quite myself yesterday, and didn't wish to look at anything; such sadness and depression had fallen upon me! My heart was cold, my mind was dark; you filled all my memory, and incessantly, my poor darling. Well, so I set to work on the copy; I wrote clearly and well, only,— I don't know exactly how to describe it to you, whether the Evil One himself tangled me up, or whether it was decreed by some mysterious fate, or simply whether it was bound to happen so, but I omitted a whole line, and the sense was utterly ruined. The Lord only knows what sense there was — simply none whatever. They were late with the papers yesterday, so they only gave this document to his Excellency for signature this morning. To-day I presented myself at the usual hour, as though nothing at all were the matter, and set myself down alongside Emelyan Ivanovitch.

I must tell you, my dear, that lately I have become twice as shamefaced as before, and more mortified. Of late I have ceased to look at any one. As soon as any one's chair squeaks, I am more dead than alive. So to-day I crept in, slipped humbly into my seat, and sat there all doubled up, so that Efim Akimovitch (he's the greatest tease in the world) remarked in such a way that all could hear him, « Why do you sit so like a y-y-y, Makar Alexievitch ? » Then he made such a grimace that everybody round him and me split with laughter, and of course at my expense. They kept it up interminably! I drooped my ears and screwed up my eyes, and sat there motionless. That's my way; they stop the quicker. All at once I heard a noise, a running and a tumult; I heard — did my ears deceive me? They were calling for me, demanding me, summoning Dyevushkin. My heart quivered in my breast, and I didn't know myself what I feared, for nothing of the sort had ever happened to me in the whole course of my life. I was rooted to my chair,— as though nothing had occurred, as though it were not I. But then they began again, nearer at hand, and nearer still. And here they were, right in my very ear: « Dyevushkin! Dyevushkin! » they called; « where's Dyevushkin ? » I raise my eyes, and there before me stands Evstafiy Ivanovitch; he says: — « Makar Alexievitch, hasten to his Excellency as quickly as possible! You've made a nice mess with that document! »

That was all he said, but it was enough, wasn't it, my dear, — quite enough to say? I turned livid, and grew as cold as ice, and lost my senses; I started, and I simply didn't know whether I was alive or dead as I went. They led me through one room, and through another room, and through a third room, to the private office, and I presented myself! Positively, I cannot give you any account of what I was thinking about. I saw his Excellency standing there, with all of them around him. It appears that I did not make my salute; I forgot it completely. I was so scared that my lips trembled and my legs shook. And there was sufficient cause, my dear. In the first place, I was ashamed of myself; I glanced to the right, at a mirror, and what I beheld therein was enough to drive any man out of his senses. And in the second place, I have always behaved as though there were no place for me in the world. So that it is not likely that his Excellency was even aware of my existence. It is possible that he may have heard it cursorily mentioned that there was a person named Dyevushkin in the department, but he had never come into any closer relations.

He began angrily, « What's the meaning of this, sir? What are you staring at? Here's an important paper, needed in haste, and you go and spoil it. And how did you come to permit such a thing?» Here his Excellency turned on Evstafiy Ivanovitch. I only listen, and the sounds of the words reach me: «It's gross carelessness. Heedlessness! You'll get yourself into trouble!» I tried to open my mouth for some purpose or other. I seemed to want to ask forgiveness, but I couldn't; to run away, but I didn't dare to make the attempt: and then — then, my dearest, something so dreadful happened that I can hardly hold my pen even now for the shame of it. My button — deuce take it — my button, which was hanging by a thread, suddenly broke loose, jumped off, skipped along (evidently I had struck it by accident), clattered and rolled away, the cursed thing, straight to his Excellency's feet, and that in the midst of universal silence. And that was the whole of my justification, all my excuse, all my answer, everything which I was preparing to say to his Excellency!

The results were terrible! His Excellency immediately directed his attention to my figure and my costume. I remembered what I had seen in the mirror; I flew to catch the button! A fit of madness descended upon me! I bent down and tried to grasp the button, but it rolled and twisted, and I couldn't get hold of it, in short, and I also distinguished myself in the matter of dexterity. Then I felt my last strength fail me, and knew that all, all was lost! My whole reputation was lost, the whole man ruined! And then, without rhyme or reason, Teresa and Faldoni began to ring in both my ears. At last I succeeded in seizing the button, rose upright, drew myself up in proper salute, but like a fool, and stood calmly there with my hands lined down on the seams of my trousers! No, I didn't, though. I began to try to fit the button on the broken thread, just as though it would stick fast by that means; and moreover, I began to smile and went on smiling.

At first his Excellency turned away; then he scrutinized me again, and I heard him say to Evstafiy Ivanovitch: — «How's this? See what a condition he is in! What a looking man! What's the matter with him?» Ah, my own dearest, think of that — «What a looking man!» and «What's the matter with him!» — «He has distinguished himself!» I heard Evstafiy say; «he has no bad marks, no bad marks on any score, and his conduct is exemplary; his salary is adequate, in accordance with the rates.» «Well then, give him some sort of assistance,» says his

Excellency; «make him an advance on his salary.»—«But he has had it, he has taken it already, for ever so long in advance. Probably circumstances have compelled him to do so; but his conduct is good, and he has received no reprimands, he has never been rebuked.» My dear little angel, I turned hot and burned as though in the fires of the bad place! I was on the point of fainting. «Well,» says his Excellency in a loud voice, «the document must be copied again as quickly as possible; come here, Dyevushkin, make a fresh copy without errors; and listen to me;» here his Excellency turned to the others and gave them divers orders, and sent them all away. As soon as they were all gone, his Excellency hastily took out his pocket-book, and from it drew a hundred-ruble bank-note. «Here,» said he, «this is all I can afford, and I am happy to help to that extent; reckon it as you please, take it,»—and he thrust it into my hand. I trembled, my angel, my whole soul was in a flutter; I didn't know what was the matter with me; I tried to catch his hand and kiss it. But he turned very red in the face, my darling, and—I am not deviating from the truth by so much as a hair's-breadth—he took my unworthy hand, and shook it, indeed he did; he took it and shook it as though it were of equal rank with his own, as though it belonged to a General like himself. «Go,» says he; «I am glad to do what I can. Make no mistakes, but now do it as well as you can.»

Now, my dear, this is what I have decided: I beg you and Feodor—and if I had children I would lay my commands upon them—to pray to God for him; though they should not pray for their own father, that they should pray daily and forever, for his Excellency! One thing more I will say, my dearest, and I say it solemnly,—heed me well, my dear,—I swear that, no matter in what degree I may be reduced to spiritual anguish in the cruel days of our adversity, as I look on you and your poverty, on myself, on my humiliation and incapacity,—in spite of all this, I swear to you that the hundred rubles are not so precious to me as the fact that his Excellency himself deigned to press my unworthy hand, the hand of a straw, a drunkard! Thereby he restored my self-respect. By that deed he brought to life again my spirit, he made my existence sweeter forevermore, and I am firmly convinced that, however sinful I may be in the sight of the Almighty, yet my prayer for the happiness and prosperity of his Excellency will reach his throne!

My dearest, I am at present in the most terrible state of spiritual prostration, in a horribly overwrought condition. My heart beats as though it would burst out of my breast, and I seem to be weak all over. I send you forty-five rubles, paper money. I shall give twenty rubles to my landlady, and keep thirty-five for myself; with twenty I will get proper clothes, and the other fifteen will go for my living expenses. But just now all the impressions of this morning have shaken my whole being to the foundations. I am going to lie down for a bit. Nevertheless, I am calm, perfectly calm. Only, my soul aches, and down there, in the depths, my soul is trembling and throbbing and quivering. I shall go to see you; but just now I am simply intoxicated with all these emotions. God sees all, my dearest, my own darling, my precious one.

Your worthy friend,

MAKAR DYEVUSHKIN.

Translation of Isabel F. Hapgood.

THE BIBLE READING

From ‹Crime and Punishment›

RASKOLNIKOFF went straight to the water-side, where Sonia was living. The three-storied house was an old building, painted green. The young man had some difficulty in finding the dvornik, and got from him vague information about the quarters of the tailor Kapernasumoff. After having discovered in a corner of the yard the foot of a steep and gloomy staircase, he ascended to the second floor, and followed the gallery facing the court-yard. Whilst groping in the dark, and asking himself how Kapernasumoff's lodgings could be reached, a door opened close to him; he seized it mechanically.

«Who is there?» asked a timid female voice.

«It is I. I am coming to see you,» replied Raskolnikoff, on entering a small ante-room. There on a wretched table stood a candle, fixed in a candlestick of twisted metal.

«Is that you? Good heavens!» feebly replied Sonia, who seemed not to have strength enough to move from the spot.

«Where do you live? Is it here?» And Raskolnikoff passed quickly into the room, trying not to look the girl in the face.

A moment afterwards Sonia rejoined him with the candle, and remained stock still before him, a prey to an indescribable agitation. This unexpected visit had upset her — nay, even frightened her. All of a sudden her pale face colored up, and tears came into her eyes. She experienced extreme confusion, united with a certain gentle feeling. Raskolnikoff turned aside with a rapid movement and sat down on a chair, close to the table. In the twinkling of an eye he took stock of everything in the room.

This room was large, with a very low ceiling, and was the only one let out by the Kapernasumoffs; in the wall, on the left-hand side, was a door giving access to theirs. On the opposite side, in the wall on the right, there was another door, which was always locked. That was another lodging, having another number. Sonia's room was more like an out-house, of irregular rectangular shape, which gave it an uncommon character. The wall, with its three windows facing the canal, cut it obliquely, forming thus an extremely acute angle, in the back portion of which nothing could be seen, considering the feeble light of the candle. On the other hand, the other angle was an extremely obtuse one. This large room contained scarcely any furniture. In the right-hand corner was the bed; between the bed and the door, a chair; on the same side, facing the door of the next set, stood a deal table, covered with a blue cloth; close to the table were two rush chairs. Against the opposite wall, near the acute angle, was placed a small chest of drawers of unvarnished wood, which seemed out of place in this vacant spot. This was the whole of the furniture. The yellowish and worn paper had everywhere assumed a darkish color, probably the effect of the damp and coal smoke. Everything in the place denoted poverty. Even the bed had no curtains. Sonia silently considered the visitor, who examined her room so attentively and so unceremoniously.

. . . .

« Her lot is fixed," thought he,—« a watery grave, the madhouse, or a brutish existence! » This latter contingency was especially repellent to him, but skeptic as he was, he could not help believing it a possibility. « Is it possible that such is really the case? » he asked himself. « Is it possible that this creature, who still retains a pure mind, should end by becoming deliberately mire-like? Has she not already become familiar with it, and if up to the present she has been able to bear with such a life, has it not been so because vice has already lost its hideousness in her eyes? Impossible again!» cried he, on his part, in the same way as Sonia had cried a moment ago. «No, that which up to the present has prevented her from throwing herself into the canal has been the fear of sin and its punishment. May she not be mad after all? Who says she is not so? Is she in full possession of all her faculties? Is it possible to speak as she does? Do people of sound judgment reason as she reasons? Can people anticipate future destruction with such tranquillity, turning a deaf ear to warnings and forebodings? Does she expect a miracle? It must be so. And does not all this seem like signs of mental derangement?»

To this idea he clung obstinately. Sonia mad! Such a prospect displeased him less than the other ones. Once more he examined the girl attentively. «And you—you often pray to God, Sonia?» he asked her.

No answer. Standing by her side, he waited for a reply. «What could I be, what should I be without God?» cried she in a low-toned but energetic voice, and whilst casting on Raskolnikoff a rapid glance of her brilliant eyes, she gripped his hand.

«Come, I was not mistaken!» he muttered to himself.—«And what does God do for you?» asked he, anxious to clear his doubts yet more.

For a long time the girl remained silent, as if incapable of reply. Emotion made her bosom heave. «Stay! Do not question me! You have no such right!» exclaimed she, all of a sudden, with looks of anger.

«I expected as much!» was the man's thought.

«God does everything for me!» murmured the girl rapidly, and her eyes sank.

«At last I have the explanation!» he finished mentally, whilst eagerly looking at her.

He experienced a new, strange, almost unhealthy feeling on watching this pale, thin, hard-featured face, these blue and soft eyes which could yet dart such lights and give utterance to such passion; in a word, this feeble frame, yet trembling with indignation and anger, struck him as weird,—nay, almost fantastic. «Mad! she must be mad!» he muttered once more. A book was lying on the chest of drawers. Raskolnikoff had noticed it more than once whilst moving about the room. He took it and examined it. It was a Russian translation of the Gospels, a well-thumbed leather-bound book.

« Where does that come from? » asked he of Sonia, from the other end of the room.

The girl still held the same position, a pace or two from the table. « It was lent me, » replied Sonia, somewhat loth, without looking at Raskolnikoff.

« Who lent it you? »

« Elizabeth — I asked her to! »

« Elizabeth. How strange! » he thought. Everything with Sonia assumed to his mind an increasingly extraordinary aspect. He took the book to the light, and turned it over. « Where is mention made of Lazarus? » asked he abruptly.

Sonia, looking hard on the ground, preserved silence, whilst moving somewhat from the table.

« Where is mention made of the resurrection of Lazarus? Find me the passage, Sonia. »

The latter looked askance at her interlocutor. « That is not the place — it is the Fourth Gospel, » said she dryly, without moving from the spot.

« Find me the passage and read it out! » he repeated, and sitting down again rested his elbow on the table, his head on his hand, and glancing sideways with gloomy look, prepared to listen.

Sonia at first hesitated to draw nearer to the table. The singular wish uttered by Raskolnikoff scarcely seemed sincere. Nevertheless she took the book. « Have you ever read the passage? » she asked him, looking at him from out the corners of her eyes. Her voice was getting harder and harder.

« Once upon a time. In my childhood. Read! »

« Have you never heard it in church? »

« I — I never go there. Do you go often yourself? »

« No, » stammered Sonia.

Raskolnikoff smiled. « I understand, then, you won't go to-morrow to your father's funeral service? »

« Oh, yes! I was at church last week. I was present at a requiem mass. »

« Whose was that? »

« Elizabeth's. She was assassinated by means of an axe. »

Raskolnikoff's nervous system became more and more irritated. He was getting giddy. « Were you friends with her? »

« Yes. She was straightforward. She used to come and see me — but not often. She was not able. We used to read and chat. She sees God. »

Raskolnikoff became thoughtful. « What, » asked he himself, « could be the meaning of the mysterious interviews of two such idiots as Sonia and Elizabeth? Why, I should go mad here myself! » thought he. « Madness seems to be in the atmosphere of the place! — Read! » he cried all of a sudden, irritably.

Sonia kept hesitating. Her heart beat loud. She seemed afraid to read. He considered « this poor demented creature » with an almost sad expression. « How can that interest you, since you do not believe? » she muttered in a choking voice.

« Read! I insist upon it! Used you not to read to Elizabeth? »

Sonia opened the book and looked for the passage. Her hands trembled. The words stuck in her throat. Twice did she try to read without being able to utter the first syllable.

« Now a certain man was sick, named Lazarus, of Bethany, » she read, at last, with an effort; but suddenly, at the third word, her voice grew wheezy, and gave way like an overstretched chord. Breath was deficient in her oppressed bosom. Raskolnikoff partly explained to himself Sonia's hesitation to obey him; and in proportion as he understood her better, he insisted still more imperiously on her reading. He felt what it must cost the girl to lay bare to him, to some extent, her heart of hearts. She evidently could not, without difficulty, make up her mind to confide to a stranger the sentiments which probably since her teens had been her support, her *viaticum* — when, what with a sottish father and a stepmother demented by misfortune, to say nothing of starving children, she heard nothing but reproach and offensive clamor. He saw all this, but he likewise saw that notwithstanding this repugnance, she was most anxious to read, — to read to him, and that now, — let the consequences be what they may! The girl's look, the agitation to which she was a prey, told him as much, and by a violent effort over herself Sonia conquered the spasm which parched her throat, and continued to read the eleventh chapter of the Gospel according to St. John. She thus reached the nineteenth verse: —

« And many of the Jews came to Martha and Mary, to comfort them concerning their brother. Then Martha, as soon as she heard that Jesus was coming, went and met him; but Mary sat still in the house. Then said Martha unto Jesus, Lord, if thou hadst been here, my brother had not died. But I know that even now, whatsoever thou wilt ask of God, God will give it thee. »

Here she paused, to overcome the emotion which once more caused her voice to tremble.

«Jesus saith unto her, Thy brother shall rise again. Martha saith unto him, I know that he shall rise again in the resurrection at the last day. Jesus said unto her, I am the Resurrection and the Life; he that believeth in me, though he were dead, yet shall he live; and whosoever liveth and believeth in me shall never die. Believest thou this? She saith unto him,»—

and although she had difficulty in breathing, Sonia raised her voice, as if in reading the words of Martha she was making her own confession of faith:—

«Yea, Lord: I believe that thou art the Christ, the Son of God, which should come into the world.»

She stopped, raised her eyes rapidly on him, but cast them down on her book, and continued to read. Raskolnikoff listened without stirring, without turning toward her, his elbows resting on the table, looking aside. Thus the reading continued till the thirty-second verse.

«Then when Mary was come where Jesus was, and saw him, she fell down at his feet, saying unto him, Lord, if thou hadst been here, my brother had not died. When Jesus therefore saw her weeping, and the Jews also weeping which came with her, he groaned in the spirit and was troubled, and said, Where have ye laid him? They said unto him, Lord, come and see. Jesus wept. Then said the Jews, Behold how he loved him. And some of them said, Could not this man, which opened the eyes of the blind, have caused that even this man should not have died?»

Raskolnikoff turned towards her and looked at her with agitation. His suspicion was a correct one. She was trembling in all her limbs, a prey to fever. He had expected this. She was getting to the miraculous story, and a feeling of triumph was taking possession of her. Her voice, strengthened by joy, had a metallic ring. The lines became misty to her troubled eyes, but fortunately she knew the passage by heart. At the last line, «Could not this man, which opened the eyes of the blind—» she lowered her voice, emphasizing passionately the doubt, the blame, the reproach of these unbelieving and blind Jews, who a moment after fell as if struck by lightning on their knees, to sob and to believe. «Yes,» thought she, deeply affected by this joyful hope, «yes, he — he who is blind, who dares not believe — he also will hear — will believe in an instant, immediately, now, this very moment!»

«Jesus therefore, again groaning in himself, cometh to the grave. It was a cave, and a stone lay upon it. Jesus said, Take ye away the stone. Martha, the sister of him that was dead, saith unto him, Lord, by this time he stinketh: for he hath been dead four days.»

She strongly emphasized the word *four*.

«Jesus saith unto her, Said I not unto thee, that if thou wouldst believe, thou shouldst see the glory of God? Then they took away the stone from the place where the dead was laid. And Jesus lifted up his eyes, and said, Father, I thank thee that thou hast heard me. And I knew that thou hearest me always; but because of the people which stand by I said it, that they may believe that thou hast sent me. And when he thus had spoken, he cried with a loud voice, Lazarus, come forth. *And he that was dead came forth,*»—

(on reading these words Sonia shuddered, as if she herself had been witness to the miracle)

«bound hand and foot with grave-clothes; and his face was bound about with a napkin. Jesus saith unto them, Loose him, and let him go. *Then many of the Jews which came to Mary, and had seen the things which Jesus did, believed on him.*»

She read no more,— such a thing would have been impossible to her,— closed the book, and briskly rising, said in a low-toned and choking voice, without turning toward the man she was talking to, «So much for the resurrection of Lazarus.» She seemed afraid to raise her eyes on Raskolnikoff, whilst her feverish trembling continued. The dying piece of candle dimly lit up this low-ceiled room, in which an assassin and a harlot had just read the Book of books.

EDWARD DOWDEN

(1843-)

"We are all hunters, skillful or skilless, in literature — hunters for our spiritual good or for our pleasure," says Edward Dowden; and to his earnest research and careful exposition many readers owe a more thorough appreciation of literature. He was educated at Queen's College, Cork (his birthplace), and then at Trinity College, Dublin, where he received the Vice-Chancellor's prize in both English verse and English prose, and also the first English Moderatorship in logic and ethics. For two years he studied divinity. Then he obtained by examination a professorship of oratory at the University of Dublin, where he was afterwards elected professor of English literature. The scholarship of his literary work has won him many honors. In 1888 he was chosen president of the English Goethe Society, to succeed Professor Müller. The following year he was appointed first Taylorian lecturer in the Taylor Institute, Oxford. The Royal Irish Academy has bestowed the Cunningham gold medal upon him, and he has also received the honorary degree LL. D. of the University of Edinburgh, and from Princeton University.

Very early in life Professor Dowden began to express his feeling for literature, and the instinct which leads him to account for a work by study of its author's personality. For more than twenty years English readers have known him as a frequent contributor of critical essays to the leading reviews. These have been collected into the delightful volumes 'Studies in Literature' and 'Transcripts and Studies.' His has been called "an honest method, wholesome as sweet." He would offer more than a mere résumé of what his author expresses. He would be one of the interpreters and transmitters of new forms of thought to the masses of readers who lack time or ability to discover values for themselves. Very widely read himself, he is fitted for just comparisons and comprehensive views. As has been pointed out, he is fond of working from a general consideration of a period with its formative influences, to the particular care of the author with whom he is dealing. Saintsbury tells us that Mr. Dowden's procedure is to ask his author a series of questions which seem to him of vital importance, and find out how he would answer them.

Dowden's style is careful, clear, and thorough, showing his scholarship and incisive thought. His form of expression is strongly picturesque. It is nowhere more so than in 'Shakespeare: a Study of His Mind and Art.' This, his most noteworthy work, has been very widely read and admired. His intimate acquaintance with German criticism upon the great Elizabethan especially fitted him to present fresh considerations to the public.

He has also written a brilliant 'Life of Shelley' (bitterly criticized by Mark Twain in the North American Review, 'A Defense of Harriet Shelley'), and a 'Life of Southey' in the English Men of Letters Series; and edited most capably 'Southey's Correspondence with Caroline Bowles,' 'The Correspondence of Sir Henry Taylor,' 'Shakespeare's Sonnets,' 'The Passionate Pilgrim,' and a collection of 'Lyrical Ballads.'

THE HUMOR OF SHAKESPEARE

From 'Shakespeare: a Critical Study of His Mind and Art'

A study of Shakespeare which fails to take account of Shakespeare's humor must remain essentially incomplete. The character and spiritual history of a man who is endowed with a capacity for humorous appreciation of the world must differ throughout, and in every particular, from that of the man whose moral nature has never rippled over with genial laughter. At whatever final issue Shakespeare arrived after long spiritual travail as to the attainment of his life, that precise issue, rather than another, was arrived at in part by virtue of the fact of Shakespeare's humor. In the composition of forces which determined the orbit traversed by the mind of the poet, this must be allowed for as a force among others, in importance not the least, and efficient at all times even when little apparent. A man whose visage "holds one stern intent" from day to day, and whose joy becomes at times almost a supernatural rapture, may descend through circles of hell to the narrowest and the lowest; he may mount from sphere to sphere of Paradise until he stands within the light of the Divine Majesty; but he will hardly succeed in presenting us with an adequate image of life as it is on this earth of ours, in its oceanic amplitude and variety. A few men of genius there have been, who with vision penetrative as lightning have gazed as it were *through* life, at some eternal significances of which life is the symbol. Intent upon its sacred meaning, they have had no eye to note the forms of the grotesque hieroglyph of human existence. Such men are not framed for laughter. To this little group the creator of Falstaff, of Bottom, and of Touchstone does not belong.

Shakespeare, who saw life more widely and wisely than any other of the seers, could laugh. That is a comfortable fact to bear in mind; a fact which serves to rescue us from the domination of intense and narrow natures, who claim authority by virtue of their grasp of one-half of the realities of our existence and their denial of the rest. Shakespeare could laugh. But we must go on to ask, "What did he laugh at? and what was the manner of his laughter?" There are as many modes of laughter as there are facets of the common soul of humanity, to reflect the humorous appearances of the world. Hogarth, in one of his pieces of coarse yet subtile engraving, has presented a group of occupants of the pit of a theatre, sketched during the performance of some broad comedy or farce. What proceeds upon the stage is invisible and undiscoverable, save as we catch its reflection on the faces of the spectators, in the same way that we infer a sunset from the evening flame upon windows that front the west. Each laughing face in Hogarth's print exhibits a different mode or a different stage of the risible paroxysm. There is the habitual enjoyer of the broad comic, abandoned to his mirth, which is open and unashamed; mirth which he is evidently a match for, and able to sustain. By his side is a companion female portrait — a woman with head thrown back to ease the violence of the guffaw; all her loose redundant flesh is tickled into an orgasm of merriment; she is fairly overcome. On the other side sits the spectator who has passed the climax of his laughter; he wipes the tears from his eyes, and is on the way to regain an insecure and temporary composure. Below appears a girl of eighteen or twenty, whose vacancy of intellect is captured and occupied by the innocuous folly still in progress; she gazes on expectantly, assured that a new blossom of the wonder of absurdity is about to display itself. Her father, a man who does not often surrender himself to an indecent convulsion, leans his face upon his hand, and with the other steadies himself by grasping one of the iron spikes that inclose the orchestra. In the right corner sits the humorist, whose eyes, around which the wrinkles gather, are half closed, while he already goes over the jest a second time in his imagination. At the opposite side an elderly woman is seen, past the period when animal violences are possible, laughing because she knows there is something to laugh at, though she is too dull-witted to know precisely what. One spectator, as we guess from his introverted air, is laughing to think what somebody else would think of this. Finally, the thin-lipped, perk-nosed person of refinement looks aside, and by his critical indifference condemns the broad, injudicious mirth of the company.

All these laughers of Hogarth are very commonplace, and some are very vulgar persons; one trivial, ludicrous spectacle is the occasion of their mirth. When from such laughter as this we turn to the laughter of men of genius, who gaze at the total play of the world's life; and when we listen to this, as with the ages it goes on gathering and swelling, our sense of hearing is enveloped and almost annihilated by the chorus of mock and jest, of antic and buffoonery, of tender mirth and indignant satire, of monstrous burlesque and sly absurdity, of desperate misanthropic derision and genial affectionate caressing of human imperfection and human folly. We hear from behind the mask the enormous laughter of Aristophanes, ascending peal above peal until it passes into jubilant ecstasy, or from the uproar springs some exquisite lyric strain. We hear laughter of passionate indignation from Juvenal, the indignation of «the ancient and free soul of the dead republics.» And there is Rabelais, with his huge buffoonery, and the earnest eyes intent on freedom, which look out at us in the midst of the zany's tumblings and indecencies. And Cervantes, with his refined Castilian air and deep melancholy mirth, at odds with the enthusiasm which is dearest to his soul. And Molière, with his laughter of unerring good sense, undeluded by fashion or vanity or folly or hypocrisy, and brightly mocking these into modesty. And Milton, with his fierce objurgatory laughter,— Elijah-like insult against the enemies of freedom and of England. And Voltaire, with his quick intellectual scorn and eager malice of the brain. And there is the urbane and amiable play of Addison's invention, not capable of large achievement, but stirring the corners of the mouth with a humane smile,— gracious gayety for the breakfast-tables of England. And Fielding's careless mastery of the whole broad common field of mirth. And Sterne's exquisite curiosity of oddness, his subtile extravagances and humors prepense. And there is the tragic laughter of Swift, which announces the extinction of reason, and loss beyond recovery of human faith and charity and hope. How in this chorus of laughters, joyous and terrible, is the laughter of Shakespeare distinguishable?

In the first place, the humor of Shakespeare, like his total genius, is many-sided. He does not pledge himself as dramatist to any one view of human life. If we open a novel by Charles Dickens, we feel assured beforehand that we are condemned to an exuberance of philanthropy; we know how the writer will insist that we must all be good friends, all be men and brothers, intoxicated with the delight of one another's presence; we expect him to hold out the right hand of fellowship to man, woman, and child; we are prepared for the bacchanalia of benevolence. The lesson we have to learn from this teacher is, that with the exception of a few inevitable and incredible monsters of cruelty, every man naturally engendered of the offspring of Adam is of his own nature inclined to every amiable virtue. Shakespeare abounds in kindly mirth: he receives an exquisite pleasure from the alert wit and bright good sense of a Rosalind; he can dandle a fool as tenderly as any nurse qualified to take a baby from the birth can deal with her charge. But Shakespeare is not pledged to deep-dyed ultra-amiability. With Jacques, he can rail at the world while remaining curiously aloof from all deep concern about its interests, this way or that. With Timon he can turn upon the world with a rage no less than that of Swift, and discover in man and woman a creature as abominable as the Yahoo. In other words, the humor of Shakespeare, like his total genius, is dramatic.

Then again, although Shakespeare laughs incomparably, mere laughter wearies him. The only play of Shakespeare's, out of nearly forty, which is farcical,—'The Comedy of Errors,'—was written in the poet's earliest period of authorship, and was formed upon the suggestion of a preceding piece. It has been observed with truth by Gervinus that the farcical incidents of this play have been connected by Shakespeare with a tragic background, which is probably his own invention. With beauty, or with pathos, or with thought, Shakespeare can mingle his mirth; and then he is happy, and knows how to deal with play of wit or humorous characterization; but an entirely comic subject somewhat disconcerts the poet. On this ground, if no other were forthcoming, it might be suspected that 'The Taming of the Shrew' was not altogether the work of Shakespeare's hand. The secondary intrigues and minor incidents were of little interest to the poet. But in the buoyant force of Petruchio's character, in his subduing tempest of high spirits, and in the person of the foiled revoltress against the law of sex, who carries into her wifely loyalty the same energy which she had shown in her virgin *sauvagerie*, there were elements of human character in which the imagination of the poet took delight.

Unless it be its own excess, however, Shakespeare's laughter seems to fear nothing. It does not, when it has once arrived at its full development, fear enthusiasm, or passion, or tragic intensity; nor do these fear it. The traditions of the English drama had favored the juxtaposition of the serious and comic: but it was reserved for Shakespeare to make each a part of the other; to interpenetrate tragedy with comedy, and comedy with tragic earnestness.

SHAKESPEARE'S PORTRAITURE OF WOMEN

From 'Transcripts and Studies'

Of all the daughters of his imagination, which did Shakespeare love the best? Perhaps we shall not err if we say one of the latest born of them all,—our English Imogen. And what most clearly shows us how Shakespeare loved Imogen is this—he has given her faults, and has made them exquisite, so that we love her better for their sake. No one has so quick and keen a sensibility to whatever pains and to whatever gladdens as she. To her a word is a blow; and as she is quick in her sensibility, so she is quick in her perceptions, piercing at once through the Queen's false show of friendship; quick in her contempt for what is unworthy, as for all professions of love from the clown-prince, Cloten; quick in her resentment, as when she discovers the unjust suspicions of Posthumus. Wronged she is indeed by her husband, but in her haste she too grows unjust; yet she is dearer to us for the sake of this injustice, proceeding as it does from the sensitiveness of her love. It is she, to whom a word is a blow, who actually receives a buffet from her husband's hand; but for Imogen it is a blessed stroke, since it is the evidence of his loyalty and zeal on her behalf. In a moment he is forgiven, and her arms are round his neck.

Shakespeare made so many perfect women unhappy that he owed us some *amende*. And he has made that *amende* by letting us see one perfect woman supremely happy. Shall our last glance at Shakespeare's plays show us Florizel at the rustic merry-making, receiving blossoms from the hands of Perdita? or Ferdinand and Miranda playing chess in Prospero's cave, and winning one a king and one a queen, while the happy fathers gaze in from the entrance of the cave? We can see a more delightful sight than these — Imogen with her arms around the neck of Posthumus, while she puts an edge upon her joy by the playful challenge and mock reproach —

> "Why did you throw your wedded lady from you?
> Think that you are upon a rock, and now
> Throw me again;"

and he responds —

> "Hang there like a fruit, my soul,
> Till the tree die."

We shall find in all Shakespeare no more blissful creatures than these two.

THE INTERPRETATION OF LITERATURE

From 'Transcripts and Studies'

The happiest moment in a critic's hours of study is when, seemingly by some divination, but really as the result of patient observation and thought, he lights upon the central motive of a great work. Then, of a sudden, order begins to form itself from the crowd and chaos of his impressions and ideas. There is a moving hither and thither, a grouping or co-ordinating of all his recent experiences, which goes on of its own accord; and every instant his vision becomes clearer, and new meanings disclose themselves in what had been lifeless and un-illuminated. It seems as if he could even stand by the artist's side and co-operate with him in the process of creating. With such a sense of joy upon him, the critic will think it no hard task to follow the artist to the sources from whence he drew his material, — it may be some dull chapter in an ancient chronicle, or some gross tale of passion by an Italian novelist, — and he will stand by and watch with exquisite pleasure the artist handling that crude material, and refashioning and refining it, and breathing into it the breath of a higher life. Even the minutest difference of text between an author's earlier and later draft, or a first and second edition, has now become a point not for dull commentatorship, but a point of life, at which he may touch with his finger the pulse of the creator in his fervor of creation.

From each single work of a great author we advance to his total work, and thence to the man himself,—to the heart and brain from which all this manifold world of wisdom and wit and passion and beauty has proceeded. Here again, before we address ourselves to the interpretation of the author's mind, we patiently submit ourselves to a vast series of impressions. And in accordance with Bacon's maxim that a prudent interrogation is the half of knowledge, it is right to provide ourselves with a number of well-considered questions which we may address to our author. Let us cross-examine him as students of mental and moral science, and find replies in his written words. Are his senses vigorous and fine? Does he see color as well as form? Does he delight in all that appeals to the sense of hearing—the voices of nature, and the melody and harmonies of the art of man? Thus Wordsworth, exquisitely organized for enjoying and interpreting all natural, and if we may so say, homeless and primitive sounds, had but little feeling for the delights of music. Can he enrich his poetry by gifts from the sense of smell, as did Keats; or is his nose like Wordsworth's, an idle promontory projecting into a desert air? Has he like Browning a vigorous pleasure in all strenuous muscular movements; or does he like Shelley live rapturously in the finest nervous thrills? How does he experience and interpret the feeling of sex, and in what parts of his entire nature does that feeling find its elevating connections and associations? What are his special intellectual powers? Is his intellect combative or contemplative? What are the laws which chiefly preside over the associations of his ideas? What are the emotions which he feels most strongly? and how do his emotions coalesce with one another? Wonder, terror, awe, love, grief, hope, despondency, the benevolent affections, admiration, the religious sentiment, the moral sentiment, the emotion of power, irascible emotion, ideal emotion—how do these make themselves felt in and through his writings? What is his feeling for the beautiful, the sublime, the ludicrous? Is he of weak or vigorous will? In the conflict of motives, which class of motives with him is likely to predominate? Is he framed to believe or framed to doubt? Is he prudent, just, temperate, or the reverse of these? These and such-like questions are not to be crudely and formally proposed, but are to be used with tact; nor should the critic press for hard and definite answers, but know how skillfully to glean its meaning from an evasion. He is a dull cross-examiner who will invariably follow the scheme which he has thought out and prepared beforehand, and who cannot vary his questions to surprise or beguile the truth from an unwilling witness. But the tact which comes from natural gift and from experience may be well supported by something of method,—method well hidden away from the surface and from sight.

This may be termed the psychological method of study. But we may also follow a more objective method. Taking the chief themes with which literature and art are conversant—God, external nature, humanity—we may inquire how our author has dealt with each of these. What is his theology, or his philosophy of the universe? By which we mean no abstract creed or doctrine, but the tides and currents of feeling and of faith, as well as the tendencies and conclusions of the intellect. Under what aspect has this goodly frame of things, in whose midst we are, revealed itself to him? How has he regarded and interpreted the life of man? Under each of these great themes a multitude of subordinate topics are included. And alike in this and in what we have termed the psychological method of study, we shall gain double results if we examine a writer's works in the order of their chronology, and thus become acquainted with the growth and development of his powers, and the widening and deepening of his relations with man, with external nature, and with that Supreme Power, unknown yet well known, of which nature and man are the manifestation. As to the study of an artist's technical qualities, this, by virtue of the fact that he is an artist, is of capital importance; and it may often be associated with the study of that which his technique is employed to express and render—the characteristics of his mind, and of the vision which he has attained of the external universe, of humanity, and of God. Of all our study, the last end and aim should be to ascertain how a great writer or artist has served the life of man; to ascertain this, to bring home to ourselves as large a portion as may be of the gain wherewith he has enriched human life, and to render access to that store of wisdom, passion, and power, easier and surer for others.

A. CONAN DOYLE

(1859–)

THE author of 'The White Company,' 'The Great Shadow,' and 'Micah Clarke' has been heard to lament the fact that his introduction to American readers came chiefly through the good offices of his accomplished friend «Sherlock Holmes.» Dr. Doyle would prefer to be judged by his more serious and laborious work, as it appears in his historic romances. But he has found it useless to protest. 'The Adventures of Sherlock Holmes' delighted a public which enjoys incident, mystery, and above all that matching of the wits of a clever man against the dumb resistance of the secrecy of inanimate things, which results in the triumph of the human intelligence. Moreover, in Sherlock Holmes himself the reader perceived a new character in fiction. The inventors of the French detective story,—that ingenious Chinese puzzle of literature,—have no such wizard as he to show. Even Poe, past master of mystery-making, is more or less empirical in his methods of mystery-solving.

A. CONAN DOYLE

But Sherlock Holmes is a true product of his time. He is an embodiment of the scientific spirit seeing microscopically and applying itself to construct, from material vestiges and psychologic remainders, an unknown body of proof. From the smallest fragments he deduces the whole structure, precisely as the great naturalists do; and so flawless are his reasonings that a course of 'The Adventures of Sherlock Holmes' would not be bad training in a high-school class in logic.

The creator of this eminent personage was born in Edinburgh in 1859, of a line of artists; his grandfather, John Doyle, having been a famous political caricaturist, whose works, under the signature «H. B.,» were purchased at a high price by the British Museum. The quaint signature of his father — a capital D, with a little bird perched on top, gained him the affectionate sobriquet of «Dicky Doyle»; and Dicky Doyle's house was the gathering-place of artists and authors, whose talk served to decide the destiny of the lad

Conan. For though he was intended for the medical profession, and after studying in Germany had kept his terms at the Medical College of Edinburgh University, the love of letters drove him forth in his early twenties to try his fortunes in the literary world of London.

Inheriting from his artist ancestry a sense of form and color, a faculty of constructiveness, and a vivid imagination, his studiousness and his industry have turned his capacities into abilities. For his romance of ‘The White Company’ he read more than two hundred books, and spent on it more than two years of labor. ‘Micah Clarke’ and ‘The Great Shadow’ involved equal wit and conscience. In his historic fiction he has described the England of Edward III., of James II., and of to-day, the Scotland of George III., the France of Edward III., of Louis XIV., and of Napoleon, and the America of Frontenac; while, in securing this correctness of historic detail, he has not neglected the first duty of a story-teller, which is to be interesting.

THE RED-HEADED LEAGUE

From ‘The Adventures of Sherlock Holmes.’ Copyright 1892, by Harper & Brothers

I HAD called upon my friend Mr. Sherlock Holmes one day in the autumn of last year, and found him in deep conversation with a very stout, florid-faced elderly gentleman, with fiery red hair. With an apology for my intrusion I was about to withdraw, when Holmes pulled me abruptly into the room and closed the door behind me.

«You could not possibly have come at a better time, my dear Watson,» he said, cordially.

«I was afraid that you were engaged.»

«So I am. Very much so.»

«Then I can wait in the next room.»

«Not at all. This gentleman, Mr. Wilson, has been my partner and helper in many of my most successful cases, and I have no doubt that he will be of the utmost use to me in yours also.»

The stout gentleman half rose from his chair and gave a bob of greeting, with a quick little questioning glance from his small, fat-encircled eyes.

«Try the settee,» said Holmes, relapsing into his arm-chair and putting his finger-tips together, as was his custom when in judicial moods. «I know, my dear Watson, that you share my love of all that is bizarre and outside the conventions and humdrum routine of every-day life. You have shown your relish for it by the enthusiasm which has prompted you to chronicle, and if you will excuse my saying so, somewhat to embellish so many of my own little adventures."

"Your cases have indeed been of the greatest interest to me," I observed.

"You will remember that I remarked the other day, just before we went into the very simple problem presented by Miss Mary Sutherland, that for strange effects and extraordinary combinations we must go to life itself, which is always far more daring than any effort of the imagination."

"A proposition which I took the liberty of doubting."

"You did, doctor; but none the less you must come round to my view, for otherwise I shall keep on piling fact upon fact on you, until your reason breaks down under them and acknowledges me to be right. Now, Mr. Jabez Wilson here has been good enough to call upon me this morning, and to begin a narrative which promises to be one of the most singular which I have listened to for some time. You have heard me remark that the strangest and most unique things are very often connected not with the larger but with the smaller crimes; and occasionally, indeed, where there is room for doubt whether any positive crime has been committed. As far as I have heard, it is impossible for me to say whether the present case is an instance of crime or not; but the course of events is certainly among the most singular that I have ever listened to. Perhaps, Mr. Wilson, you would have the great kindness to recommence your narrative. I ask you, not merely because my friend Dr. Watson has not heard the opening part, but also because the peculiar nature of the story makes me anxious to have every possible detail from your lips. As a rule, when I have heard some slight indication of the course of events, I am able to guide myself by the thousands of other similar cases which occur to my memory. In the present instance I am forced to admit that the facts are, to the best of my belief, unique."

The portly client puffed out his chest with an appearance of some little pride, and pulled a dirty and wrinkled newspaper from the inside pocket of his great-coat. As he glanced down the advertisement column, with his head thrust forward, and the paper flattened out upon his knee, I took a good look at the man, and endeavored, after the fashion of my companion, to read the indications which might be presented by his dress or appearance.

I did not gain very much, however, by my inspection. Our visitor bore every mark of being an average commonplace British tradesman, obese, pompous, and slow. He wore rather baggy gray shepherd's-check trousers, a not over clean black frock-coat unbuttoned in the front, and a drab waistcoat, with a heavy brassy Albert chain and a square pierced bit of metal dangling down as an ornament. A frayed top-hat and a faded brown overcoat with a wrinkled velvet collar lay upon a chair beside him. Altogether, look as I would, there was nothing remarkable about the man save his blazing red head, and the expression of extreme chagrin and discontent upon his features.

Sherlock Holmes's quick eye took in my occupation, and he shook his head with a smile as he noticed my questioning glances. « Beyond the obvious facts that he has at some time done manual labor, that he takes snuff, that he is a Freemason, that he has been in China, and that he has done a considerable amount of writing lately, I can deduce nothing else.»

Mr. Jabez Wilson started up in his chair, with his forefinger upon the paper, but his eyes upon my companion.

« How in the name of good fortune did you know all that, Mr. Holmes ?» he asked. « How did you know, for example, that I did manual labor ? It's as true as gospel, for I began as a ship's carpenter.»

« Your hands, my dear sir. Your right hand is quite a size larger than your left. You have worked with it, and the muscles are more developed.»

« Well, the snuff, then, and the Freemasonry ?»

« I won't insult your intelligence by telling you how I read that; especially as, rather against the strict rules of your order, you use an arc-and-compass breastpin.»

« Ah, of course, I forgot that. But the writing ?»

« What else can be indicated by that right cuff so very shiny for five inches, and the left one with the smooth patch near the elbow where you rest it upon the desk ?»

« Well, but China ?»

« The fish that you have tattooed immediately above your right wrist could only have been done in China. I have made a small study of tattoo marks, and have even contributed to the literature of the subject. That trick of staining the fishes' scales of a delicate pink is quite peculiar to China. When in addition I see a Chinese coin hanging from your watch-chain, the matter becomes even more simple."

Mr. Jabez Wilson laughed heavily. "Well, I never!" said he. "I thought at first that you had done something clever, but I see that there was nothing in it, after all."

"I begin to think, Watson," said Holmes, "that I make a mistake in explaining. 'Omne ignotum pro magnifico,' you know, and my poor little reputation, such as it is, will suffer shipwreck if I am so candid. Can you not find the advertisement, Mr. Wilson?"

"Yes, I have got it now," he answered, with his thick red finger planted half-way down the column. "Here it is. This is what began it all. You just read it for yourself, sir."

I took the paper from him, and read as follows:—

"To the Red-Headed League:—On account of the bequest of the late Ezekiah Hopkins, of Lebanon, Pa., U. S. A., there is now another vacancy open, which entitles a member of the League to a salary of £4 a week for purely nominal services. All red-headed men who are sound in body and mind, and above the age of twenty-one years, are eligible. Apply in person on Monday, at eleven o'clock, to Duncan Ross, at the offices of the League, 7 Pope's Court, Fleet Street."

"What on earth does this mean?" I ejaculated, after I had twice read over the extraordinary announcement.

Holmes chuckled, and wriggled in his chair, as was his habit when in high spirits. "It is a little off the beaten track, isn't it?" said he. "And now, Mr. Wilson, off you go at scratch, and tell us all about yourself, your household, and the effect which this advertisement had upon your fortunes. You will first make a note, doctor, of the paper and the date."

"It is the Morning Chronicle of April 27th, 1890. Just two months ago."

"Very good. Now, Mr. Wilson?"

"Well, it is just as I have been telling you, Mr. Sherlock Holmes," said Jabez Wilson, mopping his forehead: "I have a small pawnbroker's business at Coburg Square, near the city. It's not a very large affair, and of late years it has not done more than just give me a living. I used to be able to keep two assistants, but now I only keep one; and I would have a job to pay him, but that he is willing to come for half wages, so as to learn the business."

"What is the name of this obliging youth?" asked Sherlock Holmes.

"His name is Vincent Spaulding, and he's not such a youth, either. It's hard to say his age. I should not wish a smarter assistant, Mr. Holmes; and I know very well that he could better himself, and earn twice what I am able to give him. But after all, if he is satisfied, why should I put ideas in his head?"

"Why, indeed? You seem most fortunate in having an *employé* who comes under the full market price. It is not a common experience among employers in this age. I don't know that your assistant is not as remarkable as your advertisement."

"Oh, he has his faults, too," said Mr. Wilson. "Never was such a fellow for photography. Snapping away with a camera when he ought to be improving his mind, and then diving down into the cellar like a rabbit into its hole to develop his pictures. That is his main fault; but on the whole, he's a good worker. There's no vice in him."

"He is still with you, I presume?"

"Yes, sir. He and a girl of fourteen, who does a bit of simple cooking, and keeps the place clean — that's all I have in the house, for I am a widower, and never had any family. We live very quietly, sir, the three of us; and we keep a roof over our heads, and pay our debts, if we do nothing more.

"The first thing that put us out was that advertisement. Spaulding, he came down into the office just this day eight weeks, with this very paper in his hand, and he says: —

"'I wish to the Lord, Mr. Wilson, that I was a red-headed man.'

"'Why that?' I asks.

"'Why,' says he, 'here's another vacancy on the League of the Red-Headed Men. It's worth quite a little fortune to any man who gets it, and I understand that there are more vacancies than there are men, so that the trustees are at their wits' end what to do with the money. If my hair would only change color, here's a nice little crib all ready for me to step into.'

"'Why, what is it, then?' I asked. You see, Mr. Holmes, I am a very stay-at-home man, and as my business came to me instead of my having to go to it, I was often weeks on end without putting my foot over the door-mat. In that way I didn't know much of what was going on outside, and I was always glad of a bit of news.

"'Have you never heard of the League of the Red-Headed Men?' he asked, with his eyes open.

"'Never.'

"'Why, I wonder at that, for you are eligible yourself for one of the vacancies.'

"'And what are they worth?' I asked.

"'Oh, merely a couple of hundred a year; but the work is slight, and it need not interfere very much with one's other occupations.'

"Well, you can easily think that that made me prick up my ears, for the business has not been over good for some years, and an extra couple of hundred would have been very handy.

"'Tell me all about it,' said I.

"'Well,' said he, showing me the advertisement, 'you can see for yourself that the League has a vacancy, and there is the address where you should apply for particulars. As far as I can make out, the League was founded by an American millionaire, Ezekiah Hopkins, who was very peculiar in his ways. He was himself red-headed, and he had a great sympathy for all red-headed men; so when he died it was found that he had left his enormous fortune in the hands of trustees, with instructions to apply the interest to the providing of easy berths to men whose hair is of that color. From all I hear, it is splendid pay and very little to do.'

"'But,' said I, 'there would be millions of red-headed men who would apply.'

"'Not so many as you might think,' he answered. 'You see it is really confined to Londoners, and to grown men. This American had started from London when he was young, and he wanted to do the old town a good turn. Then again, I have heard it is no use your applying if your hair is light red, or dark red, or anything but real bright, blazing, fiery red. Now if you care to apply, Mr. Wilson, you would just walk in; but perhaps it would hardly be worth your while to put yourself out of the way for the sake of a few hundred pounds.'

"Now, it is a fact, gentlemen, as you may see for yourselves, that my hair is of a very full and rich tint, so that it seemed to me that if there was to be any competition in the matter, I stood as good a chance as any man that I had ever met. Vincent Spaulding seemed to know so much about it that I thought he might prove useful, so I just ordered him to put up the shutters for the day, and to come right away with me. He was very willing to have a holiday; so we shut the business up, and started off for the address that was given us in the advertisement.

«I never hope to see such a sight as that again, Mr. Holmes. From north, south, east, and west, every man who had a shade of red in his hair had tramped into the city to answer the advertisement. Fleet Street was choked with red-headed folk, and Pope's Court looked like a coster's orange-barrow. I should not have thought there were so many in the whole country as were brought together by that single advertisement. Every shade of color they were — straw, lemon, orange, brick, Irish-setter, liver, clay; but as Spaulding said, there were not many who had the real vivid flame-colored tint. When I saw how many were waiting, I would have given it up in despair; but Spaulding would not hear of it. How he did it I could not imagine, but he pushed and pulled and butted until he got me through the crowd, and right up to the steps which led to the office. There was a double stream upon the stair, some going up in hope, and some coming back dejected; but we wedged in as well as we could, and soon found ourselves in the office.»

«Your experience has been a most entertaining one,» remarked Holmes, as his client paused and refreshed his memory with a huge pinch of snuff. «Pray continue your very interesting statement.»

«There was nothing in the office but a couple of wooden chairs and a deal table, behind which sat a small man, with a head that was even redder than mine. He said a few words to each candidate as he came up, and then he always managed to find some fault in them which would disqualify them. Getting a vacancy did not seem to be such a very easy matter, after all. However, when our turn came, the little man was much more favorable to me than to any of the others, and he closed the door as we entered, so that he might have a private word with us.

«'This is Mr. Jabez Wilson,' said my assistant, 'and he is willing to fill a vacancy in the League.'

«'And he is admirably suited for it,' the other answered. 'He has every requirement. I cannot recall when I have seen anything so fine.' He took a step backward, cocked his head on one side, and gazed at my hair until I felt quite bashful. Then suddenly he plunged forward, wrung my hand, and congratulated me warmly on my success.

"'It would be injustice to hesitate,' said he. 'You will, however, I am sure, excuse me for taking an obvious precaution.' With that he seized my hair in both his hands, and tugged until I yelled with the pain. 'There is water in your eyes,' said he, as he released me. 'I perceive that all is as it should be. But we have to be careful, for we have twice been deceived by wigs and once by paint. I could tell you tales of cobbler's wax which would disgust you with human nature.' He stepped over to the window, and shouted through it at the top of his voice that the vacancy was filled. A groan of disappointment came up from below, and the folk all trooped away in different directions, until there was not a red head to be seen except my own and that of the manager.

"'My name,' said he, 'is Mr. Duncan Ross, and I am myself one of the pensioners upon the fund left by our noble benefactor. Are you a married man, Mr. Wilson? Have you a family?'

"I answered that I had not.

"His face fell immediately.

"'Dear me,' he said, gravely, 'that is very serious indeed! I am sorry to hear you say that. The fund was of course for the propagation and spread of the red-heads, as well as for their maintenance. It is exceedingly unfortunate that you should be a bachelor.'

"My face lengthened at this, Mr. Holmes, for I thought that I was not to have the vacancy after all; but after thinking it over for a few minutes, he said that it would be all right.

"'In the case of another,' said he, 'the objection might be fatal, but we must stretch a point in favor of a man with such a head of hair as yours. When shall you be able to enter upon your new duties?'

"'Well, it is a little awkward, for I have a business already,' said I.

"'Oh, never mind about that, Mr. Wilson!' said Vincent Spaulding. 'I shall be able to look after that for you.'

"'What would be the hours?' I asked.

"'Ten to two.'

"Now a pawnbroker's business is mostly done of an evening, Mr. Holmes, especially Thursday and Friday evening, which is just before pay-day; so it would suit me very well to earn a little in the mornings. Besides, I knew that my assistant was a good man, and that he would see to anything that turned up.

"'That would suit me very well,' said I. 'And the pay?'

"'Is £4 a week.'

"'And the work?'

"'Is purely nominal.'

"'What do you call purely nominal?'

"'Well, you have to be in the office, or at least in the building, the whole time. If you leave, you forfeit your whole position forever. The will is very clear upon that point. You don't comply with the conditions if you budge from the office during that time.'

"'It's only four hours a day, and I should not think of leaving,' said I.

"'No excuse will avail,' said Mr. Duncan Ross, 'neither sickness nor business nor anything else. There you must stay, or you lose your billet.'

"'And the work?'

"'Is to copy out the Encyclopædia Britannica. There is the first volume of it in that press. You must find your own ink, pens, and blotting-paper, but we provide this table and chair. Will you be ready to-morrow?'

"'Certainly,' I answered.

"'Then good-by, Mr. Jabez Wilson; and let me congratulate you once more on the important position which you have been fortunate enough to gain.' He bowed me out of the room, and I went home with my assistant, hardly knowing what to say or do, I was so pleased at my own good fortune.

"Well, I thought over the matter all day, and by evening I was in low spirits again; for I had quite persuaded myself that the whole affair must be some great hoax or fraud, though what its object might be I could not imagine. It seemed altogether past belief that any one could make such a will, or that they would pay such a sum for doing anything so simple as copying out the 'Encyclopædia Britannica.' Vincent Spaulding did what he could to cheer me up, but by bedtime I had reasoned myself out of the whole thing. However, in the morning I determined to have a look at it anyhow, so I bought a penny bottle of ink, and with a quill pen and seven sheets of foolscap paper I started off for Pope's Court.

«Well, to my surprise and delight, everything was as right as possible. The table was set out ready for me, and Mr. Duncan Ross was there to see that I got fairly to work. He started me off upon the letter A, and then he left me; but he would drop in from time to time to see that all was right with me. At two o'clock he bade me good-by, complimented me upon the amount that I had written, and locked the door of the office after me.

«This went on day after day, Mr. Holmes, and on Saturday the manager came in and planked down four golden sovereigns for my week's work. It was the same next week, and the same the week after. Every morning I was there at ten, and every afternoon I left at two. By degrees Mr. Duncan Ross took to coming in only once of a morning, and then after a time he did not come in at all. Still, of course, I never dared to leave the room for an instant, for I was not sure when he might come, and the billet was such a good one, and suited me so well, that I would not risk the loss of it.

«Eight weeks passed away like this, and I had written about Abbots and Archery and Armor and Architecture and Attica, and hoped with diligence that I might get on to the B's before very long. It cost me something in foolscap, and I had pretty nearly filled a shelf with my writings. And then suddenly the whole business came to an end.»

«To an end?»

«Yes, sir. And no later than this morning. I went to my work as usual at ten o'clock, but the door was shut and locked with a little square of card-board hammered on to the middle of the panel with a tack. Here it is, and you can read for yourself.»

He held up a piece of white cardboard about the size of a sheet of note-paper. It read in this fashion:—

THE RED-HEADED LEAGUE

IS

DISSOLVED.

October 9th, 1890.

Sherlock Holmes and I surveyed this curt announcement and the rueful face behind it, until the comical side of the affair so completely overtopped every other consideration that we both burst out into a roar of laughter.

"I cannot see that there is anything very funny," cried our client, flushing up to the roots of his flaming head. "If you can do nothing better than laugh at me, I can go elsewhere."

"No, no," cried Holmes, shoving him back into the chair from which he had half risen. "I really wouldn't miss your case for the world. It is most refreshingly unusual. But there is, if you will excuse my saying so, something just a little funny about it. Pray, what steps did you take when you found the card upon the door?"

"I was staggered, sir. I did not know what to do. Then I called at the offices round, but none of them seemed to know anything about it. Finally I went to the landlord, who is an accountant living on the ground-floor, and I asked him if he could tell me what had become of the Red-Headed League. He said that he had never heard of any such body. Then I asked him who Mr. Duncan Ross was. He answered that the name was new to him.

"'Well,' said I, 'the gentleman at No. 4.'

"'What, the red-headed man?'

"'Yes.'

"'Oh,' said he, 'his name was William Morris. He was a solicitor, and was using my room as a temporary convenience until his new premises were ready. He moved out yesterday.'

"'Where could I find him?'

"'Oh, at his new offices. He did tell me the address. Yes, 17 King Edward Street, near St. Paul's.'

"I started off, Mr. Holmes, but when I got to that address it was a manufactory of artificial knee-caps, and no one in it had ever heard of either Mr. William Morris or Mr. Duncan Ross."

"And what did you do then?" asked Holmes.

"I went home to Saxe-Coburg Square, and I took the advice of my assistant. But he could not help me in any way. He could only say that if I waited I should hear by post. But that was not quite good enough, Mr. Holmes. I did not wish to lose such a place without a struggle; so as I had heard that you were good enough to give advice to poor folk who were in need of it, I came right away to you."

"And you did very wisely," said Holmes. "Your case is an exceedingly remarkable one, and I shall be happy to look into it. From what you have told me, I think that it is possible that graver issues hang from it than might at first sight appear."

«Grave enough!» said Mr. Jabez Wilson. «Why, I have lost four pound a week.»

«As far as you are personally concerned,» remarked Holmes, «I do not see that you have any grievance against this extraordinary league. On the contrary, you are, as I understand, richer by some £30, to say nothing of the minute knowledge which you have gained on every subject which comes under the letter A. You have lost nothing by them.»

«No, sir. But I want to find out about them, and who they are, and what their object was in playing this prank — if it was a prank — upon me. It was a pretty expensive joke for them, for it cost them two-and-thirty pounds.»

«We shall endeavor to clear up these points for you. And first one or two questions, Mr. Wilson. This assistant of yours who first called your attention to the advertisement — how long had he been with you?»

«About a month then.»

«How did he come?»

«In answer to an advertisement.»

«Was he the only applicant?»

«No; I had a dozen.»

«Why did you pick him?»

«Because he was handy, and would come cheap.»

«At half wages, in fact.»

«Yes.»

«What is he like, this Vincent Spaulding?»

«Small, stout-built, very quick in his ways, no hair on his face, though he's not short of thirty. Has a white splash of acid upon his forehead.»

Holmes sat up in his chair in considerable excitement. «I thought as much,» said he. «Have you ever observed that his ears are pierced for earrings?»

«Yes, sir. He told me that a gipsy had done it for him when he was a lad.»

«Hum!» said Holmes, sinking back in deep thought. «He is still with you?»

«Oh yes, sir; I have only just left him.»

«And has your business been attended to in your absence?»

«Nothing to complain of, sir. There's never very much to do of a morning.»

«That will do, Mr. Wilson. I shall be happy to give you an opinion upon the subject in the course of a day or two. To-day is Saturday, and I hope that by Monday we may come to a conclusion."

"Well, Watson," said Holmes, when our visitor had left us, "what do you make of it all?"

"I make nothing of it," I answered, frankly. "It is a most mysterious business."

"As a rule," said Holmes, "the more bizarre a thing is, the less mysterious it proves to be. It is your commonplace, featureless crimes which are really puzzling, just as a commonplace face is the most difficult to identify. But I must be prompt over this matter."

"What are you going to do, then?" I asked.

"To smoke," he answered. "It is quite a three-pipe problem, and I beg that you won't speak to me for fifty minutes." He curled himself up in his chair, with his thin knees drawn up to his hawk-like nose, and there he sat with his eyes closed and his black clay pipe thrusting out like the bill of some strange bird. I had come to the conclusion that he had dropped asleep, and indeed was nodding myself, when he suddenly sprang out of his chair with the gesture of a man who has made up his mind, and put his pipe down upon the mantel-piece.

"Sarasate plays at the St. James's Hall this afternoon," he remarked. "What do you think, Watson? Could your patients spare you for a few hours?"

"I have nothing to do to-day. My practice is never very absorbing."

"Then put on your hat and come. I am going through the city first, and we can have some lunch on the way. I observe that there is a good deal of German music on the programme, which is rather more to my taste than Italian or French. It is introspective, and I want to introspect. Come along!"

We traveled by the Underground as far as Aldersgate; and a short walk took us to Saxe-Coburg Square, the scene of the singular story which we had listened to in the morning. It was a poky little shabby-genteel place, where four lines of dingy two-storied brick houses looked out into a small railed-in inclosure, where a lawn of weedy grass and a few clumps of faded laurel-bushes made a hard fight against a smoke-laden and uncongenial atmosphere. Three gilt balls, and a brown board with "JABEZ WILSON" in white letters, upon a corner house, announced the place where our red-headed client carried on his business. Sherlock Holmes stopped in front of it, with his head on one side, and looked it all over, with his eyes shining brightly between puckered lids. Then he walked slowly up the street, and then down again to the corner, still looking keenly at the houses. Finally he returned to the pawnbroker's, and having thumped vigorously upon the pavement with his stick two or three times he went up to the door and knocked. It was instantly opened by a bright-looking, clean-shaven young fellow, who asked him to step in.

«Thank you,» said Holmes, «I only wish to ask you how you would go from here to the Strand.»

«Third right, fourth left,» answered the assistant, promptly, closing the door.

«Smart fellow, that,» observed Holmes, as we walked away. «He is, in my judgment, the fourth smartest man in London, and for daring I am not sure that he has not a claim to be third. I have known something of him before.»

«Evidently,» said I, «Mr. Wilson's assistant counts for a good deal in this mystery of the Red-Headed League. I am sure that you inquired your way merely in order that you might see him.»

«Not him.»

«What then?»

«The knees of his trousers.»

«And what did you see?»

«What I expected to see.»

«Why did you beat the pavement?»

«My dear doctor, this is a time for observation, not for talk. We are spies in an enemy's country. We know something of Saxe-Coburg Square. Let us now explore the parts which lie behind it.»

The road in which we found ourselves as we turned round the corner from the retired Saxe-Coburg Square presented as great a contrast to it as the front of a picture does to the back. It was one of the main arteries which convey the traffic of the city to the north and west. The roadway was blocked with the immense stream of commerce, flowing in a double tide inward and outward, while the foot-paths were black with the hurrying swarm of pedestrians. It was difficult to realize, as we looked at the line of fine shops and stately business premises, that they really abutted on the other side upon the faded and stagnant square which we had just quitted.

«Let me see,» said Holmes, standing at the corner and glancing along the line, «I should like just to remember the order of the houses here. It is a hobby of mine to have an exact knowledge of London. There is Mortimer's, the tobacconist, the little newspaper shop, the Coburg branch of the City and Suburban Bank, the Vegetarian Restaurant, and McFarlane's carriage-building depot. That carries us right on to the other block. And now, doctor, we've done our work, so it's time we had some play. A sandwich and a cup of coffee, and then off to violin-land, where all is sweetness and delicacy and harmony, and there are no red-headed clients to vex us with their conundrums."

My friend was an enthusiastic musician, being himself not only a very capable performer, but a composer of no ordinary merit. All the afternoon he sat in the stalls wrapped in the most perfect happiness, gently waving his long thin fingers in time to the music, while his gently smiling face and his languid, dreamy eyes were as unlike those of Holmes the sleuth-hound, Holmes the relentless, keen-witted, ready-handed criminal agent, as it was possible to conceive. In his singular character the dual nature alternately asserted itself, and his extreme exactness and astuteness represented, as I have often thought, the reaction against the poetic and contemplative mood which occasionally predominated in him. The swing of his nature took him from extreme languor to devouring energy; and as I knew well, he was never so truly formidable as when for days on end he had been lounging in his arm-chair, amid his improvisations and his black-letter editions. Then it was that the lust of the chase would suddenly come upon him, and that his brilliant reasoning power would rise to the level of intuition, until those who were unacquainted with his methods would look askance at him as on a man whose knowledge was not that of other mortals. When I saw him that afternoon so enwrapped in the music at St. James's Hall, I felt that an evil time might be coming upon those whom he had set himself to hunt down.

"You want to go home, no doubt, doctor," he remarked as we emerged.

"Yes, it would be as well."

"And I have some business to do which will take some hours. This business at Coburg Square is serious."

"Why serious?"

"A considerable crime is in contemplation. I have every reason to believe that we shall be in time to stop it. But to-day being Saturday rather complicates matters. I shall want your help to-night."

"At what time?"

"Ten will be early enough."

"I shall be at Baker Street at ten."

"Very well. And I say, doctor, there may be some little danger, so kindly put your army revolver in your pocket." He waved his hand, turned on his heel, and disappeared in an instant among the crowd.

I trust that I am not more dense than my neighbors, but I was always oppressed with a sense of my own stupidity in my dealings with Sherlock Holmes. Here I had heard what he had heard, I had seen what he had seen, and yet from his words it was evident that he saw clearly not only what had happened, but what was about to happen, while to me the whole business was still confused and grotesque. As I drove home to my house in Kensington I thought over it all, from the extraordinary story of the red-headed copier of the 'Encyclopædia' down to the visit to Saxe-Coburg Square, and the ominous words with which he had parted from me. What was this nocturnal expedition, and why should I go armed? Where were we going, and what were we to do? I had the hint from Holmes that this smooth-faced pawnbroker's assistant was a formidable man—a man who might play a deep game. I tried to puzzle it out, but gave it up in despair, and set the matter aside until night should bring an explanation.

It was a quarter past nine when I started from home and made my way across the Park, and so through Oxford Street to Baker Street. Two hansoms were standing at the door, and as I entered the passage I heard the sound of voices from above. On entering his room I found Holmes in animated conversation with two men, one of whom I recognized as Peter Jones, the official police agent, while the other was a long thin sad-faced man, with a very shiny hat and oppressively respectable frock-coat.

"Ha! our party is complete," said Holmes, buttoning up his pea-jacket, and taking his heavy hunting crop from the rack. "Watson, I think you know Mr. Jones, of Scotland Yard? Let me introduce you to Mr. Merryweather, who is to be our companion in to-night's adventure."

"We're hunting in couples again, doctor, you see," said Jones, in his consequential way. "Our friend here is a wonderful man for starting a chase. All he wants is an old dog to help him to do the running down."

«I hope a wild goose may not prove to be the end of our chase,» observed Mr. Merryweather, gloomily.

«You may place considerable confidence in Mr. Holmes, sir,» said the police agent, loftily. «He has his own little methods, which are, if he won't mind my saying so, just a little too theoretical and fantastic, but he has the makings of a detective in him. It is not too much to say that once or twice, as in that business of the Sholto murder and the Agra treasure, he has been more nearly correct than the official force.»

«Oh, if you say so, Mr. Jones, it is all right,» said the stranger, with deference. «Still, I confess that I miss my rubber. It is the first Saturday night for seven-and-twenty years that I have not had my rubber.»

«I think you will find,» said Sherlock Holmes, «that you will play for a higher stake to-night than you have ever done yet, and that the play will be more exciting. For you, Mr. Merryweather, the stake will be some £30,000; and for you, Jones, it will be the man upon whom you wish to lay your hands.»

«John Clay, the murderer, thief, smasher, and forger. He's a young man, Mr. Merryweather, but he is at the head of his profession, and I would rather have my bracelets on him than on any criminal in London. He's a remarkable man, is young John Clay. His grandfather was a royal duke, and he himself has been to Eton and Oxford. His brain is as cunning as his fingers, and though we meet signs of him at every turn, we never know where to find the man himself. He'll crack a crib in Scotland one week, and be raising money to build an orphanage in Cornwall the next. I've been on his track for years, and have never set eyes on him yet.»

«I hope that I may have the pleasure of introducing you to-night. I've had one or two little turns also with Mr. John Clay, and I agree with you that he is at the head of his profession. It is past ten, however, and quite time that we started. If you two will take the first hansom, Watson and I will follow in the second.»

Sherlock Holmes was not very communicative during the long drive, and lay back in the cab humming the tunes which he had heard in the afternoon. We rattled through an endless labyrinth of gas-lit streets until we emerged into Farringdon Street.

«We are close there now,» my friend remarked. «This fellow Merryweather is a bank director, and personally interested in the matter. I thought it as well to have Jones with us also. He is not a bad fellow, though an absolute imbecile in his profession. He has one positive virtue. He is as brave as a bull-dog, and as tenacious as a lobster if he gets his claws upon any one. Here we are, and they are waiting for us."

We had reached the same crowded thoroughfare in which we had found ourselves in the morning. Our cabs were dismissed, and following the guidance of Mr. Merryweather, we passed down a narrow passage and through a side door, which he opened for us. Within, there was a small corridor, which ended in a very massive iron gate. This also was opened, and led down a flight of winding stone steps, which terminated at another formidable gate. Mr. Merryweather stopped to light a lantern, and then conducted us down a dark, earth-smelling passage, and so, after opening a third door, into a huge vault or cellar, which was piled all around with crates and massive boxes.

"You are not very vulnerable from above," Holmes remarked, as he held up the lantern and gazed about him.

"Nor from below," said Mr. Merryweather, striking his stick upon the flags which lined the floor. "Why, dear me, it sounds quite hollow!" he remarked, looking up in surprise.

"I must really ask you to be a little more quiet," said Holmes, severely. "You have already imperiled the whole success of our expedition. Might I beg that you would have the goodness to sit down upon one of those boxes, and not to interfere?"

The solemn Mr. Merryweather perched himself upon a crate, with a very injured expression upon his face, while Holmes fell upon his knees upon the floor, and with the lantern and a magnifying lens began to examine minutely the cracks between the stones. A few seconds sufficed to satisfy him, for he sprang to his feet again, and put his glass in his pocket.

"We have at least an hour before us," he remarked; "for they can hardly take any steps until the good pawnbroker is safely in bed. Then they will not lose a minute, for the sooner they do their work the longer time they will have for their escape. We are at present, doctor — as no doubt you have divined — in the cellar at the City branch of one of the principal London banks. Mr. Merryweather is the chairman of directors, and he will explain to you that there are reasons why the more daring criminals of London should take a considerable interest in this cellar at present."

« It is our French gold," whispered the director. « We have had several warnings that an attempt might be made upon it."

« Your French gold ? »

« Yes. We had occasion some months ago to strengthen our resources, and borrowed for that purpose 30,000 napoleons from the Bank of France. It has become known that we have never had occasion to unpack the money, and that it is still lying in our cellar. The crate upon which I sit contains 2,000 napoleons packed between layers of lead foil. Our reserve of bullion is much larger at present than is usually kept in a single branch office, and the directors have had misgivings upon the subject."

« Which were very well justified," observed Holmes. « And now it is time that we arranged our little plans. I expect that within an hour matters will come to a head. In the mean time, Mr. Merryweather, we must put the screen over that dark lantern."

« And sit in the dark ? »

« I am afraid so. I had brought a pack of cards in my pocket, and I thought that, as we were a *partie carrée*, you might have your rubber after all. But I see that the enemy's preparations have gone so far that we cannot risk the presence of a light. And first of all, we must choose our positions. These are daring men, and though we shall take them at a disadvantage, they may do us some harm unless we are careful. I shall stand behind this crate, and do you conceal yourselves behind those. Then when I flash a light upon them, close in swiftly. If they fire, Watson, have no compunction about shooting them down."

I placed my revolver, cocked, upon the top of the wooden case behind which I crouched. Holmes shot the slide across the front of his lantern, and left us in pitch darkness — such an absolute darkness as I had never before experienced. The smell of hot metal remained to assure us that the light was still there, ready to flash out at a moment's notice. To me, with my nerves worked up to a pitch of expectancy, there was something depressing and subduing in the sudden gloom, and in the cold dank air of the vault.

« They have but one retreat," whispered Holmes. « That is back through the house into Saxe-Coburg Square. I hope that you have done what I asked you, Jones ? »

« I have an inspector and two officers waiting at the front door. »

« Then we have stopped all the holes. And now we must be silent and wait.»

What a time it seemed! From comparing notes afterwards it was but an hour and a quarter, yet it appeared to me that the night must have almost gone, and the dawn be breaking above us. My limbs were weary and stiff, for I feared to change my position; yet my nerves were worked up to the highest pitch of tension, and my hearing was so acute that I could not only hear the gentle breathing of my companions, but I could distinguish the deeper, heavier in-breath of the bulky Jones from the thin, sighing note of the bank director. From my position I could look over the case in the direction of the floor. Suddenly my eyes caught the glint of a light.

At first it was but a lurid spark upon the stone pavement. Then it lengthened out until it became a yellow line, and then, without any warning or sound, a gash seemed to open and a hand appeared; a white, almost womanly hand, which felt about in the centre of the little area of light. For a minute or more the hand, with its writhing fingers, protruded out of the floor. Then it was withdrawn as suddenly as it appeared, and all was dark again save the single lurid spark which marked a chink between the stones.

Its disappearance, however, was but momentary. With a rending, tearing sound, one of the broad white stones turned over upon its side, and left a square gaping hole, through which streamed the light of a lantern. Over the edge there peeped a clean-cut, boyish face, which looked keenly about it, and then, with a hand on either side of the aperture, drew itself shoulder-high and waist-high, until one knee rested upon the edge. In another instant he stood at the side of the hole, and was hauling after him a companion, lithe and small like himself, with a pale face and a shock of very red hair.

« It's all clear,» he whispered. « Have you the chisel and the bags?—Great Scott! Jump, Archie, jump, and I'll swing for it!»

Sherlock Holmes had sprung out and seized the intruder by the collar. The other dived down the hole, and I heard the sound of rending cloth as Jones clutched at his skirts. The light flashed upon the barrel of a revolver, but Holmes's hunting crop came down on the man's wrist and the pistol clinked upon the stone floor.

"It's no use, John Clay," said Holmes, blandly. "You have no chance at all."

"So I see," the other answered, with the utmost coolness. "I fancy that my pal is all right, though I see you have got his coat-tails."

"There are three men waiting for him at the door," said Holmes.

"Oh, indeed! You seem to have done the thing very completely. I must compliment you."

"And I you," Holmes answered. "Your red-headed idea was very new and effective."

"You'll see your pal again presently," said Jones. "He's quicker at climbing down holes than I am. Just hold out, while I fix the derbies."

"I beg that you will not touch me with your filthy hands," remarked our prisoner, as the handcuffs clattered upon his wrists. "You may not be aware that I have royal blood in my veins. Have the goodness, also, when you address me always to say 'sir' and 'please.'"

"All right," said Jones, with a stare and a snigger. "Well, would you please, sir, march upstairs, where we can get a cab to carry your Highness to the police station?"

"That is better," said John Clay, serenely. He made a sweeping bow to the three of us, and walked quietly off in the custody of the detective.

"Really, Mr. Holmes," said Mr. Merryweather, as we followed them from the cellar, "I do not know how the bank car thank you or repay you. There is no doubt that you have detected and defeated in the most complete manner one of the most determined attempts at bank robbery that have ever come within my experience."

"I have had one or two little scores of my own to settle with Mr. John Clay," said Holmes. "I have been at some small expense over this matter, which I shall expect the bank to refund; but beyond that I am amply repaid by having had an experience which is in many ways unique, and by hearing the very remarkable narrative of the Red-Headed League."

"You see, Watson," he explained, in the early hours of the morning, as we sat over a glass of whisky and soda in Baker Street, "it was perfectly obvious from the first that the only possible object of this rather fantastic business of the advertisement of the League, and the copying of the 'Encyclopædia,' must be to get this not over bright pawnbroker out of the way for a number of hours every day. It was a curious way of managing it, but really, it would be difficult to suggest a better. The method was no doubt suggested to Clay's ingenious mind by the color of his accomplice's hair. The £4 a week was a lure which must draw him,—and what was it to them, who were playing for thousands? They put in the advertisement, one rogue has the temporary office, the other rogue incites the man to apply for it, and together they manage to secure his absence every morning in the week. From the time that I heard of the assistant having come for half wages, it was obvious to me that he had some strong motive for securing the situation."

"But how could you guess what the motive was?"

"Had there been women in the house, I should have suspected a mere vulgar intrigue. That however was out of the question. The man's business was a small one, and there was nothing in his house which could account for such elaborate preparations and such an expenditure as they were at. It must then be something out of the house. What could it be? I thought of the assistant's fondness for photography, and his trick of vanishing into the cellar. The cellar! There was the end of this tangled clue. Then I made inquiries as to this mysterious assistant, and found that I had to deal with one of the coolest and most daring criminals in London. He was doing something in the cellar—something which took many hours a day for months on end. What could it be, once more? I could think of nothing save that he was running a tunnel to some other building.

"So far I had got when we went to visit the scene of action. I surprised you by beating upon the pavement with my stick. I was ascertaining whether the cellar stretched out in front or behind. It was not in front. Then I rang the bell, and as I hoped, the assistant answered it. We have had some skirmishes, but we had never set eyes upon each other before. I hardly looked at his face. His knees were what I wished to see. You must yourself have remarked how worn, wrinkled, and stained they were. They spoke of those hours of burrowing. The only remaining point was what they were burrowing for. I walked round the corner, saw that the City and Suburban Bank abutted on our friend's premises, and felt that I had solved my problem. When you drove home after the concert I called upon Scotland Yard, and upon the chairman of the bank directors, with the result that you have seen."

"And how could you tell that they would make their attempt to-night?" I asked.

"Well, when they closed their League offices, that was a sign that they cared no longer about Mr. Jabez Wilson's presence—in other words, that they had completed their tunnel. But it was essential that they should use it soon, as it might be discovered, or the bullion might be removed. Saturday would suit them better than any other day, as it would give them two days for their escape. For all these reasons I expected them to come to-night."

"You reasoned it out beautifully," I exclaimed, in unfeigned admiration. "It is so long a chain, and yet every link rings true."

"It saved me from ennui," he answered, yawning. "Alas! I already feel it closing in upon me. My life is spent in one long effort to escape from the commonplaces of existence. These little problems help me to do so."

"And you are a benefactor of the race," said I.

He shrugged his shoulders. "Well, perhaps after all it is of some little use," he remarked. "'L'homme c'est rien—l'œuvre c'est tout,' as Gustave Flaubert wrote to George Sand."

THE BOWMEN'S SONG

From 'The White Company'

What of the bow?
The bow was made in England:
Of true wood, of yew wood,
The wood of English bows;
So men who are free
Love the old yew-tree
And the land where the yew-tree grows.

What of the cord?
The cord was made in England:
A rough cord, a tough cord,
A cord that bowmen love;

So we'll drain our jacks
To the English flax
And the land where the hemp was wove.

What of the shaft?
The shaft was cut in England:
A long shaft, a strong shaft,
Barbed and trim and true;
So we'll drink all together
To the gray goose feather,
And the land where the gray goose flew.

What of the men?
The men were bred in England:
The bowman — the yeoman —
The lads of dale and fell.
Here's to you — and to you!
To the hearts that are true
And the land where the true hearts dwell.

HOLGER DRACHMANN

(1846–)

HOLGER DRACHMANN, born in Copenhagen October 9th, 1846, belongs to the writers characterized by Georg Brandes as «the men of the new era.»

Danish literature had stood high during the first half of the nineteenth century. In 1850 Oehlenschläger died. In 1870 there was practically no Danish literature. The reason for this may have been that after the new political life of 1848–9 and the granting of the Danish Constitution, politics absorbed all young talent, and men of literary tastes put themselves at the service of the daily press.

HOLGER DRACHMANN

In 1872 Georg Brandes gave his lectures on 'Main Currents in the Literature of the Nineteenth Century' at the University of Copenhagen. That same year Drachmann published his first collection of 'Poems,' and so began his extraordinary productivity of poems, dramas, and novels. Of these, his lyric poems are undoubtedly of the greatest value. His is a distinctly lyric temperament. The new school had chosen for its guide Brandes's teaching that «Literature, to be of significance, should discuss problems.» In view of this fact it is somewhat hard to understand why Drachmann should be called a man of the new era. He never discusses problems. He always gives himself up unreservedly to the subject which at that special moment claims his sympathy. Taken as a whole, therefore, his writings present a certain inconsistency. He has shown himself alternately as socialist and royalist, realist and romanticist, freethinker and believer, cosmopolitan and national, according to the lyric enthusiasm of the moment. Independent of these changes, the one thing to be admired and enjoyed is his lyric feeling and the often exquisite form in which he presents it. His larger compositions, novels, and dramas do not show the same power over his subject.

If Drachmann discusses any problem, it is the problem Drachmann. He does this sometimes with what Brandes calls «a light and joking self-irony,» in a most sympathetic way. Brandes quotes one of Drachmann's early stories, where it is said of the hero:—«His name was really Palnatoke Olsen; a continually repeated discord of two tones, as he used to say.» Olsen is one of the most commonplace Danish names. Palnatoke is the name of one of the fiercest warriors of heathen antiquity, who, like a veritable Valhalla god, dared to oppose the terrible Danish king Harald Blaatand. When Olsen's parents gave him this name they unwittingly described their son, «forever drawn by two poles: one the plain Olsen, the other the hot-headed fiery Viking.» With this in mind, and considering Drachmann's literary works as a whole, one is irresistibly reminded of his friend and contemporary in Norway, Björnsterne Björnson. There is this difference between them, however, that if the irony of Palnatoke Olsen may be applied to both, one might for Drachmann use the abbreviation P. Olsen and for Björnson undoubtedly Palnatoke O.

It might be said of Drachmann, as Saüer said of the Italian poet Monti:—«Like a master in the art of appreciation, he knew how to give himself up to great time-stirring ideas; somewhat as a gifted actor throws himself into his part, with the full strength of his art, with an enthusiasm carrying all before it, and in the most expressive way; then when the part is played, lays it quietly aside and takes hold of something else.»

When a young man, Drachmann studied at the Academy of Arts in Copenhagen, and met with considerable success as a marine painter. His love for the Northern seas shows itself in his poetry and prose, and his descriptions of the sea and the life of the sailor and fisherman are of the truest and best yielded by his pen. He is the author of no less than forty-six volumes of poems, dramas, novels, short stories, and sketches, and of two unpublished dramas. His most important work is 'Forskrevet' (Condemned), which is largely autobiographical; his most attractive though not his strongest production is the opera 'Der Var Engang' (Once Upon a Time), founded on Andersen's 'The Swineherd,' with music by Sange Müller; his best poems and tales are those dealing with the sea.

At present he lives in Hamburg, where on October 10th, 1896, he celebrated his fiftieth birthday and his twenty-fifth «Author-Jubilee,» as the Danes call it. Among the features of the celebration were the sending of an enormous number of telegrams from Drachmann's admirers in Europe and America, and the performance of two of his plays,—one at the Royal Theatre in Copenhagen, the other at the Stadt Theatre in Altona.

THE SKIPPER AND HIS SHIP

From ‹Paul and Virginia of a Northern Zone›: copyright 1895, by Way and Williams, Chicago

THE Anna Dorothea, in the North Sea, was pounding along under shortened sail. The weather was thick, the air dense; there was a falling barometer.

It had been a short trip this time. Leroy and Sons, wine merchants of Havre, had made better offers than the old houses in Bordeaux. At each one of his later trips, Captain Spang had said it should be his last. He would «lay up» at home; he was growing too stout and clumsy for the sea, and now he must trust fully to Tönnes, his first mate. The captain's big broad face was flushed as usual; he always looked as if he were illuminated by a setting October sun; there was no change here—rather, the sunset tint was stronger. But Tönnes noted how the features, which he knew best in moments of simple good-nature and of sullen tumult, had gradually relaxed. He thought that it would indeed soon be time for his old skipper to «lay up»; yet perhaps a few trips might still be made.

«Holloa, Tönnes! let her go about before the next squall strikes her. She lies too dead on this bow.»

The skipper had raised his head above the cabin stairs. As usual, he was in his shirt-sleeves, and his scanty hair fluttered in the wind. When he had warned his mate, he again disappeared in the cabin.

Tönnes gave the order to the man at the helm, and hurried to help at the main-braces. The double-reefed main-topsail swung about, the Anna Dorothea caught the wind somewhat sluggishly, and not without getting considerable water over her; then followed the fore-topsail, the reefed foresail, and the trysail. When the tacking was finished and the sails had again caught the wind, the trysail was torn from the boltropes with a loud crack.

The captain's head appeared again.

«We must close-reef!» said he.

The last reef was taken in; the storm came down and lashed the sea; the sky grew more and more threatening; the waves dashed over the deck at each plunge of the old bark in the sea. The old vessel, which had carried her captain for a generation, lay heavily on the water—Tönnes thought too heavily.

The second mate — the same who had played the accordion at the inn — came over to Tönnes.

« It was wrong to stow the china-clay at the bottom and the casks on top; she lies horribly dead, and I'm afraid we shall have to use the pumps.»

« Yes, I said so to the old man, but he would have it that way,» answered Tönnes. « We shall have a wet night.»

« We shall, surely,» said the second mate.

Tönnes crawled up to the helm and looked at the compass. Two men were at the helm — lashed fast. Tönnes looked up into the rigging and out to windward; then suddenly he cried, with the full force of his lungs: —

« Look out for breakers!»

Tönnes himself helped at the wheel; but the vessel only half answered the helm. The greater portion of the sea struck the bow, the quarter, and the bulwarks and stanchions amidship, so that they creaked and groaned. One of the men at the helm had grasped Tönnes, who would otherwise have been swept into the lee scupper. When the ship had righted from the terrible blow, the captain stood on the deck in his oilcloth suit.

« Are any men missing?» cried he, through the howling of the wind and the roaring of the water streaming fore and aft, unable to escape quickly enough through the scuppers.

The storm raged with undiminished fury. The crew — and amongst them Prussian, who had been promoted to be ship's-dog — by-and-by dived forward through the seething salt water and the fragments of wreck that covered the deck.

Now it was that the second mate was missing.

The captain looked at Tönnes, and then out on the wild sea. He scarcely glanced at the crushed long-boat; even if a boat could have been launched, it would have been too late. Tönnes and his skipper were fearless men, who took things as they were. If any help could have been given, they would have given it. But their eyes sought vainly for any dark speck amidst the foaming waves — and it was necessary to care for themselves, the vessel and the crew.

« God save his soul!» murmured Captain Spang.

Tönnes passed his hand across his brow, and went to his duty.

Evening set in; the wind increased rather than decreased.

« She is taking in water,» said the captain, who had sounded the pumps.

Tönnes assented.

« We must change her course,» said the captain. « She pitches too heavily in this sea.»

The bark was held up to the wind as closely as possible. The pumps were worked steadily, but often got out of order on account of the china-clay, which mixed with the water down in the hold.

It was plain that the vessel grew heavier and heavier; her movements in climbing a wave were more and more dead.

During the night a cry arose: again one of the crew was washed overboard.

It was a long night and a wet one, as Tönnes had predicted. Several times the skipper dived down into the cabin — Tönnes knew perfectly well what for, but he said nothing. Few words were spoken on board the Anna Dorothea that night.

In the morning the captain, returning from one of his excursions down below, declared that the cabin was half full of water.

« We must watch for a sail,» he said, abruptly and somewhat huskily.

Tönnes passed the word round amongst the crew. One might read on their faces that they were prepared for this, and that they had ceased to hope, although they had not stopped work at the pumps.

The whole of the weather bulwark, the cook's cabin and the long-boat, were crushed or washed away; the water could be heard below the hatches. While keeping a sharp lookout for sails, many an eye glanced at the yawl as the last resort. But on board Captain Spang's vessel the words were not yet spoken which carried with them the doom of the ship: « We are sinking!»

In the gray-white of the dawn a signal was to be hoisted; the bunting was tied together at the middle and raised half-mast high.

Both the captain and Tönnes had lashed themselves aft; for now the bark was but little better than a wreck, over which the billows broke incessantly, as the vessel, reeling like a drunken man, exposed herself to the violent attacks of the sea instead of parrying them.

« A sail to windward, captain!» cried Tönnes.

Captain Spang only nodded.

« She holds her course!» cried one of the crew excitedly.

« No,» said Tönnes, quietly. « She has seen us, and is bearing down upon us!»

The captain again nodded.

«'Tis a brig!» cried one of the crew.

«A schooner-brig!» Tönnes corrected. «She carries her sails finely. I am sure she is a fruit-trader.»

At last the strange vessel was so near that they could see her deck each time she was thrown upon her side in the violent seething sea.

«Yes, 'tis the schooner-brig!» exclaimed Tönnes. «Do you remember, captain, the time when—»

Again Captain Spang nodded. He acted strangely. Tönnes looked sharply at him, and shook his head.

Now Tönnes hailed the vessel:—

«Help us!—We are sinking!»

At this moment two or three of the bark's crew rushed toward the yawl, although Tönnes warned them back.

Captain Spang seemed changed. Evidently some opposing feelings contended within him. Seeing the insubordination of the men, he only shrugged his shoulders, and let Tönnes take full charge.

The men were in the yawl, still hanging under the iron davits. Now they cut the ropes; the yawl touched the water. The crew of the other vessel gestured warningly; but it was too late. A sea seized the yawl with its small crew, and the next moment crushed it against the main chains of the bark. Their shipmates raised a cry, and rushed to help them; but help was impossible. Boat and crew had disappeared.

«Didn't I say so?» cried Tönnes, with flaming eyes.

Over there in the schooner-brig all was activity. From the Anna Dorothea they could plainly see how the captain gave his orders. He manœuvred his vessel like a true sailor. To board the wreck in such a sea would be madness. Therefore they unreeved two long lines and attached them to the long-boat, one on each side. Then they laid breeching under the boat, and hauled it up amidships by means of tackle. Taking advantage of a moment when their vessel was athwart the seas, they unloosed the tackle, and the boat swung out over the side; then they cut the breeching, the boat fell on the water aft, and now both lines were eased off quickly; while the brig caught the wind, the boat drifted toward the stern-sheets of the bark.

Tönnes was ready with a boat-hook, and connections were quickly made between the boat and the wreck.

«Quick now!» cried Tönnes. «Every man in the boat. No one takes his clothes with him! We may be thankful if we save our lives.»

The men were quickly over the stern-sheets and down in the boat. Prussian whined, and kept close to Captain Spang, who had not moved one step on the deck.

«Come, captain!» cried Tönnes, taking the skipper by the arm.

«What's the matter?» asked the old man angrily.

Tönnes looked at him. Prussian barked.

«We must get into the boat, captain. The vessel may sink at any moment. Come!»

The captain pressed his sou'wester down over his forehead, and glanced around his deck.

The men in the boat cried out to them to come.

«Well!» said Captain Spang, but with an air so absent-minded and a bearing so irresolute that Tönnes at last took a firm hold on him.

Prussian showed his teeth at his former master.

«You go first!» exclaimed Tönnes, snatching the dog and throwing him down to the men, who were having hard work to keep the boat from wrecking.

When the dog was no longer on the deck, it seemed as if Captain Spang's resistance was broken. Tönnes did not let go his hold on him; but the young mate had to use almost superhuman strength to get the heavy old man down over the vessel's side and placed on a seat in the boat.

As soon as they had observed from the brig that this had been done, they hauled in both lines. The boat moved back again; but it was a dangerous voyage, and all were obliged to lash themselves fast to the thwarts with ropes placed there for that purpose.

Captain Spang was like a child. Tönnes had to lash him to the seat. The old man sat with his face hidden in his hands, his back turned toward his ship, inactive, and seemingly unconscious of what took place around him.

At last, when after a hard struggle all were on the deck of the schooner-brig, her captain came forward, placed his hand on his old friend's shoulder, and said:—

«It is the second time, you see! Well, we all cling to life, and the vessel over there is pretty old.»

Captain Spang started. He scarcely returned his friend's hand-shaking.

«My vessel, I say! My papers! All that I have is in the vessel. I must go aboard, do you hear? I must go aboard. How could I forget?»

The other skipper and Tönnes looked at each other.

Captain Spang wrung his hands and stamped on the deck, his eyes fixed on his sinking vessel. She was still afloat; what did he care for the gale and the heavy sea? He belonged to the old school of skippers; he was bound to his vessel by ties longer than any life-line, heavier than any hawser; he had left his ship in a bewildered state, and had taken nothing with him that might serve to prove what he possessed and how long he had possessed it. His good old vessel was still floating on the water. He must, he would go there; if nobody would go with him, he would go alone.

All remonstrances were in vain.

Tönnes pressed the other skipper's hand.

«There is nothing else to be done. I know him,» said he.

«So do I,» was the answer.

Captain Spang and his mate were again in the boat. As they were on the point of starting, a loud whine and violent barking sounded from the deck, and Prussian showed his one eye over the railing.

«Stay where you are!» cried Tönnes. «We shall be back soon.»

But the dog did not understand him. Perhaps he had his doubts; no one can say. He sprang overboard; Tönnes seized him by the ear, and hauled him into the boat.

And then the two men and the dog ventured back to the abandoned vessel.

This time the old man climbed on board without assistance.

Prussian whined in the boat.

«Throw that dog up to me!» cried the master.

Tönnes did so.

«Shall I come up and help you?» he called out.

«No, I can find my own way.»

«But hurry, captain! do you understand?» said Tönnes, who anxiously noticed that the motions of the vessel were becoming more and more dangerous, while he needed all his strength to keep the boat clear of the wreck.

An answer came from the bark, but he could not catch it. In this moment Tönnes recalled the day when he rowed the captain out on the bay to the brig. His next thought was of Nanna. Oh, if she knew where they were!

And at this thought the mate's breast was filled with conflicting emotions. The dear blessed girl!—Oh, if her father would only come!

«Captain!» cried Tönnes; «Captain Spang! for God's sake, come! Leave those papers alone. The vessel is sinking. We may at any moment—»

He paused.

The captain stood at the stern-sheets. At his side was Prussian, squinting down into the boat. There was an entirely strange expression in Andreas Spang's face; a double expression—one moment hard and defiant, the next almost solemn.

The sou'wester had fallen from his old head. His scanty hairs fluttered in the wind. He held in his hand a parcel of papers and a coil of rope. He pointed toward the brig.

«There!» he cried, throwing the package and the rope down to Tönnes. «Give the skipper this new line for his trouble. He has used plenty of rope for us. You go back. I stay here. Give—my—love—to the girl at home.—You and she—You two—God bless you!»

«Captain!» cried Tönnes in affright; «you are sick; come, let me—»

He prepared to climb on board.

Captain Spang lifted his hand threateningly, and Prussian barked furiously.

«Stay down there, boy, I say! The vessel and I, we belong together. You shall take care of the girl. Good-by!»

The Anna Dorothea rolled heavily over on one side, righted again, and then began to plunge her head downwards, like a whale that, tired of the surface, seeks rest at the bottom. The crew of the brig hauled in the lines of the boat. Tossed on the turbid sea, Tönnes saw his old skipper leaning against the helm, the dog at his side. His gray hairs fluttered in the wind as if they wafted a last farewell; and down with vessel and dog went the old skipper—down into the wild sea that so long had borne him on its waves.

THE PRINCE'S SONG

From ‹Once Upon a Time›

PRINCESS, I come from out a land that lieth—
  I know not in what arctic latitude;
Though high in the bleak north, it never sigheth
  For sunny smiles; they wait not to be wooed.
Our privilege we know: the bright half-year
  Illumines sea and shore with sunlit glory;
In twilight then our fertile fields we ear,
  And round our brows we twine a wreath of story.

When winter decks with frost the bearded oak,
  In songs and sagas we our youth recover;
Around the hearthstone crowd the listening folk,
  While on the wall mysterious shadows hover.
The summer night, suffused with loving glow,
  The future, dawning in a golden chalice,
Enkindles hope in hearts of high and low,
  From peasant's cottage to the royal palace.

The snow of winter spreads o'er hill and valley
  Its soft and silken blue-white veil of sleep;
The springtime bids the green-clad earth to rally,
  When through the budding leaves the sunbeams peep.
The autumn brings fresh breezes from the ocean
  And paints the lad's fair cheeks a rosy red;
The maiden's heart is stirred with new emotion,
  When summer's fragrance o'er the world is spread.

To roam in our fair land is like a dream,
  Through these still woods, renowned in ancient story,
Along the shores, deep-mirrored in the gleam
  Of fjords that shine beneath the sky's blue glory.
Upon the meadows where the flowers bloom
  The elfin maidens hide themselves in slumbers,
But soon along the lakes where shadows gloom
  In every bosky nook they'll dance their numbers.

There are no frowning crags on our green mountains,
  No dark, forbidding cliffs where gorges yawn;
The streams flow gently seaward from their fountains,
  As through the silent valley steals the dawn.

Here nature smoothes the rugged, tames the savage,
And men born here in victory are kind,
Forbearing still the foeman's land to ravage,
And in defeat they bear a steadfast mind.

I'm proud of land, of kindred, and of nation,
I'm proud my home is where the waters flow;
Afar I see in golden radiation
My native land like sun through amber glow.
Its warmth revives my heart, however lonely:
Forgive me, Princess, if my soul's aflame,—
But rather be at home, a beggar only,
Than, exiled thence, have universal fame.

Translation of Charles Harvey Genung.

JOSEPH RODMAN DRAKE

(1795–1820)

Conspicuous among the young poets, essayists, and journalists, who made up literary New York in the early part of the century, was Joseph Rodman Drake, the friend of Halleck, and the best beloved perhaps of all that brilliant group. Hardly known to this generation save by 'The Culprit Fay' and 'The American Flag,' Drake was essentially a true poet and a man of letters. His work was characteristic of his day. He had a certain amount of classical knowledge, a certain eighteenth-century grace and style, yet withal, an instinctive Americanism which flowered out into our first true national literature. The group of writers among whom were found Irving, Halleck, Willis, Dana, Hoffman, Verplanck, Brockden Brown, and a score of others, reflected that age in which they sought their literary models. With the exception of Poe, who belonged to a somewhat later time and whose genius was purely subjective, much of the production of these Americans followed the lines of their English predecessors,—Johnson, Goldsmith, Addison, and Steele. It is only in their deeper moments of thought and feeling that there sounds that note of love of country, of genuine Americanism, which gives their work individuality, and which will keep their memory green.

Joseph Rodman Drake

Drake was born in New York, in August 1795. He was descended from the same family as the great admiral of Elizabethan days, the American branch of which had served their country honorably both in colonial and Revolutionary times. The scenes of his boyhood were the same as those that formed the environment of Irving, memories of which are scattered thick through the literature of the day. New York was still a picturesque, hospitable, rural capital, the centre of the present town being miles distant in the country. The best families were all intimately associated in a social life that was cultivated and refined at the same time that it was gay and unconventional; and in this society Drake occupied a place which his lovable qualities and fine talents must have won, even had it been denied him by birth. He was a precocious boy, for whom a career was anticipated by his friends while he was yet a mere child; and when he met Halleck, in his eighteenth year, he had already won some reputation.

The friendship of Drake and Halleck was destined to prove infinitely valuable to both. A discussion between Cooper, Halleck, and Drake, upon the poetic inspiration of American scenery, prompted Drake to write 'The Culprit Fay'—a poem without any human character. This he completed in three days, and offered it as the argument on his side. The scene of the poem is laid in the Highlands of the Hudson, but Drake added many pictures suggested by memories of Long Island Sound, whose waters he haunted with boat and rod. He apologized for this by saying that the purposes of poetry alone could explain the presence so far up the Hudson of so many salt-water emigrants. 'The Culprit Fay' is a creation of pure fancy, full of delicate imagery, and handled with an ethereal lightness of touch. Its exquisite grace, its delicate coloring, its prodigality of charm, explain its immediate popularity and its lasting fame. But the Rip Van Winkle legend is a far more genuine product of fancy.

Drake's few shorter lyrics throb with genuine poetic feeling, and show the loss sustained by literature in the author's early death. Best known of these is 'The American Flag,' which appeared in the Evening Post as one of a series of *jeux d'esprit*, the joint productions of Halleck and Drake, who either alternated in the composition of the numbers or wrote them together. The last four lines only of 'The American Flag' are Halleck's. The entire series appeared between March and July, 1819, under the signature of «The Croakers.» Literary New York was mystified as to the authorship of these skits, which hit off the popular fads, follies, and enthusiasms of the day with so easy and graceful a touch. Politics, music, the drama, and domestic life alike furnished inspiration for the numbers; some of whose titles, as 'A Sketch of a Debate in Tammany' and 'The Battery War,' suggest the local political issues of the present day. There is now in existence a handsome edition of these verses, with the names of the authors of the several pieces appended, and in the case of the joint ownership with the initials D. and H. subscribed.

Drake's complete poems were not published during his lifetime. Sixteen years after his death by consumption in his twenty-sixth year, his daughter issued a volume dedicated to Halleck, in which were included the best specimens of her father's work. Many of the lesser known verses indicate his true place as a poet. In the touching poem 'Abelard to Eloise,' in the third stanza of 'The American Flag,' and in innumerable beautiful lines scattered throughout his work, appears a genuine inspiration.

In his own day, Drake filled a place which his death left forever vacant. His rare and winning personality, his generous friendships, his joy in life, and his courage in the contemplation of his inevitable fate, still appeal to a generation to whom they are but traditions. The exquisite monody in which Halleck celebrated his loss, links their names and decorates their friendship with imperishable garlands.

A WINTER'S TALE

From ‹The Croakers›

«*A merry heart goes all the way,*
A sad one tires in a mile-a.»
—WINTER'S TALE.

THE man who frets at worldly strife
Grows sallow, sour, and thin;
Give us the lad whose happy life
Is one perpetual grin:
He, Midas-like, turns all to gold;
He smiles when others sigh;
Enjoys alike the hot and cold,
And laughs through wet and dry.

There's fun in everything we meet;
The greatest, worst, and best
Existence is a merry treat,
And every speech a jest:
Be 't ours to watch the crowds that pass
Where mirth's gay banner waves;
To show fools through a quizzing glass,
And bastinade the knaves.

The serious world will scold and ban,
In clamor loud and hard,
To hear Meigs* called a Congressman,
And Paulding called a bard:
But come what may, the man's in luck
Who turns it all to glee,
And laughing, cries with honest Puck,
«Good Lord! what fools ye be!»

*Henry Meigs of New York, a Congressman from 1819 to 1821 in the Sixteenth Congress.

THE CULPRIT FAY

My visual orbs are purged from film, and lo!
  Instead of Anster's turnip-bearing vales,
I see old Fairyland's miraculous show!
  Her trees of tinsel kissed by freakish gales,
Her ouphs that, cloaked in leaf-gold, skim the breeze,
  And fairies, swarming. . . . .
— TENNANT'S 'ANSTER FAIR'

'TIS the middle watch of a summer's night—
  The earth is dark, but the heavens are bright;
  Naught is seen in the vault on high
But the moon, and the stars, and the cloudless sky,
And the flood which rolls its milky hue,
A river of light on the welkin blue.
The moon looks down on old Cronest;
She mellows the shades on his shaggy breast,
And seems his huge gray form to throw
In a silver cone on the wave below;
His sides are broken by spots of shade,
By the walnut bough and the cedar made,
And through their clustering branches dark
Glimmers and dies the firefly's spark—
Like starry twinkles that momently break
Through the rifts of the gathering tempest's rack.

The stars are on the moving stream,
  And fling, as its ripples gently flow,
A burnished length of wavy beam
  In an eel-like, spiral line below;
The winds are whist, and the owl is still;
  The bat in the shelvy rock is hid;
And naught is heard on the lonely hill
But the cricket's chirp, and the answer shrill
    Of the gauze-winged katydid;
And the plaint of the wailing whippoorwill,
Who moans unseen, and ceaseless sings,
  Ever a note of wail and woe,
Till morning spreads her rosy wings,
  And earth and sky in her glances glow.

'Tis the hour of fairy ban and spell:
The wood-tick has kept the minutes well;

He has counted them all with click and stroke
Deep in the heart of the mountain oak,
And he has awakened the sentry elve
  Who sleeps with him in the haunted tree,
To bid him ring the hour of twelve,
  And call the fays to their revelry;
Twelve small strokes on his tinkling bell —
('Twas made of the white snail's pearly shell)
«Midnight comes, and all is well!
Hither, hither, wing your way!
'Tis the dawn of the fairy day.»

They come from beds of lichen green,
They creep from the mullein's velvet screen;
Some on the backs of beetles fly
  From the silver tops of moon-touched trees,
Where they swung in their cobweb hammocks high,
  And rocked about in the evening breeze;
Some from the hum-bird's downy nest —
  They had driven him out by elfin power,
And pillowed on plumes of his rainbow breast,
  Had slumbered there till the charmèd hour;
Some had lain in the scoop of the rock,
  With glittering ising-stars inlaid;
And some had opened the four-o'clock,
  And stole within its purple shade.
And now they throng the moonlight glade,
  Above, below, on every side,
Their little minim forms arrayed
  In the tricksy pomp of fairy pride!

They come not now to print the lea,
In freak and dance around the tree,
Or at the mushroom board to sup,
And drink the dew from the buttercup; —
A scene of sorrow waits them now,
For an ouphe has broken his vestal vow;
He has loved an earthly maid,
And left for her his woodland shade;
He has lain upon her lip of dew,
And sunned him in her eye of blue,
Fanned her cheek with his wing of air,
Played in the ringlets of her hair,
And nestling on her snowy breast,
Forgot the lily-king's behest.

For this the shadowy tribes of air
  To the elfin court must haste away:
And now they stand expectant there,
  To hear the doom of the culprit fay.

The throne was reared upon the grass,
Of spice-wood and of sassafras;
On pillars of mottled tortoise-shell
  Hung the burnished canopy—
And o'er it gorgeous curtains fell
  Of the tulip's crimson drapery.
The monarch sat on his judgment seat;
  On his brow the crown imperial shone;
The prisoner fay was at his feet,
  And his peers were ranged around the throne.
He waved his sceptre in the air,
  He looked around and calmly spoke;
His brow was grave and his eye severe,
  But his voice in a softened accent broke:—

"Fairy! Fairy! list and mark:
  Thou hast broke thine elfin chain;
Thy flame-wood lamp is quenched and dark,
  And thy wings are dyed with a deadly stain—
Thou hast sullied thine elfin purity
  In the glance of a mortal maiden's eye;
Thou hast scorned our dread decree,
  And thou shouldst pay the forfeit high.
But well I know her sinless mind
  Is pure as the angel forms above,
Gentle and meek, and chaste and kind,
  Such as a spirit well might love;
Fairy! had she spot or taint,
Bitter had been thy punishment:
Tied to the hornet's shardy wings;
Tossed on the pricks of nettles' stings;
Or seven long ages doomed to dwell
With the lazy worm in the walnut-shell;
Or every night to writhe and bleed
Beneath the tread of the centipede;
Or bound in a cobweb dungeon dim,
Your jailer a spider, huge and grim,
Amid the carrion bodies to lie
Of the worm, and the bug, and the murdered fly:

These it had been your lot to bear,
Had a stain been found on the earthly fair.
Now list, and mark our mild decree—
Fairy, this your doom must be:—

"Thou shalt seek the beach of sand
Where the water bounds the elfin land;
Thou shalt watch the oozy brine
Till the sturgeon leaps in the bright moonshine,
Then dart the glistening arch below,
And catch a drop from his silver bow.
The water-sprites will wield their arms
  And dash around, with roar and rave,
And vain are the woodland spirits' charms;
  They are the imps that rule the wave.
Yet trust thee in thy single might:
If thy heart be pure and thy spirit right,
Thou shalt win the warlock fight.

"If the spray-bead gem be won,
  The stain of thy wing is washed away;
But another errand must be done
  Ere thy crime be lost for aye:
Thy flame-wood lamp is quenched and dark,—
Thou must re-illume its spark.
Mount thy steed and spur him high
To the heaven's blue canopy;
And when thou seest a shooting star,
Follow it fast, and follow it far—
The last faint spark of its burning train
Shall light the elfin lamp again.
Thou hast heard our sentence, fay;
Hence! to the water-side, away!"

The goblin marked his monarch well;
  He spake not, but he bowed him low,
Then plucked a crimson colen-bell,
  And turned him round in act to go.
The way is long; he cannot fly;
  His soilèd wing has lost its power,
And he winds adown the mountain high
  For many a sore and weary hour.
Through dreary beds of tangled fern,
Through groves of nightshade dark and dern,

Over the grass and through the brake,
Where toils the ant and sleeps the snake;
Now o'er the violet's azure flush
  He skips along in lightsome mood;
And now he thrids the bramble-bush,
  Till its points are dyed in fairy blood.
He has leaped the bog, he has pierced the brier,
He has swum the brook and waded the mire,
Till his spirits sank and his limbs grew weak,
And the red waxed fainter in his cheek.
He had fallen to the ground outright,
  For rugged and dim was his onward track,
But there came a spotted toad in sight,
  And he laughed as he jumped upon her back:
He bridled her mouth with a silkweed twist,
  He lashed her sides with an osier thong.
And now, through evening's dewy mist,
  With leap and spring they bound along,
Till the mountain's magic verge is past,
And the beach of sand is reached at last.

. . . .

Up, fairy! quit thy chickweed bower,
The cricket has called the second hour;
Twice again, and the lark will rise
To kiss the streaking of the skies—
Up! thy charmèd armor don;
Thou'lt need it ere the night be gone.

He put his acorn helmet on:
It was plumed of the silk of the thistle-down;
The corselet plate that guarded his breast
Was once the wild bee's golden vest;
His cloak, of a thousand mingled dyes,
Was formed of the wings of butterflies;
His shield was the shell of a lady-bug queen,
Studs of gold on a ground of green;
And the quivering lance which he brandished bright
Was the sting of a wasp he had slain in fight.
Swift he bestrode his firefly steed;
  He bared his blade of the bent-grass blue;
He drove his spurs of the cockle-seed,
  And away like a glance of thought he flew,
To skim the heavens, and follow far
The fiery trail of the rocket-star.

The moth-fly, as he shot in air,
Crept under the leaf and hid her there;
The katydid forgot its lay,
The prowling gnat fled fast away,
The fell mosquito checked his drone
And folded his wings till the fay was gone,
And the wily beetle dropped his head,
And fell on the ground as if he were dead;
They crouched them close in the darksome shade,
They quaked all o'er with awe and fear,
For they had felt the blue-bent blade,
And writhed at the prick of the elfin spear;
Many a time, on a summer's night,
When the sky was clear, and the moon was bright,
They had been roused from the haunted ground
By the yelp and bay of the fairy hound;
They had heard the tiny bugle-horn,
They had heard the twang of the maize-silk string,
When the vine-twig bows were tightly drawn,
And the needle-shaft through air was borne,
Feathered with down of the hum-bird's wing.
And now they deemed the courier ouphe
Some hunter-sprite of the elfin ground;
And they watched till they saw him mount the roof
That canopies the world around;
Then glad they left their covert lair,
And freaked about in the midnight air.

Up to the vaulted firmament
His path the firefly courser bent,
And at every gallop on the wind,
He flung a glittering spark behind;
He flies like a feather in the blast
Till the first light cloud in heaven is past.
But the shapes of air have begun their work,
And a drizzly mist is round him cast;
He cannot see through the mantle murk;
He shivers with cold, but he urges fast;
Through storm and darkness, sleet and shade,
He lashes his steed, and spurs amain—
For shadowy hands have twitched the rein,
And flame-shot tongues around him played,
And near him many a fiendish eye
Glared with a fell malignity,

And yells of rage, and shrieks of fear,
Came screaming on his startled ear.

His wings are wet around his breast,
The plume hangs dripping from his crest,
His eyes are blurred with the lightning's glare,
And his ears are stunned with the thunder's blare.
But he gave a shout, and his blade he drew;
He thrust before and he struck behind,
Till he pierced their cloudy bodies through,
And gashed their shadowy limbs of wind;
Howling the misty spectres flew;
They rend the air with frightful cries;
For he has gained the welkin blue,
And the land of clouds beneath him lies.

Up to the cope careering swift,
In breathless motion fast,
Fleet as the swallow cuts the drift,
Or the sea-roc rides the blast,
The sapphire sheet of eve is shot,
The spherèd moon is past,
The earth but seems a tiny blot
On a sheet of azure cast.
Oh! it was sweet, in the clear moonlight,
To tread the starry plain of even!
To meet the thousand eyes of night,
And feel the cooling breath of heaven!
But the elfin made no stop or stay
Till he came to the bank of the Milky Way;
Then he checked his courser's foot,
And watched for the glimpse of the planet-shoot.

Sudden along the snowy tide
That swelled to meet their footsteps' fall,
The sylphs of heaven were seen to glide,
Attired in sunset's crimson pall;
Around the fay they weave the dance,
They skip before him on the plain,
And one has taken his wasp-sting lance,
And one upholds his bridle rein;
With warblings wild they lead him on
To where, through clouds of amber seen,
Studded with stars, resplendent shone
The palace of the sylphid queen.

Its spiral columns, gleaming bright,
Were streamers of the northern light;
Its curtain's light and lovely flush
Was of the morning's rosy blush;
And the ceiling fair that rose aboon,
The white and feathery fleece of noon.

. . . .

Borne afar on the wings of the blast,
Northward away he speeds him fast,
And his courser follows the cloudy wain
Till the hoof-strokes fall like pattering rain.
The clouds roll backward as he flies,
Each flickering star behind him lies,
And he has reached the northern plain,
And backed his firefly steed again,
Ready to follow in its flight
The streaming of the rocket-light.

The star is yet in the vault of heaven,
  But it rocks in the summer gale;
And now 'tis fitful and uneven,
  And now 'tis deadly pale;
And now 'tis wrapped in sulphur-smoke,
  And quenched is its rayless beam;
And now with a rattling thunder-stroke
  It bursts in flash and flame.
As swift as the glance of the arrowy lance
  That the storm spirit flings from high,
The star-shot flew o'er the welkin blue,
  As it fell from the sheeted sky.
As swift as the wind in its train behind
  The elfin gallops along:
The fiends of the clouds are bellowing loud,
  But the sylphid charm is strong;
He gallops unhurt in the shower of fire,
  While the cloud-fiends fly from the blaze;
He watches each flake till its sparks expire,
  And rides in the light of its rays.

But he drove his steed to the lightning's speed,
  And caught a glimmering spark;
Then wheeled around to the fairy ground,
  And sped through the midnight dark.

. . . .

Ouphe and goblin! imp and sprite!
   Elf of eve! and starry fay!
Ye that love the moon's soft light,
   Hither, hither, wend your way;
Twine ye in a jocund ring,
   Sing and trip it merrily,
Hand to hand, and wing to wing,
   Round the wild witch-hazel tree.

Hail the wanderer again
   With dance and song, and lute and lyre;
Pure his wing and strong his chain,
   And doubly bright his fairy fire.
Twine ye in an airy round,
   Brush the dew and print the lea;
Skip and gambol, hop and bound,
   Round the wild witch-hazel tree.

The beetle guards our holy ground,
   He flies about the haunted place,
And if mortal there be found,
   He hums in his ears and flaps his face;
The leaf-harp sounds our roundelay,
   The owlet's eyes our lanterns be;
Thus we sing and dance and play,
   Round the wild witch-hazel tree.

But hark! from tower on tree-top high,
   The sentry elf his call has made;
A streak is in the eastern sky;
   Shapes of moonlight! flit and fade!
The hill-tops gleam in Morning's spring,
The skylark shakes his dappled wing,
The day-glimpse glimmers on the lawn,—
The cock has crowed, and the fays are gone.

THE AMERICAN FLAG

When Freedom from her mountain height
Unfurled her standard to the air,
She tore the azure robe of night,
And set the stars of glory there;
She mingled with its gorgeous dyes
The milky baldric of the skies,
And striped its pure celestial white
With streakings of the morning light;
Then from his mansion in the sun
She called her eagle-bearer down,
And gave unto his mighty hand
The symbol of her chosen land.

Majestic monarch of the cloud!
Who rear'st aloft thy regal form,
To hear the tempest-trumpings loud,
And see the lightning lances driven,
When strive the warriors of the storm,
And rolls the thunder-drum of heaven—
Child of the sun! to thee 'tis given
To guard the banner of the free,
To hover in the sulphur-smoke,
To ward away the battle-stroke,
And bid its blendings shine afar,
Like rainbows on the cloud of war,
The harbingers of victory!

Flag of the brave! thy folds shall fly,
The sign of hope and triumph high,
When speaks the signal trumpet-tone,
And the long line comes gleaming on:
Ere yet the life-blood, warm and wet,
Has dimmed the glistening bayonet,
Each soldier eye shall brightly turn
To where the sky-born glories burn,
And as his springing steps advance,
Catch war and vengeance from the glance;
And when the cannon-mouthings loud
Heave in wild wreaths the battle-shroud,
And gory sabres rise and fall,
Like shoots of flame on midnight's pall;—

Then shall thy meteor-glances glow,
  And cowering foes shall sink beneath
Each gallant arm that strikes below
  That lovely messenger of death.

Flag of the seas! on ocean wave
Thy stars shall glitter o'er the brave;
When death, careering on the gale,
Sweeps darkly round the bellied sail,
And frighted waves rush wildly back
Before the broadside's reeling rack,
Each dying wanderer of the sea
Shall look at once to heaven and thee,
And smile to see thy splendors fly
In triumph o'er his closing eye.

Flag of the free heart's hope and home!
  By angel hands to valor given;
Thy stars have lit the welkin dome,
  And all thy hues were born in heaven.
Forever float that standard sheet!
  Where breathes the foe but falls before us,
With Freedom's soil beneath our feet,
  And Freedom's banner streaming o'er us!

JOHN WILLIAM DRAPER

(1811–1882)

The subject of this sketch was born at St. Helen's, near Liverpool, England, on the 5th of May, 1811. His earliest education was obtained at a Wesleyan Methodist school, but after a time he came under private teachers, with whose help he made rapid progress in the physical sciences, thus showing in his boyhood the natural bent of his mind and the real strength of his intellect. He afterwards studied for a time at the University of London, but in 1833 came to the United States, and three years later graduated at the University of Pennsylvania with the degree of M. D. In 1839 he was elected to the chair of chemistry in the University of New York, a position which he held until his death in 1882.

JOHN WILLIAM DRAPER

Draper's contributions to science were of a high order. He discovered some of the facts that lie at the basis of spectrum analysis; he was one of the first successful experimenters in the art of photography; and he made researches in radiant energy and other scientific phenomena. He published in 1858 a treatise on 'Human Physiology,' which is a highly esteemed and widely used text-book. He died on the 4th of January, 1882.

Draper's chief contributions to literature are three works: 'History of the Intellectual Development of Europe' (1863), a 'History of the American Civil War' (1867–1870), and 'The History of the Conflict between Religion and Science,' which appeared in the International Scientific Series in 1873. Of these works, the one on the intellectual development of Europe is the ablest, and takes a place beside the works of Lecky and Buckle as a contribution to the history of civilization. The history of the Civil War was written too soon after the events described to have permanent historical value. 'The History of the Conflict between Religion and Science' is a judicial presentation of the perennial controversy from the standpoint of the scientist.

Draper's claims to attention as a philosophic historian rest mainly on his theory of the influence of climate on human character and development. He maintains that «For every climate, and indeed for every geographical locality, there is an answering type of humanity»; and in his history of the American Civil War, as well as in his work on the intellectual development of Europe, he endeavored to prove that doctrine. Another theory which is prominent in his principal work is, that the intellectual development of every people passes through five stages; namely, 1, the Agê of Credulity; 2, the Age of Inquiry; 3, the Age of Faith; 4, the Age of Reason; 5, the Age of Decrepitude. Ancient Greece, he thinks, passed through all those stages, the age of reason beginning with the advent of physical science. Europe as a whole has now also entered the age of reason, which as before he identifies with the age of physical science; so that everywhere in his historical works, physical influences and the scientific knowledge of physical phenomena are credited with most of the progress that mankind has made. Draper has left a distinct mark upon the scientific thought of his generation, and made a distinct and valuable contribution to the literature of his adopted country.

THE VEDAS AND THEIR THEOLOGY

From ‹History of the Intellectual Development of Europe.› Copyright 1876, by Harper & Brothers

The Vedas, which are the Hindu Scriptures, and of which there are four,—the Rig, Yagust, Saman, and Atharvan,—are asserted to have been revealed by Brahma. The fourth is however rejected by some authorities, and bears internal evidence of a later composition, at a time when hierarchical power had become greatly consolidated. These works are written in an obsolete Sanskrit, the parent of the more recent idiom. They constitute the basis of an extensive literature, Upavedas, Angas, etc., of connected works and commentaries. For the most part they consist of hymns suitable for public and private occasions, prayers, precepts, legends, and dogmas. The Rig, which is the oldest, is composed chiefly of hymns; the other three of liturgical formulas. They are of different periods and of various authorship, internal evidence seeming to indicate that if the later were composed by priests, the earlier were the production of military chieftains. They answer to a state of society advanced from the nomad to the municipal condition. They are based upon an acknowledgment of a universal Spirit, pervading all things. Of this God they therefore necessarily acknowledge the unity: «There is in truth but one Deity, the Supreme Spirit, the Lord of the universe, whose work is the universe.» «The God above all gods, who created the earth, the heavens, and waters.» The world, thus considered as an emanation of God, is therefore a part of him; it is kept in a visible state by his energy, and would instantly disappear if that energy were for a moment withdrawn. Even as it is, it is undergoing unceasing transformations, everything being in a transitory condition. The moment a given phase is reached, it is departed from, or ceases. In these perpetual movements the present can scarcely be said to have any existence, for as the Past is ending, the Future has begun.

In such a never-ceasing career all material things are urged, their forms continually changing, and returning as it were through revolving cycles to similar states. For this reason it is that we may regard our earth and the various celestial bodies as having had a moment of birth, as having a time of continuance, in which they are passing onward to an inevitable destruction; and that after the lapse of countless ages similar progresses will be made, and similar series of events will occur again and again.

But in this doctrine of universal transformation there is something more than appears at first. The theology of India is underlaid with Pantheism. «God is One because he is All.» The Vedas, in speaking of the relation of nature to God, make use of the expression that he is the material as well as the cause of the universe, «the clay as well as the Potter.» They convey the idea that while there is a pervading spirit existing everywhere, of the same nature as the soul of man, though differing from it infinitely in degree, visible nature is essentially and inseparably connected therewith; that as in man the body is perpetually undergoing changes, perpetually decaying and being renewed,— or as in the case of the whole human species, nations come into existence and pass away,— yet still there continues to exist what may be termed the universal human mind, so forever associated and forever connected are the material and the spiritual. And under this aspect we must contemplate the Supreme Being, not merely as a presiding intellect, but as illustrated by the parallel case of man, whose mental principle shows no tokens except through its connection with the body: so matter, or nature, or the visible universe, is to be looked upon as the corporeal manifestation of God.

PRIMITIVE BELIEFS DISMISSED BY SCIENTIFIC KNOWLEDGE

From ‹History of the Intellectual Development of Europe.› Copyright 1876, by Harper & Brothers

As man advances in knowledge, he discovers that of his primitive conclusions some are doubtless erroneous, and many require better evidence to establish their truth incontestably. A more prolonged and attentive examination gives him reason, in some of the most important particulars, to change his mind. He finds that the earth on which he lives is not a floor covered over with a starry dome, as he once supposed, but a globe self-balanced in space. The crystalline vault, or sky, is recognized to be an optical deception. It rests upon the earth nowhere, and is no boundary at all; there is no kingdom of happiness above it, but a limitless space adorned with planets and suns. Instead of a realm of darkness and woe in the depths on the other side of the earth, men like ourselves are found there, pursuing, in Australia and New Zealand, the innocent pleasures and encountering the ordinary labors of life. By the aid of such lights as knowledge gradually supplies, he comes at last to discover that this our terrestrial habitation, instead of being a chosen, a sacred spot, is only one of similar myriads, more numerous than the sands of the sea, and prodigally scattered through space.

Never, perhaps, was a more important truth discovered. All the visible evidence was in direct opposition to it. The earth, which had hitherto seemed to be the very emblem of immobility, was demonstrated to be carried with a double motion, with prodigious velocity, through the heavens; the rising and setting of the stars were proved to be an illusion; and as respects the size of the globe, it was shown to be altogether insignificant when compared with multitudes of other neighboring ones — insignificant doubly by reason of its actual dimensions, and by the countless numbers of others like it in form, and doubtless like it the abodes of many orders of life.

And so it turns out that our earth is a globe of about twenty-five thousand miles in circumference. The voyager who circumnavigates it spends no inconsiderable portion of his life in accomplishing his task. It moves round the sun in a year, but at so great a distance from that luminary that if seen from him, it would look like a little spark traversing the sky. It is thus recognized as one of the members of the solar system. Other similar bodies, some of which are of larger, some of smaller dimensions, perform similar revolutions round the sun in appropriate periods of time.

If the magnitude of the earth be too great for us to attach to it any definite conception, what shall we say of the compass of the solar system? There is a defect in the human intellect, which incapacitates us for comprehending distances and periods that are either too colossal or too minute. We gain no clearer insight into the matter, when we are told that a comet which does not pass beyond the bounds of the system may perhaps be absent on its journey for more than a thousand years. Distances and periods such as these are beyond our grasp. They prove to us how far human reason excels imagination; the one measuring and comparing things of which the other can form no conception, but in the attempt is utterly bewildered and lost.

But as there are other globes like our earth, so too there are other worlds like our solar system. There are self-luminous suns, exceeding in number all computation. The dimensions of this earth pass into nothingness in comparison with the dimensions of the solar system, and that system in its turn is only an invisible point if placed in relation with the countless hosts of other systems, which form with it clusters of stars. Our solar system, far from being alone in the universe, is only one of an extensive brotherhood, bound by common laws and subject to like influences. Even on the very verge of creation, where imagination might lay the beginning of the realms of chaos, we see unbounded proofs of order, a regularity in the arrangement of inanimate things, suggesting to us that there are other intellectual creatures like us, the tenants of those islands in the abysses of space.

Though it may take a beam of light a million years to bring to our view those distant worlds, the end is not yet. Far away in the depths of space we catch the faint gleams of other groups of stars like our own. The finger of a man can hide them in their remoteness. Their vast distances from one another have dwindled into nothing. They and their movements have lost all individuality; the innumerable suns of which they are composed blend all their collected light into one pale milky glow.

Thus extending our view from the earth to the solar system, from the solar system to the expanse of the group of stars to which we belong, we behold a series of gigantic nebular creations rising up one after another, and forming greater and greater colonies of worlds. No numbers can express them, for they make the firmament a haze of stars. Uniformity, even though it be the uniformity of magnificence, tires at last, and we abandon the survey; for our eyes can only behold a boundless prospect, and conscience tells us our own unspeakable insignificance.

But what has become of the time-honored doctrine of the human destiny of the universe?—that doctrine for the sake of which the controversy I have described in this chapter was raised? It has disappeared. In vain was Bruno burnt and Galileo imprisoned; the truth forced its way, in spite of all opposition, at last. The end of the conflict was a total rejection of authority and tradition, and the adoption of scientific truth.

THE KORAN

From ‹History of the Intellectual Development of Europe.› Copyright 1876, by Harper & Brothers

ARABIAN influence, thus imposing itself on Africa and Asia by military successes, and threatening even Constantinople, rested essentially on an intellectual basis, the value of which it is needful for us to consider. The Koran, which is that basis, has exercised a great control over the destinies of mankind, and still serves as a rule of life to a very large portion of our race. Considering the asserted origin of this book,—indirectly from God himself,—we might justly expect that it would bear to be tried by any standard that man can apply, and vindicate its truth and excellence in the ordeal of human criticism. In our estimate of it, we must constantly bear in mind that it does not profess to be successive revelations made at intervals of ages and on various occasions, but a complete production delivered to one man. We ought therefore to look for universality, completeness, perfection. We might expect that it would present us with just views of the nature and position of this world in which we live, and that whether dealing with the spiritual or the material, it would put to shame the most celebrated productions of human genius, as the magnificent mechanism of the heavens and the beautiful living forms of the earth are

AFRICAN ARABIC MANUSCRIPT.

Thirteenth Century. National Library, Paris.

Reduced fac-simile of part of a page of an Arabic Koran, in the African character, captured at Tunis by Charles V.

The scribes of the East are distinguished by their efforts to acquire a perfect style of execution; and their success merits the greater praise, since they generally stand while writing, resting only on the left arm; and notwithstanding the inferiority of the reed to the modern pen, the Arabs have succeeded in producing the most excellent specimens of calligraphy.

superior to the vain contrivances of man. Far in advance of all that has been written by the sages of India, or the philosophers of Greece, on points connected with the origin, nature, and destiny of the universe, its dignity of conception and excellence of expression should be in harmony with the greatness of the subject with which it is concerned.

We might expect that it should propound with authority, and definitively settle, those all-important problems which have exercised the mental powers of the ablest men of Asia and Europe for so many centuries, and which are at the foundation of all faith and all philosophy; that it should distinctly tell us in unmistakable language what is God, what is the world, what is the soul, and whether man has any criterion of truth; that it should explain to us how evil can exist in a world the Maker of which is omnipotent and altogether good; that it should reveal to us in what the affairs of men are fixed by Destiny, in what by free-will; that it should teach us whence we came, what is the object of our continuing here, what is to become of us hereafter. And since a written work claiming a divine origin must necessarily accredit itself even to those most reluctant to receive it, its internal evidences becoming stronger and not weaker with the strictness of the examination to which they are submitted, it ought to deal with those things that may be demonstrated by the increasing knowledge and genius of man; anticipating therein his conclusions.

Such a work, noble as may be its origin, must not refuse but court the test of natural philosophy, regarding it not as an antagonist but as its best support. As years pass on, and human science becomes more exact and more comprehensive, its conclusions must be found in unison therewith. When occasion arises, it should furnish us at least the foreshadowings of the great truths discovered by astronomy and geology, not offering for them the wild fictions of earlier ages, inventions of the infancy of man. It should tell us how suns and worlds are distributed in infinite space, and how in their successions they come forth in limitless time. It should say how far the dominion of God is carried out by law, and what is the point at which it is his pleasure to resort to his own good providence or his arbitrary will. How grand the description of this magnificent universe, written by the Omnipotent hand! Of man it should set forth his relations to other living beings, his place among them, his privileges and responsibilities. It should not leave him to grope his way through the vestiges of Greek philosophy, and to miss the truth at last; but it should teach him wherein true knowledge consists, anticipating the physical science, physical power, and physical well-being of our own times, nay, even unfolding for our benefit things that we are still ignorant of. The discussion of subjects so many and so high is not outside the scope of a work of such pretensions. Its manner of dealing with them is the only criterion it can offer of its authenticity to succeeding times.

Tried by such a standard, the Koran altogether fails. In its philosophy it is incomparably inferior to the writings of Chakia Mouni, the founder of Buddhism; in its science it is absolutely worthless. On speculative or doubtful things it is copious enough; but in the exact, where a test can be applied to it, it totally fails. Its astronomy, cosmogony, physiology, are so puerile as to invite our mirth, if the occasion did not forbid. They belong to the old times of the world, the morning of human knowledge. The earth is firmly balanced in its seat by the weight of the mountains; the sky is supported over it like a dome, and we are instructed in the wisdom and power of God by being told to find a crack in it if we can. Ranged in stories, seven in number, are the heavens, the highest being the habitation of God, whose throne — for the Koran does not reject Assyrian ideas — is sustained by winged animal forms. The shooting stars are pieces of red-hot stone, thrown by angels at impure spirits when they approach too closely. Of God the Koran is full of praise, setting forth, often in not unworthy imagery, his majesty. Though it bitterly denounces those who give him any equals, and assures them that their sin will never be forgiven; that in the Judgment Day they must answer the fearful question, "Where are my companions about whom ye disputed?" — though it inculcates an absolute dependence on the mercy of God, and denounces as criminals all those who make a merchandise of religion, — its ideas of the Deity are altogether anthropomorphic. He is only a gigantic man, living in a paradise. In this respect, though exceptional passages might be cited, the reader rises from a perusal of the one hundred and fourteen chapters of the Koran with a final impression that they have given him low and unworthy thoughts; nor is it surprising that one of the Mohammedan sects reads it in such a way as to find no difficulty in asserting that "from the crown of the head to the breast God is hollow, and from the breast downward he is solid;" that he "has curled black hair, and roars like a lion at every watch of the night." The unity asserted by Mohammed is a unity in special contradistinction to the Trinity of the Christians, and the doctrine of a Divine generation. Our Savior is never called the Son of God, but always the Son of Mary. Throughout there is a perpetual acceptance of the delusion of the human destiny of the universe. As to man, Mohammed is diffuse enough respecting a future state, speaking with clearness of a resurrection, the Judgment Day, Paradise, the torment of hell, the worm that never dies, the pains that never end; but with all this precise description of the future, there are many errors as to the past. If modesty did not render it unsuitable to speak of such topics here, it might be shown how feeble is his physiology when he has occasion to allude to the origin or generation of man. He is hardly advanced beyond the ideas of Thales. One who is so untrustworthy a guide as to things that are past cannot be very trustworthy as to events that are to come.

Of the literary execution of his work, it is perhaps scarcely possible to judge fairly from a translation. It is said to be the oldest prose composition among the Arabs, by whom Mohammed's boast of the unapproachable excellence of his work is almost universally sustained; but it must not be concealed that there have been among them very learned men who have held it in light esteem. Its most celebrated passages, as those on the nature of God, in Chapters ii., xxiv., will bear no comparison with parallel ones in the Psalms and Book of Job. In the narrative style, the story of Joseph in Chapter xii., compared with the same incidents related in Genesis, shows a like inferiority. Mohammed also adulterates his work with many Christian legends, derived probably from the apocryphal gospel of St. Barnabas; he mixes with many of his own inventions the Scripture account of the temptation of Adam, the Deluge, Jonah and the whale, enriching the whole with stories like the later Night Entertainments of his country, the seven sleepers, Gog and Magog, and all the wonders of genii, sorcery, and charms.

An impartial reader of the Koran may doubtless be surprised that so feeble a production should serve its purpose so well. But the theory of religion is one thing, the practice another. The Koran abounds in excellent moral suggestions and precepts; its composition is so fragmentary that we cannot turn to a single page without finding maxims of which all men must approve. This fragmentary construction yields texts and mottoes and rules complete in themselves, suitable for common men in any of the incidents of life. There is a perpetual insisting on the necessity of prayer, an inculcation of mercy, almsgiving, justice, fasting, pilgrimage, and other good works; institutions respecting conduct, both social and domestic, debts, witnesses, marriage, children, wine, and the like; above all, a constant stimulation to do battle with the infidel and blasphemer. For life as it passes in Asia, there is hardly a condition in which passages from the Koran cannot be recalled suitable for instruction, admonition, consolation, encouragement. To the Asiatic and to the African, such devotional fragments are of far more use than any sustained theological doctrine. The mental constitution of Mohammed did not enable him to handle important philosophical questions with the well-balanced ability of the great Greek and Indian writers; but he has never been surpassed in adaptation to the spiritual wants of humble life, making even his fearful fatalism administer thereto. A pitiless destiny is awaiting us; yet the prophet is uncertain what it may be. «Unto every nation a fixed time is decreed. Death will overtake us even in lofty towers, but God only knoweth the place in which a man shall die.» After many an admonition of the resurrection and the Judgment Day, many a promise of Paradise and threat of hell, he plaintively confesses, «I do not know what will be done with you or me hereafter.»

The Koran thus betrays a human and not a very noble intellectual origin. It does not however follow that its author was, as is so often asserted, a mere impostor. He reiterates again and again, «I am nothing more than a public preacher.» He defends, not always without acerbity, his work from those who even in his own life stigmatized it as a confused heap of dreams, or what is worse, a forgery. He is not the only man who has supposed himself to be the subject of supernatural and divine communications, for this is a condition of disease to which any one, by fasting and mental anxiety, may be reduced.

In what I have thus said respecting a work held by so many millions of men as a revelation from God, I have endeavored to speak with respect and yet with freedom, constantly bearing in mind how deeply to this book Asia and Africa are indebted for daily guidance, how deeply Europe and America for the light of science.

As might be expected, the doctrines of the Koran have received many fictitious additions and sectarian interpretations in the course of ages. In the popular superstition angels and genii largely figure. The latter, being of a grosser fabric, eat, drink, propagate their kind, are of two sorts, good and bad, and existed long before men, having occupied the earth before Adam. Immediately after death, two greenish livid angels, Monkir and Nekkar, examine every corpse as to its faith in God and Mohammed; but the soul, having been separated from the body by the angel of death, enters upon an intermediate state, awaiting the resurrection. There is however much diversity of opinion as to its precise disposal before the Judgment Day: some think that it hovers near the grave; some, that it sinks into the well Zemzem; some, that it retires into the trumpet of the angel of the resurrection; the difficulty apparently being that any final disposal before the Day of Judgment would be anticipatory of that great event, if indeed it would not render it needless. As to the resurrection, some believe it to be merely spiritual, others corporeal; the latter asserting that the *os coccygis*, or last bone of the spinal column, will serve as it were as a germ; and that, vivified by a rain of forty days, the body will sprout from it. Among the signs of the approaching resurrection will be the rising of the sun in the west. It will be ushered in by three blasts of a trumpet: the first, known as the blast of consternation, will shake the earth to its centre, and extinguish the sun and stars; the second, the blast of extermination, will annihilate all material things except Paradise, hell, and the throne of God. Forty years subsequently, the angel Israfil will sound the blast of resurrection. From his trumpet there will be blown forth the countless myriads of souls who have taken refuge therein, or lain concealed. The Day of Judgment has now come. The Koran contradicts itself as to the length of this day; in one place making it a thousand, in another fifty thousand years. Most Mohammedans incline to adopt the longer period, since angels, genii, men, and animals have to be tried.

As to men, they will rise in their natural state, but naked; white-winged camels, with saddles of gold, awaiting the saved. When the partition is made, the wicked will be oppressed with an intolerable heat, caused by the sun, which, having been called into existence again, will approach within a mile, provoking a sweat to issue from them; and this, according to their demerits, will immerse them from the ankles to the mouth; but the righteous will be screened by the shadow of the throne of God. The Judge will be seated in the clouds, the books open before him, and everything in its turn called on to account for its deeds. For greater dispatch, the angel Gabriel will hold forth his balance, one scale of which hangs over Paradise and one over hell. In these all works are weighed. As soon as the sentence is delivered, the assembly, in a long file, will pass over the bridge Al-Sirat. It is as sharp as the edge of a sword, and laid over the mouth of hell. Mohammed and his followers will successfully pass the perilous ordeal; but the sinners, giddy with terror, will drop into the place of torment. The blessed will receive their first taste of happiness at a pond which is supplied by silver pipes from the river Al-Cawthor. The soil of Paradise is of musk. Its rivers tranquilly flow over pebbles of rubies and emeralds. From tents of hollow pearls the Houris, or girls of Paradise, will come forth, attended by troops of beautiful boys. Each saint will have eighty thousand servants and seventy-two girls. To these, some of the more merciful Mussulmans add the wives they have had upon earth; but the grimly orthodox assert that hell is already nearly filled with women. How can it be otherwise, since they are not permitted to pray in a mosque upon earth?

I have not space to describe the silk brocades, the green clothing, the soft carpets, the banquets, the perpetual music and songs. From the glorified body all impurities will escape, not as they did during life, but in a fragrant perspiration of camphor and musk. No one will complain, "I am weary;" no one will say, "I am sick."

From the contradictions, puerilities, and impossibilities indicated in the preceding paragraphs, it may be anticipated that the faith of Mohammed has been broken into many sects. Of such it is said that not less than seventy-three may be numbered. Some, as the Sonnites, are guided by traditions; some occupy themselves with philosophical difficulties,—the existence of evil in the world, the attributes of God, absolute predestination and eternal damnation, the invisibility and non-corporeality of God, his capability of local motion. . . . But the great Mohammedan philosophers, simply accepting the doctrine of the oneness of God as the only thing of which man can be certain, look upon all the rest as idle fables—having however this political use: that they furnish contention and therefore occupation to disputatious sectarians, and consolation to illiterate minds.

MICHAEL DRAYTON

(1563-1631)

While London still crowded to the new «Theatre» in Shoreditch, the first built in England; while Ben Jonson was still soldiering in the Low Countries; while Marlowe was working out the tragedy that was to revolutionize all stage traditions, and Shakespeare was yet but a «looker-on at greatness,»—there came up from Warwickshire a young man of good family who had served as page in a noble house, who had studied possibly at Oxford, and who in the first flush of manhood aspired to a place among those prodigies who made the later Elizabethan period immortal. This was Michael Drayton, whose gentle birth and breeding, education and talents, knowledge of the world and of men, together with a most sweet and lovable disposition, made him at once welcome in the literary Bohemia of the day. He became the «deare and bosom friend» of Beaumont and Fletcher, and his work received unquestioned honor from his illustrious contemporaries.

MICHAEL DRAYTON

As a child he had demanded of his elders to know what kind of beings poets were, had spent many hours in writing childishly fantastic verses, and had begged of his tutor to make a poet of him. And although he seems to have been poor and to have lived by the gifts of wealthy patrons, he cast in his lot with literature, and cherished no other ambition than that of writing well. His first book, a volume of spiritual poems, or metrical renderings of the Bible, was published in 1590 under the title 'The Harmony of the Church.' It is difficult to see why this commonplace and orthodox performance should have given such umbrage that the Archbishop of Canterbury condemned the entire edition to destruction. Yet this was its fate, with the exception of forty copies which Archbishop Whitgift ordered to be reserved for the ecclesiastical library at Lambeth Palace. Undiscouraged, the poet next produced a cycle of sixty-four sonnets and a collection of pastorals entitled 'Idea: the Shepherd's Garland,' in which under the name «Rowland» he celebrated an early love. It is strange that the intrinsic merit of these verses, and their undoubted popularity, should not have urged Drayton to continue in the same vein. Instead, however, he set about the composition of a series of historical poems which extended over the next twenty-four years, and to which he gave the best energies of his life. Beginning with the epic 'Matilda,' studied from English history, the series was continued by a poem on the 'Wars of the Roses,' afterward enlarged into 'The Barons' Wars.' This was followed by the epic 'Robert, Duke of Normandy.' Destitute of imagination, prolix and tedious, these verses were yet so popular in Drayton's day that in 1612 he began the publication of a poem in thirty books, meant to include the entire chronology and topography of Great Britain, from the earliest times. This was the famous 'Poly-Olbion,' in which, in spite of the inspiring work of his contemporaries, Drayton harked back in spirit to the dreary monotony of the Saxon Chronicle; the detail is so minute, the matter so unimportant, and the absence of discrimination so apparent, that notwithstanding many noticeable beauties of thought and style, it is hard to realize that this poem was a favorite with that brilliant group which had known Shakespeare, and still delighted in Ben Jonson. After issuing eighteen books of 'Poly-Olbion,' his publishers — with whom he was always quarreling, and whom he declared that he "despised and kicked at"— refused to undertake the remaining twelve books of the second part. His friends, however, loyal in their love and praise of him, secured a more complaisant tradesman to bring out the rest of the already famous poem.

Fortunately for his fame, Drayton had in the mean time produced two other volumes of verse, which displayed the real grace and fancifulness of his charming muse. The first of these, 'Poems Lyrical and Pastoral,' included the satire 'The Man in the Moon'; while in the second were printed the 'Ballad of Agincourt,' the most spirited of English martial lyrics, and that delightful fantasy 'Nymphidia, or the Court of Faery,' in which the touch is so light, the fancy so dainty, and the conceit so delicate, that the poem remains immortally fresh and young. Because everybody wrote plays, Drayton turned playwright, and is said to have collaborated with Massinger and Ford. Of his long works, the 'Heroicall Episodes' is perhaps the most readable. His last effort was 'The Muses' Elizium,' published in 1630. A year later he died, and was buried in Westminster, where a monument was erected to him by the Countess of Dorset.

Drayton's place in English literature is with that considerable and not unimportant band who have done somewhat, but whose repute is much more for what they were in their friends' eyes than for what they did. In an age of great intellectual achievement, he yet managed, in spite of the stimulus of kindred minds and his own undoubted gift, to produce little that has sustained the reputation accorded him by his acquaintances. Most of his work lives chiefly to afford pleasing studies for the literary antiquary, to whom the tide of time brings nothing uninteresting. Yet in the art of living, in the unselfish devotion of his powers to his chosen calling, in the graces of affection and the offices of noble friendship, he was so excellent and exemplary that he won and kept the undying regard of the most able men of the most brilliant period of English literature — men who felt a personal and unrequitable loss when he passed away, and who spoke of him always with admiring tenderness.

In person he seems to have been small and dark. He describes himself as of «swart and melancholy face.» Yet his talk was most delightful, and a strong proof of his wide popularity appears in the fact that he is quoted not less than one hundred and fifty times in ‘England's Parnassus,’ published as early as 1600. The tributes of his friends are innumerable, from the «good Rowland» of Barnfield to the «golden-mouthèd Drayton, musicall,» of Fitz-Geoffrey, the «man of vertuous disposition, honest conversation, and well-preserved carriage» of Meres, or the tender lines of his friend Ben Jonson:—

«Do, pious marble, let thy readers know
What they and what their children owe
To Drayton's name; whose sacred dust
We recommend unto thy trust.
Protect his memory, and preserve his story,
Remain a lasting monument of his glory.
And when thy ruins shall disclaim
To be the treasurer of his name,
His name, that cannot die, shall be
An everlasting monument to thee.»

SONNET

Since there's no help, come, let us kiss and part,—
Nay, I have done, you get no more of me;
And I am glad, yea, glad with all my heart,
That thus so clearly I myself can free:
Shake hands forever, cancel all our vows,
And when we meet at any time again,
Be it not seen in either of our brows
That we one jot of former love retain.
Now, at the last gasp of Love's latest breath,
When, his pulse failing, Passion speechless lies,
When Faith is kneeling by his bed of death,
And Innocence is closing up his eyes,—
Now, if thou wouldst, when all have given him over,
From death to life thou mightst him yet recover!

THE BALLAD OF AGINCOURT

Fair stood the wind for France,
When we our sails advance,
Nor now to prove our chance
Longer will tarry;
But putting to the main,
At Kaux, the mouth of Seine,
With all his martial train,
Landed King Harry.

And taking many a fort,
Furnished in warlike sort,
Marched towards Agincourt
In happy hour —
Skirmishing day by day
With those that stopped his way,
Where the French gen'ral lay
With all his power,

Which in his height of pride,
King Henry to deride,
His ransom to provide
To the King sending;
Which he neglects the while,
As from a nation vile,
Yet, with an angry smile,
Their fall portending.

And turning to his men,
Quoth our brave Henry then:—
«Though they to one be ten,
Be not amazed;
Yet have we well begun —
Battles so bravely won
Have ever to the sun
By fame been raised.

«And for myself,» quoth he,
«This my full rest shall be;
England ne'er mourn for me,
Nor more esteem me;
Victor I will remain,
Or on this earth lie slain;
Never shall she sustain
Loss to redeem me.

«Poitiers and Cressy tell,
When most their pride did swell,
Under our swords they fell;
No less our skill is
Than when our grandsire great,
Claiming the regal seat,
By many a warlike feat
Lopped the French lilies.»

The Duke of York so dread
The eager vaward led;
With the main Henry sped,
Amongst his henchmen.
Excester had the rear —
A braver man not there:
O Lord! how hot they were
On the false Frenchmen!

They now to fight are gone;
Armor on armor shone;
Drum now to drum did groan —
To hear was wonder;
That with the cries they make
The very earth did shake;
Trumpet to trumpet spake,
Thunder to thunder.

Well it thine age became,
O noble Erpingham!
Which did the signal aim
To our hid forces;
When from a meadow by,
Like a storm suddenly,
The English archery
Struck the French horses,

With Spanish yew so strong,
Arrows a cloth-yard long,
That like to serpents stung,
Piercing the weather;
None from his fellow starts,
But playing manly parts,
And like true English hearts,
Stuck close together.

When down their bows they threw,
And forth their bilbows drew,
And on the French they flew,
    Not one was tardy;
Arms were from shoulders sent;
Scalps to the teeth were rent;
Down the French peasants went;—
    Our men were hardy.

This while our noble king,
His broadsword brandishing,
Down the French host did ding,
    As to o'erwhelm it;
And many a deep wound lent,
His arm with blood besprent,
And many a cruel dent
    Bruisèd his helmet.

Glo'ster, that duke so good,
Next of the royal blood,
For famous England stood,
    With his brave brother—
Clarence, in steel so bright,
Though but a maiden knight,
Yet in that furious fight
    Scarce such another.

Warwick in blood did wade;
Oxford the foe invade,
And cruel slaughter made,
    Still as they ran up.
Suffolk his axe did ply;
Beaumont and Willoughby
Bare them right doughtily,
    Ferrers and Fanhope.

Upon Saint Crispin's day
Fought was this noble fray,
Which fame did not delay
    To England to carry;
Oh, when shall Englishmen
With such acts fill a pen,
Or England breed again
    Such a King Harry?

QUEEN MAB'S EXCURSION

From ‹Nymphidia, the Court of Faery›

Her chariot ready straight is made;
Each thing therein is fitting laid,
That she by nothing might be stay'd,
For naught must her be letting:
Four nimble gnats the horses were,
The harnesses of gossamer,
Fly Cranion, her charioteer,
Upon the coach-box getting.

Her chariot of a snail's fine shell,
Which for the colors did excel,—
The fair Queen Mab becoming well,
So lively was the limning;
The seat the soft wool of the bee,
The cover (gallantly to see)
The wing of a py'd butterflee,—
I trow, 'twas simple trimming.

The wheels composed of crickets' bones,
And daintily made for the nonce;
For fear of rattling on the stones,
With thistle-down they shod it:
For all her maidens much did fear,
If Oberon had chanced to hear
That Mab his queen should have been there,
He would not have abode it.

She mounts her chariot with a trice,
Nor would she stay for no advice,
Until her maids, that were so nice,
To wait on her were fitted,
But ran away herself alone;
Which when they heard, there was not one
But hasted after to be gone,
As she had been diswitted.

Hop, and Mop, and Drap so clear,
Pip, and Trip, and Skip, that were
To Mab their sovereign dear,
Her special maids of honor;

Fib, and Tib, and Pinck, and Pin,
 Tick, and Quick, and Jill, and Jin,
Tit, and Nit, and Wap, and Win,
 The train that wait upon her.

Upon a grasshopper they got,
And what with amble and with trot,
For hedge nor ditch they sparèd not,
 But after her they hie them.
A cobweb over them they throw,
To shield the wind if it should blow;
Themselves they wisely could bestow,
 Lest any should espy them.

GUSTAVE DROZ

(1832–1895)

Gustave Droz enjoyed for a time the distinction of being the most popular writer of light literature in France, and his fame extended throughout Europe and to America, several of his books having been translated into English. Essentially a Parisian of the day,—gay, droll, adroit,—he not only caught and reflected the humor of his countrymen, but with a new, fresh touch, reached below the surface of their volatile emotions. Occasionally striking the note of deeper feeling, he avoided as a rule the more serious sides of life, as well as the sensational tendencies of most of his contemporaries. His friends claimed for him a distinctive *genre*, and on that account presented him as a candidate for the Academy; but he failed of election.

Gustave Droz

The son of a well-known sculptor, he was born in Paris, and followed the traditions of his family in entering the École des Beaux-Arts, where he developed some aptitude with his brush; but a preference for writing beguiled him from the studio, and an acquaintance with Marcellin the illustrator, founder of La Vie Parisienne, led him to follow literature. At first he was timid, dreading the test of publication, but presently he gave himself up unreservedly to his pen. Within a year he was established as a favorite of the people, and his friend's journal was on the highway to success. For this he wrote a series of sketches of every-day life that were subsequently collected and published in book form, under the titles 'Monsieur, Madame, et Bébé,' 'Entre Nous,' and 'La Cahier Bleu de Mlle. Cibot.' Within two years these books had reached their twentieth edition, and of the first, nearly one hundred and fifty editions have been demanded since it was issued. He has written several novels, the best known of which are 'Babolein,' 'Les Étangs' (The Ponds), and 'Autour d'une Source' (Around a Spring), but they did not fully sustain the reputation gained by his short sketches; a fact which induced him in 1884 to return to his earlier form in 'Tristesses et Sourires' (Sorrows and Smiles), a volume of light dissertations on things grave and gay that at once revived his popularity.

The peculiarity of the work of Gustave Droz is its delicacy both in humor and pathos. He surprised the French by making them all laugh without making any of them wince; the sharp wits of his day were forgotten in the unalloyed enjoyment of his simple quaintness, in which there was neither affectation nor sarcasm. Yet as has been said, he was a Parisian of the Parisians, quick to perceive the ludicrous, ready to weep with the afflicted, and to laugh again with the happy. His studies of children are among his best, on account of their extreme naturalness, and are never uninteresting, despite the simplicity of the incidents and observations on which they are founded. In 'Le Cahier Bleu de Mlle. Cibot' he has used striking colors to paint the petty afflictions that beset most lives; but lest these pictures should leave an unpleasant impression, they are set off by others of a happier sort, making a collection that constitutes a most effective lesson in practical philosophy.

HOW THE BABY WAS SAVED

From 'The Seamstress's Story'

«Yes, Ma'm'selle Adèle," said the seamstress, «the real happiness of this world is not so unevenly distributed after all." Louise, as she said this, took from the reserve in the bosom of her dress a lot of pins, and applied them deftly to the trimming of a skirt which I was holding for her.

«A sufficiently comfortable doctrine," I answered; «but it does seem to me as if some people were born to live and to die unhappy."

«It is only folks who never find anybody to love enough; and I think it's nobody's fault but their own."

«But my good Louise, wouldn't you have suffered much less last year, when you came so near losing your boy, if you hadn't cared so much for him?"

I was only drawing her on, you see; Louise's chat was the greatest resource to me at that time.

«Why, Ma'm'selle Adèle, you are surely joking. You'd as well tell me to cut off my feet to save my shoes. You'll know one of these days—and not so far off neither, maybe—how mighty easy and sensible it would be not to love your children. They *are* a worry, too; but oh the delight of 'em! I'd like to have had anybody tell me not to love my darling because it might grieve me, when he lay there in his mother's lap, with blue lips, gasping for his breath, and well-nigh dead, his face blackish, and his hands like this piece of wax. You could see that everything was going against him; and with his great big eyes he was staring in my face, until I felt as if the child was tugging at my very heart-strings. I kept smiling at him, though, through the tears that blinded me, hard as I tried to hide them. Oh! such tears are bitter salt indeed, Ma'm'selle! And there was my poor husband on his knees, making paper figures to amuse him, and singing a funny song he used to laugh at. Now and then the corners of his mouth would pucker, and his cheeks would wrinkle a little bit under the eyes. You could tell he was still amused, but in such a dreamy way. Oh! our child seemed no longer with us, but behind a veil, like. Wait a minute. You must excuse me, for I can't help crying when I think of it."

And the poor creature drew out her handkerchief and fairly sobbed aloud. In the midst of it however she smiled and said: "Well, that's over now; 'twas nothing, and I'm too silly. And Ma'm'selle, here I've gone and cried upon your mother's dress, and that's a pretty business."

I took her hand in mine and pressed it.

"Aren't you afraid you'll stick yourself, Ma'm'selle? I've got my needle in that hand," she said playfully. "But you did not mean what you said just now, did you?"

"What did I say?"

"That it would be better not to love your children with all your heart, on account of the great anxiety. Don't you know such thoughts are wicked? When they come into your head your mind wants purifying. But I'm sure I beg your pardon for saying so."

"You are entirely right, Louise," I returned.

"Ah! so I thought. And now let me see. Let's fix this ruche; pull it to the left a little, please."

"But about the sick boy. Tell me about his recovery."

"That was a miracle — I ought to say two miracles. It was a miracle that God restored him to us, and a miracle to find anybody with so much knowledge and feeling,— such talent, such a tender heart, and so much, so much —! I'm speaking of the doctor. A famous one he was, too, you must know; for it was no less than Doctor Faron. Heaven knows how he is run after, and how rich and celebrated he is! Aren't you surprised to hear that it was he who attended *our* little boy? Indeed, the wonders begin with that. You may imagine my husband was at his wits' end when he saw how it was with the child; and all of a sudden I saw him jump up, get out his best coat and hat, and put them on.

"'Where are you going?' I asked.

"'To bring Doctor Faron.'

"Why, if he had said, 'To bring the Prime Minister,' it would have seemed as likely.

"'Don't you believe Doctor Faron is going to trouble himself about such as we. They will turn you out of doors.'

"But 'twas no use talking, my dear. He was already on the stairs, and I heard him running away as if the house was on fire. Fire, indeed; worse, far worse than any fire!

"And there I was, left alone with the child upon my knees. He wouldn't stay in bed, and was quieter so, wrapped up in his little blanket. 'Here will he die,' I thought. 'Soon will his eyes close, and then it will be all over;' and I held my own breath to listen to his feeble and oppressed pantings.

"About an hour had passed, when I heard a rapid step upon the stairs (we are poor, and live in attic rooms). The door opened, and my husband came in, wet with perspiration and out of breath. If I live a century, I'll not forget his look when he said:—

"'Well?'

"I answered, 'No worse. But the doctor?'

"'He's coming.'

"Oh, those blessed words! It actually seemed as if my child were saved already. If you but knew how folks love their little ones! I kissed the darling, I kissed his father, I laughed, I cried, and I no longer felt the faintest doubt. It is by God's mercy that such gleams of hope are sent to strengthen us in our trials. It was very foolish, too; for something might easily have prevented the doctor's coming, after all.

"'You found him at home, then?' I asked my husband.

"Then he told me in an undertone what he had done, stopping every now and then to wipe his face and gather breath.

. . . .

"My husband had scarcely uttered these words," continued Louise, "when I heard a step on the stairs. It was he! it was that blessed angel of a doctor, come to help us in our sore distress.

« And what do you think he said in his deep voice when he got into the room?

« 'God bless you, my friends, but I nearly broke my neck on those stairs. Where's that child?'

« 'Here he is, my dear, darling doctor.' I knew no better way to speak to him, with his dress cravat showing over his greatcoat, and his decorations dangling like a little bunch of keys at his buttonhole.

« He took off his wrappings, stooped over the child, turned him over, more gently even than his mother could have done, and laid his own head first against his back, then against his breast. How I tried to read his eyes! but they know how to hide their thoughts.

« 'We must perform an operation here,' says he; 'and it is high time.'

« Just at this moment the hospital doctor came in, and whispered to him, 'I'm afraid you didn't want to be disturbed, sir.'

« 'Oh, never mind. I am sorry it wasn't sooner, though. Get everything ready now.'

« But Ma'm'selle Adèle, why should I tell you all this? I'd better mind my work.»

« Oh, go on, Louise, go on!»

« Well then, Ma'm'selle, if you believe me, those two doctors — neither of 'em kin, or even friends till then — went to work and made all the preparations, while my husband went off to borrow lights. The biggest one tied a mattress on the table, and the assistant spread out the bright little knives.

« You who have not been through it all, Ma'm'selle, can't know what it is to have your own little one in your lap, to know that those things are to be used upon him to pierce his tender flesh, and if the hand that guides them be not sure, that they may kill him.

« When all was ready, Doctor Faron took off his cravat, then lifted my child from my arms and laid him on the mattress, in the midst of the lamps, and said to my poor man: —

« 'You will hold his head, and your wife his feet. Joseph will pass me the instruments. You've brought a breathing-tube with you, my son?'

« 'Yes, sir.'

"My husband was as white as a sheet by this; and when I saw him about to take his place with his hands shaking so much, it scared me, so I said: —

"'Doctor, please let me hold his head!'

"'But my poor woman, if you should tremble?'

"'Please let me do it, doctor!'

"'Be it so, then;' and then added with a bright look at me, and a cheering smile, 'we shall save him for you, my dear; you are a brave little woman and you deserve it.'

"Yes, and save him he did! God bless him! saved him as truly as if he had snatched him from the depths of the river."

"And you didn't tremble, Louise?"

"You may depend on that. If I had, it would have been the last of my child."

"How in the world did you keep yourself steady?"

"The Lord knows; but I was like a rock. When you must, you must, I suppose."

"And you had to bchold every detail of that operation?"

"Yes, indeed; and often have I dreamed it over since. His poor little neck laid open, and the veins, which the doctor pushed aside with his fingers, and the little silver tube which he inserted, and all that; and then the face of the child, changing as the air passed into his lungs. You've seen a lamp almost out, when you pour in oil? It was like that. They had laid him there but half alive, with his eyes all but set; and they gave him back to me, pale and with bloodless lips, it is true, but with life in his looks, and breathing — breathing the free, fresh air.

"'Kiss him, mother,' says the doctor, 'and put him to bed. Cover the place with some light thing or other, and Joseph must stay with you to-night; won't you, Joseph? Ah, well, that's all arranged.'

"He put on his things and wrapped himself up to go. He was shaking hands with my husband, when I seized one hand, and kissed it — like a fool, as I was; but I didn't stop to think. He laughed heartily, and said to my husband, 'Are you not jealous, friend? Your wife is making great advances to me. But I must be off now. Good night, good people.'

"And from that night he always talks so friendly and familiarly to us, not a bit contemptuously either, but as if he liked us, and was glad to be of service to us."

A FAMILY NEW-YEAR'S

From ‹Monsieur, Madame, and Baby›

It is barely seven o'clock. A pale ray of wan light filters through the double curtains, and some one is already at the door. In the next room I hear the stifled laughs and silvery voice of my little child, who trembles with impatience and begs to come.

«But father dear,» he cries, «it's Baby. It's your own little boy — to wish you ‹Happy New Year.›»

«Come in, darling; come quick and give me a kiss,» I cry.

The door opens, and my boy, with shining eyes and his arms in the air, rushes toward the bed. Long curls, escaping from the nightcap which imprisons his blond head, fall over his forehead. His loose night-shirt, embarrassing his little feet, adds to his impatience and makes him trip at every step. He has crossed the room at last, and stretching his hands toward mine, «Baby wishes you a happy New Year,» he says earnestly.

«Poor darling, with his bare feet! Come, dear! Come and get warm under the covers; come and hide in the quilt.»

I draw him to me; but at this movement my wife wakes up suddenly. . . . «How you frightened me! I was dreaming that there was a fire, and these voices in the midst of it! You are indiscreet with your cries!»

«*Our* cries! So you forget, dear mamma, that this is New-Year's day. Baby is waiting for you to wake up, and so am I.»

I wrap up my little man in the soft quilt, I bury him in the eiderdown, and warm his frozen feet with my hands.

«Mother dear, this is New Year,» he cries. He draws our two heads together with his arms, and kisses us anywhere at random, with his fresh lips. I feel his dimpled hand wandering about my neck; his little fingers are entangled in my beard. My mustache pricks the end of his nose. He bursts out laughing, and throws his head back.

His mother, who has recovered from her fright, draws him into her arms. She pulls the bell.

«The year begins well, my dears,» she says, «but we need a little light.»

«Tell me, mamma, do naughty children have presents at New-Year's?» says the young dissembler, with an eye on the mountain of boxes and packages visible in the corner, in spite of the gloom.

The curtains are drawn apart, the blinds are opened, there is a flood of daylight, the fire crackles gayly on the hearth, and two large packages, carefully wrapped up, are placed on the bed. One is for my wife; the other for the boy.

What is it? What will it be? I have heaped up knots, and tripled the wrappings; and I watch with delight their nervous fingers, lost in the strings.

My wife gets impatient, smiles, is vexed, kisses me, and asks for scissors. Baby on his side bites his lips, pulls with all his might, and at last asks me to help him. He longs to see through the paper. Desire and expectation are painted on his face. The convulsive movement of his hand in the folds of the quilt rustles the silk, and he makes a sound with his lips as though a savory fruit were approaching them.

The last paper is off, finally the cover is lifted, there is an outcry of joy.

"My tippet!"

"My menagerie!"

"Like my muff,— my dear husband!"

"With a real shepherd, on wheels, dear papa, *how* I love you!"

They hug me, four arms at once wind round and press me close. I am stirred — a tear comes to my eyes; two come to those of my wife; and Baby, who loses his head, utters a sob as he kisses my hand.

How absurd! you will say. I don't know whether it is absurd or not, but it is charming, I promise you. After all, does not sorrow wring tears enough from us to make up for the solitary one which joy may call forth? Life is less happy when one chances it alone; and when the heart is empty, the way seems long. It is so good to feel one's self loved; to hear the regular steps of one's fellow travelers beside one; and to think, "They are there, our three hearts beat together;" and once a year, when the great clock strikes the first of January, to sit down beside the way with hands clasped together and eyes fixed upon the dusty unknown road stretching on to the horizon, and to embrace and say:— "We will always love each other, my dear ones; you depend upon me and I on you. Let us trust and keep straight on."

And that is how I explain that we weep a little in looking at a tippet and opening a menagerie.

Translated by Jane G. Cooke, for 'A Library of The World's Best Literature.'

THEIR LAST EXCURSION

From ‹Making an Omelette›: from Lippincott's Magazine, 1871, copyrighted

IN THIS strange, rude interior, how refined and delicate Louise looked, with all her dainty appointments of long undressed kid gloves, jaunty boots, and looped-up petticoat! While I talked to the wood-cutters she shielded her face from the fire with her hands, and kept her eye on the butter beginning to sing in the pan.

Suddenly she rose, and taking the pan-handle from the old woman, said, « Let me help you make the omelette, will you? » The good woman let go with a smile, and Louise found herself alone, in the attitude of a fisherman who has just had a nibble. She stood in the full light of the fire, her eyes fixed on the melted butter, her arms tense with effort; she was biting her lips, probably in order to increase her strength.

« It's rather hard on madame's little hands,» said the old man. « I bet it's the first time you ever made an omelette in a wood-cutter's hut — isn't it, my young lady? »

Louise nodded yes, without turning her eyes from the omelette.

« The eggs! the eggs! » she suddenly exclaimed, with such a look of uneasiness that we all burst out laughing — « hurry with the eggs! The butter is all puffing up! Be quick — or I can't answer for the consequences.»

The old woman beat the eggs energetically.

« The herbs! » cried the old man. « The lard and salt! » cried the young ones. And they all set to work chopping, cutting, piling up, while Louise, stamping with excitement, called out, « Make haste! make haste! » Then there was a tremendous bubbling in the pan, and the great work began. We were all round the fire, gazing with an anxious interest inspired by our all having had a finger in the pie.

The old woman, on her knees beside a large dish, slipped a knife under the edge of the omelette, which was turning a fine brown. « Now, madame, you've only got to turn it over,» she said.

« Just one little quick blow,» suggested the old man.

« Mustn't be violent,» counseled the young one.

« All at once; up with it, dear! » I said.

« If you all talk at once — »

« Make haste, madame! »

« If you all talk at once I never shall manage it. It is too awfully heavy. »

« One quick little blow. »

« But I can't; it's going over. Oh gracious! »

In the heat of action, her hood had fallen off. Her cheeks were like a peach, her eyes shone, and though she lamented her fate, she burst into peals of laughter. At last by a supreme effort the pan moved, and the omelette rolled over, somewhat heavily, I confess, into the large dish which the old woman was holding. Never did an omelette look better!

« I am sure the young lady's arms must be tired, » said the old man, as he began cutting a round loaf into enormous slices.

« Oh no, not so very, » my wife answered with a merry laugh; « only I am crazy to taste my — our omelette. »

We had seated ourselves round the table. When we had eaten and drunk with the good souls, we rose and made ready to go home. The sun had set, and the whole family came out of the cabin to see us off and say good-night.

« Don't you want my son to go with you? » the old woman called after us.

It was growing dark and chilly under the trees, and we gradually quickened our pace. « Those are happy people, » said Louise. « We will come some morning and breakfast with them, — shan't we? We can put the baby in one of the donkey panniers, and in the other a large pasty and a bottle of wine. — You are not afraid of losing your way, George? »

« No, dear; no fear of that. »

« A pasty and a bottle of wine — What is that? »

« Nothing; the stump of a tree. »

« The stump of a tree — the stump of a tree, » she muttered. « Don't you hear something behind us? »

« It is only the wind in the leaves, or the breaking of a dead branch. »

He is fortunate who at night, in the heart of a forest, feels as calm as at his own fireside. You do not tremble, but you feel the silence. Involuntarily you look for eyes peering out of the darkness, and you try to define the confused forms appearing and changing every minute. Something breaks and sounds beneath your tread, and if you stop you hear the distant melancholy howl of your watch-dog, the scream of an owl, and other noises, far and near, not so easily explained. A sense of strangeness surrounds you and weighs you down. If you are alone, you walk faster; if there are two of you, you draw close to your companion. My wife clung to my arm.

« Let us turn wood-cutters. We could build a pretty little hut, simple, but nice enough. I would have curtains to the windows, and a carpet, and put my piano in one corner.» She spoke very low, and occasionally I felt my hand tremble on her arm.

« You would soon get enough of that, dearest.»

« It isn't fair to say so.» And in another minute she went on:—« You think I don't love you, you and our boy? Oh yes, dear, I love you. Yes, yes, yes! The happiness that comes every day can't be expressed: we live on it, so we don't think of it. Like our daily bread—who thinks of that? But when you are thinking of yourself, when you put your head down, and really think, then you say, 'I am ungrateful, for I am happy, and I give no thanks for it.' Or when we are alone together, and walking arm-in-arm, now, at this very moment,—not that I mean only this moment,—I love you, I love you.» She put her head down on my arm and pressed it earnestly. «Oh,» she said, «if I were to lose you!» She spoke very low, as if afraid. What had frightened her? The darkness and the forest, or her own words?

She went on:—« I have often and often dreamed that I was saying good-by to you. You both cried, and I pressed you so close to my heart that there was only one of us. It was a nightmare, you know, but I don't mind it, for it showed me that my life was in your lives, dear. What is that cracking noise? Didn't you see something just in front of us?»

I answered her by taking her in my arms and folding her to my heart. We walked on, but it was impossible to go on talking. Every now and then she would stop and say, « Hush! hark! No, it is nothing.»

At last we saw ahead of us a little light, now visible, now hidden by a tree. It was the lamp set for us in our parlor window. We crossed the stile and were at home. It was high time, for we were wet through.

I brought a huge log, and when the fire had blazed up we sat down in the great chimney-place. The poor girl was shivering. I took off her boots and held her feet to the fire, screening them with my hands.

"Thanks, dear George, thanks!" she said, leaning on my shoulder and looking at me so tenderly that I felt almost ready to cry.

"What were you saying to me in that horrid wood, my darling?" I asked her, when she was better.

"You are thinking about that? I was frightened, that is all, and when you are frightened you see ghosts."

"We shall be wood-cutters, shan't we?"

And kissing me, with a laugh, she replied: "It is bedtime, Jean of the Woods."

I well remember that walk, for it was our last. Often and often since, at sunset on a dark day, I have been over the same ground; often and often I have stopped where she stood, and stooped and pulled aside the fern, seeking to find, poor fool that I am! the traces of her vanished footsteps. And I have often halted in the clearing under the birches which rained down on us, and there in the shadow I have fancied I caught the flutter of her dress; I have thought I heard her startled note of fright. And on my way home at night, at every step I have found a recollection of her in the distant barking and the breaking branches, as in the trembling of her hand on my arm and the kiss which I gave her.

Once I went into the wood-hut. I saw it all as before,—the family, the smoky interior, the little bench on which we sat,—and I asked for something to drink, that I might see the glass her lips had touched.

"The little lady who makes such good omelettes, she isn't sick, for sure?" asked the old woman.

Probably she saw the tears in my eyes, for she said no more, and I came away.

And so it is that except in my heart, where she lives and is, all that was my darling grows faint and dark and dim.

It is the law of life, but it is a cruel law. Even my poor child is learning to forget, and when I say to him most unwillingly, "Baby dear, do you remember how your mother did this or that?" he answers "Yes"; but I see, alas! that he too is ceasing to remember.

Translation of Agnes Irwin.

HENRY DRUMMOND

(1851–)

One of the most widely read of modern essayists, Henry Drummond, was born at Stirling, Scotland, in 1851. Educated for the ministry, he passed through the Universities of Edinburgh and Tübingen, and the Free Church Divinity Hall, and after ordination was appointed to a mission chapel at Malta. The beauty and the historic interest of the famous island roused in him a desire for travel, and in the intervals of his professional work he has made semi-scientific pilgrimages to the Rocky Mountains and to South Africa, as well as lecturing tours to Canada, Australia, and the United States, where his addresses on scientific, religious, and sociological subjects have attracted large audiences.

HENRY DRUMMOND

A man of indefatigable industry, he has published many books, the most widely read of these being 'Natural Law in the Spiritual World,' a study of psychological conditions from the point of view of the Evolutionist. This work has passed through a large number of editions, and been translated into French, German, Dutch, and Norwegian. Scarcely less popular were 'The Greatest Thing in the World' (love), and 'Pax Vobiscum.' In 1894 he published a volume called 'The Ascent of Man,' in which he insists that certain altruistic factors modify the process of Natural Selection. This doctrine elicited much critical commentary from the stricter sects of the scientists, but the new view commended itself at once to the general reader.

The citations here given are selected from Mr. Drummond's book of travels, 'Tropical Africa,' a book whose simplicity and vividness enable the reader to see the Dark Continent exactly as it is.

THE COUNTRY AND ITS PEOPLE

From 'Tropical Africa'

Nothing could more wildly misrepresent the reality than the idea of one's school days that the heart of Africa is a desert. Africa rises from its three environing oceans in three great tiers, and the general physical geography of these has been already sketched: — first, a coast line, low and deadly; farther in, a plateau the height of the Scottish Grampians; farther in still, a higher plateau, covering the country for thousands of miles with mountain and valley. Now fill in this sketch, and you have Africa before you. Cover the coast belt with rank yellow grass; dot here and there a palm; scatter through it a few demoralized villages; and stock it with the leopard, the hyena, the crocodile, and the hippopotamus. Clothe the mountainous plateaux next, both of them, with endless forests; not grand umbrageous forest like the forests of South America, nor matted jungle like the forests of India, but with thin, rather weak forest, — with forest of low trees, whose half-grown trunks and scanty leaves offer no shade from the tropical sun. Nor is there anything in these trees to the casual eye to remind you that you are in the tropics. Here and there one comes upon a borassus or fan-palm, a candelabra-like euphorbia, a mimosa aflame with color, or a sepulchral baobab. A close inspection also will discover curious creepers and climbers; and among the branches strange orchids hide their eccentric flowers. But the outward type of tree is the same as we have at home — trees resembling the ash, the beech, and the elm, only seldom so large except by the streams, and never so beautiful. Day after day you may wander through these forests, with nothing except the climate to remind you where you are. The beasts to be sure are different, but unless you watch for them you will seldom see any; the birds are different, but you rarely hear them; and as for the rocks, they are our own familiar gneisses and granites, with honest basalt dikes boring through them, and leopard-skin lichens staining their weathered sides. Thousands and thousands of miles, then, of vast thin forest, shadeless, trackless, voiceless, — forest in mountain and forest in plain, — this is East Central Africa.

The indiscriminate praise, formerly lavished on tropical vegetation, has received many shocks from recent travelers. In

Kaffir-land, South Africa, I have seen one or two forests fine enough to justify the enthusiasm of arm-chair word-painters of the tropics; but so far as the central plateau is concerned, the careful judgment of Mr. Alfred Russell Wallace respecting the equatorial belt in general (a judgment which has at once sobered all modern descriptions of tropical lands and made imaginative people more content to stay at home) applies almost to this whole area. The fairy labyrinth of ferns and palms, the festoons of climbing plants blocking the paths and scenting the forests with their resplendent flowers, the gorgeous clouds of insects, the gayly plumaged birds, the paroquets, the monkey swinging from his trapeze in the shaded bowers — these are unknown to Africa. Once a week you will see a palm; once in three months the monkey will cross your path; the flowers on the whole are few; the trees are poor; and to be honest, though the endless forest-clad mountains have a sublimity of their own, and though there are tropical bits along some of the mountain streams of exquisite beauty, nowhere is there anything in grace and sweetness and strength to compare with a Highland glen. For the most part of the year these forests are jaded and sun-stricken, carpeted with no moss or alchemylla or scented woodruff, the bare trunks frescoed with few lichens, their motionless and unrefreshed leaves drooping sullenly from their sapless boughs. Flowers there are, small and great, in endless variety; but there is no display of flowers, no gorgeous show of blossom in the mass, as when the blazing gorse and heather bloom at home. The dazzling glare of the sun in the torrid zone has perhaps something to do with this want of color effect in tropical nature; for there is always about ten minutes just after sunset when the whole tone of the landscape changes like magic, and a singular beauty steals over the scene. This is the sweetest moment of the African day, and night hides only too swiftly the homelike softness and repose so strangely grateful to the over-stimulated eye.

Hidden away in these endless forests, like birds' nests in a wood, in terror of one another and of their common foe the slaver, are small native villages; and here in his virgin simplicity dwells primeval man, without clothes, without civilization, without learning, without religion — the genuine child of nature, thoughtless, careless, and contented. This man is apparently quite happy; he has practically no wants. One stick, pointed, makes him a spear; two sticks rubbed together make him a fire; fifty sticks tied together make him a house. The bark he peels from them makes his clothes; the fruits which hang on them form his food. It is perfectly astonishing, when one thinks of it, what nature can do for the animal man, to see with what small capital after all a human being can get through the world. I once saw an African buried. According to the custom of his tribe, his entire earthly possessions—and he was an average commoner—were buried with him. Into the grave, after the body, was lowered the dead man's pipe, then a rough knife, then a mud bowl, and last his bow and arrows—the bowstring cut through the middle, a touching symbol that its work was done. This was all. Four items, as an auctioneer would say, were the whole belongings for half a century of this human being. No man knows what a man is till he has seen what a man can be without, and be withal a man. That is to say, no man knows how great man is till he has seen how small he has been once.

The African is often blamed for being lazy, but it is a misuse of words. He does not need to work; with so bountiful a Nature round him it would be gratuitous to work. And his indolence, therefore, as it is called, is just as much a part of himself as his flat nose, and as little blameworthy as slowness in a tortoise. The fact is, Africa is a nation of the unemployed.

THE EAST-AFRICAN LAKE COUNTRY

From 'Tropical Africa'

Somewhere in the Shiré Highlands, in 1859, Livingstone saw a large lake—Lake Shirwa—which is still almost unknown. It lies away to the east, and is bounded by a range of mountains whose lofty summits are visible from the hills round Blantyre. Thinking it might be a useful initiation to African travel if I devoted a short time to its exploration, I set off one morning, accompanied by two members of the Blantyre staff and a small retinue of natives. Steering across country in the direction in which it lay, we found, two days before seeing the actual water, that we were already on the ancient bed of the lake. Though now clothed with forest, the whole district has obviously been under water at a comparatively recent period, and the shores of Lake Shirwa probably reached at one time to within a few miles of Blantyre itself. On reaching the lake a very aged female chief came to see us, and told us how, long, long ago, a white man came to her village and gave her a present of cloth. Of the white man, who must have been Livingstone, she spoke very kindly; and indeed, wherever David Livingstone's footsteps are crossed in Africa, the fragrance of his memory seems to remain.

The waters of Shirwa are brackish to the taste, and undrinkable; but the saltness must have a peculiar charm for game, for nowhere else in Africa did I see such splendid herds of the larger animals as here. The zebra was especially abundant; and so unaccustomed to be disturbed are these creatures, that with a little care one could watch their movements safely within a very few yards. It may seem unorthodox to say so, but I do not know if among the larger animals there is anything handsomer in creation than the zebra. At close quarters his striped coat is all but as fine as the tiger's, while the form and movement of his body are in every way nobler. The gait, certainly, is not to be compared for gracefulness with that of the many species of antelope and deer who nibble the grass beside him, and one can never quite forget that scientifically he is an ass; but taking him all in all, this fleet and beautiful animal ought to have a higher place in the regard of man than he has yet received.

We were much surprised, considering that this region is almost uninhabited, to discover near the lake shore a native path so beaten, and so recently beaten, by multitudes of human feet, that it could only represent some trunk route through the continent. Following it for a few miles, we soon discovered its function. It was one of the great slave routes through Africa. Signs of the horrid traffic became visible on every side; and from symmetrical arrangements of small piles of stones and freshly cut twigs, planted semaphore-wise upon the path, our native guides made out that a slave caravan was actually passing at the time. We were in fact between two portions of it, the stones and twigs being telegraphic signals between front and rear. Our natives seemed much alarmed at this discovery, and refused to proceed unless we promised not to interfere — a proceeding which, had we attempted it, would simply have meant murder for ourselves and slavery for them. Next day from a hill-top we saw the slave encampment far below, and the ghastly procession marshaling for its march to the distant coast, which many of the hundreds who composed it would never reach alive.

Talking of native foot-paths leads me to turn aside for a moment, to explain to the uninitiated the true mode of African travel. In spite of all the books that have been lavished upon us by our great explorers, few people seem to have any accurate understanding of this most simple process. Some have the impression that everything is done in bullock wagons; an idea borrowed from the Cape, but hopelessly inapplicable to Central Africa, where a wheel at present would be as great a novelty as a polar bear. Others, at the opposite extreme, suppose that the explorer works along solely by compass, making a bee-line for his destination, and steering his caravan through the trackless wilderness like a ship at sea. Now, it may be a surprise to the unenlightened to learn that probably no explorer in forcing his passage through Africa has ever, for more than a few days at a time, been off some beaten track. Probably no country in the world, civilized or uncivilized, is better supplied with paths than this unmapped continent. Every village is connected with some other village, every tribe with the next tribe, every State with its neighbor, and therefore with all the rest. The explorer's business is simply to select from this network of tracks, keep a general direction, and hold on his way. Let him begin at Zanzibar, plant his foot on a native foot-path, and set his face towards Tanganyika. In eight months he will be there. He has simply to persevere. From village to village he will be handed on, zigzagging it may be, sometimes, to avoid the impassable barriers of nature or the rarer perils of hostile tribes; but never taking to the woods, never guided solely by the stars, never in fact leaving a beaten track, till hundreds and hundreds of miles are between him and the sea, and his interminable foot-path ends with a canoe on the shores of Tanganyika. Crossing the lake, landing near some native village, he picks up the thread once more. Again he plods on and on, now on foot, now by canoe, but always keeping his line of villages, until one day suddenly he sniffs the sea-breeze again, and his faithful foot-wide guide lands him on the Atlantic seaboard.

Nor is there any art in finding out these successive villages with their intercommunicating links. He *must* find them out. A whole army of guides, servants, carriers, soldiers, and camp-followers accompany him in his march, and this nondescript regiment must be fed. Indian corn, cassava, mawere, beans, and bananas — these do not grow wild even in Africa. Every meal has to be bought and paid for in cloth and beads; and scarcely three days can pass without a call having to be made at some village where the necessary supplies can be obtained. A caravan, as a rule, must live from hand to mouth, and its march becomes simply a regulated procession through a chain of markets. Not however that there are any real markets — there are neither bazaars nor stores in native Africa. Thousands of the villages through which the traveler eats his way may never have victualed a caravan before. But with the chief's consent, which is usually easily purchased for a showy present, the villagers unlock their larders, the women flock to the grinding-stones, and basketfuls of food are swiftly exchanged for unknown equivalents in beads and calico.

The native tracks which I have just described are the same in character all over Africa. They are veritable foot-paths, never over a foot in breadth, beaten as hard as adamant, and rutted beneath the level of the forest bed by centuries of native traffic. As a rule these foot-paths are marvelously direct. Like the roads of the old Romans, they run straight on through everything, ridge and mountain and valley, never shying at obstacles, nor anywhere turning aside to breathe. Yet within this general straightforwardness there is a singular eccentricity and indirectness in detail. Although the African foot-path is on the whole a bee-line, no fifty yards of it are ever straight. And the reason is not far to seek. If a stone is encountered, no native will ever think of removing it. Why should he? It is easier to walk round it. The next man who comes that way will do the same. He knows that a hundred men are following him; he looks at the stone; a moment, and it might be unearthed and tossed aside, but no — he also holds on his way. It is not that he resents the trouble, it is the idea that is wanting. It would no more occur to him that that stone was a displaceable object, and that for the general weal he might displace it, than that its feldspar was of the orthoclase variety. Generations and generations of men have passed that stone, and it still waits for a man with an altruistic idea. But it would be a very stony country indeed — and Africa is far from stony — that would wholly account for the aggravating obliqueness and indecision of the African foot-path. Probably each four miles, on an average path, is spun out, by an infinite series of minor sinuosities, to five or six. Now, these deflections are not meaningless. Each has some history —

a history dating back perhaps a thousand years, but to which all clue has centuries ago been lost. The leading cause probably is fallen trees. When a tree falls across a path no man ever removes it. As in the case of the stone, the native goes round it. It is too green to burn in his hut; before it is dry and the white ants have eaten it, the new detour has become part and parcel of the path. The smaller irregularities, on the other hand, represent the trees and stumps of the primeval forest where the track was made at first. But whatever the cause, it is certain that for persistent straightforwardness in the general, and utter vacillation and irresolution in the particular, the African roads are unique in engineering.

Though one of the smaller African lakes, Shirwa is probably larger than all the lakes of Great Britain put together. With the splendid environment of mountains on three of its sides, softened and distanced by perpetual summer haze, it reminds one somewhat of the Great Salt Lake simmering in the July sun. We pitched our tent for a day or two on its western shore, among a harmless and surprised people who had never gazed on the pallid countenances of Englishmen before. Owing to the ravages of the slaver, the people of Shirwa are few, scattered, and poor, and live in abiding terror. The densest population is to be found on the small island, heavily timbered with baobabs, which forms a picturesque feature of the northern end. These Wa-Nyassa, or people of the lake, as they call themselves, have been driven away by fear, and they rarely leave their lake dwelling unless under cover of night. Even then they are liable to capture by any man of a stronger tribe who happens to meet them, and numbers who have been kidnapped in this way are to be found in the villages of neighboring chiefs. This is an amenity of existence in Africa that strikes one as very terrible. It is impossible for those at home to understand how literally savage man is a chattel, and how much his life is spent in the mere safeguarding of his main asset, *i. e.*, himself. There are actually districts in Africa where *three* natives cannot be sent on a message, in case two should combine and sell the third before they return.

WHITE ANTS

From 'Tropical Africa'

The termite or white ant is a small insect, with a bloated, yellowish-white body, and a somewhat large thorax, oblong-shaped, and colored a disagreeable oily brown. The flabby, tallow-like body makes this insect sufficiently repulsive, but it is for quite another reason that the white ant is the worst abused of all living vermin in warm countries. The termite lives almost exclusively upon wood; and the moment a tree is cut or a log sawn for any economical purpose, this insect is upon its track. One may never see the insect, possibly, in the flesh, for it lives underground; but its ravages confront one at every turn. You build your house perhaps, and for a few months fancy you have pitched upon the one solitary site in the country where there are no white ants. But one day suddenly the door-post totters, and lintel and rafters come down together with a crash. You look at a section of the wrecked timbers, and discover that the whole inside is eaten clean away. The apparently solid logs of which the rest of the house is built are now mere cylinders of bark, and through the thickest of them you could push your little finger. Furniture, tables, chairs, chests of drawers, everything made of wood, is inevitably attacked, and in a single night a strong trunk is often riddled through and through, and turned into matchwood. There is no limit, in fact, to the depredation by these insects, and they will eat books, or leather, or cloth, or anything; and in many parts of Africa I believe if a man lay down to sleep with a wooden leg, it would be a heap of sawdust in the morning. So much feared is this insect now, that no one in certain parts of India and Africa ever attempts to travel with such a thing as a wooden trunk. On the Tanganyika plateau I have camped on ground which was as hard as adamant, and as innocent of white ants apparently as the pavement of St. Paul's; and wakened next morning to find a stout wooden box almost gnawed to pieces. Leather portmanteaus share the same fate, and the only substances which seem to defy the marauders are iron and tin.

But what has this to do with earth or with agriculture? The most important point in the work of the white ant remains to be noted. I have already said that the white ant is never seen. Why he should have such a repugnance to being looked at is at first sight a mystery, seeing that he himself is stone blind. But his coyness is really due to the desire for self-protection; for the moment his juicy body shows itself above ground there are a dozen enemies waiting to devour it. And yet the white ant can never procure any food until it comes above ground. Nor will it meet the case for the insect to come to the surface under the shadow of night. Night in the tropics, so far as animal life is concerned, is as the day. It is the great feeding-time, the great fighting-time, the carnival of the carnivores, and of all beasts, birds, and insects of prey, from the least to the greatest. It is clear then that darkness is no protection to the white ant; and yet without coming out of the ground it cannot live. How does it solve the difficulty? It takes the ground out along with it. I have seen white ants working on the top of a high tree, and yet they were underground. They took up some of the ground with them to the tree-top; just as the Esquimaux heap up snow, building it into the low tunnel-huts in which they live, so the white ants collect earth, only in this case not from the surface, but from some depth underneath the ground, and plaster it into tunneled ways. Occasionally these run along the ground, but more often mount in endless ramifications to the top of trees, meandering along every branch and twig, and here and there debouching into large covered chambers which occupy half the girth of the trunk. Millions of trees in some districts are thus fantastically plastered over with tubes, galleries, and chambers of earth, and many pounds' weight of subsoil must be brought up for the mining of even a single tree. The building material is conveyed by the insects up a central pipe with which all the galleries communicate, and which at the downward end connects with a series of subterranean passages leading deep into the earth. The method of building the tunnels and covered ways is as follows: At the foot of a tree the tiniest hole cautiously opens in the ground close to the bark. A small head appears, with a grain of earth clasped in its jaws. Against the tree trunk this earth-grain is deposited, and the head is withdrawn. Presently it reappears with another grain of earth; this is laid beside the first, rammed tight against it, and again the builder descends underground for more. The third grain is not placed against the tree, but against the former grain; a fourth, a fifth, and a sixth follow, and the plan of the foundation begins to suggest itself as soon as these are in position. The stones or grains or pellets of earth are arranged in a semicircular wall; the termite, now assisted by three or four others, standing in the middle between the sheltering wall and the tree, and working briskly with head and mandible to strengthen the position. The wall in fact forms a small moon-rampart, and as it grows higher and higher it soon becomes evident that it is going to grow from a low battlement into a long perpendicular tunnel running up the side of the tree. The workers, safely ensconced inside, are now carrying up the structure with great rapidity, disappearing in turn as soon as they have laid their stone, and rushing off to bring up another. The way in which the building is done is extremely curious, and one could watch the movement of these wonderful little masons by the hour. Each stone as it is brought to the top is first of all covered with mortar. Of course, without this the whole tunnel would crumble into dust before reaching the height of half an inch; but the termite pours over the stone a moist sticky secretion, turning the grain round and round with its mandibles until the whole is covered with slime. Then it places the stone with great care upon the top of the wall, works it about vigorously for a moment or two till it is well jammed into its place, and then starts off instantly for another load.

Peering over the growing wall, one soon discovers one, two, or more termites of a somewhat larger build, considerably longer, and with a very different arrangement of the parts of the head, and especially of the mandibles. These important-looking individuals saunter about the rampart in the most leisurely way, but yet with a certain air of business, as if perhaps the one was the master of works and the other the architect. But closer observation suggests that they are in no wise superintending operations, nor in any immediate way contributing to the structure, for they take not the slightest notice either of the workers or the works. They are posted there in fact as sentries; and there they stand, or promenade about, at the mouth of every tunnel, like Sister Anne, to see if anybody is coming. Sometimes somebody does come, in the shape of another ant; the real ant this time, not the defenseless *Neuropteron*, but some valiant and belted knight from the warlike *Formicidæ*. Singly or in troops, this rapacious little insect, fearless in its chitinous coat of mail, charges down the tree trunk, its antennæ waving defiance to the enemy and its cruel mandibles thirsting for termite blood. The worker white ant is a poor defenseless creature, and blind and unarmed, would fall an immediate prey to these well-drilled banditti, who forage about in every tropical forest in unnumbered legion. But at the critical moment, like Goliath from the Philistines, the soldier termite advances to the fight. With a few sweeps of its scythe-like jaws it clears the ground, and while the attacking party is carrying off its dead, the builders, unconscious of the fray, quietly continue their work. To every hundred workers in a white-ant colony, which numbers many thousands of individuals, there are perhaps two of these fighting men. The division of labor here is very wonderful; and the fact that besides these two specialized forms there are in every nest two other kinds of the same insect, the kings and queens, shows the remarkable height to which civilization in these communities has attained.

But where is this tunnel going to, and what object have the insects in view in ascending this lofty tree? Thirty feet from the ground, across innumerable forks, at the end of a long branch, are a few feet of dead wood. How the ants know it is there, how they know its sap has dried up, and that it is now fit for the termites' food, is a mystery. Possibly they do not know, and are only prospecting on the chance. The fact that they sometimes make straight for the decaying limb argues in these instances a kind of definite instinct; but on the other hand, the fact that in most cases the whole tree, in every branch and limb, is covered with termite tunnels, would show perhaps that they work most commonly on speculation, while the number of abandoned tunnels, ending on a sound branch in a *cul de sac*, proves how often they must suffer the usual disappointments of all such adventurers. The extent to which these insects carry on their tunneling is quite incredible, until one has seen it in nature with his own eyes. The tunnels are perhaps about the thickness of a small-sized gas-pipe, but there are junctions here and there of large dimensions, and occasionally patches of earthwork are found, embracing nearly the whole trunk for some feet. The outside of these tunnels, which are never quite straight, but wander irregularly along stem and branch, resembles in texture a coarse sandpaper; and the color, although this naturally varies with the soil, is usually a reddish brown. The quantity of earth and mud plastered over a single tree is often enormous; and when one thinks that it is not only an isolated specimen here and there that is frescoed in this way, but often all the trees of a forest, some idea will be formed of the magnitude of the operations of these insects, and the extent of their influence upon the soil which they are thus ceaselessly transporting from underneath the ground.

In traveling through the great forests of the Rocky Mountains or of the Western States, the broken branches and fallen trunks, strewing the ground breast-high with all sorts of decaying litter, frequently make locomotion impossible. To attempt to ride through these Western forests, with their meshwork of interlocked branches and decaying trunks, is often out of the question, and one has to dismount and drag his horse after him as if he were clambering through a wood-yard. But in an African forest not a fallen branch is seen. One is struck at first at a certain clean look about the great forests of the interior, a novel and unaccountable cleanness, as if the forest bed was carefully swept and dusted daily by unseen elves. And so indeed it is. Scavengers of a hundred kinds remove decaying animal matter, from the carcass of a fallen elephant to the broken wing of a gnat; eating it, or carrying it out of sight and burying it in the deodorizing earth. And these countless millions of termites perform a similar function for the vegetable world, making away with all plants and trees, all stems, twigs, and tissues, the moment the finger of decay strikes the signal. Constantly in these woods one comes across what appear to be sticks and branches and bundles of fagots, but when closely examined they are seen to be mere casts in mud. From these hollow tubes, which preserve the original form of the branch down to the minutest knot or fork, the ligneous tissue is often entirely removed, while others are met with in all stages of demolition. There is the section of an actual specimen, which is not yet completely destroyed, and from which the mode of attack may be easily seen. The insects start apparently from two centres. One company attacks the inner bark, which is the favorite morsel, leaving the coarse outer bark untouched, or more usually replacing it with grains of earth, atom by atom, as they eat it away. The inner bark is gnawed off likewise as they go along, but the woody tissue beneath is allowed to remain, to form a protective sheath for the second company, who begin work at the centre. This second contingent eats its way outward and onward, leaving a thin tube of the outer wood to the last, as props to the mine, till they have finished the main excavation. When a fallen trunk lying upon the ground is the object of attack, the outer cylinder is frequently left quite intact, and it is only when one tries to drag it off to his camp-fire that he finds to his disgust that he is dealing with a mere hollow tube, a few lines in thickness, filled up with mud.

But the works above ground represent only a part of the labors of these slow-moving but most industrious of creatures. The arboreal tubes are only the prolongation of a much more elaborate system of subterranean tunnels, which extend over large areas and mine the earth sometimes to a depth of many feet or even yards.

The material excavated from these underground galleries and from the succession of domed chambers — used as nurseries or granaries — to which they lead, has to be thrown out upon the surface. And it is from these materials that the huge ant-hills are reared, which form so distinctive a feature of the African landscape. These heaps and mounds are so conspicuous that they may be seen for miles, and so numerous are they and so useful as cover to the sportsman, that without them in certain districts hunting would be impossible. The first things, indeed, to strike the traveler in entering the interior are the mounds of the white ant, now dotting the plain in groups like a small cemetery, now rising into mounds, singly or in clusters, each thirty or forty feet in diameter and ten or fifteen in height; or again, standing out against the sky like obelisks, their bare sides carved and fluted into all sorts of fantastic shapes. In India these ant-heaps seldom attain a height of more than a couple of feet, but in Central Africa they form veritable hills, and contain many tons of earth. The brick houses of the Scotch mission-station on Lake Nyassa have all been built out of a single ants' nest, and the quarry from which the material has been derived forms a pit beside the settlement some dozen feet in depth. A supply of bricks as large again could probably still be taken from this convenient depot; and the missionaries on Lake Tanganyika and onwards to Victoria Nyanza have been similarly indebted to the labors of the termites. In South Africa the Zulus and Kaffirs pave all their huts with white-ant earth; and during the Boer war our troops in Pretoria, by scooping out the interior from the smaller beehive-shaped ant-heaps and covering the top with clay, constantly used them as ovens. These ant-heaps may be said to abound over the whole interior of Africa, and there are several distinct species. The most peculiar, as well as the most ornate, is a small variety from one to two feet in height, which occurs in myriads along the shores of Lake Tanganyika. It is built in symmetrical tiers, and resembles a pile of small rounded hats, one above another, the rims depending like eaves, and sheltering the body of the hill from rain. To estimate the amount of earth per acre raised from the water-line of the subsoil by white ants, would not in some districts be an impossible task; and it would be found probably that the quantity at least equaled that manipulated annually in temperate regions by the earthworm.

These mounds, however, are more than mere waste-heaps. Like the corresponding region underground, they are built into a meshwork of tunnels, galleries, and chambers, where the social interests of the community are attended to. The most spacious of these chambers, usually far underground, is very properly allocated to the head of the society, the queen. The queen termite is a very rare insect, and as there are seldom more than one or at most two to a colony, and as the royal apartments are hidden far in the earth, few persons have ever seen a queen; and indeed most, if they did happen to come across it, from its very singular appearance would refuse to believe that it had any connection with white ants. It possesses indeed the true termite head, but there the resemblance to the other members of the family stops; for the size of the head bears about the same proportion to the rest of the body as does the tuft on his Glengarry bonnet to a six-foot Highlander. The phenomenal corpulence of the royal body in the case of the queen termite is possibly due in part to want of exercise; for once seated upon her throne, she never stirs to the end of her days. She lies there, a large, loathsome, cylindrical package, two or three inches long, in shape like a sausage, and as white as a bolster. Her one duty in life is to lay eggs; and it must be confessed she discharges her function with complete success, for in a single day her progeny often amounts to many thousands, and for months this enormous fecundity never slackens. The body increases slowly in size, and through the transparent skin the long folded ovary may be seen, with the eggs, impelled by a peristaltic motion, passing onward for delivery to the workers, who are waiting to carry them to the nurseries, where they are hatched. Assiduous attention meantime is paid to the queen by other workers, who feed her diligently, with much self-denial stuffing her with morsel after morsel from their own jaws. A guard of honor in the shape of a few of the larger soldier ants is also in attendance, as a last and almost unnecessary precaution. In addition finally to the soldiers, workers, and queen, the royal chamber has also one other inmate — the king. He is a very ordinary-looking insect, about the same size as the soldiers, but the arrangement of the parts of the head and body is widely different, and like the queen he is furnished with eyes.

WILLIAM DRUMMOND OF HAWTHORNDEN

(1585–1649)

It seems to be the mission of many writers to illuminate contemporary literature and so to light the way for future students, rather than to make any vital contribution to the achievement of their time. Such writers reflect the culture of their own day and represent its ideals; and although their creative work may be slight, their loss to literature would be serious. Among these lesser men stands that sincere poet, Drummond of Hawthornden. In Scotland under the Stuarts, when the vital energy of the land was concentrated upon politics and theology, native literature was reduced to a mere reflection of the pre-Spenserian classicism of England. Into this waste of correct mediocrity entered the poetry of William Drummond, an avowed and enthusiastic follower of the Elizabethan school, a finished scholar, one of the typical Scottish gentlemen who were then making Scottish history. Courtier and trifler though he was, however, he showed himself so true a poet of nature that his felicities of phrase seem to anticipate the sensuous realism of Keats and his successors.

William Drummond

William Drummond, born in 1585, was a cadet of the historic house which in 1357 gave in marriage to King Robert III. the beautiful Annabella Drummond, who was destined to become the ancestress of the royal Stuarts of Scotland and England. In his own day the family, whose head was the Earl of Perth, was powerful in Scottish affairs, and the history of the clan Drummond would be largely a history of the events which led to the Protectorate. Throughout the storm and stress that preceded the civil war Drummond was a loyalist, though at one time he appeared to be identified with the Covenanters. His literary influence, which was considerable, was always thrown on the side of the King, while the term «Drummondism» was a popular synonym for the conservative policy. Throughout the struggle, however, Drummond seems to have been forced into activity by circumstances rather than by choice. He had the instincts of a recluse and a scholar. He delighted in the society of literary men, and he was much engrossed in philosophical speculations.

In spite of the difficulties of distance, he managed to keep abreast of the thought of literary London, the London of Drayton and Webster, of Beaumont, Fletcher, Massinger, and Ford. His chief satisfaction was to know that his own work was not unacceptable to this brilliant group, and one of the great pleasures of his life was a visit from Ben Jonson, who, making a walking tour to Scotland, found at Hawthornden that congenial hospitality in which his soul delighted. Of this famous visit, as of other important events, Drummond kept a record, in which he set down his guest's behavior, opinions, and confidential sayings. Warmly as he admired Jonson's genius, he found his personality oppressive, and intrusted his criticisms to his diary. When this was published, more than a century later, the gentle Scot was accused of bad taste, breach of confidence, and disloyalty to friendship. But his defense lies in the fact that the book was meant for no eyes but his own, and that the intimacy and candor of its revelations were intended to preserve his recollections of a memorable experience.

If his environment was not entirely favorable to literary excellences, it is yet very likely that Drummond developed the full measure of his gift. He expressed the spirit of the more imaginative generation which succeeded a hard and fettered predecessor, and it is for this that literature owes him its peculiar debt.

His career began in his twenty-ninth year with the publication of an elegy on the death of Henry, Prince of Wales, eldest son of James I. This poem, under the title 'Tears on the Death of Mœliades,' appeared in 1613, and reached a third edition within a twelvemonth. Its two hundred lines show the finished versification of the scholar, with much poetic grace. It was a product of the Spenserian school, and emphasized the fact that the representative literature of the land had abandoned the Scottish dialect for English forms. Drummond's second volume of poems commemorated the death of his wife and his love of her. It is in this work that the ultimate mood of the poet appears. Much beauty of form, a delightful sensitiveness to nature, a luxuriance of color, and a finely tempered thoughtfulness pervade the poems. His next production, celebrating the visit of James I. to his native land, was entitled 'Forth Feasting,' and represented the Forth and all its borders as rejoicing in the presence of their King. To the reader of to-day the panegyric sounds fulsome and the poetry stilted, and the once famous book has now merely an archaic interest.

Drummond's reputation is based upon the 'Poems,' and upon the Jeremy-Taylor-like 'Cypress Grove,' published in 1623 in connection with the religious verses called 'Flowers of Sion.' 'Cypress Grove' is an essay on death, akin in spirit to the religious temper of the Middle Ages, and in philosophic breadth to the diviner mood of Plato. Only a mind of a high order would have conceived so beautiful and lofty a meditation on the Final Mystery. This brief essay marks the utmost reach of Drummond's mind, and shows the strength of that serene spirituality, which could thus hold its way undisturbed by the sectarian bitterness that fixed a great gulf between England and Scotland. 'The History of the Five Jameses,' which Drummond was ten years in compiling and which was not published until six years after his death, added nothing to his reputation. It lacked alike the diligent minuteness of the chronicler and the broader view of the historian. Many minor papers on the state of religion and politics, chief of which is the political tract 'Irene,' show Drummond's aggressive interest in contemporary affairs. It is not generally known that this gentle scholar was also an inventor of military engines. In 1626 Charles I. engaged him to produce sixteen machines and "not a few inventions besides." The biographers have remained curiously ignorant of this phase of his activity, but the State papers show that the King named him "our faithful subject, William Drummond of Hawthornden." He died in 1649, his death being hastened, it was said, by his passion of grief over the martyrdom of King Charles.

SEXTAIN

The heaven doth not contain so many stars,
So many leaves not prostrate lie in woods
When autumn's old and Boreas sounds his wars,
So many waves have not the ocean floods,
As my rent mind hath torments all the night,
And heart spends sighs when Phœbus brings the light.

Why should I have been partner of the light,
Who, crost in birth by bad aspéct of stars,
Have never since had happy day or night?
Why was not I a liver in the woods,
Or citizen of Thetis's crystal floods,
Than made a man, for love and fortune's wars?

I look each day when death should end the wars,
Uncivil wars, 'twixt sense and reason's light;
My pains I count to mountains, meads, and floods,
And of my sorrow partners make the stars;
All desolate I haunt the fearful woods,
When I should give myself to rest at night.

With watchful eyes I ne'er behold the night,
Mother of peace, but ah! to me of wars,
And Cynthia, queen-like, shining through the woods,
When straight those lamps come in my thought, whose light
My judgment dazzled, passing brightest stars,
And then mine eyes en-isle themselves with floods.

Turn to their springs again first shall the floods,
Clear shall the sun the sad and gloomy night,
To dance about the pole cease shall the stars,
The elements renew their ancient wars
Shall first, and be deprived of place and light,
E'er I find rest in city, fields, or woods.

End these my days, indwellers of the woods,
Take this my life, ye deep and raging floods;
Sun, never rise to clear me with thy light,
Horror and darkness, keep a lasting night;
Consume me, care, with thy intestine wars,
And stay your influence o'er me, bright stars!

In vain the stars, indwellers of the woods,
Care, horror, wars, I call, and raging floods,
For all have sworn no night shall dim my sight.

MADRIGAL

This world a-hunting is,
The prey poor man, the Nimrod
fierce is Death;
His speedy greyhounds are
Lust, sickness, envy, care,
Strife that ne'er falls amiss,
With all those ills which haunt us while we breathe.
Now if by chance we fly
Of these the eager chase,
Old age with stealing pace
Casts up his nets, and there we panting die.

REASON AND FEELING

I know that all beneath the moon decays,
And what by mortals in this world is brought,
In Time's great periods shall return to naught;
That fairest States have fatal nights and days.
I know that all the Muse's heavenly lays,
With toil of sp'rit, which are so dearly bought,
As idle sounds, of few or none are sought,—
That there is nothing lighter than vain praise.
I know frail beauty like the purple flower,
To which one morn oft birth and death affords;
That love a jarring is of minds' accords,
Where sense and will envassal Reason's power:
Know what I list, all this cannot me move,
But that, alas! I both must write and love.

DEGENERACY OF THE WORLD

What hapless hap had I for to be born
In these unhappy times, and dying days
Of this now doting World, when Good decays,
Love's quite extinct, and Virtue's held a-scorn!
When such are only prized, by wretched ways,
Who with a golden fleece them can adorn;
When avarice and lust are counted praise,
And bravest minds live orphan-like forlorn!
Why was not I born in that golden age
When gold was not yet known? and those black arts
By which base worldlings vilely play their parts,
With horrid acts staining Earth's stately stage?
To have been then, O Heaven! 't had been my bliss;
But bless me now, and take me soon from this.

THE BRIEFNESS OF LIFE

Look, how the flower which ling'ringly doth fade,
The morning's darling late, the summer's queen,
Spoiled of that juice which kept it fresh and green,
As high as it did raise, bows low the head:
Right so my life, contentment being dead,
Or in their contraries but only seen,

With swifter speed declines than erst it spread,
And, blasted, scarce now shows what it hath been.
As doth the pilgrim, therefore, whom the night
By darkness would imprison on his way,—
Think on thy home, my soul, and think aright,
Of what's yet left thee of life's wasting day;
Thy sun posts westward, passèd is thy morn,
And twice it is not given thee to be born.

THE UNIVERSE

Of this fair volume which we World do name,
If we the leaves and sheets could turn with care—
Of Him who it corrects and did it frame
We clear might read the art and wisdom rare,
Find out his power, which wildest powers doth tame,
His providence, extending everywhere,
His justice, which proud rebels doth not spare,
In every page and period of the same.
But silly we, like foolish children, rest
Well pleased with colored vellum, leaves of gold,
Fair dangling ribands, leaving what is best;
On the great Writer's sense ne'er taking hold;
Or if by chance we stay our minds on aught,
It is some picture on the margin wrought.

ON DEATH

From ‹Cypress Grove›

Death is a piece of the order of this all, a part of the life of this world; for while the world is the world, some creatures must die and others take life. Eternal things are raised far above this orb of generation and corruption where the First Matter, like a still flowing and ebbing sea, with diverse waves but the same water, keepeth a restless and never tiring current; what is below in the universality of its kind doth not in itself abide. . . . If thou dost complain there shall be a time in the which thou shalt not be, why dost thou not too grieve that there was a time in which thou wast not, and so that thou art not as old as the enlivening planet of Time? . . . The excellent fabric of the universe itself shall one day suffer ruin, or change like ruin, and poor earthlings, thus to be handled, complain!

JOHN DRYDEN

(1631-1700)

BY THOMAS R. LOUNSBURY

John Dryden, the foremost man of letters of the period following the Restoration, was born at Aldwinkle, a village of Northamptonshire, on August 9th, 1631. He died May 1st, 1700. His life was therefore coeval with the closing period of the fierce controversies which culminated in the civil war and the triumph of the Parliamentary party; that, in turn, to be followed successively by the iron rule of Cromwell, by the restoration of the exiled Stuarts, and the reactionary tendencies in politics that accompanied that event; and finally with the effectual exclusion from the throne of this same family by the revolution of 1688, leaving behind, however, to their successors a smoldering Jacobite hostility that perpetually plotted the overthrow of the new government and later broke out twice into open revolt. All these changes of fortune, with their changes of opinion, are faithfully reflected in the productions of Dryden. To understand him thoroughly requires therefore an intimate familiarity with the civil and religious movements which characterize the whole period. Equally also do his writings, both creative and critical, represent the revolution of literary taste that took place in the latter half of the seventeenth century. It was while he was in the midst of his intellectual activity that French canons of criticism became largely the accepted rules, by which the value of English productions was tested. This was especially true of the drama. The study of Dryden is accordingly a study of the political and literary history of his times to an extent that is correspondingly true of no other English author before or since.

His family, both on the father's and the mother's side, was in full sympathy with the party opposed to the court. The son was educated at Westminster, then under the mastership of Richard Busby, whose relentless use of the rod has made his name famous in that long line of flagellants who have been at the head of the great English public schools. From Westminster he went to Trinity College, Cambridge. There he received the degree of A. B. in January 1654. Later in that same decade—the precise date is not known—he took up his residence in London; and in London the rest of his life was almost entirely spent.

Dryden's first published literary effort appeared in a little volume made up of thirty-three elegies, by various authors, on the death of a youth of great promise who had been educated at Westminster. This was Lord Hastings, the eldest son of the Earl of Huntingdon. He had died of the small-pox. Dryden's contribution was written in 1649, and consisted of but little over a hundred lines. No one expects great verse from a boy of eighteen; but the most extravagant anticipations of sorry performance will fail to come up to the reality of the wretchedness which was here attained. It was in words like these that the future laureate bewailed the death of the young nobleman and depicted the disease of which he died:—

«Was there no milder way but the small-pox,
The very filthiness of Pandora's box?
So many spots, like næves, our Venus soil?
One jewel set off with so many a foil?
Blisters with pride swelled, which through his flesh did sprout
Like rosebuds, stuck in the lily-skin about.
Each little pimple had a tear in it,
To wail the fault its rising did commit;
Which, rebel-like, with its own lord at strife,
Thus made an insurrection 'gainst his life.
Or were these gems sent to adorn his skin,
The cabinet of a richer soul within?
No comet need foretell his change drew on,
Whose corps might seem a constellation.»

Criticism cannot be rendered sufficiently vituperative to characterize properly such a passage. It is fuller of conceits than ever Cowley crowded into the same space; and lines more crabbed and inharmonious Donne never succeeded in perpetrating. Its production upsets all principles of prophecy. The wretchedest of poetasters can take courage, when he contemplates the profundity of the depth out of which uprose the greatest poet of his time.

Dryden is, in fact, an example of that somewhat rare class of writers who steadily improve with advancing years. Most poets write their best verse before middle life. Many of them after that time go through a period of decline, and sometimes of rapid decline; and if they live to reach old age, they add to the quantity of their production without sensibly increasing its value. This general truth is conspicuously untrue of Dryden. His first work gave no promise of his future excellence, and it was by very slow degrees that he attained to the mastery of his art. But the older he grew, the better he wrote; and the volume published a few months before his death, and largely composed almost under its shadow, so far from showing the

JOHN DRYDEN.

slightest sign of failing power, contains a great deal of the best poetry he ever produced.

As Dryden's relatives were Puritans, and some of them held place under the government, it was natural that upon coming to London he should attach himself to that party. Accordingly it is no surprise to find him duly mourning the death of the great Protector in certain 'Heroic Stanzas Consecrated to the Memory of Oliver Cromwell.' The first edition bears the date of 1659, and so far as we know, the production was Dryden's second venture in poetry. It was written in the measure of Davenant's 'Gondibert,' and is by no means a poor piece of work, though it has been sometimes so styled. It certainly pays not simply a high but a discerning tribute to the genius of Cromwell. Before two years had gone by, we find its author greeting the return of Charles with effusive loyalty, and with predictions of prosperity and honor to attend his reign, which events were soon woefully to belie. The poet has been severely censured for this change of attitude. It is a censure which might be bestowed with as much propriety upon the whole population of England. The joyful expectations to which he gave utterance were almost universal; and no other charge can well be brought against him than that he had the ability and took the occasion to express sentiments which were felt by nearly the entire nation.

From this time on, Dryden appears more and more in the public eye, and slowly but steadily forged his way to the front as the representative man of letters of his time. In 1670 he was appointed to the two distinct offices of poet laureate and historiographer royal. Thenceforward his relations with the court became close, and so they did not cease to be until the expulsion of James II. In 1683 he received a further mark of royal favor, in being made collector of customs of the port of London. In the political controversies which subsequently arose, Dryden's writings faithfully represented the sentiments of the side he had chosen, and expressed their prejudices and aversions not merely with force but also with virulence. His first literary activity, however, was on neutral ground. After eighteen years of compulsory closing, the Restoration opened wide once more the doors of the theatre. Dryden, like every one else possessed of literary ability, began to write for the stage. His first play, a comedy entitled 'The Wild Gallant,' was brought out in February 1663; and for the eighteen years following, it was compositions of such nature that occupied the main portion of his literary life. During that time he produced wholly or in part twenty-two comedies and tragedies. His pieces must from the outset have met with a fair degree of success, otherwise the King's Company would not have entered into a contract with him, as it did in 1667, to furnish for them each year a fixed number of plays, in consideration of his receiving a certain share of the profits of the theatre.

Yet it cannot be said that Dryden was in any respect a dramatist of a high order. As a writer of comedy he was not only inferior to contemporaries and immediate successors like Wycherley, Congreve, Vanbrugh, and Farquhar, but in certain ways he was surpassed by Shadwell, the very man whom he himself has consigned to a disagreeable immortality as the hero of the 'MacFlecknoe.' His comedies are not merely full of obscenity,— which seems to have been a necessary ingredient to suit them to the taste of the age,— but they are full of a peculiarly disagreeable obscenity. One of his worst offenses in this direction, and altogether his most impudent one, was his adaptation for the stage of Shakespeare's 'Tempest.' The two plays are worth reading together for the sake of seeing how easily a pure and perfect creation of genius can be vulgarized in language and spirit almost beyond the possibility of recognition. In his tragedies, however, Dryden was much more successful. Yet even these, in spite of the excellence of occasional passages, do not attain to a high rank. Indeed, thought and expression are at times extravagant, not to say stilted, to an extent which afterward led him himself to make them the subject of ridicule. It was in them, however, during these years that he perfected by degrees his mastery of heroic verse, of which later he was to display the capabilities in a way that had never previously been seen and has never since been surpassed.

A controversy in regard to the proper method of composing plays brought forward Dryden, at an early period in his literary career, as a writer of prose. In this he at once attained unusual eminence. In him appear for the first time united the two characters of poet and of critic. Ben Jonson had in a measure preceded him in this respect; but Jonson's criticism was not so much devoted to the examination of general principles as to the exposure of the hopeless, helpless obtuseness of the men who had a different opinion of his works from what he himself entertained. The questions discussed by Dryden were of a more general nature. With the Stuarts had come in French literary tastes and French literary methods. The age was supposed to be too refined to be pleased with what had satisfied the coarse palates of preceding generations. In stage-writing in particular, the doctrine of the unities, almost uniformly violated by Shakespeare and most of the Elizabethans, was now held up as the only correct method of composition that could be employed by any writer who sought to conform to the true principles of art. Along with this came the substitution in the drama of rhyme for blank verse. Upon the comparative merits of these two as employed in tragedy, arose the first controversy in which Dryden was engaged. This one was with his brother-in-law, Sir Robert Howard; for in 1663 Dryden had become the husband of the daughter of the Earl of Berkshire, thus marrying, as Pope expressed it, «misery in a noble wife.» Dryden was an advocate of rhyme; and the controversy on this point began with the publication in 1668 of his 'Essay of Dramatic Poesy.' It was afterward carried on by both parties, in prefaces to the plays they successively published. The prefaces to these productions regularly became later the place where Dryden laid down his critical doctrines on all points that engaged his attention; and whether we agree with his views or not, we are always sure to be charmed with the manner in which they are expressed.

In 1667 Dryden published a long poem entitled 'Annus Mirabilis.' It was in the same measure as the stanzas on Oliver Cromwell. It gave him a good deal of reputation at the time; but though it is far from being a despicable performance, few there are now who read it and still fewer who re-read it. Far different has been the fate of his next work. It was not until 1681, when England was beginning to emerge slowly from the excitement and agitation growing out of the alleged Popish plot, that he brought out his 'Absalom and Achitophel,' without question the greatest combined poetical and political satire to be found in our tongue. Here it was that for the first time he fully displayed his mastery over heroic verse. The notion once so widely prevalent — for the vogue of which, indeed, Dryden himself is mainly responsible — that Waller and Denham brought this verse to perfection, it now requires both extensive and special ignorance of our earlier authors to entertain; but on the other hand, there is no question that he himself imparted to the line a variety, vigor, and sustained majesty of movement such as the verse in its modern form had never previously received. There is therefore a fairly full measure of truth in the lines in which he was characterized by Pope: —

> «Waller was smooth; but Dryden taught to join
> The varying verse, the full resounding line,
> The long majestic march and energy divine.»

These lines of Pope, it may be added, exemplify purposely two peculiarities of Dryden's versification, — the occasional use of the triplet instead of the regular couplet, and of the Alexandrine, or line of six feet, in place of the usual line of five.

The poem is largely an attack upon the Earl of Shaftesbury, who in it bears the title of Achitophel. The portrayal of this statesman, which is given in this volume, is ample evidence of that skill of the poet in characterization which has made the pictures he drew immortal. Perhaps even more effective was the description of the

Duke of Buckingham, under the designation of Zimri. For attacking that nobleman Dryden had both political and personal reasons. Buckingham had now joined the opponents of the court. Ten years previously the poet himself had been brought by him on the stage, with the aid of others, in the play called 'The Rehearsal.' His usual actions had been mimicked, his usual expressions had been put into the mouth of the character created to represent him, who was styled Bayes. This title had been given him because Dryden figuratively wore the bays, or laurel, as poet laureate. The name henceforward stuck. Dryden's turn had now come; and it was in these following lines that he drew the unfaded and fadeless picture of this nobleman, whose reputation even then was notorious rather than famous, and whose intellect was motley-minded rather than versatile:—

«Some of their chiefs were princes of the land;
In the front rank of these did Zimri stand,
A man so various that he seemed to be
Not one, but all mankind's epitome:
Stiff in opinions, always in the wrong,
Was everything by starts and nothing long,
But in the course of one revolving moon
Was chymist, fiddler, statesman, and buffoon;
Then all for women, painting, rhyming, drinking,
Besides ten thousand freaks that died in thinking.
Blest madman, who could every hour employ
With something new to wish or to enjoy!
Railing and praising were his usual themes,
And both, to show his judgment, in extremes:
So over-violent or over-civil
That every man with him was God or Devil.
In squandering wealth was his peculiar art:
Nothing went unrewarded but desert.
Beggared by fools whom still he found too late,
He had his jest, and they had his estate.»

As an example of the loftier and more majestic style occasionally found in this poem, is the powerful appeal of Achitophel to Absalom. The latter, it is to be said, stands for the Duke of Monmouth, the eldest of the illegitimate sons of Charles II. Him many of the so-called country party, now beginning to be styled Whigs, were endeavoring to have recognized as the next successor to the throne, in place of the Roman Catholic brother of the king, James, Duke of York. As a favorite son of the monarch, he, though then in opposition, is treated tenderly by Dryden throughout; and this feeling is plainly visible in the opening of the address to him put into the mouth of Achitophel, in these words:—

«Auspicious prince, at whose nativity
Some royal planet ruled the southern sky,
Thy longing country's darling and desire,
Their cloudy pillar and their guardian fire,
Their second Moses, whose extended wand
Divides the seas and shows the promised land,
Whose dawning day in every distant age
Has exercised the sacred prophet's rage,
The people's prayer, the glad diviner's theme,
The young men's vision and the old men's dream,—
Thee savior, thee the nation's vows confess,
And never satisfied with seeing, bless.»

Dryden followed up the attack upon Shaftesbury with a poem entitled ‹The Medal.› This satire, which appeared in March 1682, was called forth by the action of the partisans of the Whig leader in having a medal struck commemorating his release from the Tower, after the grand jury had thrown out the charge of treason which had been brought against him. Both of these pieces were followed by a host of replies. Some of them did not refrain from personal attack, which indeed had a certain justification in the poet's own violence of denunciation. The most abusive of these was a poem by Thomas Shadwell, entitled ‹The Medal of John Bayes.› Such persons as fancy Dryden's subsequent punishment of that dramatist unwarranted in its severity should in justice read this ferociously scurrilous diatribe, in which every charge against the poet that malice or envy had concocted and rumor had set afloat, was here industriously raked together; and to the muck-heap thus collected, the intimacy of previous acquaintance was doubtless enabled to contribute its due quota of malignant assertion and more malignant insinuation. Shadwell was soon supplied, however, with ample reason to regret his action. Dryden's first and best known rejoinder is ‹MacFlecknoe, or a Satire on the True Blue Protestant Poet T. S.› This production has always had the reputation in literature of being the severest personal satire in the language; but it requires now for its appreciation an intimate acquaintance with Shadwell's plays, which very few possess. It is further disfigured in places by a coarseness from which, indeed, none of the poet's writings were certain to be free. Its general spirit can be indicated by a brief extract from its opening paragraph. Flecknoe, it is to be said, was a feeble poet who had died a few years before. He is here represented as having long reigned over the kingdom of dullness, but knowing that his end was close at hand, determines to settle the succession to the State. Accordingly he fixes upon his son Shadwell as the one best fitted to take his place in ruling over the realm of nonsense, and in continuing the war with wit and sense. The announcement of his intention he begins in the following words:—

«—'Tis resolved, for Nature pleads that he
Should only rule who most resembles me.
Shadwell alone my perfect image bears,
Mature in dullness from his tender years;
Shadwell alone of all my sons is he
Who stands confirmed in full stupidity.
The rest to some faint meaning make pretense,
But Shadwell never deviates into sense.»

Far more bitter, however, was the renewed attack which a month later Dryden inserted in the two hundred lines he contributed to the continuation of 'Absalom and Achitophel' that was written by Nahum Tate. In this second part, which came out in November 1682, he devoted himself in particular to two of his opponents, Settle and Shadwell, under the names respectively of Doeg and Og—«two fools,» he says, in his energetic way,—

«That crutch their feeble sense on verse;
Who by my Muse to all succeeding times
Shall live in spite of their own doggerel rhymes.»

Of Settle, whose poetry was possessed of much smoothness but little sense, he spoke in a tone of contemptuous good-nature, though the object of the attack must certainly have deemed the tender mercies of Dryden to be cruel. It was in this way he was described, to quote a few lines:—

«Spiteful he is not, though he wrote a satire,
For still there goes some thinking to ill-nature.
. . . .
Let him be gallows-free by my consent,
And nothing suffer, since he nothing meant;
Hanging supposes human soul and reason,—
This animal's below committing treason:
Shall he be hanged who never could rebel?
That's a preferment for Achitophel.
. . . .
Let him rail on; let his invective Muse
Have four-and-twenty letters to abuse,
Which if he jumbles to one line of sense,
Indict him of a capital offense.»

But it was not till he came to the portraiture of Shadwell that he gave full vent to the ferocity of his satire. He taunted him with the unwieldiness of his bulk, the grossness of his habits, with his want of wealth, and finally closed up with some lines into which he concentrated all the venom of his previous attacks:—

«But though Heaven made him poor, with reverence speaking,
He never was a poet of God's making·

The midwife laid her hand on his thick skull,
With this prophetic blessing — *Be thou dull;*
Drink, swear, and roar, forbear no lewd delight
Fit for thy bulk; do anything but write.
Thou art of lasting make, like thoughtless men;
A strong nativity — but for the pen;
Eat opium, mingle arsenic in thy drink,
Still thou mayest live, avoiding pen and ink.
I see, I see, 'tis counsel given in vain,
For treason, botched in rhyme, will be thy bane;
Rhyme is the rock on which thou art to wreck;
'Tis fatal to thy fame and to thy neck.
. . . .
«A double noose thou on thy neck dost pull,
For writing treason and for writing dull;
To die for faction is a common evil,
But to be hanged for nonsense is the devil.
Hadst thou the glories of thy King exprest,
Thy praises had been satires at the best;
But thou in clumsy verse, unlicked, unpointed,
Hast shamefully defied the Lord's anointed.
I will not rake the dunghill of thy crimes,
For who would read thy life that reads thy rhymes?
But of King David's foes be this the doom,—
May all be like the young man Absalom;
And for my foes may this their blessing be,—
To talk like Doeg and to write like thee.»

Refinement of tone is not the distinguishing characteristic of satire of this sort. It does not attack its object by delicate insinuation or remote suggestion. It operates by heavy downright blows which crush by the mere weight and power of the stroke. There was in truth in those days a certain brutality not only permitted but expected in the way men spoke of each other, and Dryden conformed in this as in other respects to the manners and methods of his age. But of its kind the attack is perfect. The blows of a bludgeon which make of the victim a shapeless mass kill as effectively as the steel or poison which leaves every feature undisturbed, and to the common apprehension it serves to render the killing more manifest. At any rate, so long as a person has been done to death, it makes comparatively little difference how the death was brought about; and the object in this instance of Dryden's attack, though a man of no mean abilities, has never recovered from the demolition which his reputation then underwent.

In 1685 Charles II. died, and his brother James ascended the throne. In the following year Dryden went over to the Roman Catholic Church. No act of his life has met with severer censure. Nor can there be any doubt that the time he took to change his religion afforded ground for distrusting the sincerity of his motives. A king was on the throne who was straining every nerve to bring the Church of England once more under the sway of the Church of Rome. Obviously the adoption of the latter faith would recommend the poet to the favor of the bigoted monarch, and tend to advance his personal interests. There is no wonder, therefore, that he should at the time have been accused of being actuated by the unworthiest of reasons, and that the charge should continue to be repeated to our day. Yet a close study of Dryden's life and writings indicates that the step he took was a natural if not an inevitable outcome of the processes through which his opinions had been passing. He had been early trained in the strict tenets of the Puritan party. From these he had been carried over to the loose beliefs and looser life that followed everywhere hard upon the Restoration. By the sentiments then prevailing he was profoundly affected. Nothing in the writings of the first half of his literary life is more marked—not even his flings at matrimony—than the scoffing way in which he usually spoke of the clergy. His tone towards them is almost always contemptuous, where it is not positively vituperative. His famous political satire began with this line—

> «In pious times, ere priestcraft did begin;»—

and a little later in the course of the same poem he observed that—

> «Fraud was used, the sacrificer's trade,»

the «sacrificer» here denoting the priest. This feeling toward the clergy never in truth deserted him entirely. But no one who reads carefully his ‘Religio Laici,’ a poem published in 1682, can fail to perceive that even then he had not only drifted far away from the faith of his childhood, but had begun to be tormented and perplexed by the insoluble problems connected with the life and destiny of man, and with his relations to his Creator. The subject was not likely to weigh less heavily upon him in the years that followed. To Dryden, as to many before and since, it may have seemed the easiest method of deliverance from the difficulties in which he found himself involved, to cast the burden of doubts which disquieted the mind and depressed the heart, upon a Church that undertakes to assume the whole responsibility for the man's future on condition of his yielding to it an unquestioning faith in the present.

An immediate result of his conversion was the production in 1687 of one of his most deservedly famous poems, ‘The Hind and the Panther.’ He began it with the idea of assisting in bringing about the reconciliation between the Panther, typifying the Church of England, and the Hind, typifying the Church of Rome. It is apparent that before he finished it he saw that the project was hopeless. It is a poem of over twenty-five hundred lines, of which the opening up to line 150 is printed in this volume. Part of the passage here cited contains, without professing it as an object, and probably without intending it, the best defense that could be made for his change of religion. The production in its entirety is remarkable for the skill which its author displayed in carrying on an argument in verse. In this he certainly had no superior among poets, perhaps no equal. The work naturally created a great sensation in those days of fierce political and religious controversy. Both it and its writer were made the object of constant attack. A criticism, in particular, appeared upon it in the shape of a dialogue in prose with snatches of verse interspersed. It is usually known by the title of 'The Town Mouse and the Country Mouse,' and was exalted at the time by unreasoning partisanship into a wonderful performance. Even to the present day, this dreary specimen of polemics is described as a very witty work by those who have never struggled to read it. It was the production of Charles Montagu, the future Earl of Halifax, and of Matthew Prior. A story too is still constantly repeated that Dryden was much hurt by the attacks of these two young men, to whom he had been kind, and wept over their ingratitude. If he shed any tears at all upon the occasion, they must have been due to the mortification he felt that any two persons who had been admitted to his friendship should have been guilty of twaddle so desperately tedious.

The flight of James and the accession of William and Mary threw Dryden at once out of the favor of the court, upon which to a large extent he had long depended for support. As a Jacobite he could not take the oath of allegiance; but there is hardly any doubt that under any circumstances he would have been deprived of the offices of place and profit he held. In the laureateship he was succeeded by his old antagonist Shadwell; and within a few years he saw the dignity of the position still further degraded by the appointment to it of Nahum Tate, one of the worst of the long procession of poetasters who have filled it. Dryden henceforth belonged to the party out of power. His feelings about his changed relations are shown plainly in the fine epistle with which he consoled Congreve for the failure of his comedy of the 'Double Dealer.' Yet displaced and unpensioned, and sometimes the object of hostile attack, his literary supremacy was more absolute than ever. All young authors, whether Whigs or Tories, sought his society and courted his favor; and his seat at Will's coffee-house was the throne from which he swayed the literary sceptre of England.

After the revolution of 1688 Dryden gave himself entirely up to authorship. He first turned to the stage; and between 1690 and 1694 he produced five plays. With the failure in the last-mentioned year of his tragi-comedy called 'Love Triumphant,' he abandoned writing for the theatre. The period immediately following he devoted mainly to his translation of Virgil, which was published in 1697. It was highly successful; but far more reputation came to him from a large folio volume that was brought out in November 1699, under the title of 'Fables.' Its contents consisted mainly of poetical narratives founded upon certain stories of the 'Decameron,' and of the modernization of some of the 'Canterbury Tales.' In certain ways these have been his most successful pieces, and have made his name familiar to successive generations of readers. Of the tales from Boccaccio, that of 'Cymon and Iphigenia' is on the whole the most pleasing. The modernizations of Chaucer were long regarded as superior to the original; and though superior knowledge of the original has effectually banished that belief, there is on the other hand no justification for the derogatory terms which are now sometimes applied to Dryden's versions.

The verse in this volume was preceded by a long critical essay in prose. Many of its views, especially those about the language of Chaucer, have been long discarded; but the criticism will always be read with pleasure for the genial spirit and sound sense which pervade it, and the unstudied ease with which it is written. Cowley and Dryden are in fact the founders of modern English prose; and the influence of the latter has been much greater than that of the former, inasmuch as he touched upon a far wider variety of topics, and for that reason obtained a far larger circle of readers in the century following his death. There was also the same steady improvement in Dryden's critical taste that there was in his poetical expression. His admiration for Shakespeare constantly improved during his whole life; and it is to be noticed that in what is generally regarded as the best of his plays—'All for Love,' brought out in the winter of 1677–78—he of his own accord abandoned rhyme for blank verse.

The publication of the 'Fables' was Dryden's last appearance before the public. In the following year he died, and was buried in Westminster Abbey by the side of Chaucer and Cowley. After his death his fame steadily increased instead of diminishing. For a long period his superiority in his particular line was ungrudgingly conceded by all, or if contested, was contested by Pope alone. His poetry indeed is not of the highest kind, though usually infinitely superior to that of his detractors. Still his excellences were those of the intellect and not of the spirit. On the higher planes of thought and feeling he rarely moves; to the highest he never aspires. The nearest he ever approaches to the former is in his later work, where religious emotion or religious zeal has lent to expression the aid of its intensity. There is a striking example of this in the personal references to his own experiences in the lines cited below from 'The Hind and the Panther.' Something too of the same spirit can be found, expressed in lofty language, in the following passage from the same poem, descriptive of the unity of the Church of Rome as contrasted with the numerous warring sects into which the Protestant body is divided:—

«One in herself, not rent by schism, but sound,
Entire, one solid shining diamond,
Not sparkles shattered into sects like you:
One is the Church, and must be to be true,
One central principle of unity.
As undivided, so from errors free;
As one in faith, so one in sanctity.
Thus she, and none but she, the insulting rage
Of heretics opposed from age to age;
Still when the giant brood invades her throne,
She stoops from heaven and meets them half-way down,
And with paternal thunders vindicates her crown.

. . . .

«Thus one, thus pure, behold her largely spread,
Like the fair ocean from her mother-bed;
From east to west triumphantly she rides,
All shores are watered by her wealthy tides.
The gospel sound diffused from Pole to Pole,
Where winds can carry and where waves can roll,
The selfsame doctrine of the sacred page
Conveyed to every clime, in every age.»

But though Dryden's poetry is not of the highest class, it is of the very highest kind in its class. Wherever the pure intellect comes into play, there he is invariably excellent. There is never any weakness; there is never any vagueness; there is never any deviation from the true path into aimless digression. His words invariably go straight to the mark, and not unfrequently with a directness and force that fully merit the epithet of «burning» applied to them by the poet Gray. His thoughts always rise naturally out of the matter in hand; and in the treatment of the meanest subjects he is not only never mean, but often falls without apparent effort into a felicity of phrase which holds the attention and implants itself in the memory. The benefit of exercise, for instance, is not a topic that can be deemed highly poetical; but in his epistle on country life addressed to his cousin John Driden, the moment he comes to speak of hunting and its salutary results his expression at once leaves the commonplace, and embodies the thought in these pointed lines:—

«So lived our sires, ere doctors learned to kill,
And multiply with theirs the weekly bill.
The first physicians by debauch were made;
Excess began, and sloth sustains the trade.
. . . .
By chase our long-lived fathers earned their food;
Toil strung the nerves and purified the blood:
But we their sons, a pampered race of men,
Are dwindled down to threescore years and ten.
Better to hunt in fields for health unbought
Than fee the doctor for a nauseous draught.
The wise for cure on exercise depend;
God never made his work for man to mend.»

In a similar way in ‹Cymon and Iphigenia› the contempt which Dryden, in common with the Tories of his time, felt for the English militia force, found vent in the following vigorous passage, really descriptive of them and their conduct though the scene is laid in Rhodes:—

«The country rings around with loud alarms,
And raw in fields the rude militia swarms;
Mouths without hands; maintained at vast expense,
In peace a charge, in war a weak defense;
Stout once a month they march, a blustering band,
And ever, but in times of need, at hand:
This was the morn when, issuing on the guard,
Drawn up in rank and file they stood prepared
Of seeming arms to make a short essay,
Then hasten to be drunk, the business of the day.»

In a world where what is feeble in expression is so often supposed to indicate peculiar delicacy; where what is vague is so often deemed peculiarly poetical; and where what is involved and crabbed and hard to comprehend is thought to denote peculiar profundity,—it is a pleasure to turn to a writer with a rank settled by the consensus of successive generations, who thought clearly and wrote forcibly, who knew always what he had to say and then said it with directness and power. There are greater poets than he; but so long as men continue to delight in vividness of expression, in majesty of numbers, in masculine strength and all-abounding vigor, so long will Dryden continue to hold his present high place among English authors.

The writings of Dryden constitute of themselves a literature. They treat of a vast variety of topics in many different departments of intellectual activity. The completest edition of his works was first published in 1808 under the editorship of Walter Scott. It fills twenty-one volumes, the first of which however is devoted to a biography. The notes to this edition are generally excellent; the text is very indifferent. A revised edition of it has been recently published under the editorship of George Saintsbury. But easily accessible is a single-volume edition of the poems alone, edited by W. D. Christie, which furnishes a superior text, and is amply supplied with all necessary annotations.

Thomas R. Lounsbury.

FROM 'THE HIND AND THE PANTHER'

A MILK-WHITE Hind, immortal and unchanged,
Fed on the lawns and in the forest ranged;
Without unspotted, innocent within,
She feared no danger, for she knew no sin.
Yet had she oft been chased with horns and hounds,
And Scythian shafts, and many wingèd wounds
Aimed at her heart; was often forced to fly,
And doomed to death, though fated not to die.
Not so her young; for their unequal line
Was hero's make, half human, half divine.
Their earthly mold obnoxious was to fate,
The immortal part assumed immortal state.
Of these a slaughtered army lay in blood,
Extended o'er the Caledonian wood,
Their native walk; whose vocal blood arose
And cried for pardon on their perjured foes.
Their fate was fruitful, and the sanguine seed,
Endued with souls, increased the sacred breed.
So captive Israel multiplied in chains,
A numerous exile, and enjoyed her pains.
With grief and gladness mixed, their mother viewed
Her martyred offspring and their race renewed;
Their corps to perish, but their kind to last,
So much the deathless plant the dying fruit surpassed.
Panting and pensive now she ranged alone,
And wandered in the kingdoms once her own.
The common hunt, though from their rage restrained
By sovereign power, her company disdained,
Grinned as they passed, and with a glaring eye
Gave gloomy signs of secret enmity.
'Tis true she bounded by and tripped so light,
They had not time to take a steady sight;

For truth has such a face and such a mien
As to be loved needs only to be seen.
The bloody Bear, an independent beast,
Unlicked to form, in groans her hate expressed.
Among the timorous kind the quaking Hare
Professed neutrality, but would not swear.
Next her the buffoon Ape, as atheists use,
Mimicked all sects and had his own to chuse;
Still when the Lion looked, his knees he bent,
And paid at church a courtier's compliment.
The bristled baptist Boar, impure as he,
But whitened with the foam of sanctity,
With fat pollutions filled the sacred place,
And mountains leveled in his furious race;
So first rebellion founded was in grace.
But since the mighty ravage which he made
In German forests had his guilt betrayed,
With broken tusks and with a borrowed name,
He shunned the vengeance and concealed the shame,
So lurked in sects unseen. With greater guile
False Reynard fed on consecrated spoil;
The graceless beast by Athanasius first
Was chased from Nice, then by Socinus nursed,
His impious race their blasphemy renewed,
And Nature's King through Nature's optics viewed;
Reversed they viewed him lessened to their eye,
Nor in an infant could a God descry.
New swarming sects to this obliquely tend,
Hence they began, and here they all will end.
What weight of ancient witness can prevail,
If private reason hold the public scale?
But gracious God, how well dost thou provide
For erring judgments an unerring guide!
Thy throne is darkness in the abyss of light,
A blaze of glory that forbids the sight.
O teach me to believe thee thus concealed,
And search no farther than thy self revealed;
But her alone for my director take,
Whom thou hast promised never to forsake!
My thoughtless youth was winged with vain desires;
My manhood, long misled by wandering fires,
Followed false lights; and when their glimpse was gone,
My pride struck out new sparkles of her own.
Such was I, such by nature still I am;
Be thine the glory and be mine the shame!

Good life be now my task; my doubts are done;
What more could fright my faith than Three in One?
Can I believe eternal God could lie
Disguised in mortal mold and infancy,
That the great Maker of the world could die?
And after that, trust my imperfect sense
Which calls in question his omnipotence?
Can I my reason to my faith compel,
And shall my sight and touch and taste rebel?
Superior faculties are set aside;
Shall their subservient organs be my guide?
Then let the moon usurp the rule of day,
And winking tapers show the sun his way;
For what my senses can themselves perceive
I need no revelation to believe.
Can they, who say the Host should be descried
By sense, define a body glorified,
Impassible, and penetrating parts?
Let them declare by what mysterious arts
He shot that body through the opposing might
Of bolts and bars impervious to the light,
And stood before his train confessed in open sight.
For since thus wondrously he passed, 'tis plain
One single place two bodies did contain;
And sure the same omnipotence as well
Can make one body in more places dwell.
Let Reason then at her own quarry fly;
But how can finite grasp infinity?
 'Tis urged again, that faith did first commence
By miracles, which are appeals to sense,
And thence concluded, that our sense must be
The motive still of credibility.
For latter ages must on former wait,
And what began belief must propagate.
 But winnow well this thought, and you shall find
'Tis light as chaff that flies before the wind.
Were all those wonders wrought by power Divine
As means or ends of some more deep design?
Most sure as means, whose end was this alone,
To prove the Godhead of the Eternal Son.
God thus asserted: Man is to believe
Beyond what Sense and Reason can conceive,
And for mysterious things of faith rely
On the proponent Heaven's authority.

If then our faith we for our guide admit,
Vain is the farther search of human wit;
As when the building gains a surer stay,
We take the unuseful scaffolding away.
Reason by sense no more can understand;
The game is played into another hand.
Why choose we then like bilanders to creep
Along the coast, and land in view to keep,
When safely we may launch into the deep?
In the same vessel which our Savior bore,
Himself the pilot, let us leave the shore,
And with a better guide a better world explore.
Could he his Godhead veil with flesh and blood
And not veil these again to be our food?
His grace in both is equal in extent;
The first affords us life, the second nourishment.
And if he can, why all this frantic pain
To construe what his clearest words contain,
And make a riddle what he made so plain?
To take up half on trust and half to try,
Name it not faith, but bungling bigotry.
Both knave and fool the merchant we may call,
To pay great sums and to compound the small,
For who would break with Heaven, and would not break for all?
Rest then, my soul, from endless anguish freed:
Nor sciences thy guide, nor sense thy creed.
Faith is the best insurer of thy bliss;
The bank above must fail before the venture miss.

TO MY DEAR FRIEND MR. CONGREVE

On His Comedy Called 'The Double Dealer'

Well then, the promised hour is come at last;
The present age of wit obscures the past:
Strong were our sires, and as they fought they writ;
Conquering with force of arms and dint of wit:
Theirs was the giant race before the flood;
And thus, when Charles returned, our empire stood.
Like Janus, he the stubborn soil manured,
With rules of husbandry the rankness cured;
Tamed us to manners, when the stage was rude,
And boisterous English wit with art endued.

Our age was cultivated thus at length,
But what we gained in skill we lost in strength.
Our builders were with want of genius curst;
The second temple was not like the first;
Till you, the best Vitruvius, come at length,
Our beauties equal, but excel our strength.
Firm Doric pillars found your solid base,
The fair Corinthian crowns the higher space;
Thus all below is strength, and all above is grace.
In easy dialogue is Fletcher's praise;
He moved the mind, but had not power to raise.
Great Jonson did by strength of judgment please,
Yet, doubling Fletcher's force, he wants his ease.
In differing talents both adorned their age,
One for the study, t'other for the stage.
But both to Congreve justly shall submit,
One matched in judgment, both o'ermatched in wit.
In him all beauties of this age we see:
Etherege his courtship, Southern's purity,
The satire, wit, and strength of manly Wycherley.
All this in blooming youth you have achieved;
Nor are your foiled contemporaries grieved.
So much the sweetness of your manners move,
We cannot envy you, because we love.
Fabius might joy in Scipio, when he saw
A beardless Consul made against the law,
And join his suffrage to the votes of Rome,
Though he with Hannibal was overcome.
Thus old Romano bowed to Raphael's fame,
And scholar to the youth he taught became.

O that your brows my laurel had sustained!
Well had I been deposed, if you had reigned:
The father had descended for the son,
For only you are lineal to the throne.
Thus, when the State one Edward did depose,
A greater Edward in his room arose:
But now, not I, but poetry, is curst;
For Tom the second reigns like Tom the first.
But let them not mistake my patron's part,
Nor call his charity their own desert.
Yet this I prophesy: Thou shalt be seen,
Though with some short parenthesis between,
High on the throne of wit, and seated there,
Not mine—that's little—but thy laurel wear.

Thy first attempt an early promise made;
That early promise this has more than paid.
So bold, yet so judiciously you dare,
That your least praise is to be regular.
Time, place, and action may with pains be wrought,
But genius must be born, and never can be taught.
This is your portion, this your native store:
Heaven, that but once was prodigal before,
To Shakespeare gave as much; she could not give him more.
Maintain your post: that's all the fame you need;
For 'tis impossible you should proceed.
Already I am worn with cares and age,
And just abandoning the ungrateful stage:
Unprofitably kept at Heaven's expense,
I live a rent-charge on His providence:
But you, whom every Muse and grace adorn,
Whom I foresee to better fortune born,
Be kind to my remains; and oh, defend,
Against your judgment, your departed friend!
Let not the insulting foe my fame pursue,
But shade those laurels which descend to you:
And take for tribute what these lines express;
You merit more, nor could my love do less.

ODE

TO THE PIOUS MEMORY OF THE ACCOMPLISHED YOUNG LADY

MRS. ANNE KILLIGREW,

EXCELLENT IN THE TWO SISTER ARTS OF POESY AND PAINTING.

THOU youngest virgin daughter of the skies,
Made in the last promotion of the blest;
Whose palms, new-plucked from Paradise,
In spreading branches more sublimely rise,
Rich with immortal green above the rest:
Whether, adopted to some neighboring star,
Thou roll'st above us in thy wandering race,
Or in procession fixed and regular
Moved with the heaven's majestic pace,
Or called to more superior bliss,
Thou tread'st with seraphims the vast abyss:
Whatever happy region be thy place,
Cease thy celestial song a little space;

Thou wilt have time enough for hymns divine,
Since Heaven's eternal year is thine.
Hear then a mortal Muse thy praise rehearse
In no ignoble verse,
But such as thy own voice did practice here,
When thy first fruits of poesy were given,
To make thyself a welcome inmate there;
While yet a young probationer,
And candidate of Heaven.

If by traduction came thy mind,
Our wonder is the less to find
A soul so charming from a stock so good;
Thy father was transfused into thy blood:
So wert thou born into the tuneful strain
(An early, rich, and inexhausted vein).
But if thy pre-existing soul
Was formed at first with myriads more,
It did through all the mighty poets roll
Who Greek or Latin laurels wore,
And was that Sappho last, which once it was before.
If so, then cease thy flight, O heaven-born mind!
Thou hast no dross to purge from thy rich ore:
Nor can thy soul a fairer mansion find
Than was the beauteous frame she left behind:
Return, to fill or mend the quire of thy celestial kind.

May we presume to say that at thy birth
New joy was sprung in heaven, as well as here on earth?
For sure the milder planets did combine
On thy auspicious horoscope to shine,
And even the most malicious were in trine.
Thy brother angels at thy birth
Strung each his lyre, and tuned it high,
That all the people of the sky
Might know a poetess was born on earth;
And then, if ever, mortal ears
Had heard the music of the spheres.
And if no clustering swarm of bees
On thy sweet mouth distilled their golden dew,
'Twas that such vulgar miracles
Heaven had not leisure to renew:
For all the blest fraternity of love
Solemnized there thy birth, and kept thy holiday above.

O gracious God! how far have we
Profaned thy heavenly gift of Poesy!
Made prostitute and profligate the Muse,
Debased to each obscene and impious use,
Whose harmony was first ordained above,
For tongues of angels and for hymns of love!
Oh wretched we! why were we hurried down
This lubric and adulterate age,
(Nay, added fat pollutions of our own,)
To increase the steaming ordures of the stage?
What can we say to excuse our second fall?
Let this thy Vestal, Heaven, atone for all:
Her Arethusian stream remains unsoiled,
Unmixed with foreign filth and undefiled;
Her wit was more than man, her innocence a child.

Art she had none, yet wanted none,
For Nature did that want supply:
So rich in treasures of her own,
She might our boasted stores defy:
Such noble vigor did her verse adorn
That it seemed borrowed, where 'twas only born.
Her morals too were in her bosom bred,
By great examples daily fed,
What in the best of books, her father's life, she read.
And to be read herself she need not fear;
Each test and every light her Muse will bear,
Though Epictetus with his lamp were there.
Even love (for love sometimes her Muse exprest)
Was but a lambent flame which played about her breast;
Light as the vapors of a morning dream,
So cold herself, whilst she such warmth exprest,
'Twas Cupid bathing in Diana's stream.

Born to the spacious empire of the Nine,
One would have thought she should have been content
To manage well that mighty government;
But what can young ambitious souls confine?
To the next realm she stretched her sway,
For Painture near adjoining lay,
A plenteous province and alluring prey.
A Chamber of Dependences was framed,
As conquerors will never want pretense,
(When armed to justify the offense,)
And the whole fief in right of Poetry she claimed.

The country open lay without defense;
For poets frequent inroads there had made,
And perfectly could represent
The shape, the face, with every lineament,
And all the large demains which the dumb Sister swayed;
All bowed beneath her government,
Received in triumph wheresoe'er she went.
Her pencil drew whate'er her soul designed,
And oft the happy draught surpassed the image in her mind;
The sylvan scenes of herds and flocks
And fruitful plains and barren rocks;
Of shallow brooks that flowed so clear,
The bottom did the top appear;
Of deeper too and ampler floods
Which, as in mirrors, showed the woods;
Of lofty trees, with sacred shades
And perspectives of pleasant glades,
Where nymphs of brightest form appear,
And shaggy satyrs standing near,
Which them at once admire and fear.
The ruins too of some majestic piece,
Boasting the power of ancient Rome or Greece,
Whose statues, friezes, columns, broken lie,
And, though defaced, the wonder of the eye;
What nature, art, bold fiction, e'er durst frame,
Her forming hand gave feature to the name.
So strange a concourse ne'er was seen before,
But when the peopled Ark the whole creation bore.

The scene then changed; with bold erected look
Our martial King the sight with reverence strook:
For, not content to express his outward part,
Her hand called out the image of his heart:
His warlike mind, his soul devoid of fear,
His high-designing thoughts were figured there,
As when by magic ghosts are made appear.
Our phœnix Queen was portrayed too so bright
Beauty alone could beauty take so right:
Her dress, her shape, her matchless grace,
Were all observed, as well as heavenly face.
With such a peerless majesty she stands,
As in that day she took the crown from sacred hands;
Before a train of heroines was seen,
In beauty foremost, as in rank the Queen.

Thus nothing to her genius was denied,
But like a ball of fire, the farther thrown,
Still with a greater blaze she shone,
And her bright soul broke out on every side.
What next she had designed, Heaven only knows:
To such immoderate growth her conquest rose
That Fate alone its progress could oppose.

Now all those charms, that blooming grace,
The well-proportioned shape and beauteous face,
Shall never more be seen by mortal eyes;
In earth the much-lamented virgin lies.
Not wit nor piety could Fate prevent;
Nor was the cruel Destiny content
To finish all the murder at a blow,
To sweep at once her life and beauty too;
But, like a hardened felon, took a pride
To work more mischievously slow,
And plundered first, and then destroyed.
O double sacrilege on things divine,
To rob the relic, and deface the shrine!
But thus Orinda died:
Heaven by the same disease did both translate;
As equal were their souls, so equal was their fate.

Meantime, her warlike brother on the seas
His waving streamers to the winds displays,
And vows for his return with vain devotion pays.
Ah, generous youth! that wish forbear,
The winds too soon will waft thee here!
Slack all thy sails, and fear to come;
Alas! thou knowest not, thou art wrecked at home.
No more shalt thou behold thy sister's face;
Thou hast already had her last embrace.
But look aloft, and if thou ken'st from far,
Among the Pleiads, a new-kindled star,
If any sparkles than the rest more bright,
'Tis she that shines in that propitious light.

When in mid-air the golden trump shall sound,
To raise the nations under ground;
When in the Valley of Jehoshaphat
The judging God shall close the book of Fate,
And there the last assizes keep
For those who wake and those who sleep;

When rattling bones together fly
From the four corners of the sky;
When sinews o'er the skeletons are spread,
Those clothed with flesh, and life inspires the dead;
The sacred poets first shall hear the sound,
And foremost from the tomb shall bound,
For they are covered with the lightest ground;
And straight, with inborn vigor, on the wing,
Like mounting larks, to the new morning sing.
There thou, sweet saint, before the quire shalt go,
As harbinger of Heaven, the way to show,
The way which thou so well hast learned below.

A SONG

Fair, sweet, and young, receive a prize
Reserved for your victorious eyes:
From crowds whom at your feet you see,
Oh pity and distinguish me!
As I from thousand beauties more
Distinguish you, and only you adore.

Your face for conquest was designed,
Your every motion charms my mind;
Angels, when you your silence break,
Forget their hymns to hear you speak;
But when at once they hear and view,
Are loth to mount, and long to stay with you.

No graces can your form improve,
But all are lost, unless you love;
While that sweet passion you disdain,
Your veil and beauty are in vain:
In pity then prevent my fate,
For after dying all reprieve's too late.

LINES PRINTED UNDER MILTON'S PORTRAIT

In Tonson's Folio Edition of the 'Paradise Lost,' 1688

Three poets, in three distant ages born,
Greece, Italy, and England did adorn.
The first in loftiness of thought surpassed,
The next in majesty, in both the last:
The force of Nature could no farther go;
To make a third she joined the former two.

ALEXANDER'S FEAST; OR, THE POWER OF MUSIC

A Song in Honor of St. Cecilia's Day: 1697

I

'Twas at the royal feast for Persia won
By Philip's warlike son:
Aloft in awful state
The godlike hero sate
On his imperial throne;
His valiant peers were placed around;
Their brows with roses and with myrtles bound:
(So should desert in arms be crowned.)
The lovely Thais, by his side,
Sate like a blooming Eastern bride,
In flower of youth and beauty's pride.
Happy, happy, happy pair!
None but the brave,
None but the brave,
None but the brave deserves the fair.

CHORUS

Happy, happy, happy pair!
None but the brave,
None but the brave,
None but the brave deserves the fair.

II

Timotheus, placed on high
Amid the tuneful quire,
With flying fingers touched the lyre:
The trembling notes ascend the sky,
And heavenly joys inspire.
The song began from Jove,
Who left his blissful seats above,
(Such is the power of mighty love.)
A dragon's fiery form belied the god:
Sublime on radiant spires he rode,
When he to fair Olympia pressed:
And while he sought her snowy breast,
Then round her slender waist he curled,
And stamped an image of himself, a sovereign of the world.

The listening crowd admire the lofty sound
A present deity, they shout around;
A present deity, the vaulted roofs rebound:
With ravished ears
The monarch hears,
Assumes the god,
Affects to nod,
And seems to shake the spheres.

CHORUS

With ravished ears
The monarch hears,
Assumes the god,
Affects to nod,
And seems to shake the spheres.

III

The praise of Bacchus then the sweet musician sung,
Of Bacchus ever fair, and ever young.
The jolly god in triumph comes;
Sound the trumpets, beat the drums;
Flushed with a purple grace
He shows his honest face:
Now give the hautboys breath; he comes, he comes.
Bacchus, ever fair and young,
Drinking joys did first ordain;
Bacchus's blessings are a treasure,
Drinking is the soldier's pleasure;
Rich the treasure,
Sweet the pleasure,
Sweet is pleasure after pain.

CHORUS

Bacchus's blessings are a treasure,
Drinking is the soldier's pleasure;
Rich the treasure,
Sweet the pleasure,
Sweet is pleasure after pain.

IV

Soothed with the sound, the king grew vain;
Fought all his battles o'er again;
And thrice he routed all his foes, and thrice he slew the slain.

The master saw the madness rise,
His glowing cheeks, his ardent eyes;
And while he heaven and earth defied,
Changed his hand, and checked his pride.
He chose a mournful Muse,
Soft pity to infuse;
He sung Darius great and good,
By too severe a fate,
Fallen, fallen, fallen, fallen,
Fallen from his high estate,
And weltering in his blood;
Deserted at his utmost need
By those his former bounty fed;
On the bare earth exposed he lies,
With not a friend to close his eyes.
With downcast looks the joyless victor sate,
Revolving in his altered soul
The various turn of chance below;
And now and then a sigh he stole,
And tears began to flow.

CHORUS

Revolving in his altered soul
The various turns of chance below;
And now and then a sigh he stole,
And tears began to flow.

V

The mighty master smiled to see
That love was in the next degree;
'Twas but a kindred sound to move,
For pity melts the mind to love.
Softly sweet, in Lydian measures,
Soon he soothed his soul to pleasures.
War, he sung, is toil and trouble;
Honor but an empty bubble,
Never ending, still beginning,
Fighting still, and still destroying:
If the world be worth thy winning,
Think, oh think it worth enjoying:
Lovely Thais sits beside thee;
Take the good the gods provide thee;
The many rend the skies with loud applause;
So Love was crowned, but Music won the cause.

The prince, unable to conceal his pain,
Gazed on the fair
Who caused his care,
And sighed and looked, sighed and looked,
Sighed and looked, and sighed again;
At length, with love and wine at once oppressed,
The vanquished victor sunk upon her breast.

CHORUS

The prince, unable to conceal his pain,
Gazed on the fair
Who caused his care,
And sighed and looked, sighed and looked,
Sighed and looked, and sighed again;
At length, with love and wine at once oppressed,
The vanquished victor sunk upon her breast.

VI

Now strike the golden lyre again;
A louder yet, and yet a louder strain.
Break his bands of sleep asunder,
And rouse him, like a rattling peal of thunder.
Hark, hark, the horrid sound
Has raised up his head;
As awaked from the dead,
And amazed, he stares around.
Revenge, revenge, Timotheus cries,
See the Furies arise;
See the snakes that they rear,
How they hiss in their hair,
And the sparkles that flash from their eyes!
Behold a ghastly band,
Each a torch in his hand!
Those are Grecian ghosts, that in battle were slain,
And unburied remain
Inglorious on the plain:
Give the vengeance due
To the valiant crew.
Behold how they toss their torches on high,
How they point to the Persian abodes,
And glittering temples of their hostile gods!
The princes applaud with a furious joy;

And the king seized a flambeau with zeal to destroy;
Thais led the way,
To light him to his prey,
And like another Helen, fired another Troy.

CHORUS

And the king seized a flambeau with zeal to destroy;
Thais led the way,
To light him to his prey,
And like another Helen, fired another Troy.

VII

Thus long ago,
Ere heaving bellows learned to blow,
While organs yet were mute,
Timotheus, to his breathing flute
And sounding lyre,
Could swell the soul to rage, or kindle soft desire.
At last divine Cecilia came,
Inventress of the vocal frame;
The sweet enthusiast, from her sacred store,
Enlarged the former narrow bounds,
And added length to solemn sounds,
With Nature's mother wit, and arts unknown before.
Let old Timotheus yield the prize,
Or both divide the crown:
He raised a mortal to the skies;
She drew an angel down.

GRAND CHORUS

At last divine Cecilia came,
Inventress of the vocal frame;
The sweet enthusiast, from her sacred store,
Enlarged the former narrow bounds,
And added length to solemn sounds,
With Nature's mother wit, and arts unknown before.
Let old Timotheus yield the prize,
Or both divide the crown:
He raised a mortal to the skies;
She drew an angel down.

ACHITOPHEL*

From ‘Absalom and Achitophel’

This plot, which failed for want of common-sense,
Had yet a deep and dangerous consequence:
For as when raging fevers boil the blood,
The standing lake soon floats into a flood,
And every hostile humor, which before
Slept quiet in its channels, bubbles o'er;
So several factions from this first ferment
Work up to foam, and threat the government.
Some by their friends, more by themselves thought wise,
Opposed the power to which they could not rise.
Some had in courts been great, and thrown from thence,
Like fiends were hardened in impenitence.
Some, by their monarch's fatal mercy, grown
From pardoned rebels kinsmen to the throne,
Were raised in power and public office high;
Strong bands, if bands ungrateful men could tie.
Of these the false Achitophel was first;
A name to all succeeding ages curst:
For close designs and crooked councils fit;
Sagacious, bold, and turbulent of wit;
Restless, unfixed in principles and place;
In power unpleased, impatient of disgrace:
A fiery soul, which, working out its way,
Fretted the pigmy body to decay,
And o'er-informed the tenement of clay.
A daring pilot in extremity;
Pleased with the danger, when the waves went high
He sought the storms; but for a calm unfit,
Would steer too nigh the sands to boast his wit.
Great wits are sure to madness near allied,
And thin partitions do their bounds divide;
Else why should he, with wealth and honor blest,
Refuse his age the needful hours of rest?
Punish a body which he could not please;
Bankrupt of life, yet prodigal of ease?
And all to leave what with his toil he won,
To that unfeathered two-legged thing, a son;
Got while his soul did huddled notions try,
And born a shapeless lump, like anarchy.

* Lord Shaftesbury.

In friendship false, implacable in hate;
Resolved to ruin or to rule the State.
To compass this the triple bond he broke,
The pillars of the public safety shook,
And fitted Israel for a foreign yoke:
Then, seized with fear yet still affecting fame,
Usurped a patriot's all-atoning name.
So easy still it proves in factious times,
With public zeal to cancel private crimes.
How safe is treason, and how sacred ill,
Where none can sin against the people's will!
Where crowds can wink, and no offense be known,
Since in another's guilt they find their own!
Yet fame deserved no enemy can grudge;
The statesman we abhor, but praise the judge.
In Israel's courts ne'er sat an Abethdin
With more discerning eyes, or hands more clean,
Unbribed, unsought, the wretched to redress;
Swift of dispatch, and easy of access.
Oh! had he been content to serve the Crown,
With virtues only proper to the gown;
Or had the rankness of the soil been freed
From cockle that oppressed the noble seed;
David for him his tuneful harp had strung,
And heaven had wanted one immortal song.
But wild Ambition loves to slide, not stand,
And Fortune's ice prefers to Virtue's land.
Achitophel, grown weary to possess
A lawful fame, and lazy happiness,
Disdained the golden fruit to gather free,
And lent the crowd his arm to shake the tree.
Now, manifest of crimes contrived long since,
He stood at bold defiance with his prince;
Held up the buckler of the people's cause
Against the Crown, and skulked behind the laws.
The wished occasion of the plot he takes;
Some circumstances finds, but more he makes.
By buzzing emissaries fills the ears
Of listening crowds with jealousies and fears
Of arbitrary counsels brought to light,
And proves the king himself a Jebusite.

MAXIME DU CAMP

(1822–1894)

"Why have I always felt happy, filled with the spirit of content and of infinite independence, whenever I have slept in the tent or in the ruins of foreign lands?" The love of change and adventure has been the spring of Du Camp's life, a life whose events are blended so intimately with his literary achievement, that to know the one is to know the other. This practical man of the world has an imaginative, beauty-loving side to his nature, which craves stimulus from tropical unfamiliar nature and exotic ways.

So, after the usual training of French boys in lycée and college,—"in those hideous houses where they wearied our childhood," as he says,—the just-emancipated youth of twenty-two left his home in Paris for an eighteen-months' trip in the far East. The color and variety of the experience whetted his love of travel, and very soon after his return he began a serious study of photography in view of future plans.

Maxime Du Camp

Then came the revolution of 1848, the overthrow of Louis Philippe; and Du Camp had an opportunity to prove his courage and patriotism in the ranks of the National Guard. In his 'Souvenirs de l'Année 1848,' he tells the story with color and interest, and with the forceful logic of an eye-witness.

His bravery and a serious wound won him the red ribbon of the Legion of Honor, bestowed by General Cavaignac. This drew attention to him, and led the minister of public instruction to intrust him a few months later with a mission of exploration to Egypt, Nubia, Palestine, and Asia Minor; a result of which trip was his first literary success. Utilizing his photographic knowledge, he collected a great many negatives for future development. Upon his return he published a volume of descriptive sketches, 'Le Nil, Egypte, et Nubie,' generously illustrated with printed reproductions of these pictures. This first combination of photography and typography was popular, and was speedily imitated, initiative of many illustrated books.

Later, Du Camp's warlike and exploring instincts led him at his own expense into Sicily with Garibaldi, where he collected matter and photographs for 'Les Deux Siciles,' another successful volume. In 1851 he associated with others to found the Revue de Paris, for which he wrote regularly until its suspension in 1858. He has also written a great deal for the Revue des Deux Mondes, in which for several years he continued a series of historical studies upon the government of Paris. The six volumes upon 'Paris: its Organs, its Functions, its Life, during the Second Half of the Nineteenth Century,' form one of his chief achievements. His personal knowledge on the subject, and his access to valuable unpublished documents, give it authoritative value.

In 'Les Ancêtres de la Commune,' and 'Les Convulsions de Paris,' he has accomplished much more in the same line. The latter, a brilliant circumstantial exposition of the Commune, a logical condemnation of its folly and ignorance, brought him gratitude from the French Academy, and aided his election to that body in 1880. For this extensive work on contemporary politics, for his illustrated travels, and his artistic and literary criticism, he is better known than for his two or three novels and volumes of poetry.

Du Camp's may be characterized as a soldierly style, strong, direct, and personal. He loves to retrace old scenes with the later visible sequence of cause and effect. Always straightforward, sometimes bluntly self-assertive, he is sometimes eloquent. Perhaps his great charm is spontaneity.

A STREET SCENE DURING THE COMMUNE

From 'The Convulsions of Paris'

There were strange episodes during this terrible evening. At half-past eight, M. Rouville, a Protestant minister, was at home in a house he owns on the Rue de Lille. He heard an alarm, the cry, « Everything is burning! Escape! » Then he went down, saw the street in flames, and the poor people weeping as they escaped. Just as he was returning to rescue a few valuables, some federates rushed into the court, crying, « Hurry! They are setting the place on fire! » He took some money and the manuscript of the sermons he had preached. Mechanically he seized his hat and cane. Then, throwing a last look around the apartment where he had long lived, invoking the memory of the great Biblical destructions familiar to him in Holy Writ, weak and trembling with emotion, he descended the staircase from his home.

There was indescribable tumult in the street, dominated by the cry of women; a shrill wordless involuntary cry of terror, vibrating above the uproar like a desperate appeal to which no supernatural power replied. Pastor Rouville stopped. The house next his own was in flames. They were setting fire to the one opposite. The houses between the Rue de Beaune and the Rue du Bac, red from cellar to garret, were vomiting flame from all the broken windows.

The pastor's family were not at Paris. He was alone with a faithful maid, who did not leave him for a moment. This doubtless determined his resolution, and gave him courage to brave all to save his house. If he had felt his wife and daughter near, he would have thought only of their safety, and would have hastened to get them away from the place, where, he said, "One could die of horror."

Pastor Rouville is a small man, whose great activity keeps him young and remarkably energetic. He belongs to the strong race of Southern Protestants, which has resisted everything to guard its faith. I should not be surprised if he has had some nimble Cévennole, companion of Jean Cavalier, among his ancestors. Chaplain in the prisons of the Seine, accustomed to sound doubtful spirits, to seek in vicious hearts some intact fibres which could re-attach them to virtue; fervent in faith, eloquent, with a high voice which could rise above the tumult, knowing by experience that there is no obscurity so profound that light cannot be made to penetrate it,—he had remained on duty at his post during the Commune; for the prisoners had more need of spiritual aid, now that the regular administration no longer watched over them. He had been indignant at the incarceration of Catholic priests, and had signed the fine protest demanding the liberty of the archbishop, which the ministers had carried to the Hôtel de Ville.

Alone in the presence of the great disaster which threatened him, he commended his spirit to God, remembering that the little stone of David had killed the giant Philistine, and he decided to fight for his home. He encamped energetically before the door, to forbid access; and using the weapons bestowed upon him by Providence and study, he spoke. The federates stopped before this man, whose simplicity rendered him heroic. One may guess what he said to them:—

"Why strike the innocent and tender, as if they were execrable? Why be enraged with a Protestant, a minister, whose religion, founded on the dogma of free examination, is naturally allied to republican ideas? The faith he teaches is that promulgated by Christ: Christ said to Peter, 'Sheathe thy sword;' he said to men, 'Love one another!' No, the people of Paris, this people whose sufferings have been shared, whose unfortunates have been succored during the siege; this people, so good when not led astray by the wicked; this people will not burn the house of a poor minister, whose whole life has been passed in the exercise of charity."

The pastor must have been eloquent and have spoken with profound conviction, for the federates who were listening to him began to weep, then seized and embraced him. Meantime the tenants of the shops in his house had lowered the iron curtains, which at least was an obstacle against the first throwing of petroleum. This lasted an hour. The federates, evidently softened and touched by the pastor's despair, remained near him and had pity upon him. An old sergeant of the National Guard stayed beside him, as if to bring him help in case of need, and to maintain a little order among his subordinates. Some hope revived in M. Rouville's heart, and he was saying to himself that perhaps his house would be spared, when some young men, wearing the braided caps of officers, arrived as if to inspect the fires. Seeing one house intact, emerging like a little island from an ocean of flames, they exclaimed. The pastor sprang forward and wanted to argue with them. It was trouble wasted. One of these young scamps said to him, "You are an old reactionist: you bore us with your talking. If you don't like it, we will pin you to the wall." Then, turning toward the federates and pointing to the houses on the Rue de Lille, he cried, "All that belongs to the people. The people have the right to burn everything."

This had perhaps decided the fate of the pastor's house, when the sergeant of federates interfered, and addressing the officer said to him, "I have received orders to stop the fire just here." "Show me your order," answered the officer. The sergeant replied, "It is a verbal order." Then there was a lively quarrel between the two men. The sergeant was firm. The officer insisted, and according to the custom of the moment, threatened to have the rebel shot.

The situation was becoming grave, when an incident resolved it. A mounted officer galloped up and ordered all the federates to retreat, because they were about to be surrounded by the troops from Versailles.

Nearly all the National Guards hurried away. The sergeant who had remained near the pastor said, « Get away, scurry, father! You will get yourself killed, and that will not save your camp. »

The other officers passed, commanded everything to be burned, and when the sergeant resisted, compelled him to leave. For half an hour the unhappy pastor remained alone, holding back the incendiaries, passing from supplications to threats, and gaining time by every possible artifice. The sergeant returned with tearful eyes, and showed the dismayed pastor a written order to burn the house, sent by his chiefs. Not yet discouraged, the pastor roused the compassion of the old sergeant, and so moved him that the rebel cried, « Ah, well! so much the worse! I'll disobey. No, I won't let your house be burned. They'll shoot me. It's all the same. I deserve to be. » Then raising his hand toward the sky, where the stars shone like sparks through the veil of wind-driven smoke, he cried « O my father, I believe in God! Fear nothing; I will stay here. They shan't touch your house. I shall know how to keep off plunderers! »

O strange deceiving people; ready for all crimes, ready for all good actions, according to the voice which speaks to thee and the emotion which carries thee away! This sergeant was indeed thy likeness, and one need not despair of thee, although thou dishearten those who love thee best!

The brandy at the wine merchants'; the ether at the druggists'; the powder and shot forgotten in stations, or secreted in cellars, burst with terrible explosions and scattered flaming coals. The pastor looked at his house, still miraculously intact. He gave it a last look, and departed sobbing. It was eleven o'clock. For three hours in the midst of this furnace he had resisted the incendiaries. His strength was exhausted. The faithful servant, who went back again and again to rescue one thing more from the burning, dragged him away. In the Rue des Saints-Pères they plunged into darkness, all the deeper for the brazier of sparkling lights behind them. They groped their way over the barricades through a shower of bullets. More than once they fell down. Finally, safe and sound despite the dangers braved, they reached the Rue de Seine, near the Rue de Bucy, where they found refuge in a lodging-house.

Next day Pastor Rouville ran towards the Rue de Lille. His house was standing intact. The old sergeant had kept his word. What became of this brave man, who at the risk of his life saved the property of a man whose speech had touched him? Perhaps he perished. Perhaps he received his due reward. Perhaps he drags out a wretched life in some workshop of a penitentiary. I know not his fate, nor even his name.

ALEXANDRE DUMAS, SENIOR

(1803?–1870)

BY ANDREW LANG

No author is less capable of being illustrated by extracts than Alexandre Dumas. Writers like Prosper Mérimée or Mr. Robert Louis Stevenson can be not inadequately represented by a short story or a brief scene. Even from Scott's work we can detach 'Wandering Willie's Tale,' or 'The Tapestried Chamber,' or the study of Effie Deans in prison, or of Jeanie Deans before the Queen. But Dumas is invariably diffuse; though, unlike other diffuse talkers and writers, he is seldom tedious. He is long without *longueurs*. A single example will explain this better than a page of disquisition. The present selector had meant to extract Dumas's first meeting with Charles Nodier at the theatre. In memory, that amusing scene appeared to occupy some six pages. In fact, it covers nearly a hundred and thirty pages of the Brussels edition of the 'Memoirs' of Dumas. One reads it with such pleasure that looked back upon, it seems short, while it is infinitely too long to be extracted. In dialogue Dumas is both excellent and copious, so that he cannot well be abbreviated. He is the Porthos of novelists, gigantic, yet (at his best) muscular and not overgrown. For these reasons, extracts out of his romances do no justice to Dumas. To read one of his novels, say 'The Three Musketeers,' even in a slovenly translation, is to know more of him than a world of critics and essayists can teach. It is also to forget the world, and to dwell in a careless Paradise. Our object therefore is not to give an «essence of Dumas,» but to make readers peruse him in his own books, and to save them trouble by indicating, among these books, the best.

It is notorious that Dumas was at the head of a «Company» like that which Scott laughingly proposed to form «for writing and publishing the class of books called Waverley Novels.» In legal phrase, Dumas «deviled» his work; he had assistants, «researchers,» collaborators. He would briefly sketch a plot, indicate the authorities to be consulted, hand his notes to Maquet or Fiorentino, receive their draught, and expand that into a romance. Work thus executed cannot be equal to itself. Many books signed by Dumas may be neglected without loss. Even to his best works, one or other of his assistants was apt to assert a claim. The answer is convincing. Not one of these ingenious men ever produced, by himself, anything that could be mistaken for the work of the master. All his good things have the same stamp and the same spirit, which we find nowhere else. Again, nobody contests his authorship of his own 'Memoirs,' or of his book about his dogs, birds, and other beasts—'The Story of My Pets.' Now, the merit of these productions is, in kind, identical with many of the merits of his best novels. There is the same good-humor, gayety, and fullness of life. We may therefore read Dumas's central romances without much fear of being grateful to the wrong person. Against the modern theory that the Iliad and Odyssey are the work of many hands in many ages, we can urge that these supposed «hands» never did anything nearly so good for themselves; and the same argument applies in the case of Alexandre Dumas.

A brief sketch of his life must now be given. «No man has had so many of his possessions disputed as myself,» says Dumas. Not only his right to his novels, but his right to his name and to legitimate birth, was contested. Here we shall follow his own account of himself in his 'Memoirs,' which do not cover nearly the whole of his life. Alexandre Dumas was born at Villers-Cotterets-sur-Aisne, on July 24th, 1803(?). He lived to almost exactly the threescore and ten years of the Psalmist. He saw the fall of Napoleon, the restoration of the rightful king, the expulsion of the Legitimate monarch in 1830, the Orleans rule, its overthrow in 1848, the Republic, the Empire, and the Terrible Year, 1870-1871. Then he died, in the hour of the sorrow of his

«Immortal and indomitable France.»

Dumas's full name was noble: he was Alexandre Dumas-Davy de la Pailleterie. His family estate, La Pailleterie, was made a marquisate by Louis XIV. in 1707. About 1760 the grandfather of Dumas sold his lands in France, and went to Hayti. There in 1762 was born his father, son of Louise Cossette Dumas and of the Marquis de la Pailleterie. The mother must have been a woman of color; Dumas talks of his father's «mulatto hue,» and he himself had undoubted traces of African blood. Yet it appears that the grandparents were duly married. In 1772, his wife having died, the old marquis returned to France. The Revolution broke out, and the father of Alexandre Dumas fought in the armies of the Republic. The cruel mob called him by way of mockery, «Monsieur Humanity,» because he endeavored to rescue the victims of their ferocity. He was a man of great courage and enormous physical strength. Napoleon, in honor of one of his feats of arms, called him in a dispatch «The Horatius Cocles of the Republic.» He was with Napoleon in

ALEXANDRE DUMAS.

Egypt, where a quarrel arose, as he suspected and opposed the ambition of the future emperor. Though Dumas found a treasure in a bey's house, he honorably presented it to his government. He died in France, a poor man, in 1806.

Dumas was not at home when his father died. He was staying, a child of four, with his cousin Marianne.

«At midnight I was awakened, or rather my cousin and I were awakened, by a great blow struck on the door of our room. By the light of a night lamp I saw my cousin start up, much alarmed. No mortal could have knocked at our chamber door, for the outer doors were locked. [He gives a plan of the house.] I got out of bed to open the door. 'Where are you going, Alexandre?' cried my cousin.

«'To let in papa, who is coming to say adieu.'

«The girl dragged me back to bed; I cried, 'Adieu, papa, adieu!' Something like a sighing breath passed over my face. . . . My father had died at the hour when we heard the knock!»

This anecdote may remind the reader of what occurred at Abbotsford on the night when Mr. Bullock died in London. Dumas tells another tale of the same kind ('Memoirs,' Vol. xi., page 255: Brussels, 1852). On the night of his mother's death he in vain sought a similar experience. These things «come not by observation»; but Dumas, like Scott, had a mind not untuned to such themes, though not superstitious.

Young Dumas, like most men of literary genius, taught himself to read. A Buffon with plates was the treasure of the child, already a lover of animals. To know more about the beasts he learned to read for his own pleasure. Of mythology he was as fond as Keats. His intellectual life began (like the imaginative life of our race) in legends of beasts and gods. For Dumas was born *un primitif*, as the French say; his taste was the old immortal human taste for romance, for tales of adventure, love, and war. This predilection is now of course often scouted by critics who are over-civilized and under-educated. Superior persons will never share the love of Dumas which was common to Thackeray and Mr. Robert Louis Stevenson. From Buffon he went on to the 'Letters to Émil' (letters on mythology), and to the 'Arabian Nights.' An imaginative child, he knew the «pains of sleep» as Coleridge did, and the terrors of vain imagination. Many children whose manhood is not marked by genius are visionaries. A visionary too was little Dumas, like Scott, Coleridge, and George Sand in childhood. To the material world he ever showed a bold face. «I have never known doubt or despair,» he says; his faith in God was always unshaken; the doctrine of immortality he regarded rather with hope than absolute belief. Yet surely it is a corollary to the main article of his creed.

At ten, Dumas went to a private school kept by an Abbé Grégoire. At the Restoration, a boy of twelve, he made and he adhered to an important resolution. He chose to keep his grandmaternal name of Dumas, like his father, and to drop the name and arms of De la Pailleterie, with all the hopes of boons from the restored Royalists. Dumas remained a man of the popular party, though he had certain relations of friendship with the house of Orléans. But he entertained no posthumous hatred of the old monarchy and the old times. His kings are nearly as good, in his romances, as Sir Walter's own, and his Henri III. and Henri IV. may be named with Scott's Gentle King Jamie and Louis XI.

Madame Dumas, marquise as she was by marriage, kept a tobacconist's shop; and in education, Dumas was mainly noted for his calligraphy. Poaching was now the boy's favorite amusement; all through his life he was very fond of sport. Napoleon returned from Elba; Dumas saw him drive through Villers-Cotterets on his way to Waterloo. Soon afterwards came in stragglers; the English, they said, had been defeated at five o'clock on June 18th, but the Prussians arrived at six o'clock and won the battle. What the English were doing between five and six does not appear; it hardly seems that they quitted the field. The theory of that British defeat at Waterloo was never abandoned by Dumas. He saw Napoleon return through Villers-Cotterets. «Wellington, Bülow, Blücher, were but masks of men; really they were spirits sent by the Most High to defeat Napoleon.» It is a pious opinion!

At the age of fifteen Dumas, like Scott, became a notary's clerk. About this time he saw 'Hamlet' played, in the version of Ducis. Corneille and Racine had always been disliked by this born romanticist. 'Hamlet' carried him off his feet. Soon afterwards he read Bürger's 'Lenore,' the ballad which Scott translated at the very beginning of his career as an author.

«Tramp! tramp! along the land they rode,
Splash! splash! along the sea;
The scourge is red, the spur drops blood,
The flashing pebbles flee.»

This German ballad, says Scott, «struck him as the kind of thing he could do himself.» And Dumas found that the refrain

«Hurrah, fantôme, les morts vont vite,»

was more to his taste than the French poetry of the eighteenth century. He tried to translate 'Lenore.' Scott finished it in a night; Dumas gave up in despair. But this, he says, was the beginning of his authorship. He had not yet opened a volume of Scott or Cooper, «ces deux grands romanciers.» With a friend named Leuven he began to try to write plays (1820–1821). He now poached his way to Paris, defraying his expenses with the game he shot on the road. Shakespeare too was a poacher; let us excuse the eccentricities of genius. He made Talma's acquaintance; he went to the play; he resigned his clerkship: «Paris was my future.» Thither he went; his father's name served him with General Foy, and he obtained a little post in the household of the Duc D'Orléans — a supernumerary secretaryship at £60 a year. At the play he met Charles Nodier, reading the rarest of Elzevirs, and at intervals (like Charles Lamb) hissing his own piece! This delightful scene, with its consequences, occupies one hundred and thirty pages!

Dumas now made the acquaintance of Frederic Soulié, and became a pillar of theatres. He began to read with a purpose: first he read Scott; «The clouds lifted, and I beheld new horizons.» Then he turned to Cooper; then to Byron. One day he entered his office, crying aloud, «Byron is dead!» «Who is Byron?» said one of his chiefs. Here Dumas breaks off in his 'Memoirs' to give a life of Byron! He fought his first duel in the snow, and won an easy, almost a bloodless victory. For years he and Leuven wrote plays together,— plays which were never accepted.

At last he, Rousseau (not Jean Jacques!), and Leuven composed a piece together. Refused at one house, it was accepted at another: 'La Chasse et l'Amour' (The Chase and Love) was presented on September 22d, 1823. It succeeded. A volume of three short stories sold to the extent of four copies. Dumas saw that he must «make a name» before he could make a livelihood. «I do not believe in neglected talent and unappreciated genius,» says he. Like Mr. Arthur Pendennis, he wrote verses «up to» pictures. Thackeray did the same. «Lady Blessington once sent him an album print of a boy and girl fishing, with a request that he would make some verses for it. 'And,' he said, 'I liked the idea, and set about it at once. I was two entire days at it,— was so occupied with it, so engrossed by it, that I did not shave during the whole time.'» So says Mr. Locker-Lampson.

We cannot all be Dumas or Thackeray. But if any literary beginner reads these lines, let him take Dumas's advice; let him disbelieve in neglected genius, and do the work that comes in his way, as best he can. Dumas had a little anonymous success in 1826, a vaudeville at the Porte-Saint-Martin. At last he achieved a serious tragedy, or melodrama, in verse, 'Christine.' He wrote to Nodier, reminding him of their meeting at the play. The author of 'Trilby' introduced him to Taylor; Taylor took him to the Théâtre Français; 'Christine' was read and accepted unanimously.

Dumas now struck the vein of his fortune. By chance he opened a volume of Anquetil, and read an anecdote of the court of Henri III.

This led him to study the history of Saint Megrin, in the Memoirs of L'Estoile, where he met Quelus, and Maugiron, and Bussy d'Amboise, with the stirring tale of his last fight against twelve men. Out of these facts he made his play 'Henri III.,' and the same studies inspired that trilogy of romances 'La Reine Margot' (Queen Margot), 'La Dame de Monsoreau' (The Lady of Monsoreau), and 'Les Quarante-Cinq' (The Forty-Five). These are, with the trilogy of the 'Mousquetaires,' his central works as a romancer, and he was twenty-five when he began to deal with the romance of history. His habit was to narrate his play or novel, to his friends, to invent as he talked, and so to arrive at his general plan. The mere writing gave him no trouble. We shall later show his method in the composition of 'The Three Musketeers.'

'Christine' had been wrecked among the cross-currents of theatrical life. 'Henri III.' was more fortunate. Dumas was indeed obliged to choose between his little office and the stage; he abandoned his secretaryship. In 1829 occurred this «duel between his past and his future.» Just before the first night of the drama, Dumas's mother, whom he tenderly loved, was stricken down by paralysis. He tended her, he watched over his piece, he almost dragged the Duc d'Orléans to the theatre. On that night he made the acquaintance of Hugo and Alfred de Vigny. Dumas passed the evening between the theatre and his mother's bedside. When the curtain fell, he was «called on»; the audience stood up uncovered, the Duc d'Orléans and all!

Next morning Dumas, like Byron, «woke to find himself famous.» He had «made his name» in the only legitimate way,—by his work. Troubles followed, difficulties with the Censorship, duels and rumors of duels, and the whole romantic upheaval which accompanied the Revolution of 1830. Dumas was attached again to the Orléans household. He dabbled in animal magnetism, which had been called mesmerism, and now is known as hypnotism. The phenomena are the same; only the explanations vary. About 1830 there was a mania for animal magnetism in Paris; Lady Louisa Stuart recounted some of the marvels to Sir Walter Scott, who treated the reports with disdain. When writing his romance 'Joseph Balsamo' (a tale of the French Revolution), Dumas made studies of animal magnetism, and was, or believed himself to be, an adept. The orthodox party of modern hypnotists merely hold that by certain physical means, a state of somnambulism can be produced in certain people. Once in that state, the patients are subject to «suggestion,» and are obedient to the will of the hypnotizer. He for his part exerts no «magnetic current,» no novel unexplained force or fluid. Some recent French and English experiments are not easily to be reconciled with this hypothesis. Dumas himself believed that he exerted a magnetic force, and without any «passes» or other mechanical means, could hypnotize persons who did not know what he was about, and so were not influenced by «suggestion.» In a few cases he held that his patients became clairvoyant; one of them made many political prophecies,—all unfulfilled. Another, in trance, improved vastly as a singer; «her normal voice stopped at *contre-si*. I bade her rise to *contre-re*, which she did; though incapable of it when awake.» So far, this justifies the plot of Mr. Du Maurier's novel 'Trilby.' Dumas offers no theory; he states facts, as he says, including «post-hypnotic suggestion.»

These experiments were made by Dumas merely as part of his studies for 'Joseph Balsamo' (Cagliostro); his conclusion was that hypnotism is not yet reduced to a scientific formula. In fiction it is already overworked. Dumas got his 'Christine' acted at last. Then broke out the Revolution of 1830. Dumas's description of his activity is «as good as a novel,» but too long and varied for condensation. It seems better to give this extract about his life of poverty before his mother died, before fame visited him. (I quote Miss Cheape's translation of the passage included in her 'Stories of Beasts,' published by Longmans, Green and Company.)

He had, in later years, named a cat Mysouff II.

«If you won't think me impertinent, sir,» said Madame Lamarque, «I should so like to know what Mysouff means.»

«Mysouff just means Mysouff, Madame Lamarque.»

«It is a cat's name, then?»

«Certainly, since Mysouff the First was so-called. It is true, Madame Lamarque, you never knew Mysouff.» And I became so thoughtful that Madame Lamarque was kind enough to withdraw quietly, without asking any questions about Mysouff the First.

That name had taken me back to fifteen years ago, when my mother was still living. I had then the great happiness of having a mother to scold me sometimes. At the time I speak of, I held a situation in the service of the Duc d'Orléans, with a salary of 1500 francs. My work occupied me from ten in the morning until five in the afternoon. We had a cat in those days, whose name was Mysouff. This cat had missed his vocation; he ought to have been a dog. Every morning I started for my office at half-past nine, and came back every evening at half-past five. Every morning Mysouff followed me to the corner of a particular street, and every evening I found him in the same street, at the same corner, waiting for me. Now the curious thing was that on the days when I had found some amusement elsewhere, and was not coming home to dinner, it was of no use to open the door for Mysouff to go and meet me. Mysouff, in the attitude of the serpent with its tail in its mouth, refused to stir from his cushion. On the other hand, on the days I did come, Mysouff would scratch at the door until some one opened it for him. My mother was very fond of Mysouff; she used to call him her barometer.

«Mysouff marks my good and my bad weather,» my dear mother would say: «the days you come in are my days of sunshine; my rainy days are when you stay away.»

When I came home I used to see Mysouff at the street corner, sitting quite still and gazing into the distance. As soon as he caught sight of me, he began to move his tail; then as I drew nearer, he rose and walked backward and forward across the pavement with his back arched and his tail in the air. When I reached him, he jumped up upon me as a dog would have done, and bounded and played round me as I walked towards the house; but when I was close to it he dashed in at full speed. Two seconds after, I used to see my mother at the door.

Never again in this world, but perhaps in the next, I shall see her standing waiting for me at the door.

That is what I was thinking of, dear readers, when the name of Mysouff brought back all these recollections; so you understand why I did not answer Madame Lamarque's question.

The life of Dumas after 1830 need not be followed step by step; indeed, for lack of memoirs, to follow it is by no means easy.

Dumas, by dint of successful plays, and later of successful novels, earned large sums of money—£40,000 in one year, it is said. He traveled far and wide, and compiled books of travel. In the forties, before the Revolution of 1848, he built a kind of Abbotsford of his own, named «Monte Cristo,» near St. Germains, and joyously ruined himself. «Monte Cristo,» like Abbotsford, has been described as a palace. Now, Abbotsford is so far from being a palace that Mr. Hope Scott, when his wife, Scott's granddaughter, inherited the place, was obliged to build an additional wing.

At Monte Cristo Dumas kept but one man-servant, Michel (his «Tom Purdie»), who was groom, keeper, porter, gardener, and everything. Nor did Dumas ruin himself by paying exorbitant prices for poor lands, as Scott did. His collection of books and curios was no rival for that of Abbotsford. But like Scott, he gave away money to right and left, and he kept open house. He was eaten up by parasites,—beggars, poor greedy hangers-on of letters, secretaries, above all by tribes of musical people. On every side money flowed from him; hard as he worked, largely as he earned, he spent more. His very dog brought in thirteen other dogs to bed and board. He kept monkeys, cats, eagles, a vulture, a perfect menagerie. His own account of these guests may be read in 'My Pets'; perhaps the most humorous, good-humored, and amusing of all his works.

The Revolution of 1848 impoverished him and drove him from Monte Cristo; not out of debt to his neighbors. Dumas was a cheerful giver, but did not love to «fritter away his money in paying bills.» He started newspapers, such as The Musketeer, and rather lost than gained by a careless editorship. A successful play would enrich him, and he would throw away his gains. He went with Garibaldi on his expedition against the King of Naples, and was received with ingratitude by the Neapolitans.

A friend of Daniel Dunglas Home, the «medium,» he accompanied him to Russia, where Home married a lady of a noble and wealthy family. Returned to France, Dumas found his popularity waning. His plays often failed; he had outlived his success and his generation; he had saved nothing; he had to turn in need to his son Alexandre, the famous dramatist. Finally he died, doubting the security of his own fame, in the year of the sorrows of France.

Dumas is described by Michelet as «a force of nature.» Never was there in modern literature a force more puissant, more capricious, or more genial. His quantity of mind was out of all proportion to its quality. He could learn everything with ease; he was a skilled cook, a fencer; he knew almost as if by intuition the technique and terminology of all arts and crafts. Ignorant of Greek, he criticized and appreciated Homer with an unmatched zest and appreciation. Into the dry bones of history he breathed life, mere names becoming full-blooded fellow-creatures under his spell. His inspiration was derived from Scott, a man far more learned than he, but scarcely better gifted with creative energy. Like Scott he is long, perhaps prolix; like him he is indifferent to niceties of style, does not linger over the choice of words, but serves himself with the first that comes to hand. Scott's wide science of human nature is not his; but his heroes, often rather ruffianly, are seldom mere exemplary young men of no particular mark. More brilliantly and rapidly than Scott, he indicates action in dialogue. He does not aim at the construction of rounded plots; his novels are chronicles which need never stop while his heroes are alive. His plan is to take a canvas of fact, in memoir or history, and to embroider his fantasies on that. Occasionally the canvas (as Mr. Saintsbury says) shows through, and we have blocks of actual history. His 'Joan of Arc' begins as a romance, and ends with a comparatively plain statement of facts too great for any art but Shakespeare's. But as a rule it is not historical facts, it is the fictitious adventures of characters living in an historical atmosphere, that entertain us in Dumas.

The minute inquirer may now compare the sixteenth-century 'Memoirs of Monsieur D'Artagnan' (fictitious memoirs, no doubt) with the use made of them by Dumas in 'The Three Musketeers' and 'Twenty Years After.' The 'Memoirs' (reprinted by the Librairie Illustrée, Paris) gave Dumas his opening scenes; gave him young D'Artagnan, Porthos, Athos, Aramis, Rosnay, De Treville, Milady, the whole complicated intrigue of Milady, D'Artagnan, and De Vardes. They gave him several incidents, duels, and «local color.» By making Milady the wife of Athos, Dumas knotted his plot; he added the journey to England, after the Queen's diamonds; from a subordinate character he borrowed the clerical character of Aramis; a mere hint in the ‹Memoirs› suggested the Bastion Saint-Gervais. The discrimination of character, the dialogue, and many adventures, are Dumas's own; he was aided by Maquet in the actual writing. In a similar way, Brantôme and L'Estoile, in their ‹Memoirs,› supply the canvas of the tales of the Valois cycle.

The beginner in Dumas will assuredly find the following his best works. For the Valois period, ‹The Horoscope› (a good deal neglected), ‹Queen Margot,› ‹The Lady of Monsoreau,› ‹The Forty-Five.› ‹Isabeau of Bavière,› an early novel, deals with the anarchy and misery before the coming of Jeanne d'Arc. For Henri II., ‹The Two Dianas› is indicated. For the times of Richelieu, Mazarin, Louis XIV., we have ‹The Three Musketeers,› ‹Twenty Years After,› and ‹The Viscount of Bragelonne.› These deal with the youth, middle age, old age, and death of D'Artagnan, Porthos, Athos, and Aramis. The Revolutionary novels, ‹Joseph Balsamo,› ‹The Queen's Necklace,› and others, are much less excellent. The Regency is not ill done in ‹The Regent's Daughter›; and ‹The Chevalier of Harmenthal,› with ‹Olympe of Cleves,› has many admirers. Quite apart from these is the immense modern fantasy of ‹The Count of Monte Cristo›; the opening part alone is worthy of the master. ‹The Black Tulip,› so warmly praised by Thackeray, is an innocent little romance of the days of Dutch William. *Les jeunes filles* may read ‹The Black Tulip›: indeed, Dumas does not sacrifice at all to «the Goddess of Lubricity,» even when he describes very lax moralities.

With a knowledge of these books, and of ‹My Pets› and the ‹Memoirs,› any student will find himself at home in Dumas, and can make wider ranges in that great wilderness of fancy. Some autobiographical details will be found in the novel called ‹Ange Pithou.› ‹Isaac Laquedem› was meant to be a romance of the Wandering Jew; only two volumes are published. Philosophy a reader will not find, nor delicate analysis, nor «chiseled style»; but he will be in touch with a great sunny life, rejoicing in all the accidents of existence.

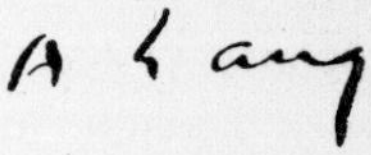

THE CURE FOR DORMICE THAT EAT PEACHES

From ‹The Count of Monte Cristo›

Not on the same night he had intended, but the next morning, the Count of Monte Cristo went out on the road to Orléans. Leaving the village of Linas, without stopping at the telegraph, which at the moment the count passed threw out its long bony arms, he reached the tower of Montlhéry, situated, as every one knows, upon the highest point of the plain of that name. At the foot of the hill the count dismounted, and began to ascend the mountain by a little winding path about eighteen inches wide; when he reached the summit he found himself stopped by a hedge, upon which green fruit had succeeded to red and white flowers.

Monte Cristo looked for the door of the inclosure, and was not long in finding it. It was a little wooden gate, working on willow hinges, and fastened with a nail and string. The count soon understood its mechanism, and the door opened. He then found himself in a little marvelously well-kept garden, about twenty feet long by twelve wide, bounded on one side by part of the hedge, in which was formed the ingenious machine we have named a door; and on the other by the old tower, covered with ivy and studded with wild flowers. Monte Cristo stopped, after having closed the door and fastened the string to the nail, and cast a look around.

«The man at the telegraph,» said he, «must either keep a gardener or devote himself passionately to horticulture.» Suddenly he struck himself against something crouching behind a wheelbarrow filled with leaves; the something rose, uttered an exclamation of astonishment, and Monte Cristo found himself facing a man about fifty years old, who was plucking strawberries, which he was placing upon vine-leaves. He had twelve leaves and about as many strawberries, which, on rising suddenly, he let fall from his hand. «You are gathering your crop, sir?» said Monte Cristo, smiling.

«Excuse me, sir,» replied the man, raising his hand to his cap; «I am not up there, I know, but I have only just come down.»

«Do not let me interfere with you in anything, my friend,» said the count; «gather your strawberries, if indeed there are any left.»

«I have ten left,» said the man, «for here are eleven, and I had twenty-one, five more than last year. But I am not surprised; the spring has been warm this year, and strawberries require heat, sir. This is the reason that, instead of the sixteen I had last year, I have this year, you see, eleven already plucked — twelve, thirteen, fourteen, fifteen, sixteen, seventeen, eighteen. Ah, I miss three! they were here last night, sir — I am sure they were here — I counted them. It must be the son of Mother Simon who has stolen them; I saw him strolling about here this morning. Ah! the young rascal! stealing in a garden; he does not know where that may lead him to.»

«Certainly, it is wrong,» said Monte Cristo, «but you should take into consideration the youth and greediness of the delinquent.»

«Of course,» said the gardener, «but that does not make it the less unpleasant. But, sir, once more I beg pardon; perhaps you are an official that I am detaining here?» And he glanced timidly at the count's blue coat.

«Calm yourself, my friend,» said the count, with that smile which at his will became so terrible or benevolent, and which this time beamed only with the latter expression; «I am not an inspector, but a traveler, conducted here by curiosity he half repents of, since he causes you to lose your time.»

«Ah! my time is not valuable,» replied the man, with a melancholy smile. «Still, it belongs to the government, and I ought not to waste it; but having received the signal that I might rest for an hour» (here he glanced at a sun-dial, for there was everything in the inclosure of Montlhéry, even a sun-dial), «and having ten minutes before me, and my strawberries being ripe, when a day longer — by-the-by, sir, do you think dormice eat them?»

«Indeed, I should think not,» replied Monte Cristo: «dormice are bad neighbors for us who do not eat them preserved, as the Romans did.»

«What! did the Romans eat them?» said the gardener; «eat dormice?»

«I have read so,» said the count.

«Really! They can't be nice, though they do say 'as fat as a dormouse.' It is not a wonder they are fat, sleeping all day, and only waking to eat all night. Listen: last year I had four apricots — they stole one; I had one nectarine, only one — well, sir, they ate half of it on the wall; a splendid nectarine — I never ate a better."

"You ate it?"

"That is to say, the half that was left — you understand; it was exquisite, sir. Ah, those gentlemen never choose the worst morsels; like Mother Simon's son, who has not chosen the worst strawberries. But this year," continued the horticulturist, "I'll take care it shall not happen, even if I should be forced to sit up the whole night to watch when the strawberries are ripe." Monte Cristo had seen enough. Every man has a devouring passion in his heart, as every fruit has its worm; that of the man at the telegraph was horticulture. He began gathering the vine-leaves which screened the sun from the grapes, and won the heart of the gardener. "Did you come here, sir, to see the telegraph?" he said.

"Yes, if not contrary to the rules."

"Oh no," said the gardener; "there are no orders against doing so, providing there is nothing dangerous, and that no one knows what we are saying."

"I have been told," said the count, "that you do not always yourselves understand the signals you repeat."

"Certainly, sir; and that is what I like best," said the man, smiling.

"Why do you like that best?"

"Because then I have no responsibility. I am a machine then, and nothing else; and so long as I work, nothing more is required of me."

"Is it possible," said Monte Cristo to himself, "that I can have met with a man that has no ambition? That would spoil my plans."

"Sir," said the gardener, glancing at the sun-dial, "the ten minutes are nearly expired; I must return to my post. Will you go up with me?"

"I follow you." Monte Cristo entered the tower, which was divided into three stages. The lowest contained gardening implements, such as spades, rakes, watering-pots, hung against the wall; this was all the furniture. The second was the usual dwelling or rather sleeping-place of the man; it contained a few poor articles of household furniture, a bed, a table, two chairs, a stone pitcher, and some dry herbs hung up to the ceiling, which the count recognized as sweet-peas, and of which the good man was preserving the seeds, having labeled them with as much care as if he had been a botanist.

« Does it require much study to learn the art of telegraphing, sir? » asked Monte Cristo.

« The study does not take long; it was acting as a supernumerary that was so tedious. »

« And what is the pay? »

« A thousand francs, sir. »

« It is nothing. »

« No; but then we are lodged, as you perceive. »

Monte Cristo looked at the room. They passed on to the third stage; it was the room of the telegraph. Monte Cristo looked in turns at the two iron handles by which the machine was worked. « It is very interesting, » he said; « but it must be very tedious for a lifetime. »

« Yes. At first my neck was cramped with looking at it, but at the end of a year I became used to it; and then we have our hours of recreation, and our holidays when we have a fog. »

« Ah, to be sure. »

« Those are indeed holidays to me; I go into the garden, I plant, prune, trim, and kill the insects all day long. »

« How long have you been here? »

« Ten years, and five as a supernumerary make fifteen. »

« You are — »

« Fifty-five years old. »

« How long must you serve to claim the pension? »

« Oh, sir, twenty-five years. »

« And how much is the pension? »

« A hundred crowns. »

« Poor humanity! » murmured Monte Cristo.

« What did you say, sir? » asked the man.

« I was saying it was very interesting. »

« What was? »

« All you were showing me. And you really understand none of these signals? »

« None at all. »

« And have you never tried to understand them? »

« Never. Why should I? »

« But still there are some signals only addressed to you. »

« Certainly. »

« And do you understand them? »

«They are always the same.»

«And they mean —»

«*Nothing new; You have an hour;* or *To-morrow.*»

«This is simple enough,» said the count; «but look! is not your correspondent putting himself in motion?»

«Ah yes; thank you, sir.»

«And what is it saying — anything you understand?»

«Yes; it asks if I am ready.»

«And you reply?»

«By the same sign, which at the same time tells my right-hand correspondent that I am ready, while it gives notice to my left-hand correspondent to prepare in his turn.»

«It is very ingenious,» said the count.

«You will see,» said the man, proudly; «in five minutes he will speak.»

«I have then five minutes,» said Monte Cristo to himself; «it is more time than I require. My dear sir, will you allow me to ask you a question?»

«What is it, sir?»

«You are fond of gardening?»

«Passionately.»

«And you would be pleased to have, instead of this terrace of twenty feet, an inclosure of two acres?»

«Sir, I should make a terrestrial paradise of it.»

«You live badly on your thousand francs?»

«Badly enough; but yet I do live.»

«Yes; but you have only a small garden.»

«True, the garden is not large.»

«And then, such as it is, it is filled with dormice, who eat everything.»

«Ah! they are my scourges.»

«Tell me, should you have the misfortune to turn your head while your right-hand correspondent was telegraphing —»

«I should not see him.»

«Then what would happen?»

«I could not repeat the signals.»

«And then?»

«Not having repeated them, through negligence, I should be fined.»

«How much?»

«A hundred francs.»

«The tenth of your income — that would be fine work.»

« Ah! » said the man.

« Has it ever happened to you? » said Monte Cristo.

« Once, sir, when I was grafting a rose-tree.»

« Well, suppose you were to alter a signal, and substitute another? »

« Ah, that is another case; I should be turned off, and lose my pension.»

« Three hundred francs.»

« A hundred crowns; yes, sir; so you see that I am not likely to do any of these things.»

« Not even for fifteen years' wages? Come, it is worth thinking about? »

« For fifteen thousand francs! »

« Yes.»

« Sir, you alarm me.»

« Nonsense! »

« Sir, you are tempting me? »

« Just so; fifteen thousand francs, do you understand? »

« Sir, let me see my right-hand correspondent! »

« On the contrary, do not look at him, but on this.»

« What is it? »

« What! do you not know these little papers? »

« Bank-notes! »

« Exactly; there are fifteen of them.»

« And whose are they? »

« Yours, if you like.»

« Mine! » exclaimed the man, half suffocated.

« Yes; yours — your own property.»

« Sir, my right-hand correspondent is signaling.»

« Let him.»

« Sir, you have distracted me; I shall be fined.»

« That will cost you a hundred francs; you see it is your interest to take my bank-notes.»

« Sir, my right-hand correspondent redoubles his signals; he is impatient.»

« Never mind — take these; » and the count placed the packet in the hands of the man. « Now, this is not all,» he said; « you cannot live upon your fifteen thousand francs.»

« I shall still have my place.»

« No! you will lose it, for you are going to alter the sign of your correspondent.»

« Oh, sir, what are you proposing? »

« A jest! »

« Sir, unless you force me — »

« I think I can effectually force you; » and Monte Cristo drew another packet from his pocket. « Here are ten thousand more francs,» he said; « with the fifteen thousand already in your pocket, they will make twenty-five thousand. With five thousand you can buy a pretty little house with two acres of land; the remaining twenty thousand will bring you in a thousand francs a year.»

« A garden with two acres of land! »

« And a thousand francs a year.»

« Oh heavens! »

« Come, take them! » and Monte Cristo forced the bank-notes into his hand.

« What am I to do? »

« Nothing very difficult.»

« But what is it? »

« To repeat these signs; » Monte Cristo took a paper from his pocket, upon which were drawn three signs, with numbers to indicate the order in which they were to be worked.

« There, you see it will not take long.»

« Yes; but — »

« Do this, and you will have nectarines and all the rest.» The mark was hit: red with fever, while the large drops fell from his brow, the man executed, one after the other, the three signs given by the count; notwithstanding the frightful contortions of the right-hand correspondent, who, not understanding the change, began to think the gardener had become mad. As to the left-hand one, he conscientiously repeated the same signals, which were definitively carried to the Minister of the Interior. « Now you are rich,» said Monte Cristo.

« Yes,» replied the man, « but at what a price! »

« Listen, friend,» said Monte Cristo. « I do not wish to cause you any remorse; believe me, then, when I swear to you that you have wronged no man, but on the contrary have benefited mankind.» The man looked at the bank-notes, felt them, counted them; he turned pale, then red; then rushed into his room to drink a glass of water, but he had no time to reach the water-jug, and fainted in the midst of his dried herbs. Five minutes after the new telegram reached the minister, Debray had the horses put to his carriage, and drove to Danglars's.

«Has your husband any Spanish bonds?» he asked of the baroness.

«I think so, indeed! He has six millions' worth.»

«He must sell them at whatever price.»

«Why?»

«Because Don Carlos has fled from Bourges, and has returned to Spain.»

«How do you know?»—Debray shrugged his shoulders. «The idea of asking how I hear the news!» he said. The baroness did not wait for a repetition; she ran to her husband, who immediately hastened to his agent and ordered him to sell at any price. When it was seen that Danglars sold, the Spanish funds fell directly. Danglars lost five hundred thousand francs; but he rid himself of all his Spanish shares. The same evening the following was read in Le Messager:—

«Telegraphic dispatch. The King, Don Carlos, has escaped the vigilance exercised over him at Bourges, and has returned to Spain by the Catalonian frontier. Barcelona has risen in his favor.»

All that evening nothing was spoken of but the foresight of Danglars, who had sold his shares, and of the luck of the stock-jobber, who only lost five hundred thousand francs by such a blow. Those who had kept their shares, or bought those of Danglars, looked upon themselves as ruined, and passed a very bad night. Next morning Le Moniteur contained the following:

«It was without any foundation that Le Messager yesterday announced the flight of Don Carlos and the revolt of Barcelona. The King (Don Carlos) has not left Bourges, and the peninsula is in the enjoyment of profound peace. A telegraphic signal, improperly interpreted owing to the fog, was the cause of this error.»

The funds rose one per cent. higher than before they had fallen. This, reckoning his loss, and what he had missed gaining, made the difference of a million to Danglars. «Good!» said Monte Cristo to Morrel, who was at his house when the news arrived of the strange reverse of fortune of which Danglars had been the victim. «I have just made a discovery for twenty-five thousand francs, for which I would have paid a hundred thousand.»

«What have you discovered?» asked Morrel.

«I have just discovered the method of ridding a gardener of the dormice that eat his peaches.»

THE SHOULDER OF ATHOS, THE BELT OF PORTHOS, AND THE HANDKERCHIEF OF ARAMIS

From 'The Three Musketeers'

Furious with rage, D'Artagnan crossed the ante-room in three strides, and began to descend the stairs four steps at a time, without looking where he was going; when suddenly he was brought up short by knocking violently against the shoulder of a musketeer who was leaving the apartments of M. De Treville. The young man staggered backwards from the shock, uttering a cry, or rather a yell.

«Excuse me,» said D'Artagnan, trying to pass him, «but I am in a great hurry.»

He had hardly placed his foot on the next step, when he was stopped by the grasp of an iron wrist on his sash.

«You are in a great hurry!» cried the musketeer, whose face was the color of a shroud; «and you think that is enough apology for nearly knocking me down? Not so fast, my young man. I suppose you imagine that because you heard M. De Treville speaking to us rather brusquely to-day, that everybody may treat us in the same way? But you are mistaken, and it is as well you should learn that you are not M. De Treville.»

«Upon my honor,» replied D'Artagnan, recognizing Athos, who was returning to his room after having his wound dressed, «upon my honor, it was an accident, and therefore I begged your pardon. I should have thought that was all that was necessary. I repeat that I am in a very great hurry, and I should be much obliged if you would let me go my way.»

«Monsieur,» said Athos, loosening his hold, «you are sadly lacking in courtesy, and one sees that you must have had a rustic upbringing.»

D'Artagnan was by this time half-way down another flight; but on hearing Athos's remark he stopped short.

«My faith, monsieur!» exclaimed he, «however rustic I may be, I shall not come to you to teach me manners.»

«I am not so sure of that,» replied Athos.

«Oh, if I was only not in such haste,» cried D'Artagnan; «if only I was not pursuing somebody —»

«Monsieur, you will find me without running after me. Do you understand?»

« And where, if you please? »

« Near Carmes-Deschaux. »

« At what hour? »

« Twelve o'clock. »

« Very good. At twelve I will be there. »

« And don't be late, for at a quarter past twelve I will cut off your ears for you. »

« All right, » called out D'Artagnan, dashing on down-stairs after his man; « you may expect me at ten minutes before the hour. »

But he was not to escape so easily. At the street door stood Porthos, talking to a sentry, and between the two men there was barely space for a man to pass. D'Artagnan took it for granted that he could get through, and darted on, swift as an arrow, but he had not reckoned on the gale that was blowing. As he passed, a sudden gust wrapped Porthos's mantle tight round him; and though the owner of the garment could easily have freed him had he so chosen, for reasons of his own he preferred to draw the folds still closer.

D'Artagnan, hearing the volley of oaths let fall by the musketeers, feared he might have damaged the splendor of the belt, and struggled to unwind himself; but when he at length freed his head, he found that like most things in this world the belt had two sides, and while the front bristled with gold, the back was mere leather; which explains why Porthos always had a cold and could not part from his mantle.

« Confound you! » cried Porthos, struggling in his turn, « have you gone mad, that you tumble over people like this? »

« Excuse me, » answered D'Artagnan, « but I am in a great hurry. I am pursuing some one, and — »

« And I suppose that on such occasions you leave your eyes behind you? » asked Porthos.

« No, » replied D'Artagnan, rather nettled; « and thanks to my eyes, I often see things that other people don't. »

Possibly Porthos might have understood this allusion, but in any case he did not attempt to control his anger, and said sharply: —

« Monsieur, we shall have to give you a lesson if you take to tumbling against the musketeers like this! »

« A lesson, monsieur! » replied D'Artagnan; « that is rather a severe expression. »

«It is the expression of a man who is always accustomed to look his enemies in the face.»

«Oh, if that is all, there is no fear of *your* turning your back on anybody,» and enchanted at his own wit, the young man walked away in fits of laughter.

Porthos foamed with rage, and rushed after D'Artagnan.

«By-and-by, by-and-by,» cried the latter; «when you have not got your mantle on.»

«At one o'clock then, behind the Luxembourg.»

«All right; at one o'clock,» replied D'Artagnan as he vanished around the corner.

But he could see no one either in the street he had passed through, or in the one his eager gaze was searching; however slowly the stranger might have walked, he had gone his way, or perhaps into some house. D'Artagnan inquired of everybody he met, but could find nothing at all about him. This chase however did him good in one way; for in proportion as the sweat started out on his forehead, his heart began to cool.

He began to think over the many unlucky things which had happened. It was scarcely eleven in the morning, and yet this morning had already brought him into disgrace with M. Treville, who must think the way D'Artagnan had left him was rather boorish.

Moreover, he had gotten himself into two fierce duels with two men, each able to kill three D'Artagnans; in a word, with two musketeers,—beings he set so high that he placed them above all other men.

It was a sad lookout. To be sure, as the youth was certain to be killed by Athos, he was not much disturbed about Porthos. As hope is the last thing to die in a man's heart, however, he ended by hoping that he might come out alive from both duels, even if dreadfully injured; and on that supposition he scored himself in this way for his conduct:—

«What a rattle-headed dunce I am! That brave and unfortunate Athos was wounded right on that shoulder I ran against head-foremost, like a ram. The only thing that surprises me is that he didn't strike me dead on the spot; he had provocation enough, for I must have hurt him savagely. As to Porthos—oh! as to Porthos—that's a funny affair!»

And the youth began to laugh aloud in spite of himself; looking round carefully, however, to see if his laughing alone in public without apparent cause aroused any suspicion.

"As to Porthos, it is funny enough, to be sure, but I am a crazy blockhead all the same. Are people to be run into without warning? No! And have I any right to peep under their cloaks to see what they haven't got? He would have forgiven me, I am sure, if I had said nothing to him about that cursed cloak,—with a double meaning, it is true, but too broad a joke in one of them! Ah! cursed Gascon that I am, I believe I should crack a joke if I was being roasted over a slow fire. Friend D'Artagnan," he went on, speaking to himself with the gentleness he thought fair, "if you get away, which there is not much chance of, I would advise you to practice entire politeness for the future. You must henceforth be admired and quoted as a model of it. To be obliging and civil does not necessarily make a man a coward. Look at Aramis, now: mildness and grace embodied; and did anybody ever dream of calling Aramis a coward? No indeed, and from this instant I will try to model myself after him. And luckily, here he is."

D'Artagnan, walking and soliloquizing, had come within a few steps of the Aiguillon House, and in front of it saw Aramis chatting gayly with three of the King's Guards. Aramis also saw D'Artagnan; but not having forgotten that it was in his presence M. de Treville had got so angry in the morning, and as a witness of the rebuke was not at all pleasant, he pretended not to see him. D'Artagnan, on the other hand, full of his plans of conciliation and politeness, approached the young man with a profound bow accompanied by a most gracious smile. Aramis bowed slightly but did not smile. Moreover, all four immediately broke off their conversation.

D'Artagnan was not so dull as not to see he was not wanted; but he was not yet used enough to social customs to know how to extricate himself dexterously from his false position, which his generally is who accosts people he is little acquainted with, and mingles in a conversation which does not concern him. He was mentally casting about for the least awkward manner of retreat, when he noticed that Aramis had let his handkerchief fall, and (doubtless by mistake) put his foot on it. This seemed a favorable chance to repair his mistake of intrusion: he stooped down, and with the most gracious air he could assume, drew the handkerchief from under the foot in spite of the efforts made to detain it, and holding it out to Aramis, said:—

"I believe, sir, this is a handkerchief you would be sorry to lose?"

The handkerchief was in truth richly embroidered, and had a cornet and a coat of arms at one corner. Aramis blushed excessively, and snatched rather than took the handkerchief.

"Ha! ha!" exclaimed one of the guards, "will you go on saying now, most discreet Aramis, that you are not on good terms with Madame de Bois-Tracy, when that gracious lady does you the favor of lending you her handkerchief!"

Aramis darted at D'Artagnan one of those looks which tell a man that he has made a mortal enemy; then assuming his mild air he said:—

"You are mistaken, gentlemen: this handkerchief is not mine, and I cannot understand why this gentleman has taken it into his head to offer it to me rather than to one of you. And as a proof of what I say, here is mine in my pocket."

So saying, he pulled out his handkerchief, which was also not only a very dainty one, and of fine linen (though linen was then costly), but was embroidered and without arms, bearing only a single cipher, the owner's.

This time D'Artagnan saw his mistake; but Aramis's friends were by no means convinced, and one of them, addressing the young musketeer with pretended gravity, said:—

"If things were as you make out, I should feel obliged, my dear Aramis, to reclaim it myself; for as you very well know, Bois-Tracy is an intimate friend of mine, and I cannot allow one of his wife's belongings to be exhibited as a trophy."

"You make the demand clumsily," replied Aramis; "and while I acknowledge the justice of your reclamation, I refuse it on account of the form."

"The fact is," D'Artagnan put in hesitatingly, "I did not actually see the handkerchief fall from M. Aramis's pocket. He had his foot on it, that's all, and I thought it was his."

"And you were deceived, my dear sir," replied Aramis coldly, very little obliged for the explanation; then turning to the guard who had professed himself Bois-Tracy's friend—"Besides," he went on, "I have reflected, my dear intimate friend of Bois-Tracy, that I am not less devotedly his friend than you can possibly be, so that this handkerchief is quite as likely to have fallen from your pocket as from mine!"

"On my honor, no!"

"You are about to swear on your honor, and I on my word; and then it will be pretty evident that one of us will have lied.

Now here, Montaran, we will do better than that: let each take a half."

"Perfectly fair," cried the other two guardsmen; "the judgment of Solomon! Aramis, you are certainly full of wisdom!"

They burst into a loud laugh, and as may be supposed, the incident bore no other fruit. In a minute or two the conversation stopped, and the three guards and the musketeer, after heartily shaking hands, separated, the guards going one way and Aramis another.

"Now is the time to make my peace with this gentleman," said D'Artagnan to himself, having stood on one side during all the latter part of the conversation; and in this good spirit drawing near to Aramis, who was going off without paying any attention to him, he said:—

"You will excuse me, I hope."

"Ah!" interrupted Aramis, "permit me to observe to you, sir, that you have not acted in this affair as a man of good breeding ought."

"What!" cried D'Artagnan, "do you suppose —"

"I suppose that you are not a fool, and that you knew very well, even though you come from Gascony, that people do not stand on handkerchiefs for nothing. What the devil! Paris is not paved with linen!"

"Sir, you do wrong in trying to humiliate me," said D'Artagnan, in whom his native pugnacity began to speak louder than his peaceful resolutions. "I come from Gascony, it is true; and since you know it, there is no need to tell you that Gascons are not very patient, so that when they have asked pardon once, even for a folly, they think they have done at least as much again as they ought to have done."

"Sir, what I say to you about this matter," said Aramis, "is not for the sake of hunting a quarrel. Thank Heaven, I am not a swashbuckler, and being a musketeer only for a while, I only fight when I am forced to do so, and always with great reluctance; but this time the affair is serious, for here is a lady compromised by you."

"By us, you mean," cried D'Artagnan.

"Why did you give me back the handkerchief so awkwardly?"

"Why did you let it fall so awkwardly?"

"I have said that the handkerchief did not fall from my pocket."

«Well, by saying that you have told two lies, sir; for I saw it fall.»

«Oh ho! you take it up that way, do you, Master Gascon? Well, I will teach you how to behave yourself.»

«And I will send you back to your pulpit, Master Priest. Draw, if you please, and instantly —»

«Not so, if you please, my good friend; not here, at least. Do you not see that we are opposite Aiguillon House, full of the Cardinal's creatures? How do I know that it is not his Eminence who has honored you with the commission to bring him in my head? Now, I entertain an absurd partiality for my head, it seems to suit my shoulders so finely. I have no objection to killing you, you may be sure, but quietly, in a snug, distant spot, where you will not be able to boast of your death to anybody.»

«I agree, but don't be too confident; and take away your handkerchief — whether it belongs to you or somebody else, perhaps you may stand in need of it to bandage up a wound. As a Gascon, I don't put off engagements for prudence's sake.»

«Prudence is a virtue useless enough to musketeers, I know, but indispensable to churchmen; and as I am only a temporary musketeer, I hold it best to be prudent. At two o'clock I shall have the honor of expecting you at Treville's. There I will point out the best place and time to you.»

The two bowed and separated. Aramis went up the street which led to the Luxembourg; while D'Artagnan, seeing that the appointed hour was coming near, took the road to the Carmes-Deschaux, saying to himself, «I certainly cannot hope to come out of these scrapes alive; but if I am doomed to be killed, it will be by a royal musketeer.»

THE DEFENSE OF THE BASTION SAINT-GERVAIS

From ‹The Three Musketeers›

When D'Artagnan arrived, he found his three friends all together. Athos was thinking deeply, Porthos was twirling his mustache, and Aramis was reading his prayers out of a beautiful little book bound in blue velvet.

«My faith, gentlemen!» exclaimed he, «I hope that what you have to tell me is very important, or I shall owe you a grudge for dragging me here, out of my bed, after a whole night passed in taking and dismantling a bastion! Ah, it is a thousand pities you were not there! It was warm work!»

«We were somewhere else, where it was not very cold either,» replied Porthos, giving his mustache another twist. . . .

«Aramis,» said Athos, «didn't you breakfast the other day at Parpaillot's?»

«Yes.»

«Were you comfortable there?»

«No, I did not like it at all. It was a fast day, and they had nothing but meat.»

«What, no fish to be had in a seaport town?»

«They say,» replied Aramis, taking up his book, «that they have all taken to the deep sea, since the Cardinal built that dike.»

«That is not what I was asking,» replied Athos. «Were you quite free and at your ease, or did any one pay attention to you?»

«Oh, nobody paid any attention to me. And if *that* is your object, Athos, Parpaillot's will suit us very well.»

«Let us go at once then,» said Athos, «for these walls are like paper.»

On the way they met Grimaud [the valet of Athos], whom Athos beckoned silently to follow them. Grimaud, according to his custom, obeyed without a word. The poor fellow had almost forgotten how to speak!

It did not take them long to reach Parpaillot's, but unluckily the hour was ill chosen for a private conference. The *réveille* had just been sounded, and the sleepy soldiers were all pouring into the inn. This state of matters delighted the landlord, but was hardly so agreeable to the four friends, who merely nodded sulkily at the salutations of the crowd.

«If we are not careful,» said Athos, rousing himself, «we shall find ourselves landed in some quarrel, which would be highly inconvenient at this moment. D'Artagnan, tell us about your night's work, and then we will tell you about ours.»

«Ah yes,» said a light-horse soldier, who was slowly sipping a glass of brandy, «you were down at the trenches last night, I think, and I believe you had a brush with the Rochellois.»

D'Artagnan looked at Athos, to see if he ought to answer or not.

«My dear fellow,» replied Athos, «I don't think you are aware that M. De Busigny did you the honor to address you! Since these gentlemen are interested in last night's affair, tell them about it.»

«Is it true that you captured a bastion?» asked a Swiss, who had filled his beer up with rum.

«Yes, monsieur,» replied D'Artagnan, «we had that honor. We also introduced a barrel of powder into a corner, which in exploding opened a really beautiful breach; and as the bastion was not built yesterday, the whole building was severely shaken.»

«What bastion was it?» said a dragoon, who was holding a goose on the point of his sword, and cooking it at the fire.

«The Bastion Saint-Gervais,» replied D'Artagnan; «the Rochellois behind it were always annoying our men.»

«And there was a good deal of sharp-shooting?»

«A good deal. We lost five men, and the Rochellois eight or ten.»

«But this morning,» went on the light-horseman, «they will probably send down some pioneers to rebuild the bastion.»

«Yes, probably,» answered D'Artagnan.

«Gentlemen,» broke in Athos, «I want to propose a bet.»

«What bet?» asked the light-horseman.

«I bet you, M. De Busigny, that I and my three friends Porthos, Aramis, and D'Artagnan, will breakfast in the Bastion Saint-Gervais, and will hold it an hour by the clock, against all comers.»

Porthos and Aramis looked at each other. They were beginning to understand what Athos had in his head.

«But,» objected D'Artagnan, leaning over to whisper to Athos, «we shall be killed without a chance of escape.»

«We shall be killed a great deal more certainly if we don't go,» replied Athos.

«Ah!» ejaculated Porthos, twirling his mustache, «that is a grand bet.»

«I take it,» said M. De Busigny; «let us fix the stakes.»

«That is easily done,» replied Athos. «We are four and you are four. The loser shall give the whole eight a dinner.»

«Very well, let us agree to that,» said M. De Busigny and the dragoon.

«Your breakfast is ready, gentlemen,» broke in the landlord at this instant.

"Then bring it here," answered Athos.

The landlord obeyed, and Athos, making a sign to Grimaud, pointed out a large basket standing in a corner, which he was to fill with wine and food.

"But where are you going to eat it?" asked the landlord.

"What does that matter to you as long as you are paid?" replied Athos, throwing two pistoles on the table. Then, turning to M. De Busigny, he observed:—

"Will you have the kindness, monsieur, to set your watch by mine, or let me set mine by yours?"

"Certainly, monsieur," said the light-horseman, drawing out a beautiful watch incrusted with diamonds; "half-past seven."

"Five-and-twenty minutes to eight. So I am five minutes faster than you;" and bowing to the rest of the company, the four young men took the road to the Bastion Saint-Gervais, followed by Grimaud carrying the basket. He had not the faintest idea where they were going, or what they were to do, but Athos had given his orders, and he always obeyed without questioning.

As long as they were within the camp, the four friends remained silent; but once they had passed the wall of circumvallation, D'Artagnan, who was completely in the dark, thought it was time to ask for an explanation.

"And now, my dear Athos," said he, "will you be good enough to tell me where we are bound for?"

"Why, for the bastion, of course."

"And what are we to do when we get there?"

"I told you before. We are going to breakfast."

"But why didn't we do that at Parpaillot's?"

"Because we had some important matters to discuss, and it was impossible to talk for five minutes at that inn, with all those people coming and going, and perpetually bowing and speaking to you. Here at least," continued Athos, pointing to the bastion, "we shall not be interrupted."

"It seems to me," said D'Artagnan, with the caution which was as much his characteristic as his foolhardy courage, "it seems to me that we might have found some secluded place among the sand-hills on the sea-shore."

"Oh, somebody would have seen, and in a quarter of an hour spies would have informed the Cardinal that we were holding council."

«Yes,» said Aramis. «Athos is right. *Animadvertuntur in desertis.*»

«A desert would have done very well,» replied Porthos; «but first we should have to find it.»

«There is no desert where a bird cannot fly overhead, or a fish jump out of the water, or a rabbit run out of his hole; and bird, fish, and rabbit have all become spies of the Cardinal. Much better to go on with our adventure, which we cannot now give up without dishonor. We have made a bet, and a bet on the spur of the moment; a bet of which I defy any one to guess the true meaning. To win it, we must hold the bastion for an hour. Either they will attack us, or they won't. If we are left unmolested, we shall have plenty of time to talk without any one overhearing us, for I will answer for the walls of this bastion having no ears. If they try to dislodge us, we can talk all the same, and in defending our position shall cover ourselves with glory. You see that from every point of view we have the whip hand.»

«Yes,» said D'Artagnan, «but most certainly we shall attract some stray bullet.»

«My good fellow,» remarked Athos, «do you really think that the enemy's bullets are those we have most cause to fear?»

«But surely, if we were embarking on such an expedition, we ought to have brought our muskets?»

«Porthos, you are a goose! What would be the good of burdening ourselves with anything so useless?»

«I should hardly think that a heavy musket, a dozen cartridges, and a powder flask would be useless when one is in the presence of an enemy.»

«Dear me!» said Athos, «didn't you hear what D'Artagnan was saying?»

«What did D'Artagnan say?» asked Porthos.

«He said that during last night's attack eight or ten Frenchmen were killed, and as many Rochellois.»

«Well?»

«Well, hasn't everybody been too busy ever since to think of stripping the dead bodies?»

«What then?»

«What then? Why, we shall find their muskets, their flasks, and their cartridges, all waiting for us; and instead of four muskets and twelve charges, there will be fifteen pieces and a hundred bullets.»

«O Athos,» exclaimed Aramis, «you are a great man!»

Porthos nodded approval; only D'Artagnan did not seem to be convinced; and Grimaud appeared to have his doubts, for seeing they were still making for the bastion (which up to that moment he had declined to believe), he plucked his master by the coat.

«Where are we going?» he asked by a sign.

Athos pointed out the bastion.

«But,» objected Grimaud, speaking always in pantomime, «we shall leave our bodies there.»

Athos raised his hands and eyes to heaven. Grimaud placed his basket on the ground and sat down, shaking his head.

Athos took a pistol from his belt, looked to see if it was well primed, cocked it, and approached the barrel to Grimaud's ear. Grimaud was on his legs again, as if by magic. Athos then signed to him to take up the basket and go on.

Grimaud obeyed.

When they reached the bastion, the four friends turned round and beheld over three hundred soldiers assembled at the gate of the camp; M. De Busigny, the dragoon, the Swiss, and their silent companion forming a group apart.

Athos removed his hat, put it on the edge of his sword, and waved it in the air.

The spectators returned his salute and gave a great hurrah, which penetrated to their ears even at that distance. Then all four disappeared inside the bastion, where Grimaud had preceded them.

THE CONSULTATION OF THE MUSKETEERS

From ‹The Three Musketeers›

As Athos had assumed, the bastion was only occupied by a dozen dead men, French and Rochellois.

«Gentlemen,» said Athos, to whom the command of the expedition naturally fell, «while Grimaud lays out breakfast, we will begin by picking up the muskets and cartridges, and of course there is nothing in this employment to prevent our talking. Our friends here,» he added, pointing to the dead, «will pay no attention to us.»

«But after we have made sure they have nothing in their pockets, we had better throw them into the trench,» said Porthos.

« Yes, » replied Athos, « that is Grimaud's business. »

« Well then, » said D'Artagnan, « let Grimaud search them, and after he has done so, throw them over the wall. »

« He shall do nothing of the sort, » replied Athos; « we may find them useful yet. »

« You are going mad, my good fellow! Of what use can these dead men be? »

« Don't judge hastily, say the gospel and the Cardinal, » replied Athos. « How many guns have we got? »

« Twelve, » said Aramis.

« How many charges? »

« A hundred. »

« That will do. Now let us load. »

They set to work; and as they finished loading the last gun, Grimaud made a sign that breakfast was ready.

By a gesture Athos replied that they were ready also, and then pointed out a pepper-box turret, where Grimaud was to keep watch. To help him pass the time Athos allowed him to take some bread, two cutlets, and a bottle of wine. . . .

« Now, » said D'Artagnan, « that there is no chance of our being overheard, I hope you will tell us your secret. »

« I trust, gentlemen, to give you both pleasure and glory at once, » replied Athos. « I have made you take a charming walk, and now here is an excellent breakfast; while below, as you may see through the loop-holes, are five hundred persons, who consider us to be either lunatics or heroes,—two classes of idiots who have much in common. . . . »

« What is the matter, Grimaud? As the circumstances are grave, I will allow you to speak, but be short, I beg. What is it? »

« A troop. »

« How many? »

« Twenty? »

« What are they? »

« Sixteen pioneers, four soldiers. »

« How far off? »

« Five hundred paces. »

« Then we have just time to finish this fowl and drink your health, D'Artagnan. »

A few minutes later the troop hove in sight, marching along a narrow trench that connected the bastion and the town.

«Bah!» said Athos. «It was scarcely worth while disturbing ourselves for a mere handful of rascals armed with pickaxes, hoes, and shovels. Grimaud had only got to make them a sign to return whence they came, and I am sure they would have left us in peace.»

«I doubt it,» said D'Artagnan, «for they are advancing steadily. And besides the sappers, there are four soldiers and a brigadier, all armed with muskets.»

«It is only because they have not seen us,» replied Athos.

«Upon my honor,» cried Aramis, «I feel quite ashamed to fire on poor devils like that.»

«False priest!» exclaimed Porthos, «to have pity on heretics.»

«Aramis is right,» said Athos. «I will warn them.»

«What on earth are you doing?» said D'Artagnan. «You will get yourself shot, my good fellow.»

But Athos paid no attention to this remark, and mounting the breach, his hat in one hand and his musket in the other, he addressed the troop, who were so astonished at this unexpected apparition that they halted about fifty paces distant. «Gentlemen,» he said, bowing courteously as he spoke, «I am at this moment breakfasting with some friends in the shelter of this bastion. As you know, there is nothing so unpleasant as to be disturbed during your meals; therefore we should be greatly obliged if you would postpone any business you may have here, till we have finished, or else call again. Unless, indeed, you have the happy inspiration to quit the side of rebellion, and to drink, with us, to the health of the King of France.»

«Do take care, Athos!» exclaimed D'Artagnan; «don't you see they are aiming at you?»

«Oh, yes, of course,» said Athos; «but they are only civilians, who don't know how to shoot; and they will never touch me.»

He had scarcely uttered the words when four muskets fired simultaneously. The balls fell round Athos, but not one grazed him.

Four muskets immediately answered, but these were better directed than the others. Three of the soldiers fell dead, and one of the sappers was wounded.

«Grimaud, another musket,» said Athos, who was still on the breach. Grimaud obeyed; a second volley was fired; the brigadier and two pioneers fell dead, and the rest of the troop took flight.

«Now we must make a sortie,» cried Athos; and the four comrades dashed out of the fort, picked up the muskets belonging to the dead soldiers, and retreated to the bastion, carrying the trophies of their victory. . . .

«To arms!» called Grimaud.

The young men jumped up and ran for their muskets.

This time the advancing troop was composed of twenty or twenty-five men, but they were no longer sappers, but soldiers of the garrison.

«Hadn't we better return to the camp?» said Porthos. «The fight is not equal at all.»

«Impossible, for three reasons,» said Athos. «First, because we haven't finished breakfast; second, because we have several important things to discuss; and third, because there are still ten minutes before the hour is up.»

«Well, anyway,» remarked Aramis, «we had better have some plan of campaign.»

«It is very simple,» replied Athos. «The moment the enemy is within reach, we fire. If they still come on, we fire again, and go on firing as long as our guns are loaded. If any of them are left, and they try to carry the place by assault, we will let them get well into the ditch, and then drop on their heads a piece of the wall, that only keeps poised by a kind of miracle.»

«Bravo,» cried Porthos. «Athos, you were born to be a general; and the Cardinal, who thinks himself a great commander, is not to be compared to you.»

«Gentlemen,» replied Athos, «remember, one thing at a time. Cover your man well.»

«I have mine,» said D'Artagnan.

«And I,» said Porthos and Aramis.

«Then fire;» and as Athos gave the word, the muskets rang out and four men fell. Then the drum beat, and the little army advanced to the charge, while all the while the fire was kept up, irregularly, but with a sure aim. The Rochellois however did not flinch, but came on steadily.

When they reached the foot of the bastion, the enemy still numbered twelve or fifteen. A sharp fire received them, but they never faltered, and leaping the trench, prepared to scale the breach.

«Now, comrades!» cried Athos. «Let us make an end of them. To the wall!»

And all four, aided by Grimaud, began to push with their guns a huge block of wall, which swayed as if with the wind, and then rolled slowly down into the trench. A horrible cry was heard, a cloud of dust mounted upwards; and all was silent.

« Have we crushed them all, do you think? » asked Athos.

« It looks like it, » answered D'Artagnan.

« No, » said Porthos, « for two or three are limping off. »

Athos looked at his watch.

« Gentlemen, » he said, « an hour has elapsed since we came here, and we have won our bet. » . . .

« What is going on in the town? » asked Athos.

« It is a call to arms. »

They listened, and the sound of a drum reached their ears.

« They must be sending us an entire regiment, » said Athos.

« You don't mean to fight a whole regiment? » said Porthos.

« Why not? » asked the musketeer. « If we had only had the sense to bring another dozen bottles, I could make head against an army! »

« As I live, the drum is coming nearer, » said D'Artagnan.

« Let it, » replied Athos. « It takes a quarter of an hour to get from here to the town, so it takes a quarter of an hour to get from the town here. That is more than enough time for us to arrange our plans. If we leave this, we shall never find such a good position. . . . But I must first give Grimaud his orders; » and Athos made a sign to his servant.

« Grimaud, » said he, pointing to the dead who were lying on the bastion, « you will take these gentlemen and prop them up against the wall, and put their hats on their heads and their guns in their hands. »

« Great man! » ejaculated D'Artagnan; « I begin to see. »

« You do? » asked Porthos.

« Do *you* understand, Grimaud? » said Aramis.

Grimaud nodded.

« Then we are all right, » said Athos. . . .

« On guard! » cried D'Artagnan. « Look at those red and black points moving down there! A regiment, did you call it, Athos? — it is a perfect army! »

« My word, yes! » said Athos, « there they come! How cunning to beat neither drums nor trumpets. Are you ready, Grimaud? »

Grimaud silently nodded, and showed them a dozen dead men, arranged skillfully in various attitudes, some porting arms, some taking aim, others drawing their swords.

«Well done!» exclaimed Athos, «it does honor to your imagination.»

«If it is all the same to you,» said Porthos, «I should like to understand what is going on.»

«Let us get away first,» replied D'Artagnan, «and you will understand after.»

«One moment, please! Give Grimaud time to clear away the breakfast.»

«Ah!» said Aramis; «the red and black specks are becoming more distinct, and I agree with D'Artagnan that we have no time to lose before we regain the camp.»

«Very well,» rejoined Athos, «I have nothing to say against retreating. The wager was for an hour, and we have been here an hour and a half. Let us be off at once.»

The four comrades went out at the back, following Grimaud, who had already departed with the basket.

«Oh!» cried Athos, stopping suddenly, «what the devil is to be done?»

«Has anything been forgotten?» asked Aramis.

«Our flag, man, our flag! We can't leave our flag in the enemy's hands, if it is nothing but a napkin.» And Athos dashed again into the bastion, and bore away the flag unhurt, amid a volley of balls from the Rochellois.

He waved his flag, while turning his back on the troops of the town, and saluting those of the camp. From both sides arose great cries, of anger on the one hand and enthusiasm on the other, and the napkin, pierced with three bullet-holes, was in truth transformed into a flag. «Come down, come down!» they shouted from the camp.

Athos came down, and his friends, who had awaited him anxiously, received him with joy.

«Be quick, Athos,» said D'Artagnan; «now that we have got everything but money, it would be stupid to get killed.»

But Athos would not hurry himself, and they had to keep pace with him.

By this time Grimaud and his basket were well beyond bullet range, while in the distance the sounds of rapid firing might be heard.

«What are they doing?» asked Porthos; «what are they firing at?»

«At our dead men,» replied Athos.

«But they don't fire back.»

«Exactly so; therefore the enemy will come to the conclusion that there is an ambuscade. They will hold a council, and send an envoy with a flag of truce, and when they at last find out the joke, we shall be out of reach. So it is no use getting apoplexy by racing.»

«Oh, I understand,» said Porthos, full of astonishment.

«That is a mercy!» replied Athos, shrugging his shoulders, as they approached the camp, which was watching their progress in a ferment of admiration.

This time a new fusillade was begun, and the balls whistled close to the heads of the four victors and fell about their ears. The Rochellois had entered the bastion.

«What bad shooting!» said D'Artagnan. «How many was it we killed? Twelve?»

«Twelve or fifteen.»

«And how many did we crush?»

«Eight or ten.»

«And not a scratch to show for it.»

«Ah, what is that on your hand, D' Artagnan? It looks to me like blood.»

«It's nothing,» replied D'Artagnan.

«A spent ball?»

«Not even that.»

«But what is it, then?» As we have said, the silent and resolute Athos loved D'Artagnan like his own son, and showed every now and then all the anxiety of a father.

«The skin is rubbed off, that is all,» said D'Artagnan. «My fingers were caught between two stones — the stone of the wall and the stone of my ring.»

«That is what comes of having diamonds,» remarked Athos disdainfully. . . .

«Here we are at the camp, and they are coming to meet us and bring us in triumphantly.»

And he only spoke the truth, for the whole camp was in a turmoil. More than two thousand people had gazed, as at a play, at the lucky bit of braggadocio of the four friends,— braggadocio of which they were far from suspecting the real motive. The cry of «Long live the musketeers,» resounded on all sides, and M. De Busigny was the first to hold out his hand to Athos and to declare that he had lost his wager. The dragoon and the

Swiss had followed him, and all the others had followed the dragoon and the Swiss. There was nothing but congratulations, hand-shakings, embraces; and the tumult became so great that the Cardinal thought there must be a revolt, and sent La Houdinière, his captain of guards, to find out what was the matter.

« Well ? » asked the Cardinal, as his messenger returned.

« Well, monseigneur, » replied La Houdinière, « it is about three musketeers and a guardsman who made a bet with M. De Busigny to go and breakfast at the Bastion Saint-Gervais, and while breakfasting, held it for two hours against the enemy, and killed I don't know how many Rochellois. »

« You asked the names of these gentlemen ? »

« Yes, monseigneur. »

« What are they ? »

« Athos, Porthos, and Aramis. »

« Always my three heroes, » murmured the Cardinal. « And the guardsman ? »

« M. D'Artagnan. »

« Always my young rogue! I must gain over these men. »

And the same evening, the Cardinal had a conversation with M. De Treville about the morning's exploit, with which the whole camp was still ringing. M. De Treville, who had heard it all at first hand, gave his Eminence all the details, not forgetting the episode of the napkin.

« Very good, M. De Treville, » said the Cardinal; « but you must get me that napkin, and I will have three golden lilies embroidered on it, and give as a banner to your company. »

« Monseigneur, » replied M. De Treville, « that would be an injustice to the guards. M. D'Artagnan does not belong to me, but to M. Des Essarts. »

« Then you must take him, » said the Cardinal. « As these four brave soldiers love each other so much, they ought certainly to be in the same regiment. »

That evening M. De Treville announced the good news to the three musketeers and to D'Artagnan, and invited them all to breakfast the following day.

D'Artagnan was nearly beside himself with joy. As we know, it had been the dream of his life to be a musketeer.

THE MAN IN THE IRON MASK

From 'The Viscount of Bragelonne'

[Dumas adopts the theory that the Man in the Iron Mask was the suppressed twin brother of Louis XIV.]

"What is all this noise?" asked Philippe, turning towards the door of the concealed staircase. And as he spoke a voice was heard saying, "This way, this way. Still a few steps, sire."

"It is M. Fouquet's voice," said D'Artagnan, who was standing near the Queen Mother.

"Then M. D'Herblay will not be far off," added Philippe; but little did he expect to see the person who actually entered.

All eyes were riveted on the door, from which the voice of M. Fouquet proceeded; but it was not he who came through.

A cry of anguish rang through the room, breaking forth simultaneously from the King and the spectators, and surely never had been seen a stranger sight.

The shutters were half closed, and only a feeble light struggled through the velvet curtains, with their thick silk linings, and the eyes of the courtiers had to get accustomed to the darkness before they could distinguish between the surrounding objects. But once discerned, they stood out as clear as day.

So, looking up, they saw Louis XIV. in the doorway of the private stair, his face pale and his brows bent; and behind him stood Fouquet.

The Queen Mother, whose hand held that of Philippe, uttered a shriek at the sight, thinking that she beheld a ghost.

Monsieur staggered for a moment and turned away his head, looking from the King who was facing him to the King who was by his side.

Madame on the contrary stepped forward, thinking it must be her brother-in-law reflected in a mirror. And indeed, this seemed the only rational explanation of the double image.

Both young men, agitated and trembling, clenching their hands, darting flames of fury from their eyes, dumb, breathless, ready to spring at each other's throats, resembled each other so exactly in feature, figure, and even, by pure accident, in dress, that Anne of Austria herself stood confounded. For as yet the truth had not dawned on her. There are some torments that we all instinctively reject. It is easier far to accept the supernatural, the impossible.

That he should encounter such obstacles had never for one moment occurred to Louis. He imagined he had only to show himself, for the world to fall at his feet. The Sun-king could have no rival; and where his rays did not fall, there must be darkness—

As to Fouquet, who could describe his bewilderment at the sight of the living portrait of his master? Then he thought that Aramis was right, and that the new-comer was every whit as much a king as his double, and that after all, perhaps he had made a mistake when he had declined to share in the *coup d'état* so cleverly plotted by the General of the Jesuits.

And then, it was equally the blood royal of Louis XIII. that Fouquet had determined to sacrifice to blood in all respects identical; a noble ambition, to one that was selfish. And it was the mere aspect of the pretender which showed him all these things.

D'Artagnan, leaning against the wall and facing Fouquet, was debating in his own mind the key to this wonderful riddle. He felt instinctively, though he could not have told why, that in the meeting of the two Louis XIV.s lay the explanation of all that had seemed suspicious in the conduct of Aramis during the last few days.

Suddenly Louis XIV., by nature the most impatient of the two young men, and with the habit of command that was the result of training, strode across the room and flung open one of the shutters. The flood of light that streamed through the window caused Philippe involuntarily to recoil, and to step back into the shelter of an alcove.

The movement struck Louis, and turning to the Queen he said:

«Mother, do you not know your own son, although every one else has denied his King?»

Anne trembled at his voice and raised her arms to heaven, but could not utter a single word.

«Mother,» retorted Philippe in his quietest tones, «do you not know your own son?»

And this time it was Louis who stepped back.

As for Anne, pierced to the heart with grief and remorse, she could bear it no longer. She staggered where she stood, and unaided by her attendants, who seemed turned into stone, she sank down on a sofa with a sigh.

This spectacle was too much for Louis. He rushed to D'Artagnan, whose brain was going round with bewilderment, and who clung to the door as his last hope.

«To me, musketeer! Look us both in the face, and see which is the paler, he or I.»

The cry awoke D'Artagnan from his stupor, and struck the chord of obedience strong in the bosom of every soldier. He lifted his head, and striding straight up to Philippe laid his hand on his shoulder, saying quietly:—

«Monsieur, you are my prisoner.»

Philippe remained absolutely still, as if nailed to the floor, his eyes fixed despairingly on the King who was his brother. His silence reproached him as no words could have done, with the bitterness of the past and the tortures of the future.

And the King understood, and his soul sank within him. His eyes fell, and drawing his brother and sister-in-law with him, he hastily quitted the room; forgetting in his agitation even his mother, lying motionless on the couch beside him, not three paces from the son whom for the second time she was allowing to be condemned to a death in life.

Philippe drew near to her, and said softly:—

«If you had not been my mother, madame, I must have cursed you for the misery you have caused me.»

D'Artagnan overheard, and a shiver of pity passed through him. He bowed respectfully to the young prince, and said:—

«Forgive me, monseigneur; I am only a soldier, and my faith is due to him who has left us.»

«Thank you, M. D'Artagnan. But what has become of M. D'Herblay?»

«M. D'Herblay is safe, monseigneur,» answered a voice behind them; «and while I am alive and free, not a hair of his head shall be hurt.»

«M. Fouquet!» said the prince, smiling sadly.

«Forgive me, monseigneur,» cried Fouquet, falling on his knees; «but he who has left the room was my guest.»

«Ah!» murmured Philippe to himself with a sigh, «you are loyal friends and true hearts. You make me regret the world I am leaving. M. D'Artagnan, I will follow you.»

As he spoke, Colbert entered and handed to the captain of the musketeers an order from the King; then bowed, and went out.

D'Artagnan glanced at the paper, and in a sudden burst of wrath crumpled it in his hand.

« What is the matter? » asked the prince.

« Read it, monseigneur, » answered the musketeer.

And Philippe read these words, written hastily by the King himself: —

« M. D'Artagnan will conduct the prisoner to the Îles Sainte-Marguerite. He will see that his face is covered with an iron mask, which must never be lifted on pain of death. »

« It is just, » said Philippe; « I am ready. »

« Aramis was right, » whispered Fouquet to D'Artagnan, « this is as good a king as the other. »

« Better, » replied D'Artagnan; « he only needed you and me. »

A TRICK IS PLAYED ON HENRY III. BY AID OF CHICOT

From 'The Lady of Monsoreau'

The King and Chicot remained quiet and silent for the next ten minutes. Then suddenly the King sat up, and the noise he made roused Chicot, who was just dropping off to sleep.

The two looked at each other with sparkling eyes.

« What is it? » asked Chicot in a low voice.

« Do you hear that sighing sound? » replied the King in a lower voice still. « Listen! »

As he spoke, one of the wax candles in the hand of the golden satyr went out; then a second, then a third. After a moment, the fourth went out also.

« Oh, oh! » cried Chicot, « that is more than a sighing sound. » But he had hardly uttered the last word when in its turn the lamp was extinguished, and the room was in darkness, save for the flickering glow of the dying embers.

« Look out! » exclaimed Chicot, jumping up.

« He is going to speak, » said the King, shrinking back into his bed.

« Then listen and let us hear what he says, » replied Chicot, and at the same instant a voice which sounded at once both piercing and hollow, proceeded from the space between the bed and the wall.

« Hardened sinner, are you there? »

« Yes, yes, Lord, » gasped Henri with chattering teeth.

« Dear me! » remarked Chicot, « that is a very hoarse voice to have come from heaven! I feel dreadfully frightened; but never mind! »

« Do you hear me? » asked the voice.

« Yes, Lord, » stammered Henri; « and I bow before your anger. »

« Do you think you are carrying out my will by performing all the mummeries you have taken part in to-day, while your heart is full of the things of this world? »

« Well said! » cried Chicot; « you touched him there! »

The King's hands shook as he clasped them, and Chicot went up to him.

« Well, » murmured Henri, « are you convinced now? »

« Wait a bit, » answered Chicot.

« What do you want more? »

« Hush! listen to me. Creep softly out of bed, and let me take your place. »

« Why? »

« Because then the anger of the Lord will fall first upon me. »

« And do you think I shall escape? »

« We will try, anyway; » and with affectionate persistence he pushed the King out of bed, and took his place.

« Now, Henri, » he said, « go and lie on my sofa, and leave all to me. »

Henri obeyed; he began to understand Chicot's plan.

« You are silent, » continued the voice, « which proves that your heart is hardened. »

« Oh, pardon, pardon, Lord! » exclaimed Chicot, imitating the King's nasal twang. Then, stretching himself out of bed, he whispered to the King, « It is very odd, but the heavenly voice does not seem to know that it is Chicot who is speaking. »

« Oh! » replied Henri, « what do you suppose is the meaning of that? »

« Don't be in a hurry; plenty of strange things will happen yet! »

« Miserable creature that you are! » went on the voice.

« Yes, Lord, yes! » answered Chicot. « I am a horrible sinner, hardened in crime. »

« Then confess your sins, and repent. »

« I acknowledge, » said Chicot, « that I dealt wickedly by my cousin Condé, whose wife I betrayed; and I repent bitterly. »

« What is that you are saying? » cried the King. « There is no good in mentioning that. It has all been forgotten long ago. »

« Oh, has it? » replied Chicot; « then we will pass on to something else. »

« Answer, » said the voice.

« I acknowledge, » said the false Henri, « that I behaved like a thief toward the Poles, who had elected me their king, in stealing away to France one fine night, carrying with me all the crown jewels; and I repent bitterly. »

« Idiot! » exclaimed Henri, « what are you talking about now? Nobody remembers anything about that. »

« Let me alone, » answered Chicot, « I must go on pretending to be the King. »

« Speak, » said the voice.

« I acknowledge, » continued Chicot, « that I snatched the throne from my brother D'Alençon, who was the rightful heir, since I had formally renounced my claims when I was elected King of Poland; I repent bitterly. »

« Rascal! » cried the King.

« There is yet something more, » said the voice.

« I acknowledge to have plotted with my excellent mother, Catherine de' Medicis, to hunt from France my brother-in-law the King of Navarre, after first destroying all his friends, and my sister Queen Marguerite, after first destroying all her lovers; and I repent bitterly. »

« Scoundrel! Cease! » muttered the King, his teeth clenched in anger.

« Sire, it is no use trying to hide what Providence knows as well as we do. »

« There is a crime unconfessed that has nothing to do with politics, » said the voice.

« Ah, now we are getting to it, » observed Chicot dolefully; « it is about my conduct, I suppose? »

« It is, » answered the voice.

« I cannot deny, » continued Chicot, always speaking in the name of the King, « that I am very effeminate, very lazy; a hopeless trifler, an incorrigible hypocrite. »

« It is true, » said the voice.

« I have behaved ill to all women, to my own wife in particular; and such a good wife too.»

« A man should love his wife as himself, and above all the world,» cried the voice angrily.

« Oh dear!» wailed Chicot in despairing tones; « then I certainly have sinned terribly.»

« And by your example you have caused others to sin.»

« That is true, sadly true.»

« You very nearly sent that poor Saint-Luc to perdition.»

« Bah!» said Chicot, « are you sure I did not send him there quite?»

« No; but such a fate may befall both of you if you do not let him go back to his family at break of day.»

« Dear me!» said Chicot to the King, « the voice seems to take a great interest in the house of Cossé.»

« If you disobey me, you will suffer the same torments as Sardanapalus, Nabuchodnosor, and the Marshal De Retz.»

Henry III. gave a loud groan; at this threat he became more frightened than ever.

« I am lost,» he ejaculated wildly; « I am lost. That voice from on high will be my death-warrant.»

ALEXANDRE DUMAS, JUNIOR

(1824–1895)

BY FRANCISQUE SARCEY

We shall not say much about the life of Alexandre Dumas the younger. The history of a great writer is the history of his works. He was born in Paris, on July 27th, 1824. His name on the register of births appears as «Alexandre, son of Marie Catherine Lebay, seamstress.» He was not acknowledged by his father until he had reached his sixth year, March 7th, 1830. I emphasize this particular because it had great influence on the bent of his genius. During all his life Dumas was haunted by a desire of rehabilitating illegitimate children, of creating a reaction against their treatment by the Civil Code and the prejudice which makes of them something little better than outcasts in society.

«When seven years old,» he himself says, «I entered as a boarder the school of Monsieur Vauthier, on Rue Montagne Saint-Geneviève. Thence I passed, about two years later, to the Saint-Victor School; the principal was Monsieur Goubaux, a friend of my father, with whom he collaborated under the *nom de plume* of Dinaux. This school, which numbered two hundred and fifty boarding pupils, and with the rather strange habits which I tried to depict in 'The Clémenceau Case,' occupied all the ground covered to-day by the Casino de Paris and the 'Pôle-Nord' establishment. When about fifteen I left the Saint-Victor School for Monsieur Hénon's school, which was situated in the Rue de Courcelles and has now disappeared. It is in the Collège Bourbon (now the Lycée Condorcet) that I received all my instruction, as the pupils of the two schools where I lived attended the college classes. I never belonged to any of the higher State schools,—I have not even the degree of bachelor.»

At the end of his years of study he returned to his father. He did not stay there more than six months. The rather tumultuous life which he saw in the house disturbed his proud mind, already filled with serious yearnings.

«You have debts,» his father said to him. «Do as I do: work, and you will pay them.»

Such was indeed the young man's intention. His first work was a one-act play in verse, 'The Queen's Jewel,' which no one, assuredly, would mention to-day but for his signature. The date was 1845, and the author was then twenty-one. Other works by him were published at various times in the Journal des Demoiselles.

«I was,» he has said, «the careless, lazy, and spoilt child of all my father's friends. I believed in the eternity of youth, of strength, of joy. I spent the whole day laughing, the whole night sleeping, unless I had some reason for writing verses.»

About 1846 he set resolutely to work. He turned to novel-writing, which seemed to him to offer greater facilities for reaching the public and greater chances of immediate income than dramatic composition. Only two of his novels have survived: 'La Dame aux Camélias' ('Camille': 1848), because from this book came the immortal drama by the same title; and 'The Clémenceau Case,' because the author wrote it when he was in complete possession of his talent, and because moreover it is a first-rate work.

It was in 1852 that the Vaudeville Theatre gave the first performance of 'Camille,' the fortune of which was to be so extraordinary. For two or three years the play had been tossed from theatre to theatre. Nobody wanted it. To the ideas of the time it seemed simply shocking, and the play was still forbidden in London after its performances in France were numbered by the hundreds.

There is this special trait in 'Camille'—it was a work all instinct with the spirit of youth. Dumas twenty years later sadly said: «I might perhaps make another 'Demi-Monde'; I could not make another 'Camille.'» There existed, indeed, other works which have all the fire and charm of the twentieth year. 'Polyeucte' is Corneille's masterpiece; his 'Cid' breathes the spirit of youth: Corneille at forty could not have written the 'Cid.' Racine's first play is 'Andromaque': Beaumarchais's is the 'Barber of Seville'; Rossini, when young, enlivened it with his light and sparkling airs. Fifteen years later he himself wrote his 'William Tell,' a higher work, but a work which was not young.

If the theatrical managers had recoiled from 'Camille' in spite of the great names that recommended it, it is because it was cut after a pattern to which neither they nor the public were accustomed; it is because it contained the germ of a whole dramatic revolution. Now, the author was not a theatrical revolutionist. He had not said to himself, «I am going to throw down the old fabric of the drama, and erect a new one on its ruins.» To tell the truth, he had no idea of what he was doing. He had witnessed a love drama. He had thrown it still throbbing upon the stage, without any regard for the dramatic conventions which were then imposed upon playwrights, and which were almost accepted as laws. He had simply depicted what he had seen. All the managers, attached as they were to the

ALEX. DUMAS, FILS.

old customs, and respectful of the traditions, had trembled with horror when they saw moving around Camille the ignoble Prudence, the idiotic Duc de Varville, the silly Saint-Gaudens. But the public—though the fact was suspected neither by them nor by the public itself—yearned for more truth upon the boards. When 'Camille' was presented to them, the play-goers uttered a cry of astonishment and joy: that was the thing! that was just what they wanted! From that day, which will remain as a date in the history of the French stage, the part of Camille has been performed by all the celebrated actresses. The part has two sides: one may see in it a degraded woman who has fallen profoundly in love, rather late in life; one may also see in it a woman, already poetical in her own nature, suddenly carried away by a great passion into the sacred regions of the Ideal.

Almost any young man in Dumas's place would have lost his head after so astounding a success, and might not have resisted the temptation of at once working out the vein. For on coming out of the theatre after the first performance, the author had all the managers at his feet, and the smallest trifle was sure to be accepted if it only had his signature. But he had learned, by the side of «a prodigal father,» the art of husbanding his talent. He declined to front the footlights again, save with a work upon which he had been able to bestow all the care and labor it deserved: he waited a year before he gave, at the Gymnase theatre, 'Diane de Lys.'

'Diane de Lys' undoubtedly pleased the public, but its success was not exactly brilliant. It is full of great qualities, it is strongly conceived, constructed with rare power and logic, but it added nothing to his reputation. The play as a whole seemed long and melancholy. It is a curious subject for critical study, as one of the stages in which the genius of the author stopped awhile, on its way to higher works. It will leave no great trace in his career.

Two years later he gave at the Gymnase theatre—I do not dare to say his masterpiece, but certainly the best constructed and most enjoyable play he ever wrote, 'Le Demi-Monde' (The Other Half-World). In this play he discovered and defined the very peculiar world of those women who live on the margin of regular «society,» and try to preserve its tone and demeanor. What scientific and strong construction are here! What an admirable disposition of the scenes, both flexible and logical! And through the action, which moves on with wonderful straightforwardness and breadth, how many portraits, drawn with a steady hand, each one bearing such distinctive features that you would know them if you met them on the street! Olivier de Jalin, the refined Parisian, the dialectician of the play, who is no other than Dumas himself; Raymond de Nanjac, handsome and honest, but not keen or Parisian; and that giddy Valentine de Sanctis, whose head turns with the wind, whose tongue cannot rest one moment; and especially Suzanne d'Ange, so witty, so complex, so devious in her motions, so *roublarde*, as a Parisian of to-day would say.

Between 'The Demi-Monde,' and 'La Question d'Argent' (The Money Question), which followed, Dumas spent two years at work. 'La Question d'Argent' is a favorite play with the connoisseurs; but its reception by the public was of the coldest. It is a noteworthy fact that plays turning upon money have never been successful. Le Sage's 'Turcaret' is a dramatic masterpiece: it never had the luck to please the crowd. Dumas's Jean Giraud is, however, a very curiously studied character. The author has represented in him the commonest type of the shady money-man, the unconscious rascal. And very skillfully he made an individual out of that general type, by giving to Jean Giraud a certain rough good-nature; the appearance of a good fellow, with a certain degree of fineness; a mixture of humility and self-conceit, of awkwardness and impudence, and even some ideas as to the power of money that do not lack dignity, and some real liberality of sentiment and act,—for wealth alone, though acquired by ignominious means, suggests and dictates to the great robbers some advantageous movements which the small rascal cannot indulge in: and around this Turcaret of the Second Empire how many pictures of honest people, every one of whom, in his or her way, is good and fine!

One year later Dumas carried to the Gymnase, his favorite theatre, 'Le Fils Naturel' (The Natural Son); and the next year 'Un Père Prodigue' (A Prodigal Father; known also in English through a free adaptation as 'My Awful Dad').

In 'Le Fils Naturel' Dumas for the first time wrote a theme-play, a kind of work in which he was to become a master. Hitherto we have seen him drawing pictures of manners. To be sure, philosophical considerations on the period depicted are not wanting, but the play has not the form and does not assume the movement of a thesis. It does not take up one special trait of our social order, one of our worldly prejudices, in order to show its strong and weak sides. 'Le Fils Naturel' is the work of a moralist as well as of a playwright; or rather, it is the work of a playwright who was a born moralist.

'Un Père Prodigue' originally excited great curiosity. It escaped no one that in his Count Fernand de la Rivonnière, Dumas had shown us some traits of his illustrious father, who *had* been a prodigal father; and that he had depicted himself in Viscount André. Every one made comparisons; some, of course, accused the author of filial disrespect. The accusation was ridiculous, and he did not even answer it. He had so well disguised the persons, he had transported them into such different surroundings, that no one could recognize in them their true prototypes. Then — and this is no small praise — if Count de la Rivonnière is guilty of one fault, that of throwing to the wind his fortune, he is a most amiable nobleman, full of broad ideas and generous sentiments,— has a warm heart. The fourth act, in which the father sacrifices himself in order to save his son's life, is pathetic in the extreme. But nothing equals the first act, which is a model of animated and picturesque composition. No one ever painted in more vivid colors the pillage of a household, and a family without so much as a shadow of discipline. It is an accumulation of small details, not one of which is of an indifferent nature, and which, taken together, drive into our minds the idea that this nobleman, so well-mannered, so charming in conversation, so sober for himself, is running to ruin as gayly as he can.

For four years after the production of ‹Un Père Prodigue› Dumas wrote nothing. But in 1864 he reappeared at the Gymnase with a strange play, ‹L'Ami des Femmes› (A Friend of the Sex), which completely failed. After ‹L'Ami des Femmes› there was another interruption, not of Dumas's labors but of his dramatic production. Perhaps he was sick of an art which had caused him a cruel disappointment. He turned again to novel-writing, and published (1866) ‹L'Affaire Clémenceau› (The Clémenceau Case), the success of which was not as great as he had hoped. In France, when a man is superior in one specialty people will not let him leave it. He is not allowed to be at once an unequaled novelist and a first-rate dramatist.

At that time Dumas hesitated which road to follow. An incident which created a great deal of comment threw him back towards the stage, and towards a new form of comedy.

M. Émile de Girardin, one of the best known publicists of the Second Empire, had bethought himself, when over fifty years of age, and knowing nothing of this kind of work, to write a play. He had been a great friend of Dumas père, and had kept up the most affectionate intercourse with his son. He had asked him to fit his play for the stage. It possessed one really dramatic idea. Dumas, in order to oblige his father's friend, made out of it ‹Le Supplice d'une Femme› (A Woman's Torture). Émile de Girardin, who was self-conceited and somewhat despotic, refused to recognize his offspring in the bear that Dumas had licked. He declined to sign the play: «Neither shall I,» Dumas retorted.

‹A Woman's Torture› was acted at the Comédie Française with extraordinary success. This success was for Dumas a warning and a lesson. ‹A Woman's Torture› was a three-act play, short, concise, panting, which hurried to the *coup de théâtre* of the second act, upon which the drama revolved, and rushed to its conclusion. The time of five-act comedies, with ample expositions, copious developments, philosophical disquisitions, curious and fanciful episodes, was gone. Henceforth the dramatist had to deal with a hurried and *blasé* public, which, taking dinner at eight, could give to the theatre but a short time, and an attention disturbed by the labor of digestion. 'A Woman's Torture,' which lasted only an hour and a half, and proceeded only by rapid strokes, was exactly what that public wanted. After that time Dumas wrote only three-act and one-act plays; using four acts only for 'Les Idées de Madame Aubray' (Madame Aubray's Ideas); and these four acts are very short. In 1867 this play announced Dumas's return to the stage; and Dumas is here more paradoxical than he had ever been. His theme looked like a wager not simply against bourgeois prejudices, but even against good sense, and, I dare to say, against justice. This wager was won by Dumas, thanks to an incredible display of skill. He took up the thesis a second time in 'Denise,' and won his wager again, but with less difficulty. In 'Denise' the lover struggles only against social prejudices, and allows himself to be carried away by one of those emotional fits which disturb and confound human reason. In 'Madame Aubray's Ideas' the triumph is one of pure logic.

'Une Visite de Noces' (A Wedding Call) and 'La Princesse Georges' followed rather closely on 'Madame Aubray's Ideas.' 'A Wedding Call'!—what a thunderbolt then! It was of but one act, *but* one act the effect of which was prodigious, the echo of which is still heard. Time and familiarity have now softened for us the too sharp outlines of this bitter play. It has been acknowledged a masterpiece. It is certainly one of the boldest works of this extraordinary magician, who, thanks to his unerring skill and to the dazzling wit of his dialogue, brought the public to listen to whatever he chose to put upon the stage. It seemed that, like a lion tamer in the arena, Dumas took pleasure in belaboring and exasperating this many-headed monster, in order to prove to his own satisfaction that he could subdue its revolts.

'La Princesse Georges' is a work of violent and furious passion. We find in it Madame de Terremonde, the good woman who adores her husband, but who adores him with fury, who wants him all to herself, and who, when sure that she is betrayed, passes from the most exasperated rage to tears and despair. There is in the first act a scene of exposition which has become celebrated. No one ever so rapidly mastered the public; no one ever from the first stroke so painfully twisted the heart of the spectators.

Let us pass rapidly over 'La Femme de Claude' (Claude's Wife: 1873). Of all his plays it is the one Dumas said he liked best, the one he most passionately defended with all sorts of commentaries, letters, prefaces, etc.; the one which he insisted on having revived, a long time after it had failed. To my mind that play was a mistake: and the public, in spite of Dumas's arguments, in spite of the protests of the critics, who are often very glad to distinguish themselves by not yielding to the common voice,—the public insisted on agreeing with me.

Only a few months later, Dumas brilliantly retrieved himself with 'Monsieur Alphonse.' His Madame Guichard is the most cheerfully vulgar type of the *parvenue* which any one ever dared to put upon the stage. She can hardly read and write; she is no longer young, and she is "to boot" very proud of her money; she has no tact and no taste; but at heart she is a good sort of woman. Her morality is as primitive as her education. But deceit disgusts her; she hates but one thing, she says,—lying. She is not troubled by conventionalities, and her speech has all the color and energy of popular speech. But see! Dumas in depicting this woman preserved exquisite measure. Madame Guichard says many pert and droll things; she never utters a coarse word. Her language is picturesque; it is free from slang. Hers is a vulgar nature, but she does not offend delicate ears by the grossness of her utterance. Dumas never drew a more living picture; she is the joy of this rather sad play.

All that remain to be reviewed are 'L'Étrangère,' 'La Princesse de Bagdad,' and 'Francillon'; all of which were given at the Comédie Française. 'L'Étrangère' is indeed a melodrama, with an admixture of comedy. Had he gone further in that direction, Dumas might have made a new sort of play, which would perhaps have reigned a long time on the stage. But after this trial, successful though it was, he stopped. 'La Princesse de Bagdad' entirely failed. 'Francillon' was Dumas's last success at the Comédie Française.

After 1887 Dumas gave nothing to the stage. He had completed a great five-act play, 'The Road to Thebes,' which the manager of the Comédie Française hoped every year to put on the boards. Dumas kept promising it; but either from distrust of himself or of the public, or from fatigue, or fear of meeting with failure, he asked for new delays, until the day when he declared that not only the play would not be acted during his life, but that he would not even allow it to be acted after his death.

This death he saw coming, with sad but calm eyes. It was a sorrow for us to see this man, whom we had known so quick and alert, grow weaker every day, showing the progress of disease in his shriveled features and body. The complexion had lost all color, the cheeks had become flaccid, the eye had no life left.

On October 1st, 1895, he wrote to his friend Jules Claretie:—"Do not depend upon me any more; I am vanquished. There are moments when I mourn my loss, as Madame D'Houdetot said when dying." He was at Puys, by the seaside, when he wrote that despairing letter. He returned to Marly, there to die, surrounded by his family, on November 28th, 1895, in a house which he loved and which had been bequeathed to him years before by an intimate friend.

His loss threw into mourning the world of letters, and the whole of Paris. People discovered then — for death loosens every tongue and every pen — how kind and generous in reality was Dumas, who had often been accused of avarice by those who contrasted him with his father; how many services he had discreetly rendered, how open his hand always was. His constant cheerfulness and good-nature had finally caused him to be forgiven for his wit, which was sarcastic and cutting, and for his success, which had thrown so many rivals into the shade. This witty man, who was always obliging and even tender-hearted, had no envy, and gave his applause without a shadow of reserve to the successes of others. Every young author found in him advice and support; he did not expect gratitude, and therefore was soured by no disappointment. He was a good man, partly from nature, partly from determination; for he deemed that, after all, the best way to live happy in this world is to make happy as many people as possible.

If in this long essay I have not spoken of Dumas as a moralist, it is because, in my opinion, in spite of all that has been said, Dumas was a dramatist a great deal more than a philosopher. In his comedies he discussed a great many moral and social questions, without giving a solution for any; or rather, the solutions that he gave were due not to any set of fixed principles, but to the conclusion which he was preparing for this play or that. He said, indifferently, «Kill her» or «Forgive her,» according to the requirements of the subject which he had selected; and he would afterwards write a sensational preface with a view to demonstrate that the solution this time given by him was the only legitimate one. These prefaces are very amusing reading; for he wrote them with all the fire of his nature, and he had the gift of movement. But they were a strange medley of incongruous and contradictory statements. Every idea that he expresses can be grasped and understood; but it is impossible to see how it agrees with those that precede and follow. It is a chaos of clear ideas.

Dumas was not a philosopher, but an agitator. He stirred up a great many questions; he drew upon them our distracted attention; he compelled us to think of them. Therein he did his duty as a dramatist.

He gave much thought to the fate of woman in our civilization. We may say, however, that though loving her much, he still more feared her; and I shall even add, despised her. All his characters who have the mission of defending morality and good sense are very attentive to her, but keep her at arm's-length. They are affectionate counselors, not lovers. They hold her to be a frail being, who must be controlled and guided. Some one has said that there was in Dumas something of the Catholic priest. It is true. He was to women a lay director of conscience.

He was a great connoisseur of pictures and a great art lover. Music, I think, is the only art that did not affect him much. He was a dazzling talker; his plays teem with bright sayings; his conversation sparkled with them. I did not know him in his prime, when he delighted his friends and companions by his unceasing flow of spirits. I became intimate with him only later. If you knew how to start him, he simply coruscated. I never knew any one, save Edmond About, who was as witty, and who, like About, always paid you back in good sounding coin.

Dumas was a member of the French Academy. He had not wished for that honor, because it had been denied to his father. He desired, in his reception speech, to call up the great spirit of this illustrious father and make it share his academician's chair. He had this joy; the two Dumas were received on the same day. Their two names will never perish.

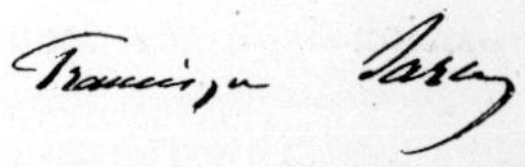

[The editors have been compelled, for lack of space, to leave out that part of M. Sarcey's valuable essay which is a professional analysis of several of Dumas's plays, and which would be of interest, chiefly, to special students of the French drama and stage.]

THE PLAYWRIGHT IS BORN—AND MADE

From the Preface to 'A Prodigal Father'

OF ALL the various forms of thought, the stage is that which nearest approaches the plastic arts—inasmuch as we cannot work in it unless we know its material processes; but with this difference: that in the other arts one learns these processes, while in play-writing one guesses them; or to speak more accurately, they are in us to begin with.

One can become a painter, a sculptor, a musician, by sheer study: one does not become a dramatic author in this fashion. A caprice of nature makes your eye in such a way that you can see a thing after a particular manner, not absolutely correct, but which must nevertheless appear, to any other persons that you wish to have so think, the only correct point of view. The man really called to write for the stage reveals what is an extremely rare faculty, in his very first attempts,—say in a farce in school, or a drawing-room charade. There is a sort of science of optics and of perspective that enables one to draw a personage, a character, a passion, an impulse of the soul, with a single stroke of the pen. Dramatic *cheating of the eye* is so complete that often the spectator, when he is a mere reader of the play, desiring to give himself once more the same emotion that he has felt as one of the audience, not only cannot recapture that emotion in the written words before him, but often cannot even distinguish the passage where the emotion lies hid. It was a word, a look, a silence, a gesture, a purely atmospheric combination, that held him spellbound. So comes in the genius of the playwright's trade, if those two words can be associated. One may compare writing for the stage in relation to other phases of literature, as we compare ceiling painters with [painters of] pictures for the wall or the easel. Woe to the painter if he forget that his composition is to be looked at from a distance, with a light below it!

A man without merit as a thinker, a moralist, a philosopher, an author, may turn out to be a dramatic author of the first class; that is to say, in the work of setting in motion before you the purely external movements of mankind; and on the other hand, to become in the theatre the thinker, the moralist, the philosopher, or the author to whom one listens, one must indispensably be furnished with the particular and natural qualities of a man of much lower grade. In short, to be a master in the art of writing for the stage, you must be a poor hand in the superior art. . . .

That dramatic author who shall know mankind like Balzac, and who shall know the theatre like Scribe, will be the greatest dramatic author that has ever existed.

Translated for ‹A Library of the World's Best Literature,› by E. Irenæus Stevenson

AN ARMED TRUCE

From ‹A Friend of the Sex›

[The following conversation in the first act of the play takes place in the pleasant morning-room of a country-house near Paris, the home of M. and Madame Leverdet. M. Leverdet is asleep in his chair. The speakers are Madame Leverdet, a coquettish, sprightly lady approaching middle age, and young M. De Ryons, a friend and neighbor. Madame Leverdet is determined to marry off De Ryons advantageously, and as soon as possible. Unfortunately he is a confirmed bachelor, not to say woman-hater, whose cynicism is the result of severely disappointing experiences. Under that cynicism there is however genuine respect and even chivalry as to the right sort of woman,—the superior and sincere type, which he does not happen often to encounter.]

MADAME LEVERDET — Let us come to serious topics while we are alone, my friend.

De Ryons — And apropos of them?

Madame Leverdet — Are you willing to be married off yet?

De Ryons [*with a start of terror*] — Pardon me, my dear lady! At what hour can I take the first train for Paris?

Madame Leverdet — Now listen to me, at least.

De Ryons — What! Here it is two years since I have called on you; I come to make you a little visit of a morning, in all good friendship, with the thermometer forty, centigrade; I am totally unsuspecting; all I ask is to have a little lively chat with a clever woman — and see how you receive me.

Madame Leverdet [*continuing*] — A simple, charming young girl —

De Ryons [*interrupting her, and in the same tone*] — — musical, speaks English, draws nicely, sings agreeably, a society woman, a domestic woman,— all at the choice of the applicant.

Madame Leverdet [*laughing*] — Yes, and pretty and graceful and rich; and, by-the-by, one who finds you a charming fellow.

De Ryons — She is quite right there. I shall make a charming husband — I shall; I know it. Only thirty-two years old; all my teeth, all my hair (no such very common detail, the way young men are nowadays); lively, sixty thousand livres income as a landed proprietor — oh, I am an excellent match: only unfortunately I am not a marrying man.

Madame Leverdet — And why not, if you please?

De Ryons [*smiling*] — It would interfere severely with my studies.

Madame Leverdet — What sort of studies?

De Ryons — My studies of — woman.

Madame Leverdet — Really! I don't understand you.

De Ryons — What! Do you not know that I am making women my particular, my incessant study, and that I am reckoning on leaving some new and very interesting documents dealing with that branch of natural history? — a branch very little understood just at present, in spite of all that has been written on the topic. My friend, I cannot sacrifice the species to the individual; I belong to science. It is quite impossible for me to give myself wholly and completely — as one certainly should do when he marries — to one of those charming and terrible little carnivora for whose sake men dishonor themselves, ruin themselves, kill themselves; whose sole preoccupation, in the midst of the universal carnage that they make, is to dress themselves now like umbrellas and now like table bells.

Madame Leverdet [*scornfully*] — So you really think you understand women, do you?

De Ryons — I rather think I do. Why, just as you see me this instant, at the end of five minutes' study or conversation I can tell you to what class a woman belongs, — whether to the middle class, to women of rank, artists, or whatever you please; what are her tastes, her characteristics, her antecedents, the state of her heart, — in a word, everything that concerns my special science.

Madame Leverdet — Really! Will you have a glass of water?

De Ryons — Not yet, thank you.

Madame Leverdet — I suppose, then, you are under the impression that you know me too.

De Ryons — As if I did not!

Madame Leverdet — Well, and I am — what?

De Ryons — Oh, you are a clever woman. It is for that reason that I call on you [*aside:* every two years].

Madame Leverdet — Will you kindly give me the sum of your observations in general? You can tell me so much, since I am a clever woman.

De Ryons — The true, the true, the true sum?

Madame Leverdet — Yes.

De Ryons — Simply that woman of our day is an illogical, subordinate, and mischief-making creature. [*In saying this De Ryons draws back and crouches down as if expecting to be struck.*]

Madame Leverdet — So then, you detest women?

De Ryons — I? I detest women? On the contrary, I adore them; but I hold myself in such a position toward them that they cannot bite me. I keep on the outside of the cage.

Madame Leverdet — Meaning by that — what?

De Ryons — Meaning by that, that I am a friend of the sex; for I have long perceived that just as truly as women are dangerous in love, just so much are they adorable in friendship, with men; — that is to say, with no obligations, and therefore no treasons; no rights, and in consequence no tyrannies. One assists, too, as a spectator, often as a collaborator, in the comedy of love. A man under such conditions sees before his nose the stage tricks, the machinery, the changes of scenes, all that stage mounting so dazzling at a distance and so simple when one is near by. As a friend of the sex and on a basis of friendship, one estimates the causes, the contradictions, the incoherences, of that phantasmagoric changeableness that belongs to the heart of a woman. So you have something that is interesting and instructive. Under such circumstances a man is the consoler, and gives his advice; he wipes away tears; he brings quarrelsome lovers together; he asks for the letters that must be returned; he hands back the photographs (for you know that in love affairs photographs are taken only in order to be returned, and it is nearly always the same photograph that serves as many times as may be necessary. I know one photograph that I have had handed back by three different men, and it ended its usefulness by being given for good and all to a fourth one, who was — not single). . . . In short, you see, my dear madam, I am above all the friend of those women — who have known what it is to be in love. And moreover inasmuch, just as Rochefoucauld says, as women do not think a great deal of their first experience, — why, one fine day or another —

Madame Leverdet — You prove to be the second one.

De Ryons — No, no; I have no number, I! A well-brought-up woman never goes from one experience of the heart to another one, without a decent interval of time, more or less long. Two railroad accidents never come together on the same railway. During the *intervals* a woman really needs a friend, a good confidant; and it is then that I turn up. I let her tell me all the melancholy affairs in question; I see the unhappy victim in tears after the traitor has called; I lament with her, I weep with her, I make her laugh with me: and little by little I replace the delinquent without her seeing that I am doing so. But then I know very well that I am without importance, that I am a mere politician of the moment, a cabinet minister without a portfolio, a sentimental distraction without any consequences; and some fine day, after having been the confidential friend as to past events, I become the confidential friend as to future ones,— for the lady falls in love for the second time with somebody who knows nothing of the first experience, who will never know anything about it, and who of course must be made to suppose he represents the first one. Then I go away for a little time and leave them to themselves, and then I come back like a new friend to the family. By-and-by, when the dear creature is reckoning up the balance-sheet of her past, when her conscience pours into her ear the names that she would rather not remember, and my name comes with the others, she reflects an instant,— and then she says resolutely and sincerely to herself, "Oh, *he* does not count!" My friend, I am always the one that does not count, and I like it extremely.

Madame Leverdet [*indignantly*] — You are simply a monster!

De Ryons — Oh no, oh no, oh no, I am not!

Madame Leverdet — According to your own account, you have no faith in women. . . . Wretch! Ungrateful creature! And yet it is woman who inspires all the great things in this life.

De Ryons — But somehow forbids us to accomplish them.

Madame Leverdet — Go out from here, my dear De Ryons, and never let me see you again.

De Ryons [*rising promptly and making a mocking bow*] — My dear lady —

Madame Leverdet — No, I will *not* shake hands with you.

De Ryons — Then I shall die of chagrin — that's all about it.

Madame Leverdet — Do you know how you will end, you incorrigible creature? When you are fifty years old you will have rheumatism.

De Ryons — Yes, or sciatica. But I shall find some one who will embroider me warm slippers.

Madame Leverdet — Indeed you will not! You will marry your cook.

De Ryons — That depends on how well she cooks. Again farewell, dear madam.

Madame Leverdet — No, stay one moment.

De Ryons — It is you who are keeping me; so look out.

Madame Leverdet — Let me have really your last word on the whole matter.

De Ryons — It is very easily given. There are just two kinds of women: those who are good women, and those who are not.

Madame Leverdet — Without fine distinctions?

De Ryons — Without fine distinctions.

Madame Leverdet — What is one to do in the case of those who are not — good women?

De Ryons — They must be consoled.

Madame Leverdet — And those who are?

De Ryons — They must be guaranteed against being anything else; and as to that process of guarantee I have taken a patent.

Madame Leverdet — Come now, if you are playing in parlor theatricals, say so. What are you trying to be, — Lovelace or Don Quixote?

De Ryons — I am neither the one nor the other. I am a man who, having nothing else to do, took to studying women just as another man studies beetles and minerals, only I am under the impression that my scientific study is more interesting and more useful than that of the other savant — because we meet your sex everywhere. We meet the mother, the sister, the daughter, the wife, the woman who is in love; and it is important to be well informed upon such an eternal associate in our lives. Now I am a man of my time, exercised over one theory or another, hardly knowing what he must believe, good or bad, but inclined to believe in good when occasion presents itself. I respect women who respect themselves. . . . It is not I who created the world; I take it as I find it. . . . And as to marriage, the day when I shall find a young girl with the four qualities of goodness of heart, sound health, thorough self-respect, and cheerfulness, — the squaring of the conjugal hypothenuse, — then I count for nothing all my long term of waiting; like the great Doctor Faust, I become young again, and such as I am, I give myself to her. My friend, if this same young girl of whom you have been speaking (and by the way, I know her just as well as you do) really unites these conditions, — I do not believe she does so, though I shall see very soon, — why then, I will marry her to-morrow — I will marry her to-night. But in the mean time, as I have positively nothing to do, — if you happen to know a self-respecting woman who needs to be kept from a bit of folly . . . why, I am wholly at your service.

Translated for ‹A Library of the World's Best Literature,› by E. Irenæus Stevenson

TWO VIEWS OF MONEY

From 'The Money Question'

[The following passage occurs in the first act of Dumas's play. The characters include the young parvenu Jean Giraud, the aristocratic M. De Cayolle, and several others, all guests in the drawing-room of the country-house of Madame Durieu. In course of the conversation Giraud refers to his father, at one time a gardener on the estate of M. De Charzay.]

JEAN GIRAUD—Oh, yes, yes, I have got along in the world, as people say. There are people who blush for their fathers; I make a brag of mine—that's the difference.

René de Charzay—And what is Father Giraud nowadays? Oh, I beg your pardon—

Jean—Don't be embarrassed—we keep on calling him Father Giraud all the same. He is a gardener still, only he gardens on his own account. He owns the house that your father was obliged to sell a while ago. My father has never had but one idea,—our Father Giraud,—and that is to be a land-owner; I bought that piece of property for him, and so he is as happy as a fish in the water. If you like, we will go and take breakfast with him to-morrow morning. He will be delighted to see you. How things change, eh? There, where a while ago we were the servants, now we are the masters; though we are not so very proud, for all that.

Countess Savelli [*aside*]—He has passed the Rubicon of parvenus! He has confessed his father! Now nothing can stop his way!

Jean [*to De Charzay*]—I have wanted to see you for a long time, but I have not been sure how you would meet me.

René—I would have met you with pleasure, as my uncle would have met you. One cannot utter reproaches to a man who has made his own fortune, except when he has made it by dishonest means; a man who owes it to his intelligence and his probity, who uses it worthily, everybody is ready to meet kindly, as you are met here.

Jean—Sir, it is not necessary that a man should use his fortune nobly, provided it is made—that is the main thing!

Madame Durieu—Oh, oh, M. Giraud! there you spoil everything that you have said.

Jean—I don't say that of my own case, madam, but I say just what I say,—money is money, whatever may be the kind of hands where it sticks. It is the sole power that one never disputes. You may dispute virtue, beauty, courage, genius; but you can't dispute money. There is not one civilized being, rising in the morning, who does not recognize the sovereignty of money, without which he would have neither the roof which shelters him, nor the bed in which he sleeps, nor the bread that he eats. Whither are bound these masses of people crowding in the streets?—from the employé sweating under his too heavy burden, to the millionaire hurrying down to the Bourse behind his two trotters? The one is running after fifteen sous, the other after one hundred thousand francs. Why do we all have these shops, these railroads, these factories, these theatres, these museums, these lawsuits between brothers and sisters, between fathers and sons, these revelations, these divisions in families, these murders? All for pieces, more or less numerous, of that white or yellow metal which people call silver or gold. And pray who will be the most thought of at the end of this grand race after money? The man who brings back the most of it. Ah, nowadays a man has no business to have more than one object in life—and that is to become as rich as possible! For my part, that has always been my idea; I have carried it out: I congratulate myself on it. Once upon a time everybody found me homely, stupid, a bore; to-day everybody finds me handsome, witty, amiable,—and the Lord knows if *I* am witty, amiable, handsome! On the day when I might be stupid enough to let myself be ruined, to become plain «Jean» as before, there would not be enough stones in the Montmartre quarries to throw at my head. But there, that day is a good way off, and meantime many of my business acquaintances have been ruined for the sake of keeping me from ruin. The last word, too, the greatest praise that I could give to wealth, certainly is, that such a circle as I find myself in at present has had the patience to listen so long to the son of a gardener, who has no other right to their attention than the poor little millions that he has made.

Durieu [*aside*]—It is all absolutely true, every word that he has been saying—gardener's son that he is! He sees our epoch just as it really is.

Madame Durieu—Come now, my dear M. De Cayolle, what do you think of what M. Giraud has been telling us?

Cayolle—I think, madam, that the theories of M. Giraud are sound, but sound only as to that society in which M. Giraud has lived until now: a world of speculation, whose one object naturally ought to be to make money. As to wealth itself, it brings about infamous things, but it also brings about great and noble things. In that respect it is like human speech: a bad thing for some people, a good thing for others, according to the use they make of it. This obligation of our state of society that makes a man wake up each morning with taking thought of the necessary sum for his personal wants, lest he take what does not belong to him, has created the finest intelligence of all the ages! It is simply to this need of money every day that we owe Franklin, who began the world by being a printer's apprentice; Shakespeare, who used to hold horses at the door of the theatre which later he was going to immortalize; Machiavelli, who was secretary to the Florentine republic at fifteen crowns a month; Raphael, the son of a mere dauber; Jean Jacques Rousseau, a notary's clerk and an engraver,—one who did not have a dinner every day; Fulton, once upon a time a mechanic, who gave us steam: and so many others. Had these same people been born with an income of half a million livres apiece, there would have been a good many chances that not one of them would ever have become what he did become. [*To M. Giraud.*] This race after wealth, of which you speak, M. Giraud, has good in it: even if it enriches some silly people or some rascals, if it procures for them the consideration of those in a humble station of life,—of the lower classes, of those who have cash relations with society, on the other hand there is a great deal of good in the spur given to faculties which would otherwise remain stationary; enough good to pardon some errors in the distribution of wealth. Just in proportion as you enter into the true world of society—a world which is almost unknown to you, M. Giraud—you will find that a man who is received there is received only in proportion to his personal value. Look around here where we are, without taking the trouble to go any further, and you will see that money has not the influence you ascribe to it. For proof, here is Countess Savelli, with half a million francs income, who in place of dining out with millionaires besieging her house every day, comes quietly here to dine with our friends the Durieus, people without title, poor people measured by her fortune; and she comes here for the pleasure of meeting M. De Charzay, who has not more than a thousand crowns income, but who, for all the millionaires in the world, would never do a thing a man ought not to do; and she meets here M. De Roncourt, who has a business of fifteen hundred francs because he gave up his fortune to creditors who were not his own creditors. There is Mademoiselle De Roncourt, who sacrificed her dowry to the same sentiment of honor; yonder is Mademoiselle Durieu, who would never be willing to become the wife of any other than an honest man, even if he had for his rivals all the Crœsuses present and to come; and last of ali, one meets me here,— a man who has for money (in the acceptation that you give the word) the most profound contempt. Now, M. Giraud, if we listened to you for so long a time, it is because we are well-bred people, and besides, you talk very well; but there has been no flattery for your millions in our attention, and the proof is that everybody has been listening to me a longer time than to you,— listening to me, who have not like you a thousand-franc note to put along with every one of my phrases!

Jean—Who is that gentleman who has just been speaking?

Durieu—That is M. De Cayolle.

Jean—The railway director?

Durieu—Yes.

Jean [*going to M. De Cayolle*]—M. De Cayolle, I hope you will believe that I am very glad to meet you.

Cayolle—I dare say you are, monsieur. [*M. De Cayolle as he utters the words turns his back upon Giraud and steps aside.*]

Translated for ‹A Library of the World's Best Literature,› by E. Irenæus Stevenson

M. DE RÉMONIN'S PHILOSOPHY OF MARRIAGE

From ‹L'Étrangère›

MADAME DE RUMIÈRES—See here, now, Rémonin, you who claim to explain everything as a learned man—can you solve this proposition? Why is it that with all the quantity of love in this world, there are so many unhappy marriages?

M. Rémonin—I could give you a perfect explanation, my dear lady, if you were not a woman.

Madame de Rumières—You mean that the explanation is not decent?

M. Rémonin — No, I mean that it is a matter based on the abstract. . . . It is this. The reason why marriages are rarely happy, in spite of the « quantity of love » in question, is because love and marriage, scientifically considered, have no relationship. They belong to two sorts of things, completely differing. Love is of the physical. Marriage is a matter of chemistry.

Madame de Rumières — Explain yourself.

Rémonin — Certainly. Love is an element of the natural evolution of our being; it comes to us of itself in course of our life, at one time or another, independent of all our will, and even without a definite object. The human creature can wish to be in love before really loving any one! . . . But marriage is a social combination, an adjustment, that refers itself to chemistry, as I have said; since chemistry concerns itself with the action of one element on another and the phenomena resulting: . . . . to the end of bringing about family life, morality, and labor, and in consequence the welfare of man, as involved in all three. Now, so often as you really can conform to the theory of such a blending of things, so long as you happen to have effected in marriage such a combination of the physical *and* chemical, all goes well; the experiment is happy, it results well. But if you are ignorant or maladroit enough to seek and to make a combination of two refractory chemical forces in the matrimonial experiment, then in the place of a fusion you will find you have only inert forces; and the two elements remain there, together but unfused, eternally opposed to each other, never able to be united! . . . Or else there is not merely inertia — there are shocks, explosions, catastrophes, accidents, dramas. . . .

Madame de Rumières — Have you ever been in love?

M. Rémonin — I? My dear marquise, I am a scientist — I have never had time! And you?

Madame de Rumières — I have loved my children. M. de Rumières was a charming man all his life; but he didn't expect me really to love him. My son tells me his affairs of the heart; . . . my daughter has already made me a grandmother. . . . I have little to reproach myself as to my past life, and now I look on at the lives of others, sometimes much interested. I am like the subscribers to the Opéra, who know the whole repertory by heart, but who can always hear some passages with pleasure and who encourage the débutants.

Condensed and translated for 'A Library of the World's Best Literature,' by E. Irenæus Stevenson.

REFORMING A FATHER

From ‹A Prodigal Father›

[The ensuing dialogue occurs in the first act of the play. The Count de Ravonnières and his son André reside together in their comfortable bachelor's establishment in Paris, and are devotedly attached to one another. The count, unfortunately, has only grown more careless of money, more a gay man of the world, as he has grown older; and blessed with a youthfulness of physique and temperament that nothing impairs, he is as thriftless as he is fascinating. His son, accordingly, has had to be the economist of their resources, which are at a dangerous ebb. As the scene opens, the count is preparing to take luncheon, with Joseph, the confidential servant of the house, in attendance.]

JOSEPH — Monsieur is served.

Count de Ravonnières —Very well. You will please go to my florist Lemoine, the Opera florist,— you know who I mean,— and tell him to send, to-day, with my card,— he has a lot of cards of mine in advance,— to Mademoiselle Albertine de la Borde, 26 or 28 Rue de la Paix — I don't exactly remember the number that the lady gave me —

Joseph — No. 26.

Count — Ah! You know her address, do you?

Joseph — Yes, sir.

Count — To send her a bouquet of white lilacs and roses. And I don't need you any more: go at once. [*Joseph bows, and hands the Count a large envelope.*] What's all this?

Joseph — Some law papers that have come in your absence, sir, which I did not think ought to be forwarded to Dieppe.

Count [*without taking the papers*] — Quite right. Has my son seen them?

Joseph — No, sir.

Count —Very well; don't let him see them. Put them away with the others.

Joseph — May I beg monsieur to say a good word for me to his son?

Count — As to what, Joseph?

Joseph —Your son, sir, has just told me to look out for another situation; and I am so attached to the family —

Count — Oh, I will straighten all that out; if my son sends you away I will take you into our service again. Come now, get off to my florist; be quick about it.

As Joseph *goes out,* André *enters. He does not at first perceive his father, but on turning toward the table discovers him.*

André — Ah! you are here, are you?

Count — Yes, I have been here during an hour; and moreover, a very agreeable person has been doing the honors of your establishment on my behalf.

André — It is a fine time to talk about agreeable persons! You are a very agreeable person —

Count — What in the world is the matter with you?

André — I am perfectly furious.

Count — Against whom?

André — Against you.

Count — Why? What have I been doing?

André — You have drawn on me at sight this draft here.

Count — Oh yes, I know very well what that means. It comes from London; it is to pay for the boat, you know.

André — Oh yes, it comes from London, and it is to pay for the boat! That is no excuse for it. And what about the boat, if you please?

Count — But my dear fellow, they had no business to present it until the 15th.

André — Well?

Count — Why, to-day *is* the 15th!

André — You ought to know it.

Count — I thought that to-day was only the 14th! Have you paid it?

André — Of course.

Count — Ah! then I owe you six thousand francs. That's all there is to the matter.

André — Yes, that's all! But you never said a word to me about it; I had no money in the house: I had to send to our man of business. May I beg of you in the future to be so good as to —

Count — Poor boy! poor boy! Really, between ourselves, you would have done a great deal better (as it is a month since you have seen me, and since you are really very fond of me) to embrace me in meeting me again, rather than to say all these things to me that you have been saying!

André [*embracing his father heartily*] — Oh, of course they make no difference, when it comes to *that!*

Count—Your second impulse is a very good one; but you ought to have begun with it. All the same, I do not in the less ask pardon for the inconvenience that I have caused you, my boy. [*Takes some bank-notes from his pocket.*] Here are your six thousand francs, and [*holding out the remainder of the notes to André*] since you need money, help yourself.

André—Where in the world does that money come from?

Count—Oh, it is some money that I have received.

André—There was none coming to you from anywhere!

Count—There is always something to come to one, if he looks around carefully. And now let us speak of serious things.

André—Yes, by all means. Father, are you not disposed to settle down?

Count—What do you mean by «settle down»?

André—To save money, for one thing.

Count—Save money! I should be charmed to do so; but I really do not see how we can do it. We certainly live as modestly as possible. This house belongs to us; we have only four saddle horses, four carriage horses, a couple of extra horses for evening service (we could not get along with less), two coachmen, two valets, two grooms, one cook. Why, we haven't even a housekeeper.

André—No, we only want that!

Count—We never receive any except masculine society; we certainly are not extravagant as to the table. Look at me here: I am breakfasting this minute on two eggs and a glass of water. It seems to me that with our fortune—

André—Our fortune? Would you like to know in what condition our fortune is?

Count—You ought to know better than I, since it is you who have had the running of affairs since your majority.

André—Well then, I *do* know the expenses; and let me tell you that you have counted up only those that are part of our life in Paris, and you have not said a syllable of those that belong to our country one.

Count—Those that belong to our country one! Those are all just so much economy.

André—So then the place at Vilsac is just so much economy?

Count—Of course. We get everything from it, from eggs up to oxen.

André— Yes, and even to wild boars, when it suits you to shoot one. Now be so good as to consider the place at Vilsac, which you call a matter of economy. First of all, it brings us in absolutely nothing.

Count— It never has brought us in anything.

André— It is mortgaged for two hundred thousand francs.

Count— That happened when I was young.

André— Are you under the impression that there comes a time when mortgages wear themselves out? I wish they did. But I am afraid that you deceive yourself; and in the mean time, you are paying every year a mortgagor's interest. Furthermore, at Vilsac—

Count— Where, remember, we spend September, October, November, all of which is positively an economy—

André— Furthermore, as to Vilsac, this summer place where we pass September, October, and November,—all of which is positively an economy,— the proof of its being an economy is that here we are in the middle of September, and we are just setting out for Dieppe.

Count— For one time only, by chance! And moreover, we will have to go down to Vilsac by the end of the month, for I have asked those fellows to come down there for the shooting.

André— Yes, in this economical country place, where you have asked all those gentlemen to come down for the shooting, at the end of the month—

Count— Really, one would be bored to death without that!

André— In this same economical establishment, I say, you have twelve keepers.

Count— Quite true; but it is one of the best preserves in France, and really, there are so many poachers—

André— You have two masters of hounds, you have ten horses, —in short, a whole hunting equipage; and I don't speak of the indemnities that you pay year by year, if only for the rabbits that you kill.

Count— The fact is, there *are* thousands of rabbits; but shooting rabbits is such fun!

André— Add to that the entertainments that it occurs to you to give every now and then, with fireworks and so on, during the evening.

Count— Oh, yes, but that pleases all the peasants of the neighborhood, who adore me; between ourselves it *is* rather—

Oh, my dear boy! if I had only been rich, what fine things I would have done! In France, people do not know how to spend money. In Russia it is quite another matter! Now, there you have people who understand how to give an entertainment. But then what can anybody do with two hundred thousand livres for an income?

André—Father, one can do exactly what you have done,—one can ruin himself.

Count—What! ruin himself?

André—Yes. When my mother died your personal fortune brought you, as you say, an income of two hundred thousand livres; and the money which my mother left to me, of which you have had the use until I came of age, amounted to a hundred and twenty thousand livres.

Count—I certainly have made an accounting to you in the matter.

André—A perfectly exact one, only—

Count—Only—?

André—Only in doing so you have seriously impaired your own capital.

Count—Why did you not say that to me at the time?

André—Because I too—I was thinking of nothing but spending money.

Count—You ought to have warned me about this before now.

André—But I—I was doing then just what I see you doing; I was taking life exactly as you had taught me to take it.

Count—André, I hope that is not a reproach.

André—God bless me, no. I am only saying to you why I have not looked after your interests better than you have ever done so yourself.

Count—Very good. Then I am going to explain to you why I brought you up—

André—Not worth while, my dear father. There is no good in going back to that, and I know quite well—

Count—On the contrary, you know nothing at all about the matter, and you will please allow me to speak. It will be a consolation. You are perfectly right as to things that have no common-sense in them; and if I have brought you up after a certain manner, it is just because I myself suffer from a different kind of education. *I* was brought up very severely; at twenty-two years I knew nothing of life. I was born, I was kept hanging on at Vilsac, with my father and my mother, who were saints on earth, with my great-uncle, who had the gout, and with my tutor, who was an abbé. I was born with a constitution like iron. I went hunting day by day for whole months, on foot or on horseback. I ate my meals like an ogre. I rode every sort of a horse, and I was a swordsman like St. George himself. As for other things, my dear fellow, there was no use dreaming about them: I had not a crown in my pocket. The other sex — well, I had heard it said that there was a world of women somewhere, but I certainly did not know where it was. One day my father asked me if I was willing to marry, and I cried out, « Oh yes, yes! » with such an explosion that my father himself could not help laughing — he who never laughed. I was presented to a young girl, virtuous and beautiful; and I fell in love with her with a passion which at first fairly frightened the delicate and timid creature. Such was your mother, my dear André, and to her I owe the two happiest years of my life; it is true that I owe to her also my greatest grief, for at the end of those two years she died. But it must be said, either to the blame or to the praise of nature, that organizations such as mine are proof against the severest shocks. At twenty-four years I found myself rich, a widower, free to do what I pleased, and thrown — with a child a year old — into the midst of this world called Paris, of which I knew nothing whatever. Ought I to have condemned you to this sort of life that I had led at Vilsac, and which had been for me so often an intolerable bore? No, I obeyed my real nature. I gave you my qualities and my shortcomings, without reckoning closely in the matter; I have sought in your case your affection rather than your obedience or your respect. I have never taught you economy, it is true, but then I did not know anything about that myself; and besides, I had not a business and a business name to leave you. To have everything in common between us, one heart and one purse, to be able to give each other everything and say everything to each other,— that has been our motto. The puritans will think that they have a right to blame this intimacy as too close: let them say so if they choose. We have lost, it seems, some hundreds of thousands of francs; but we have gained this,— that we can always count upon each other, you upon me and I upon you. Either of us will be ready at any moment to kill himself for the other, and that is the most important matter between a father and a son;

all the rest is not worth the trouble that one takes to reason about it. Don't you think I am right?

André—All that is true, my dear father! and I am just as much attached to you as you are to me. Far be it from me to reproach you; but now in my turn I want to make a confession to you. You are an exception in our society; your fettered youth, your precocious widowerhood, are your excuses, if you need any. You were born at a time when all France was in a fever, and when the individual, as well as the great mass of people, seemed to be striving to spend by every possible means a superabundance of vitality. Urged toward active life by nature, by curiosity, by temperament, you have cared for things that were worth caring for,—for them only; for entertaining yourself, for hunting, for fine horses, for the artist world, for people of rank and distinction. In such an environment as this you have paid your tribute to your country, you have paid the debt of your rank in life and of your name. But I, on the other hand, like almost all my generation, brought in contact with a fashionable world from the time that I began life,—I, born in an epoch of lassitude and transition,—I led for a while this life by mere imitation in laziness. . . . It is a kind of existence that no longer amuses me; and moreover, I can tell you that it never did amuse me. To sit up all night turning over cards; to get up at two o'clock in the afternoon, to have horses put to the carriage and go for the drive around the Lake, or to ride horseback; to live by day with idlers and to pass my evenings with such parasites as your friend M. De Tournas—all that seems to me the height of foolishness. And at the bottom of your own thoughts you think just as I do. So now, now that you really have got to a serious explanation of affairs, let us reach a real irrevocable determination of them. Are you willing to let me arrange your life for you in the future exactly as I would wish to arrange my own life? Are you willing to have confidence in me, and after having brought me up in your way, are you willing that in turn, while there is still time for it, I should—bring you up in mine?

Count—Yes, go on.

André—Very well,—to severe diseases strong remedies. You think a great deal of our Vilsac estate?

Count—I was born there. I should not be sorry to end my days there.

André—Very well. We will keep Vilsac for you, and find money in some other way to pay off the mortgage.

Count—How?

André—That's my business; only you must send away the two piqueurs, and six of the keepers.

Count—Poor fellows!

André—And only four horses are to be kept. No more entertainments are to be given, no more fireworks. You will entertain only two or three intimate friends now and then,—if we find as many friends as that among all those that are about us nowadays here,—and you will stay at Vilsac seven or eight months of the year.

Count—Alone?

André—Wait a little. I have not finished yet. This house where we are must be sold. We must put out of doors these servants, who are just so many thieves; and we will keep at Paris only a very modest stopping-place.

Count—Will you kindly allow me to get my breath?

André—Don't stir, or my surgical operation will not be successful. Now that your debts are paid there will be left to you—

Count—There will be left to me—

André—Forty thousand livres income, and as much for me,—no more; and with all that, during three or four years you will not have the capital at your disposition.

Count—Heavens, what a smash!

André—Are you willing to accept my scheme?

Count—I must.

André—Very well, then: sign these papers!

Count—What are they?

André—They are papers which I have just got from the notary, and which I have been expecting to make you sign while at Dieppe and send to me; but since you are here—

Count [*signs*]—Since I am here, I may as well sign at once: you are quite right,—there you are.

André—Very well; now as, according to my notions, just as much as you are left to yourself you will slip back into the same errors as in the past—

Count—What are you going to do further?

André—Guess.

Count—You are going to forbid—

André—Are you out of your senses? I am going to marry you off.

Count—Marry me off!

André—Without permission.

Count—And how about yourself?

André—I am going to marry myself off—afterwards. You must begin as an example.

Count—André, do you know something?

André—What?

Count—Some one has told you the very thing I have had in mind.

André—Nobody has told me anything.

Count—Your word on it?

André—My word on it.

Count—Explain yourself. You, all by yourself, have had this idea of marriage?

André—I myself.

Count—Deny now the sympathy between us!

André—Well?

Count—It exists [*putting his arms around his son*]. There, embrace me!

André—And you accept?

Count—As if I would do anything else!

Translated for ‹A Library of the World's Best Literature,› by E. Irenæus Stevenson

MR. AND MRS. CLARKSON

From ‹L'Étrangère›

[These scenes, the final ones of the drama, occur in the private drawing-room of Catherine, the young Duchess of Septmonts. Mr. Clarkson, a wealthy American man of business, a Californian, has just received a note from the Duke of Septmonts, a blasé young roué of high family, requesting him to call at once. He has come, in some bewilderment, to find the duke. Mr. Clarkson has only a formal acquaintance with the duke, but Mrs. Clarkson, who resides much of the time in Paris, acting as Mr. Clarkson's business representative, knows the duke confidentially. The Duchess of Septmonts receives Clarkson.]

Mr. Clarkson—I beg your pardon, madam, for having insisted on making my way in here; but a few moments ago I found on returning to my house, a letter from your husband. It asked me for a rendezvous as soon as possible, without giving me a reason for it. I find M. de Septmonts not at home. May I ask you if you know how I can be of service to him?

Catherine—I was under the impression that in his letter, M. de Septmonts explained to you the matter in which he wishes your assistance.

Clarkson—No.

Catherine—Did not his letter contain another letter, sealed, which he purposed leaving in your hands?

Clarkson—No.

Catherine—Are you really telling me the truth?

Clarkson—I never lie, madam: I have too much business on my hands; it would mix me up quite too much in my affairs.

Catherine—Then perhaps it is to Mrs. Clarkson that my husband has intrusted that letter.

Clarkson—No. She would have mentioned it; for I told her that I had received a line from the Duke, and was on my way to this house.

Catherine—Perhaps your wife did not tell you—all.

Clarkson—She has no earthly reason to conceal anything from me!

Catherine—True! I know very well that she is your wife only in name; she told me as much when I was at her house yesterday.

Clarkson—Really! She must be very much pleased with you, for she does not talk readily about her personal affairs.

Catherine—Unfortunately, it is quite otherwise as far as I am concerned; she has not hidden from me the fact that she detests me, and that she will do me all the injury she possibly can.

Clarkson—You? Injury? For what reason? Pray, what have you done to her?

Catherine—Nothing! I have known her only two days. Nevertheless—

Clarkson—Nevertheless—

Catherine—What I was going to say is not my secret, sir, it is hers, and she alone has the right to tell it to you. But as to this letter that my husband has told my father he has sent to you—it is I who wrote that letter. You may as well know, too, that it was abstracted from my possession; and moreover, that with that letter any one can indeed do me all the mischief with which your wife, Mrs. Clarkson, has threatened me.

Clarkson [*very gravely*]—Then we must know at once if my wife has that letter. I will write her to come here immediately and join us—that I have something very important to communicate to her—here. Are you willing to have her come? [*He writes while he speaks.*]

Catherine—Certainly.

Clarkson—Then we can have a general explanation. You may be sure, madam, that I shall never lend my hand to anything that means harm to you, or to any woman: I come from the country where we respect women.

Catherine [*rings the bell, and says to a servant who answers it*]—See that this letter is sent immediately. Be careful that it does not go astray. It is not my letter. This gentleman has written it. [*Exit servant.*]

Clarkson—And now, madam, do you know why M. de Septmonts wishes to have an interview with me?

Catherine—Yes, I can guess. It concerns me, perhaps; but I have no right to discuss the matter. It is something which belongs to the Duke, and he alone has the right to impart it to you. All I can do is to beg of you to have all details thoroughly explained to you, and to look into them very carefully.

A Servant *enters*

Servant—M. le Duc has come in; he will be glad to have Mr. Clarkson come to him.

Clarkson—Very good. [*Going.*] I bid you good evening, madam.

Catherine [*to the servant*]—Wait a moment. [*Going to Clarkson and speaking in a low voice.*] Suppose I were to ask you a very great service.

Clarkson—Ask it, madam.

Catherine—Suppose I were to ask you to say to my husband that you are waiting for him here in this drawing-room—that you will be glad to speak with him *here*.

Clarkson—Nothing but that? With great pleasure. [*To the servant.*] Say to M. de Septmonts that I shall be obliged if he will join me—here. [*Servant goes out.*]

Catherine—I shall leave you; for if I know what is going to be discussed in this interview, I neither could nor should take part in it; but whatever may come of it, I shall never forget that you have done everything that you could do as a courtesy to me,—and that you are a gentleman. [*Exit Catherine.*]

Clarkson [*alone*]—Charming! She is charming, that little woman; but may I be hanged if I understand one word of what is going on here.

The Duke of Septmonts *comes in hastily, and advances to* Clarkson

Septmonts—I have just come from your house, Mr. Clarkson. Mrs. Clarkson told me you were here. I returned at once. Pardon me for troubling you. If when I came in I asked you to come to my own drawing-room, and have thus troubled you once more, it is because I was told you were expecting me here, with the duchess. This is her private parlor; and as what we have to say is a matter for men—

Clarkson—Therefore the duchess went to her own room when your return here was announced.

Septmonts—Mr. Clarkson, did *she* tell the servant that you would prefer to hold our conversation here?

Clarkson—No, I told him.

[*Septmonts goes to the door of the room by which Catherine went out, and closes the portière.*]

Clarkson [*in a scornful aside*]—What an amount of mystery and precaution!

Septmonts—The matter is this, Mr. Clarkson. I must fight a duel to-morrow morning. This duel can terminate only in the death of one or other of the contestants. I am the insulted one, therefore I have the choice of weapons. I choose the sword.

Clarkson—Do you fence well?

Septmonts—I believe I am one of the best fencers in Paris. But another friend on whom I could count is one of those men of the world who discuss all the details of an affair, and with whom the preliminaries of such a meeting might last several days. I want to get through with the matter at once.

Clarkson—Ah! The fact is, you *do* give an importance and a solemnity to such things in France that we don't understand, we Americans, who settle the question in five minutes on the first corner of the street, in the sight of everybody.

Septmonts—That is just the reason that I allowed myself to apply to you, Mr. Clarkson. Now, are you disposed to be present as my second?

Clarkson — Bless me, with all my heart! Besides, when I mentioned your letter to Mrs. Clarkson she told me to do all I could to serve you. Have you and my wife known each other long?

Septmonts — About four years; and I owe your wife a great deal, morally speaking. I have no desire to conceal the fact. I was not yet married when I met Mrs. Clarkson. One day I had lost a large sum at play, — a hundred and fifty thousand francs, — which I did not have, and tried in vain to procure; for at that time I was completely ruined. Mrs. Clarkson very generously lent me the sum, and I repaid it, with interest equivalent to the capital.

Clarkson — But as you were ruined, duke, how could you pay this large capital and this large interest? Did your father or mother die? In France the death of parents is a great resource, I know.

Septmonts — No. I was an orphan, and I had no expectations. I married.

Clarkson — Ah, true! You French people make much of marriages for money! It's a great advantage over us Americans, who only marry for love. Now with us, in such a case as yours, a man goes into some business or other; he goes to mining; he works. But every country has its own customs. I beg your pardon for interrupting you. After all, it doesn't concern me. Come back to our duel.

Septmonts — I have a letter here in my hands —

Clarkson — Ah! You have a letter in your hands —

Septmonts — A letter which compromises my wife —

Clarkson — Ah! I am completely at your service. I belong to the sort of men who do not admit any compromises in matters of that kind.

Septmonts — I may be killed — one has to look ahead. If I lose my life, I lose it by having been so injured by my wife that I intend to be revenged on her.

Clarkson — And how?

Septmonts — I wish that the contents of this letter, which I have in my possession, shall become public property if I am killed.

Clarkson [*coldly*] — Ah! And how can I serve you as to that?

Septmonts — I will intrust this sealed letter to you. [*He takes the letter from his pocket.*] Here it is.

Clarkson [*still more coldly*] — Very well.

Septmonts — Now, if I survive, you will restore it to me as it is. If not, then in the trial which will follow, you will read it in a court. I wish the letters to become public. Then it will be known that I avenged my honor under a feigned pretext; and M. Gérard and the duchess will be so situated that they will never be able to see each other again.

Clarkson — Nonsense! Once dead, what does it matter to you?

Septmonts — I am firm there. Will you kindly accept the commission?

Clarkson [*in a formal tone*] — Surely.

Septmonts — Here is the letter.

Clarkson [*takes it and holds it as he speaks*] — But, duke, now that I think about it, when this trial occurs it is probable, even certain, that I shall not be in France. I was expecting to leave Paris on business to-morrow morning at the latest. I can wait until to-morrow evening to please you, and to help you with this duel of yours; but that is really all the time I can spare.

Septmonts — Very well; then you will have the goodness to give this letter to Mrs. Clarkson with the instructions I have just given you, and it will be in equally good hands.

Clarkson [*looking at the letter*] — All right. A blank envelope. What is there to indicate that this letter was addressed to M. Gérard?

Septmonts — The envelope with his name on it is inside.

Clarkson — You found this letter?

Septmonts — I found it — before it was mailed.

Clarkson — And as you had your suspicions you — opened it?

Septmonts — Yes.

Clarkson — I beg your pardon for questioning you so, but you yourself did me the honor to say that you wished me to be *fully* informed. Do you know whether the sentiments between M. Gérard and the duchess were of long standing?

Septmonts — They date from before my marriage.

Clarkson [*looking toward the apartment of the duchess*] — Oh, I see. That is serious!

Septmonts — They loved each other, they wanted to marry each other, but my wife's father would not consent.

Clarkson [*reflectively*] — M. Gérard wanted to marry her, did he?

Septmonts — Yes; but when he learned that Mademoiselle Mauriceau was a millionaire, as he had nothing and had no title other than his plain name Gérard, he withdrew his pretensions.

Clarkson — That was a very proper thing for the young man to do. It doesn't surprise me!

Septmonts — Yes; but now, Mr. Clarkson, this young gentleman has come back —

Clarkson — And is too intimate a friend to your wife?

Septmonts — Ah, I do not say that!

Clarkson — What do you say, then?

Septmonts — That as the letter in question gives that impression, the situation amounts to the same thing as far as a legal process is concerned.

Clarkson [*thoughtfully and coldly*] — Oh-h-h!

Septmonts — Don't you agree with me, Mr. Clarkson?

Clarkson — No, not at all. I can understand revenge on those who have injured us, but not on those who haven't done so. And I don't like vengeance on a woman anyway, even when she is guilty; and certainly not when she is innocent; and you owe your wife a great deal — between ourselves, you owe your wife a great deal, duke. I understand now why, for once, your father-in-law M. Mauriceau sides with his daughter and M. Gérard against you. He is sure they both are innocent. By-the-by, does M. Mauriceau also know of this letter?

Septmonts — Yes. He even tried to take it from me by force.

Clarkson — Why did he not take it?

Septmonts — Ah, because you see, I had the presence of mind to tell him that I did not have it any longer — that I had sent it to you!

Clarkson [*ironically*] — That *was* very clever!

Septmonts — And then when M. Gérard had challenged me, M. Mauriceau thought he would make an impression by saying to him before me, "I will be your second."

Clarkson — Well, is that the whole story?

Septmonts — Yes.

Clarkson — Very well, my dear sir: to speak frankly, all those people whom you characterize so slightingly seem to me the right kind of people — excellent people. Your little wife seems to be the victim of prejudices, of morals, and of combinations about which we mere American savages don't know anything at all. In our American society, which of course I can't compare with yours, as we only date from yesterday,—if Mademoiselle Mauriceau had loved a fine young fellow like M. Gérard, her father would have given her to the man she loved; or if he had refused that, why she would have gone quite simply and been married before the justice of the peace! Perhaps her father wouldn't have portioned her; but then the husband would have worked, gone into business, and the two young people would have been happy all the same. As to your M. Gérard here, he is an honest man and a clever one. We like people who work, we Americans, and to whatever country they belong, we hold them as compatriots—because we are such savages, I suppose. So you understand that I don't at all share your opinion of this question.

Septmonts—And so speaking, you mean—?

Clarkson—That if I give you this explanation, it is because I think I understand that in paying me the honor of choosing me as a second, you thought that the men of my country were less clear-sighted, less scrupulous than the men of yours. In short, duke, you thought I would lend my hand to all these social pettinesses, these little vilenesses which you have just recounted with a candor that honors you.

Septmonts—Do you happen to remember, Mr. Clarkson, that you are talking to *me*—in this way?

Clarkson—To you. Because there are only two of us here! But if you like, we will call in other people to listen.

Septmonts—Then, sir, you tell me to my face—

Clarkson—I tell you to your face that to squander your inheritance—to have gambled away money you did not have—to borrow it from a woman without knowing when or how you could return it—to marry in order to pay your debts and continue your dissipations—to revenge yourself now on an innocent woman—to steal letters—to misapply your skill in arms by killing a brave man—why, I tell you to your face that all that is the work of a rascal, and that therefore a rascal you are. Oh, what astonishes me is that fifty people haven't told you so already, and that I have had to travel three thousand leagues to inform you on the subject! For you don't seem to have ever suspected it, and you don't look thoroughly convinced even now.

Septmonts [*controlling himself with the greatest difficulty*]—Mr. Clarkson, you know that I cannot call you to account until I have settled with your friend M. Gérard. You take a strange advantage of the fact, sir. But we shall meet again. Please return me the paper you have had from me.

Clarkson—Your wife's letter? Never in the world! As it was addressed to M. Gérard, it belongs to M. Gérard. I intend to give it to M. Gérard. If *he* wants to return it to you, I won't stand in the way; but I doubt whether he will return it.

Septmonts—You will fight me, then, you mean?

Clarkson—Oh! as for that; yes, fight as much as you like.

Septmonts—Very well; when I have finished with the other, you and I will have our business together.

Clarkson—Say the day after to-morrow, then?

Septmonts—The day after to-morrow.

Clarkson—Stop; I must start off by to-morrow night, at the latest.

Septmonts—You can wait. And while waiting, leave me!

Clarkson—Duke, do I look like a man to whom to say «leave» in that tone, and who goes? Now look at me; it isn't hard to see what I have decided. I don't mean you to fight with Gérard before you have fought with me. If Gérard kills you, I shan't have the pleasure of crossing swords with «one of the first fencers in Paris,» which it will amuse me to do. If you kill him, you cause irreparable misfortunes. If you think I'm going to let you kill a man who has saved me twenty-five per cent. in the cost of washing gold, you are mistaken! Come, prove you are brave, even when you aren't sure of being the stronger! Go and get a good pair of swords from your room (since the sword is your favorite weapon—mine, too, for the matter of that), and follow me to those great bare grounds back of your house. On my way here I was wondering why in goodness's name they were not utilized. In the heart of the city they must be worth a good deal! We will prove it. As for seconds, umpires of the point of honor, we'll have the people who pass by in the street—if any do pass.

[*Septmonts rushes in a fury toward the door, but when there stretches his hand toward the bell. Clarkson throws himself between him and the bell.*]

Clarkson—Ah! no ringing, please! Don't play the Louis XV. gentleman, and order your servants to cudgel a poor beggar! or as sure as my name is Clarkson, I'll slap your face, sir, before all your lackeys!

Septmonts—Very well, so be it! I *will* begin with you. [*Angrily hastens from the room for the weapons.*]

Clarkson—Quite right! [*Looking coolly at his watch.*] Let me see; why, perhaps I *can* get away from Paris this evening after all. [*He goes calmly out at the back toward the darkened garden.*]

[*The Duchess of Septmonts has pulled aside the portière and looks toward the door by which her husband and Mr. Clarkson have gone out. She is very much agitated, and can hardly walk. She rings the bell, and then makes an effort to appear calm. The servant comes in.*]

Catherine [*tremulously, to the servant*]—Ask my father to come here, immediately. [*The servant goes out. Catherine looks toward the window and makes a movement to go to it.*] No, I will not look out! I will not know anything! I do not know anything; I have *heard* nothing; the minutes that that hand marks upon the clock, no one knows what they say to me. One of them will decide my life! Even if I had heard nothing, things would take the turn that they have, and I should merely be amazed in knowing of them. Instead of knowing nothing, I have merely to remember nothing. But no, no,—I am trying in vain to smother the voice of my own conscience! What I am doing is wicked. From the moment that I have known anything about this, I am an accomplice; and if one of these two men is killed he has been killed with my consent. No, I cannot and I will not. [*She runs toward the door. As she does so Mrs. Clarkson enters hastily.*] You, you, madam!

Mrs. Clarkson—Were you not really expecting me to-day, madam? My husband sends me a note to say that you—and he—wish to speak to me immediately.

Catherine—Madam, since Mr. Clarkson has written you, there has occurred a thing which neither your husband, nor I, nor you yourself could foresee.

Mrs. Clarkson—What do you mean?

Catherine—While my husband the duke has been explaining to Mr. Clarkson the reasons of the duel,—which you, you, madam, have provoked,—your husband, who did not find these reasons either sufficient or honorable, has undertaken to defend us—Gérard, yes, Gérard, and me,—and so very forcibly, that at this instant—

Mrs. Clarkson—They are fighting?

Catherine—Yes, yes, only a few steps away from here!

Mrs. Clarkson — Ah! That sounds like Clarkson! [*She takes a step toward the door.*]

Catherine — Madam, that duel must not go on.

Mrs. Clarkson — Why not?

Catherine — I will not permit these two men to lose their lives on my account.

Mrs. Clarkson — You? What difference does it make to you? They are not doing anything but what they chose to do. « Hands off," as the officials at the gaming-tables say when the ball has stopped rolling. You have wished to be free, haven't you? and you are perfectly right; you never said so to anybody, but you begged it all the same of One who can do anything. He has heard your prayer, and he has made use of me to save you; of me, who have been anxious to destroy you! That is justice; and do you think that I object — I who am to be the loser? In the game that I play with Destiny, every time I make up my mind that God is against me, I bow my head and throw up the game. I don't fear any one except God. He is on your side. Let us talk no more about it.

[*Just as she is speaking the last words, Clarkson comes in. He is very grave.*]

Mrs. Clarkson — See there. You are a widow.

Clarkson [*to Mrs. Clarkson*] — My dear Noémi, will you be so kind as to hand that paper to our friend the duchess. She will perhaps feel some embarrassment in taking it directly from my hand — and it is a thing that must be returned to her. Such was the last wish of her husband; he really did not have time to tell me as much, but I fancy that I guess it right.

[*Mrs. Clarkson calmly takes the letter and goes to Catherine.*]

Mrs. Clarkson — I once said to your friend M. Rémonin that if I lost my game I would lose like one who plays fair. Madam, it was through me that your marriage came to pass; and now it is through me that your marriage — is dissolved. [*Turning to Clarkson.*] And now, Clarkson, my dear, let us get out of this. You are a good and a brave fellow. I will go anywhere with you. I have had enough of Europe — things here are too small. Do you know, I really believe I am going to find myself in love with you! Come, let us go! I am positively smothering.

Clarkson — Yes, let us go.

[*At the moment that Mr. and Mrs. Clarkson are going out, servants and police officials, accompanied by a commissioner of the police service, appear in the door. Clarkson is pointed out.*]

Commissioner — I beg your pardon, monsieur,— there seems to have been — a murder here.

Clarkson — Oh no, monsieur, not at all a murder — only a duel.

Commissioner — And am I to understand, monsieur, that it is you who —

Clarkson — Oh yes, monsieur, it is I. You have come to take me into custody?

Commissioner — Yes, monsieur.

Clarkson — What a ridiculous country! I am ready to follow you, monsieur. But I am an American citizen. I shall give you bail — but of course, the law before anything. . . .

Mrs. Clarkson — Reckon on me, Clarkson. *I* shall take charge of this matter.

Clarkson — How are you going to do that?

Mrs. Clarkson — Oh, that's my affair.

[*Mrs. Clarkson crosses the stage and whispers a word to the commissioner. The commissioner bows very respectfully. Mrs. Clarkson goes out.*]

Commissioner [*to Dr. Rémonin*] — You are a doctor, monsieur?

Rémonin — Yes, monsieur.

Commissioner — Will you have the goodness to give a certificate of death?

Rémonin [*significantly*] — With great pleasure!

Translated for 'A Library of the World's Best Literature,' by E. Irenæus Stevenson

GEORGE DU MAURIER

(1834–1896)

George Louis Palmella Busson du Maurier was born in Paris on March 6th, 1834, and his early life was passed there. His father was a Frenchman, who had married an Englishwoman in Paris. The Du Mauriers came of an old family in Brittany, Du Maurier's grandfather having been a small *rentier*, who derived his living from glass-works. During Du Maurier's childhood his parents removed to Belgium and thence to London. At seventeen years of age he tried for a degree at the Sorbonne in Paris, but was not successful; and he was put, much against his will, to study chemistry under Dr. Williamson at University College, London. Du Maurier's father, whose characteristics are described in 'Peter Ibbetson,' was an amateur of science. It has been hinted by the son that certain unlucky experiments, which were the result of the elder Du Maurier's fancy for the natural sciences, considerably impaired the family fortunes. The father had bent his heart on the son's being a man of science, but the son's tastes were all for art. He did therefore little good in his chemical studies.

George du Maurier

Du Maurier's father died in 1856, and he then devoted himself definitely to art. He worked at the British Museum, and made considerable progress there. He next went to Paris, and lived the life which he has described in 'Trilby.' In 1857 he attended the Academy at Antwerp, and studied under De Kaiser and Van Lerius. His severe studies at Antwerp had the result that his sight was seriously impaired, and he lost the use of his left eye. After two years of enforced idleness he went to London to seek his fortune. An old acquaintance of his student life in Paris introduced him to Charles Reade, who in turn introduced him to Mark Lemon, the editor of Punch. Through these acquaintances he obtained employment in drawing for Once a Week, Punch, and the Cornhill Magazine. On the death of Leech in 1864 he was regularly attached to the staff of Punch, and till the time of his death continued to work for that periodical with ever-increasing success. It is not too much to say that for many years Punch was chiefly and mainly Du Maurier. He early marked out for himself an entirely new path, which was not in the direction of caricature or broad comedy; grace, sentiment, and wit, rather than fun, were the characteristics of his work. He confined himself almost entirely to society, so that his field was a narrower one than that of some of his coadjutors. He had not, for instance, the masculine breadth of Leech, who represented with great strength and humor the chief characters of English life,—the parson, the soldier, the merchant, the farmer, etc.

Du Maurier was almost entirely a carpet knight. He drew London society, and a certain phase of London society. The particular society which he represented is of very recent existence. Thirty years ago there was but one society in London. This was simply the ancient aristocratic society of England, which gathered in London in the season. It is true that there was an artistic society in London at that time, but it was quite apart and of little general recognition or influence. But since then there has come up in London a society made up chiefly of artists, professional people, and successful merchants (having moreover its points of contact with the old society), which is very strong and influential. It is this which Du Maurier knew, and which he represented. Even here, however, the types he has selected for description were very special. But they were presented with so much grace and charm that the public never tired of them. To his type of woman he was especially faithful: the tall woman with long throat and well-defined chin, much resembling the figures of Burne-Jones and Rossetti, only somewhat more mundane. We have the same woman in the heroine of 'Trilby.'

Though Du Maurier, before beginning 'Peter Ibbetson,' had never written a book, he had had considerable literary experience, for he is said to have spent as much time upon the construction of the dialogues which accompanied his pictures as upon the pictures themselves. The story of 'Peter Ibbetson' he had often related to his friends, who had urged him to write it down. This he finally did,—at the special instance, it is said, of Henry James. It appeared in Harper's Magazine in 1891. 'Trilby' was published in 1894 in Harper's Magazine, and at once attained a great popular success. The publishers estimate that about 250,000 copies of the book have been sold. Du Maurier had sold the book outright for £2,000, but when it became apparent that the work was to be a success, the publishers admitted the author to a royalty, paying at one time $40,000. They also shared with him the large sums paid for the dramatization of the work. For 'The Martian,' his last novel, he received £10,000 outright. This also was published in Harper's Magazine.

It is perhaps too early to pass judgment upon the merits of these works. They have, no doubt, grave faults. The story of 'Peter Ibbetson' has been completed when it is but two-thirds told. The remaining portion of the book is a dream. This is of course a dangerous reversal of the usual method of the story-teller, which is to make dreams seem like facts. The hypnotic part of 'Trilby' is said by the professional authorities on the subject to be bad science. The hypnotism in 'Trilby' was perhaps a journalist's idea, that subject being much talked of at the time the book was written. Du Maurier, it need hardly be said, was by training a journalist, although the training had been of the pencil rather than of the pen. The literary style of the novels is curious. It makes no pretensions to finish; the grammar even is sometimes at fault. But on the other hand, it has decided merits. It is particularly easy, flowing, and simple. These are not the qualities we should have expected from the nature of Du Maurier's literary training. The brief dialogues which he has for so many years appended to his sketches in 'Punch' would have educated, we should have thought, the qualities of brevity and point rather than those of ease and fullness. Certain peculiarities of the style cannot be defended, but the author produces his effects in spite of such solecisms. This is true of the matter of his stories as well as of the style. They are at many points inartistically constructed; but the stuff is good, and the works therefore hold their own in spite of these drawbacks. They certainly have one virtue, which is most necessary to the success of any work of the imagination: they have reality. We believe as we read, and continue to believe after we have ceased reading, that the Major and Mimsey and Taffy and Trilby are real persons. They are real to us because they have in the first case been real to their creator. It is possible, however, that the pictures which accompany the text may increase the strength of the illusion.

No book, in recent years at any rate, has had so instantaneous and prodigious a popular success as 'Trilby.' Popularity is always hard to explain with any certainty. It seems to be a quality in the warp and woof of the mind of the man that has it. One condition appears to be that he shall be in sympathy with the minds of the mass of his fellow-beings. There was such a sympathy in Du Maurier's case; and to be more particular, his kindly and friendly enthusiasm was a quality to commend him to men. He had a power of enjoying beauty in his fellow-beings. Then he had had a long education in the qualities that make popularity. He had long studied the art of pleasing. It is not improbable that in these novels, which were intended for the American public, he may have played upon certain of our national susceptibilities. We in this country like to have our literature taken seriously by the European. It may be that Du Maurier may have had an inkling of this, for it is curious to note how much of our poetry appears in these novels. Du Maurier had a very nice taste in poetry, a genuine enthusiasm for it which it is heartily to be wished were shared by all college professors of English literature. Thus, he could not have chosen better lines than those which Peter Ibbetson was in the habit of reciting to Mimsey, 'The Water-fowl' of Bryant,—perhaps the most perfect poem ever produced in this country,—a poem so «beautifully carried,» as Matthew Arnold once described it to the present writer. Poe's beautiful and musical lines, written by him at fourteen,—'Helen, thy beauty is to me,'—are also made use of. We have a good deal of Longfellow and other American writers. 'Ben Bolt' is of course an American song. These appeals to our national predilections may have influenced us. But the interest and curiosity of our practical and hard-working American public in the Bohemian art life of the Latin Quarter was also, no doubt, a chief cause of the popularity of 'Trilby.'

Du Maurier did not live long to enjoy his success. He had always been known to his friends as a sensitive man, this quality being ascribed to ill health. Ill health was no doubt a chief cause of the vexation with which he received certain comments upon his books, in some cases inspired by envy of his success. Many of his recent contributions to Punch have been at the expense of the unsuccessful author, and have supported the thesis that ill success was not an indubitable proof of genius. When Lord Wolseley asked him what would be the title of his next novel, he said 'Soured by Success.' He died in London on October 8th, 1896.

AT THE HEART OF BOHEMIA

From 'Trilby.' Copyright 1894, by Harper & Brothers

AND then—well, I happen to forget what sort of a day this particular day turned into, about six of the clock.

If it was decently fine, the most of them went off to dine at the Restaurant de la Couronne, kept by the Père Trin, in the Rue de Monsieur, who gave you of his best to eat and drink for twenty sols Parisis, or one franc in the coin of the empire. Good distending soups, omelets that were only too savory, lentils, red and white beans, meat so dressed and sauced and seasoned that you didn't know whether it was beef or mutton, flesh, fowl, or good red herring,—or even bad, for that matter,—nor very greatly care.

And just the same lettuce, radishes, and cheese of Gruyère or Brie as you got at the Trois Frères Provençaux (but not the same butter!). And to wash it all down, generous wine in wooden «brocs,» that stained a lovely æsthetic blue everything it was spilled over.

And you hobnobbed with models, male and female, students of law and medicine, painters and sculptors, workmen and blanchisseuses and grisettes, and found them very good company, and most improving to your French, if your French was of the usual British kind, and even to some of your manners, if these were very British indeed. And the evening was innocently wound up with billiards, cards, or dominoes at the Café du Luxembourg opposite; or at the Théâtre du Luxembourg, in the Rue de Madame, to see funny farces with screamingly droll Englishmen in them; or still better, at the Jardin Bullier (la Closerie des Lilas), to see the students dance the cancan, or try and dance it yourself, which is not so easy as it seems; or best of all, at the Théâtre de l'Odéon, to see Fechter and Madame Doche in the 'Dame aux Camélias.'

Or if it were not only fine, but a Saturday afternoon into the bargain, the Laird would put on a necktie and a few other necessary things, and the three friends would walk arm-in-arm to Taffy's hotel in the Rue de Seine, and wait outside till he had made himself as presentable as the Laird, which did not take very long. And then (Little Billee was always presentable) they would, arm-in-arm, the huge Taffy in the middle, descend the Rue de Seine and cross a bridge to the Cité, and have a look in at the Morgue. Then back again to the quays on the Rive Gauche by the Pont Neuf, to wend their way westward; now on one side to look at the print and picture shops and the magasins of bric-à-brac, and haply sometimes buy thereof, now on the other to finger and cheapen the second-hand books for sale on the parapet, and even pick one or two utterly unwanted bargains, never to be read or opened again.

When they reached the Pont des Arts they would cross it, stopping in the middle to look up the river towards the old Cité and Notre Dame, eastward, and dream unutterable things and try to utter them. Then turning westward, they would gaze at the glowing sky and all it glowed upon — the corner of the Tuileries and the Louvre, the many bridges, the Chamber of Deputies, the golden river narrowing its perspective and broadening its bed, as it went flowing and winding on its way between Passy and Grenelle to St. Cloud, to Rouen, to the Havre, to England perhaps—where *they* didn't want to be just then; and they would try and express themselves to the effect that life was uncommonly well worth living in that particular city at that particular time of the day and year and century, at that particular epoch of their own mortal and uncertain lives.

Then, still arm-in-arm and chatting gayly, across the courtyard of the Louvre, through gilded gates well guarded by reckless imperial Zouaves, up the arcaded Rue de Rivoli as far as the Rue Castiglione, where they would stare with greedy eyes at the window of the great corner pastry-cook, and marvel at the beautiful assortment of bonbons, pralines, dragées, marrons glacés—saccharine, crystalline substances of all kinds and colors, as charming to look at as an illumination; precious stones, delicately frosted sweets, pearls and diamonds so arranged as to melt in the mouth; especially, at this particular time of the year, the monstrous Easter eggs of enchanting hue, enshrined like costly jewels in caskets of satin and gold; and the Laird, who was well read in his English classics and liked to show it, would opine that «they managed these things better in France.»

Then across the street by a great gate into the Allée des Feuillants, and up to the Place de la Concorde—to gaze, but quite without base envy, at the smart people coming back from the Bois de Boulogne. For even in Paris «carriage people» have a way of looking bored, of taking their pleasure sadly, of having nothing to say to each other, as though the vibration of so many wheels all rolling home the same way every afternoon had hypnotized them into silence, idiocy, and melancholia.

And our three musketeers of the brush would speculate on the vanity of wealth and rank and fashion; on the satiety that follows in the wake of self-indulgence and overtakes it; on the weariness of the pleasures that become a toil—as if they knew all about it, had found it all out for themselves, and nobody else had ever found it out before!

Then they found out something else—namely, that the sting of healthy appetite was becoming intolerable; so they would betake themselves to an English eating-house in the Rue de la Madeleine (on the left-hand side near the top), where they would renovate their strength and their patriotism on British beef and beer, and household bread, and bracing, biting, stinging yellow mustard, and horseradish, and noble apple-pie, and Cheshire cheese; and get through as much of these in an hour or so as they could for talking, talking, talking; such happy talk! as full of sanguine hope and enthusiasm, of cocksure commendation or condemnation of all painters, dead or alive, of modest but firm belief in themselves and each other, as a Paris Easter egg is full of sweets and pleasantness (for the young).

And then a stroll on the crowded, well-lighted boulevards, and a bock at the café there, at a little three-legged marble table right out on the genial asphalt pavement, still talking nineteen to the dozen.

Then home by dark old silent streets and some deserted bridge to their beloved Latin Quarter, the Morgue gleaming cold and still and fatal in the pale lamplight, and Notre Dame pricking up its watchful twin towers, which have looked down for so many centuries on so many happy, sanguine, expansive youths walking arm-in-arm by twos and threes, and forever talking, talking, talking. . . .

The Laird and Little Billee would see Taffy safe to the door of his *hôtel garni* in the Rue de Seine, where they would find much to say to each other before they said good-night — so much that Taffy and Little Billee would see the Laird safe to *his* door, in the Place St. Anatole des Arts. And then a discussion would arise between Taffy and the Laird on the immortality of the soul, let us say, or the exact meaning of the word "gentleman," or the relative merits of Dickens and Thackeray, or some such recondite and quite unhackneyed theme, and Taffy and the Laird would escort Little Billee to *his* door, in the Place de l'Odéon, and he would re-escort them both back again, and so on till any hour you please.

Or again, if it rained, and Paris through the studio window loomed lead-colored, with its shiny slate roofs under skies that were ashen and sober, and the wild west wind made woeful music among the chimney-pots, and little gray waves ran up the river the wrong way, and the Morgue looked chill and dark and wet, and almost uninviting (even to three healthy-minded young Britons), they would resolve to dine and spend a happy evening at home.

Little Billee, taking with him three francs (or even four), would dive into back streets and buy a yard or so of crusty new bread, well burned on the flat side, a fillet of beef, a litre of wine, potatoes and onions, butter, a little cylindrical cheese called «bondon de Neufchâtel,» tender curly lettuce, with chervil, parsley, spring onions, and other fine herbs, and a pod of garlic, which would be rubbed on a crust of bread to flavor things with.

Taffy would lay the cloth English-wise, and also make the salad, for which, like everybody else I ever met, he had a special receipt of his own (putting in the oil first and the vinegar after); and indeed, his salads were quite as good as everybody else's.

The Laird, bending over the stove, would cook the onions and beef into a savory Scotch mess so cunningly that you could not taste the beef for the onions — nor always the onions for the garlic!

And they would dine far better than at le Père Trin's, far better than at the English Restaurant in the Rue de la Madeleine — better than anywhere else on earth!

And after dinner, what coffee, roasted and ground on the spot, what pipes and cigarettes of «caporal,» by the light of the three shaded lamps, while the rain beat against the big north window, and the wind went howling round the quaint old mediæval tower at the corner of the Rue Vieille des Mauvais Ladres (the old street of the bad lepers), and the damp logs hissed and crackled in the stove!

What jolly talk into the small hours! Thackeray and Dickens again, and Tennyson and Byron (who was «not dead yet» in those days); and Titian and Velasquez, and young Millais and Holman Hunt (just out); and Monsieur Ingres and Monsieur Delacroix, and Balzac and Stendhal and George Sand; and the good Dumas! and Edgar Allan Poe; and the glory that was Greece and the grandeur that was Rome. . . .

Good, honest, innocent, artless prattle — not of the wisest, perhaps, nor redolent of the very highest culture (which by the way can mar as well as make), nor leading to any very practical result; but quite pathetically sweet from the sincerity and fervor of its convictions, a profound belief in their importance, and a proud trust in their lifelong immutability.

Oh happy days and happy nights, sacred to art and friendship! oh happy times of careless impecuniosity, and youth and hope and health and strength and freedom — with all Paris for a playground, and its dear old unregenerate Latin Quarter for a workshop and a home!

CHRISTMAS IN THE LATIN QUARTER

From 'Trilby.' Copyright, 1894, by Harper & Brothers

Christmas was drawing near.

There were days when the whole Quartier Latin would veil its iniquities under fogs almost worthy of the Thames Valley between London Bridge and Westminster, and out of the studio window the prospect was a dreary blank. No Morgue! no towers of Notre Dame! not even the chimney-pots over the way —not even the little mediæval toy turret at the corner of the Rue Vieille des Mauvais Ladres, Little Billee's delight!

The stove had to be crammed till its sides grew a dull deep red, before one's fingers could hold a brush or squeeze a bladder; one had to box or fence at nine in the morning, that one might recover from the cold bath and get warm for the rest of the day!

Taffy and the Laird grew pensive and dreamy, childlike and bland; and when they talked, it was generally about Christmas at home in merry England and the distant land of cakes, and how good it was to be there at such a time—hunting, shooting, curling, and endless carouse!

It was Ho! for the jolly West Riding, and Hey! for the bonnets of Bonnie Dundee, till they grew quite homesick, and wanted to start by the very next train.

They didn't do anything so foolish. They wrote over to friends in London for the biggest turkey, the biggest plum-pudding, that could be got for love or money, with mince-pies, and holly and mistletoe, and sturdy, short, thick English sausages, half a Stilton cheese, and a sirloin of beef—two sirloins, in case one should not be enough.

For they meant to have a Homeric feast in the studio on Christmas Day—Taffy, the Laird, and Little Billee—and invite all the delightful chums I have been trying to describe; and that is just why I tried to describe them—Durien, Vincent, Antony, Lorrimer, Carnegie, Petrolicoconose, l'Zouzou, and Dodor!

The cooking and waiting should be done by Trilby, her friend Angèle Boisse, M. et Mme. Vinard, and such little Vinards as could be trusted with glass and crockery and mince-pies; and if that was not enough, they would also cook themselves and wait upon each other.

When dinner should be over, supper was to follow, with scarcely any interval to speak of; and to partake of this, other guests should be bidden — Svengali and Gecko, and perhaps one or two more. No ladies!

For as the unsusceptible Laird expressed it, in the language of a gillie he had once met at a servants' dance in a Highland country-house, « Them wimmen spiles the ball! »

Elaborate cards of invitation were sent out, in the designing and ornamentation of which the Laird and Taffy exhausted all their fancy (Little Billee had no time).

Wines and spirits and English beers were procured at great cost from M. E. Delevigne's, in the Rue St. Honoré, and liqueurs of every description — chartreuse, curaçoa, ratafia de cassis, and anisette; no expense was spared.

Also truffled galantines of turkey, tongues, hams, rillettes de Tours, pâtés de foie gras, « fromage d'Italie » (which has nothing to do with cheese), saucissons d'Arles et de Lyon, with and without garlic, cold jellies, peppery and salt — everything that French charcutiers and their wives can make out of French pigs, or any other animal whatever, beast, bird, or fowl (even cats and rats), for the supper; and sweet jellies and cakes, and sweetmeats, and confections of all kinds, from the famous pastry-cook at the corner of the Rue Castiglione.

Mouths went watering all day long in joyful anticipation. They water somewhat sadly now at the mere remembrance of these delicious things — the mere immediate sight or scent of which in these degenerate latter days would no longer avail to promote any such delectable secretion. Hélas! ahimè! ach weh! ay de mi! eheu! οἴμοι — in point of fact, *alas!*

That is the very exclamation I wanted.

Christmas eve came round. The pieces of resistance and plum-pudding and mince-pies had not yet arrived from London — but there was plenty of time.

Les trois Angliches dined at le Père Trin's, as usual, and played billiards and dominoes at the Café du Luxembourg, and possessed their souls in patience till it was time to go and hear the midnight mass at the Madeleine, where Roucouly, the great baritone of the Opéra Comique, was retained to sing Adam's famous Noël.

The whole Quarter seemed alive with the réveillon. It was a clear frosty night, with a splendid moon just past the full, and most exhilarating was the walk along the quays on the Rive Gauche, over the Pont de la Concorde and across the Place thereof, and up the thronged Rue de la Madeleine to the massive Parthenaic place of worship that always has such a pagan, worldly look of smug and prosperous modernity.

They struggled manfully, and found standing and kneeling room among that fervent crowd, and heard the impressive service with mixed feelings, as became true Britons of very advanced liberal and religious opinions; not with the unmixed contempt of the proper British Orthodox (who were there in full force, one may be sure).

But their susceptible hearts soon melted at the beautiful music, and in mere sensuous *attendrissement* they were quickly in unison with all the rest.

For as the clock struck twelve, out pealed the organ, and up rose the finest voice in France:

«Minuit, Chrétiens! c'est l'heure solennelle
Où l'Homme-Dieu descendit parmi nous!»

And a wave of religious emotion rolled over Little Billee and submerged him; swept him off his little legs, swept him out of his little self, drowned him in a great seething surge of love—love of his kind, love of love, love of life, love of death, love of all that is and ever was and ever will be—a very large order indeed, even for Little Billee.

And it seemed to him that he stretched out his arms for love to one figure especially beloved beyond all the rest—one figure erect on high, with arms outstretched to him, in more than common fellowship of need: not the sorrowful Figure crowned with thorns, for it was in the likeness of a woman; but never that of the Virgin Mother of our Lord.

It was Trilby, Trilby, Trilby! a poor fallen sinner and waif, all but lost amid the scum of the most corrupt city on earth. Trilby, weak and mortal like himself, and in woeful want of pardon! and in her gray dove-like eyes he saw the shining of so great a love that he was abashed; for well he knew that all that love was his, and would be his forever, come what would or could.

«Peuple, debout! Chante ta délivrance!
Noël! Noël! Voici le Rédempteur!»

So sang and rang and pealed and echoed the big deep metallic baritone bass — above the organ, above the incense, above everything else in the world — till the very universe seemed to shake with the rolling thunder of that great message of love and forgiveness!

Thus at least felt Little Billee, whose way it was to magnify and exaggerate all things under the subtle stimulus of sound, and the singing human voice had especially strange power to penetrate into his inmost depths — even the voice of man!

And what voice but the deepest and gravest and grandest there is, can give worthy utterance to such a message as that,— the epitome, the abstract, the very essence of all collective humanity's wisdom at its best!

«DREAMING TRUE»

From ‹Peter Ibbetson.› Copyright, 1891, by Harper & Brothers

As I SAT down on a bench by the old willow (where the rat lived), and gazed and gazed, it almost surprised me that the very intensity of my desire did not of itself suffice to call up the old familiar faces and forms, and conjure away these modern intruders. The power to do this seemed almost within my reach: I willed and willed and willed with all my might, but in vain; I could not cheat my sight or hearing for a moment. There they remained, unconscious and undisturbed, those happy, well-mannered, well-appointed little French people, and fed the gold and silver fish; and there with an aching heart I left them.

Oh, surely, surely, I cried to myself, we ought to find some means of possessing the past more fully and completely than we do. Life is not worth living for many of us, if a want so desperate and yet so natural can never be satisfied. Memory is but a poor rudimentary thing that we had better be without, if it can only lead us to the verge of consummation like this, and madden us with a desire it cannot slake. The touch of a vanished hand, the sound of a voice that is still, the tender grace of a day that is dead, should be ours forever at our beck and call, by some exquisite and quite conceivable illusion of the senses.

Alas! alas! I have hardly the hope of ever meeting my beloved ones again in another life. Oh, to meet their too dimly remembered forms in this, just as they once were, by some trick of my own brain! To see them with the eye, and hear them with the ear, and tread with them the old obliterated ways as in a waking dream! It would be well worth going mad, to become such a self-conjurer as that.

I GOT back to my hotel in the Rue de la Michodière.

Prostrate with emotion and fatigue, the tarantella still jingling in my ears, and that haunting, beloved face, with its ineffable smile, still printed on the retina of my closed eyes, I fell asleep.

And then I dreamed a dream, and the first phase of my real, inner life began!

All the events of the day, distorted and exaggerated and jumbled together after the usual manner of dreams, wove themselves into a kind of nightmare and oppression. I was on my way to my old abode; everything that I met or saw was grotesque and impossible, yet had now the strange, vague charm of association and reminiscence, now the distressing sense of change and desolation.

As I got near to the avenue gate, instead of the school on my left there was a prison; and at the door a little thick-set jailer, three feet high and much deformed, and a little deformed jaileress no bigger than himself, were cunningly watching me out of the corners of their eyes, and toothlessly smiling. Presently they began to waltz together to an old familiar tune, with their enormous keys dangling at their sides; and they looked so funny that I laughed and applauded. But soon I perceived that their crooked faces were not really funny; indeed, they were fatal and terrible in the extreme, and I was soon conscious that these deadly dwarfs were trying to waltz between me and the avenue gate for which I was bound — to cut me off, that they might run me into the prison, where it was their custom to hang people of a Monday morning.

In an agony of terror I made a rush for the avenue gate, and there stood the Duchess of Towers, with mild surprise in her eyes and a kind smile — a heavenly vision of strength and reality.

«You are not dreaming true!» she said. «Don't be afraid — those little people don't exist! Give me your hand and come in here.»

And as I did so she waved the troglodytes away, and they vanished; and I felt that this was no longer a dream, but something else — some strange thing that had happened to me, some new life that I had woke up to.

For at the touch of her hand my consciousness, my sense of being I, myself, which hitherto in my dream (as in all previous dreams up to then) had been only partial, intermittent, and vague, suddenly blazed into full, consistent, practical activity — just as it is in life, when one is well awake and much interested in what is going on; only with perceptions far keener and more alert.

I knew perfectly who I was and what I was, and remembered all the events of the previous day. I was conscious that my real body, undressed and in bed, now lay fast asleep in a small room on the fourth floor of an *hôtel garni* in the Rue de la Michodière. I knew this perfectly; and yet here was my body too, just as substantial, with all my clothes on; my boots rather dusty, my shirt collar damp with the heat, for it was hot. With my disengaged hand I felt in my trousers pocket; there were my London latch-key, my purse, my penknife; my handkerchief in the breast pocket of my coat, and in its tail pockets my gloves and pipe-case, and the little water-color box I had bought that morning. I looked at my watch; it was going, and marked eleven. I pinched myself, I coughed, I did all one usually does under the pressure of some immense surprise, to assure myself that I was awake; and I *was*, and yet here I stood, actually hand in hand with a lady to whom I had never been introduced (and who seemed much tickled at my confusion); and staring now at her, now at my old school.

The prison had tumbled down like a house of cards, and lo! in its place was M. Saindou's *maison d'éducation*, just as it had been of old. I even recognized on the yellow wall the stamp of a hand in dry mud, made fifteen years ago by a day boy called Parisot, who had fallen down in the gutter close by, and thus left his mark on getting up again; and it had remained there for months, till it had been whitewashed away in the holidays. Here it was anew, after fifteen years.

The swallows were flying and twittering. A yellow omnibus was drawn up to the gates of the school; the horses stamped and neighed, and bit each other, as French horses always did in those days. The driver swore at them perfunctorily.

A crowd was looking on — le Père et la Mère François, Madame Liard the grocer's wife, and other people, whom I remembered at once with delight. Just in front of us a small boy and girl were looking on, like the rest, and I recognized the back and the cropped head and thin legs of Mimsey Seraskier.

A barrel organ was playing a pretty tune I knew quite well, and had forgotten.

The school gates opened, and M. Saindou, proud and full of self-importance (as he always was), and half a dozen boys whose faces and names were quite familiar to me, in smart white trousers and shining boots, and silken white bands round their left arms, got into the omnibus, and were driven away in a glorified manner — as it seemed — to heaven in a golden chariot. It was beautiful to see and hear.

I was still holding the duchess's hand, and felt the warmth of it through her glove; it stole up my arm like a magnetic current. I was in Elysium; a heavenly sense had come over me that at last my periphery had been victoriously invaded by a spirit other than mine — a most powerful and beneficent spirit. There was a blessed fault in my impenetrable armor of self, after all, and the genius of strength and charity and loving-kindness had found it out.

« Now you're dreaming true,» she said. « Where are those boys going?»

« To church, to make their *première communion*,» I replied.

« That's right. You're dreaming true because I've got you by the hand. Do you know that tune?»

I listened, and the words belonging to it came out of the past, and I said them to her, and she laughed again, with her eyes screwed up deliciously.

« Quite right — quite!» she exclaimed. « How odd that you should know them! How well you pronounce French for an Englishman! For you are Mr. Ibbetson, Lady Cray's architect?»

I assented, and she let go my hand.

The street was full of people — familiar forms and faces and voices, chatting together and looking down the road after the yellow omnibus; old attitudes, old tricks of gait and manner, old forgotten French ways of speech — all as it was long ago. Nobody noticed us, and we walked up the now deserted avenue.

The happiness, the enchantment of it all! Could it be that I was dead, that I had died suddenly in my sleep, at the hotel in the Rue de la Michodière? Could it be that the Duchess of Towers was dead too—had been killed by some accident on her way from St. Cloud to Paris? and that, both having died, so near each other, we had begun our eternal after-life in this heavenly fashion?

That was too good to be true, I reflected; some instinct told me that this was not death, but transcendent earthly life—and also, alas! that it would not endure forever!

I was deeply conscious of every feature in her face, every movement of her body, every detail of her dress,—more so than I could have been in actual life,—and said to myself, « Whatever this is, it is no dream.» But I felt there was about me the unspeakable elation which can come to us only in our waking moments when we are at our very best; and then only feebly, in comparison with this, and to many of us never. It never had to me, since that morning when I had found the little wheelbarrow.

I was also conscious, however, that the avenue itself had a slight touch of the dream in it. It was no longer quite right, and was getting out of drawing and perspective, so to speak. I had lost my stay—the touch of her hand.

« Are you still dreaming true, Mr. Ibbetson?»

« I am afraid not quite,» I replied.

« You must try by yourself a little—try hard. Look at this house; what is written on the portico?»

I saw written in gold letters the words « Tête Noire,» and said so.

She rippled with laughter, and said, « No, try again;» and just touched me with the tip of her finger for a moment.

I tried again, and said « Parvis Notre Dame.»

« That's rather better,» she said, and touched me again; and I read, « Parva sed Apta,» as I had so often read there before in old days.

«And now look at that old house over there,» pointing to my old home; « how many windows are there in the top story?»

I said seven.

« No; there are five. Look again!» and there were five; and the whole house was exactly, down to its minutest detail, as it had been once upon a time. I could see Thérèse through one of the windows, making my bed.

« That's better,» said the duchess; « you will soon do it—it's very easy—*ce n'est que le premier pas!* My father taught me;

you must always sleep on your back with your arms above your head, your hands clasped under it and your feet crossed, the right one over the left, unless you are left-handed; and you must never for a moment cease thinking of where you want to be in your dream till you are asleep and get there; and you must never forget in your dream where and what you were when awake. You must join the dream on to reality. Don't forget. And now I will say good-by; but before I go, give me both your hands, and look round everywhere as far as your eye can see."

It was hard to look away from her; her face drew my eyes, and through them all my heart; but I did as she told me, and took in the whole familiar scene, even to the distant woods of Ville d'Avray, a glimpse of which was visible through an opening in the trees; even to the smoke of a train making its way to Versailles, miles off; and the old telegraph, working its black arms on the top of Mont Valérien.

"Is it all right?" she asked. "That's well. Henceforward, whenever you come here, you will be safe as far as your sight can reach,—from this spot,—all through my introduction. See what it is to have a friend at court! No more little dancing jailers! And then you can gradually get farther by yourself.

"Out there, through that park, leads to the Bois de Boulogne—there's a gap in the hedge you can get through; but mind and make everything plain in front of you—*true*, before you go a step farther, or else you'll have to wake and begin it all over again. You have only to will it, and think yourself as awake, and it will come—on condition, of course, that you have been there before. And mind, also, you must take care how you touch things or people—you may hear, see, and smell; but you mustn't touch, nor pick flowers or leaves, nor move things about. It blurs the dream, like breathing on a window-pane. I don't know why, but it does. You must remember that everything here is dead and gone by. With you and me it is different; we're alive and real—that is, *I* am; and there would seem to be no mistake about your being real too, Mr. Ibbetson, by the grasp of your hands. But you're *not;* and why you are here, and what business you have in this my particular dream, I cannot understand; no living person has ever come into it before. I can't make it out. I suppose it's because I saw your reality this afternoon, looking out of the window at the Tête Noire, and you are just a stray figment of my over-tired brain — a very agreeable figment, I admit; but you don't exist here just now — you can't possibly; you are somewhere else, Mr. Ibbetson; dancing at Mabille, perhaps, or fast asleep somewhere, and dreaming of French churches and palaces, and public fountains, like a good young British architect — otherwise I shouldn't talk to you like this, you may be sure!

"Never mind. I am very glad to dream that I have been of use to you, and you are very welcome here, if it amuses you to come — especially as you are only a false dream of mine, for what else *can* you be? And now I must leave you: so good-by."

She disengaged her hands and laughed her angelic laugh, and then turned towards the park. I watched her tall straight figure and blowing skirts, and saw her follow some ladies and children into a thicket that I remembered well, and she was soon out of sight.

I felt as if all warmth had gone out of my life; as if a joy had taken flight; as if a precious something had withdrawn itself from my possession, and the gap in my periphery had closed again.

Long I stood in thought, with my eyes fixed on the spot where she had disappeared; and I felt inclined to follow, but then considered this would not have been discreet. For although she was only a false dream of mine, a mere recollection of the exciting and eventful day, a stray figment of my over-tired and excited brain — a *more* than agreeable figment (what else *could* she be!) — she was also a great lady, and had treated me, a perfect stranger and a perfect nobody, with singular courtesy and kindness; which I repaid, it is true, with a love so deep and strong that my very life was hers to do what she liked with, and always had been since I first saw her, and always would be as long as there was breath in my body! But this did not constitute an acquaintance without a proper introduction, even in France — even in a dream. Even in dreams one must be polite, even to stray figments of one's tired, sleeping brain.

And then what business had *she* in *this*, *my* particular dream — as she herself had asked of me?

But *was* it a dream? I remembered my lodgings at Pentonville, that I had left yesterday morning. I remembered what I was — why I came to Paris; I remembered the very bedroom at the Paris hotel where I was now fast asleep, its loudly ticking clock, and all the meagre furniture. And here was I, broad awake and conscious in the middle of an old avenue that had long ceased to exist — that had been built over by a huge brick edifice covered with newly painted trellis-work. I saw it,— this edifice,— myself, only twelve hours ago. And yet here was everything as it had been when I was a child; and all through the agency of this solid phantom of a lovely young English duchess, whose warm gloved hands I had only this minute been holding in mine! The scent of her gloves was still in my palm. I looked at my watch; it marked twenty-three minutes to twelve. All this had happened in less than three-quarters of an hour!

Pondering over all this in hopeless bewilderment, I turned my steps towards my old home, and to my surprise, was just able to look over the garden wall, which I had once thought about ten feet high.

Under the old apple-tree in full bloom sat my mother, darning small socks; with her flaxen side-curls (as it was her fashion to wear them) half concealing her face. My emotion and astonishment were immense. My heart beat fast. I felt its pulse in my temples, and my breath was short.

At a little green table that I remembered well sat a small boy, rather quaintly dressed in a bygone fashion, with a frill round his wide shirt collar, and his golden hair cut quite close at the top, and rather long at the sides and back. It was Gogo Pasquier. He seemed a very nice little boy. He had pen and ink and copy-book before him, and a gilt-edged volume bound in red morocco. I knew it at a glance; it was 'Elegant Extracts.' The dog Médor lay asleep in the shade. The bees were droning among the nasturtiums and convolvulus.

A little girl ran up the avenue from the porter's lodge and pushed the garden gate, which rang the bell as it opened, and she went into the garden, and I followed her; but she took no notice of me, nor did the others. It was Mimsey Seraskier.

I went and sat at my mother's feet, and looked long in her face.

I must not speak to her nor touch her — not even touch her busy hand with my lips, or I should «blur the dream.»

I got up and looked over the boy Gogo's shoulder. He was translating Gray's Elegy into French; he had not got very far, and seemed to be stumped by the line —

«And leaves the world to darkness and to me.»

Mimsey was silently looking over his other shoulder, her thumb in her mouth, one arm on the back of his chair. She seemed to be stumped also; it was an awkward line to translate.

I stooped and put my hand to Médor's nose, and felt his warm breath. He wagged his rudiment of a tail, and whimpered in his sleep. Mimsey said: —

« Regarde Médor, comme il remue la queue! *C'est le Prince Charmant qui lui chatouille le bout du nez.* »

Said my mother, who had not spoken hitherto: —

« Do speak English, Mimsey, please. »

O my God! My mother's voice, so forgotten, yet so familiar, so unutterably dear! I rushed to her and threw myself on my knees at her feet, and seized her hand and kissed it, crying, « Mother, mother! »

A strange blur came over everything; the sense of reality was lost. All became as a dream — a beautiful dream, but only a dream; and I woke.

BARTY JOSSELIN AT SCHOOL

From ‹The Martian›

INDEED, even from his early boyhood, he was the most extraordinarily gifted creature I have ever known, or even heard of; a kind of spontaneous humorous Crichton to whom all things came easily — and life itself as an uncommonly good joke. During that summer term of 1847 I did not see very much of him. He was in the class below mine, and took up with Laferté and little Bussy-Rabutin, who were first-rate boys, and laughed at everything he said, and worshiped him. So did everybody else, sooner or later; indeed, it soon became evident that he was a most exceptional little person.

In the first place, his beauty was absolutely angelic, as will be readily believed by all who have known him since. The mere sight of him as a boy made people pity his father and mother for being dead!

Then he had a charming gift of singing little French and English ditties, comic or touching, with his delightful fresh young pipe, and accompanying himself quite nicely on either piano or guitar without really knowing a note of music. Then he could draw caricatures that we boys thought inimitable, much funnier than Cham's or Bertall's or Gavarni's, and collected and treasured up. I have dozens of them now — they make me laugh still, and bring back memories of which the charm is indescribable; and their pathos to me!

And then how funny he was himself, without effort, and with a fun that never failed! He was a born buffoon of the graceful kind,— more whelp or kitten than monkey — ever playing the fool, in and out of season, but somehow always apropos; and French boys love a boy for that more than anything else; or did in those days.

. . . .

His constitution, inherited from a long line of frugal seafaring Norman ancestors (not to mention another long line of well-fed, well-bred Yorkshire squires), was magnificent. His spirits never failed. He could see the satellites of Jupiter with the naked eye; this was often tested by M. Dumollard, maître de mathématiques (et de cosmographie), who had a telescope, which, with a little good-will on the gazer's part, made Jupiter look as big as the moon, and its moons like stars of the first magnitude.

His sense of hearing was also exceptionally keen. He could hear a watch tick in the next room, and perceive very high sounds to which ordinary human ears are deaf (this was found out later); and when we played blindman's buff on a rainy day, he could, blindfolded, tell every boy he caught hold of — not by feeling him all over like the rest of us, but by the mere smell of his hair, or his hands, or his blouse! No wonder he was so much more alive than the rest of us! According to the amiable, modest, polite, delicately humorous, and ever tolerant and considerate Professor Max Nordau, this perfection of the olfactory sense proclaims poor Barty a degenerate! I only wish there were a few more like him, and that I were a little more like him myself!

By the way, how proud young Germany must feel of its enlightened Max, and how fond of him, to be sure! *Mes compliments!*

But the most astounding thing of all (it seems incredible, but all the world knows it by this time, and it will be accounted for later on) is that at certain times and seasons Barty knew by an infallible instinct *where the north was*, to a point. Most of my readers will remember his extraordinary evidence as a witness in the « Rangoon » trial, and how this power was tested in open court, and how important were the issues involved, and how he refused to give any explanation of a gift so extraordinary.

It was often tried at school by blindfolding him, and turning him round and round till he was giddy, and asking him to point out where the North Pole was, or the North Star, and seven or eight times out of ten the answer was unerringly right. When he failed, he knew beforehand that for the time being he had lost the power, but could never say why. Little Doctor Larcher could never get over his surprise at this strange phenomenon, nor explain it; and often brought some scientific friend from Paris to test it, who was equally nonplussed.

When cross-examined, Barty would merely say: —

« Quelquefois je sais — quelquefois je ne sais pas — mais quand je sais, je sais, et il n'y pas à s'y tromper! »

Indeed, on one occasion that I remember well a very strange thing happened; he not only pointed out the north with absolute accuracy, as he stood carefully blindfolded in the gymnastic ground, after having been turned and twisted again and again — but still blindfolded, he vaulted the wire fence and ran round to the refectory door, which served as the home at rounders, all of us following; and there he danced a surprising dance of his own invention, that he called 'La Paladine,' the most humorously graceful and grotesque exhibition I ever saw; and then, taking a ball out of his pocket, he shouted, « À l'amandier! » and threw the ball. Straight and swift it flew, and hit the almond tree, which was quite twenty yards off; and after this he ran round the yard from base to base, as at « la balle au camp, » till he reached the camp again.

« If ever he goes blind, » said the wondering M. Mérovée, « he'll never need a dog to lead him about. »

« He must have some special friend above! » said Madame Germain (Mérovée's sister, who was looking on).

Prophetic words! I have never forgotten them, nor the tear that glistened in each of her kind eyes as she spoke. She was a deeply religious and very emotional person, and loved Barty almost as if he were a child of her own.

Such women have strange intuitions.

Barty was often asked to repeat this astonishing performance before skeptical people — parents of boys, visitors, etc. — who had been told of it, and who believed he could not have been properly blindfolded; but he could never be induced to do so.

There was no mistake about the blindfolding — I helped in it myself; and he afterwards told me the whole thing was «aussi simple que bonjour» if once he felt the north — for then, with his back to the refectory door, he knew exactly the position and distance of every tree from where he was.

«It's all nonsense about my going blind and being able to do without a dog,» he added; «I should be just as helpless as any other blind man, unless I was in a place I knew as well as my own pocket — like this play-ground! Besides, *I* shan't go blind; nothing will ever happen to *my* eyes — they're the strongest and best in the whole school!»

He said this exultingly, dilating his nostrils and chest; and looked proudly up and around, like Ajax defying the lightning.

«But what *do* you feel when you feel the north, Barty — a kind of tingling?» I asked.

«Oh — I feel where it is — as if I'd got a mariner's compass trembling inside my stomach — and as if I wasn't afraid of anybody or anything in the world — as if I could go and have my head chopped off and not care a fig.»

«Ah, well — I can't make it out — I give it up,» I exclaimed.

«So do I,» exclaims Barty.

«But tell me, Barty,» I whispered — «*have* you — have you *really* got a — a — *special friend above?*»

«Ask no questions and you'll get no lies,» said Barty, and winked at me one eye after the other — and went about his business, and I about mine.

WILLIAM DUNBAR

(1465?–1530?)

A picturesque figure in a picturesque age is that of William Dunbar, court minstrel to James IV., and as Sir Walter Scott declared, "a poet unrivaled by any that Scotland has ever produced." Little of his personal history is known. Probably he was a native of East Lothian, a member of the family of the Earl of March, and a graduate of St. Andrews University about the year 1479. After his college days he joined the order of Franciscans and became a mendicant friar, preaching the queer sermons of his time, and begging his way through England and France. Yet in these pilgrimages the young scholar learned useful habits of self-denial, saw new phases of human character, and above all enjoyed that close communion with nature which is the need of the poet. Over and over there is a reflection of this life in that fanciful verse, which has caught the color of the morning hours when the hedgerows are wet and the grass dewy, when the wild roses scent the roadside and the lark is at matins — verse full of the joy of life and the hope of youth.

After some years of this vagabond life, Dunbar left the Franciscans and attached himself to the court, where he speedily became a favorite. His day was one of pageant and show, of masque and spectacle, and into its gay assemblage of knights and courtiers, ladies and great nobles, Dunbar fitted perfectly. When an embassy was sent to England to negotiate the royal marriage with Margaret Tudor, Dunbar went along, being specially accredited by the king. He became a favorite with the young Princess, and a poem written in honor of the city of London, and one descriptive of the Queen's Progress, afford a faithful and valuable memorial of this mission. History is fortunate when she secures a poet as her scribe. Dunbar is principally known by his three poems 'The Thistle and the Rose,' 'The Golden Targe,' and 'The Dance of the Seven Deadly Sins.'

The first of these is an allegory celebrating the nuptials of the king. It suggests of course the allegories of Chaucer; but Dunbar's muse is his own, and the poem springs fresh and clear from native fonts. The poet represents himself as awakened by Aurora on a spring morning and told to do homage to May. Through the symbolism of the court of Nature, who crowns the Lion and Eagle, commissions the Thistle and Rose as her handmaidens, and orders their praises sung by the assembled birds of earth, the political significance of the allegory appears. But ‹The Thistle and the Rose,› which is thus made to illustrate the union between the two great houses of Scotland and England, is far more than the poem of an occasion. It is full of the melody and fragrance of spring, saturated with that sensuous delight which at this bountiful season fills the veins of Nature. Here Dunbar is no longer the court laureate, but the begging friar, wandering through the green lanes and finding bed and board under the free skies.

‹The Golden Targe› is more artificial in construction. It is another allegory, descriptive of an encounter between Cupid and Reason, who is defended by a golden targe or shield from the attacks of love. Here again the rural landscape forms a background to his mimic action. Amazons dressed in green fight the battle of Cupid, and vanquish Reason, then magically vanish and leave the poet to awake from his dream. ‹The Golden Targe› was a poem to be read in the royal presence, when the court assembled after a day's hunting or an afternoon of archery; but it is filled with the ethereal loveliness which only the true poet beholds.

It is in ‹The Dance of the Seven Deadly Sins› that Dunbar touches the note of seriousness, which characterizes his race and his individual genius. This satire is not so unsparing an indictment as the vision of Piers Ploughman, and yet it provokes inevitable comparison with the older poem. In a dream the poet sees heaven and hell opened. It is the eve of Ash Wednesday, and the Devil has commanded a dance to be performed by those spirits that had never received absolution. In obedience to this command the Seven Deadly Sins present a masque before his Satanic Majesty, and it is in the description of this grisly performance that Dunbar reveals a new aspect of power. The comedy here is not comic, but grotesque and horrid. The vision of the Scot is the vision that came to the poets of the ‹Inferno› and ‹Paradise Lost,› and it shows that his imagination was capable of the loftiest flights.

After the melancholy day of Flodden Field, the Scottish laureateship ceased to exist, but it is remarkable that so prominent a man as Dunbar should so completely have disappeared from contemporary view that his subsequent career and the time of his death are matters of doubt. His period is given as between the years 1465 and 1530, but these dates are only approximate.

Had Dunbar held his genius in hand as completely as did Chaucer, his accomplishment would doubtless have been greater than it was. Yet his place in literature is that of one of the most important poets of the fifteenth century, the age of Caxton and book-making, the time of that first flush of radiance which ushered in the full day of Spenser and Shakespeare.

THE THISTLE AND THE ROSE

QUHEN Merche wes with variand windis past,
And Appryle had, with her silver schouris,
Tane leif at Nature with ane orient blast,
And lusty May, that muddir is of flouris,
Had maid the birdis to begyn thair houris
Amang the tendir odouris reid and quhyt,
Quhois armony to heir it wes delyt:

In bed at morrow, sleiping as I lay,
Me thocht Aurora with hir cristall ene
In at the window lukit by the day,
And halsit me, with visage paill and grene;
On quhois hand a lark sang fro the splene:—
Awalk, luvaris, out of you slomering;
Sé hou the lusty morrow dois up spring.

Me thocht fresche May befoir my bed up stude,
In weid depaynt of mony diverss hew,
Sobir, benyng, and full of mansuetude,
In brycht atteir of flouris forgit new,
Hevinly of color, quhyt, reid, broun and blew,
Balmit in dew, and gilt with Phebus bemys;
Quhyll all the house illumynit of her lemys.

Slugird, sche said, awalk annone for schame,
And in my honour sum thing thou go wryt;
The lark hes done the mirry day proclame,
To raise up luvaris with confort and delyt;
Yit nocht incressis thy curage to indyt,
Quhois hairt sum tyme hes glaid and blisfull bene,
Sangis to mak undir the levis grene.

Than callit sche all flouris that grew on feild,
Discirnyng all thair fassionis and effeiris,
Upone the awfull Thrissil sche beheld,
And saw him kepit with a busche of speiris;
Considering him so able for the weiris,
A radius croun of rubeis sche him gaif,
And said, In feild go furth and fend the laif:

And sen thou art a King, thou be discreit;
Herb without vertew thow hald nocht of sic pryce
As herb of vertew and of odour sueit;

And lat no nettill vyle, and full of vyce,
Hir fallow to the gudly flour-de-lyce;
Nor latt no wyld weid, full of churlicheness,
Compair hir till the lilleis nobilness.

Nor hald non udir flour in sic denty
As the fresche Rois, of cullour reid and quhyt:
For gife thow dois, hurt is thyne honesty;
Considring that no flour is so perfyt,
So full of vertew, plesans, and delyt,
So full of blisful angeilik bewty,
Imperiall birth, honour and dignité.

FROM ‹THE GOLDEN TARGE›

Bryght as the stern of day begouth to schyne
Quhen gone to bed war Vesper and Lucyne,
I raise, and by a rosere did me rest:
Up sprang the goldyn candill matutyne,
With clere depurit bemes cristallyne
Glading the mery foulis in thair nest;
Or Phebus was in purpur cape revest
Up raise the lark, the hevyn's menstrale fyne
In May, in till a morrow myrthfullest.

Full angellike thir birdis sang thair houris
Within thair courtyns grene, in to thair bouris,
Apparalit quhite and red, wyth blomes suete;
Anamalit was the felde with all colouris,
The perly droppis schuke in silvir schouris;
Quhill all in balme did branch and levis flete,
To part fra Phebus did Aurora grete;
Hir cristall teris I saw hyng on the flouris
Quhilk he for lufe all drank up with his hete.

For mirth of May, wyth skippis and wyth hoppis,
The birdis sang upon the tender croppis,
With curiouse notis, as Venus chapell clerkis;
The rosis yong, new spreding of their knoppis,
War powderit brycht with hevinly beriall droppis,
Throu bemes rede, birnyng as ruby sperkis;
The skyes rang for schoutyng of the larkis.

NO TREASURE AVAILS WITHOUT GLADNESS

Be merry, man, and tak not sair in mind
The wavering of this wretchit warld of sorrow;
To God be humble, and to thy friend be kind,
And with thy neighbour gladly lend and borrow:
His chance to-nicht, it may be thine to-morrow;
Be blyth in heart for ony aventúre;
For oft with wise men't has been said aforrow
Without Gladnéss availis no Treasúre.

Mak thee gude cheer of it that God thee sendis,
For warldis wrak but weilfare nocht availis;
Nae gude is thine, save only that thou spendis,
Remenant all thou brukis but with bailis:
Seek to soláce when sadness thee assailis;
In dolour lang thy life may not indure,
Wherefore of comfort set up all thy sailis;
Without Gladnéss availis no Treasúre.

Follow on pitý, flee trouble and debate,
With famous folkis hald thy company;
Be charitáble and humble in thine estate,
For warldly honour lastis but a cry:
For trouble in erd tak no mélancholý;
Be rich in patience, give thou in guids be puir;
Who livis merry he livis michtily;
Without Gladnéss availis no Treasúre.

Thou sees thir wretches set with sorrow and care
To gather guids in all their livis space;
And when their bags are full, their selves are bare,
And of their riches but the keeping has:
While others come to spend it that has grace,
Whilk of thy winning no labour had nor cure.
Tak thou example, and spend with merriness;
Without Gladnéss availis no Treasúre.

Though all the work that e'er had living wicht
Were only thine, no more thy part does fall
But meat, drink, clais, and of the lave a sicht,
Yet to the Judge thou sall give compt of all;
Ane reckoning richt comes of ane ragment small:
But just and joyous, do to none injúre,
Ane Truth sall mak thee strang as ony wall;
Without Gladnéss availis no Treasúre.

JEAN VICTOR DURUY

(1811–1894)

Duruy, whose monumental works upon Grecian and Roman history have been worthily reproduced in England under the editorship of Professor Mahaffy, and in America in sumptuous illustrated editions, was a figure of the first importance both in the educational and in the distinctly literary history of France, throughout nearly half the present century. He became one of the «Immortals» in 1884, succeeding to the chair of Mignet; but his ‹History of Ancient Greece,› which was published in 1862, had been already crowned by the Academy. His more extensive ‹History of the Grecian People,› published in 1885–1887, won from the Academy the Jean Renaud prize of 10,000 francs.

Jean Victor Duruy

He was born September 11th, 1811, of a family employed in the Gobelins tapestry works in Paris. His predilection for study secured him an opportunity to enter the College of Sainte-Barbe, whence he passed to the Normal School.

When he was twenty-two he began teaching history, first at Rheims, and then in the College of Henry IV. in Paris. Here he began his literary work, mostly upon school-books, of which he wrote many, mainly historical and geographical. He received the degree of Doctor of Letters in 1853, and became successively Inspector of the Academy of Paris, Master of Conferences at the Normal School, Professor of History at the Polytechnic School, and Inspector-General of Secondary Instruction. During the whole of this period he had been engaged with secondary classes, and had become strongly impressed by the faulty condition of the primary and secondary schools. In 1863 Louis Napoleon put him at the head of the educational system of the empire as Minister of Public Instruction. This appointment gave him the opportunity to carry out numerous and important secularizing reforms which brought him into sharp collision with the clerical party. He held his post as minister for six years — six years of struggle with the parsimonious disposition of the administration upon the one hand, and with the hostile clericals upon the other.

The measures in which he was especially interested were the reorganization of the Museum of Natural History, the extension of scientific study, the introduction of the study of modern and contemporary history in the lyceums (a dreadful experiment, according to his opponents), gratuitous and compulsory primary education, the improvement of the night schools, and popular classes for adults. He was to a large extent successful in all these, except in the direction of compulsory education. The efforts which he made to improve the instruction given to young girls brought upon him the tempest. The bishops, with Monsignor Dupanloup of Orléans at their head, raised a veritable crusade, and Pope Pio Nono himself at length entered the hostile ranks. Probably in part because of this conflict, he was superseded in 1869 and was made a member of the Senate, from which he retired to private life, and the prosecution of his literary labors on the fall of the empire, in the following year. He died in 1894.

As an author his style is clear and direct. Among his numerous works the most important are the two great histories, for which, as for other achievements, honors were heaped upon him. In these he laid particular stress upon the *milieu* — the conditions of place, time, and race. Consequently he has therein written the history of the Greek and Roman peoples, and not merely the history of Greece and Rome, — and has pictured them, so far as possible, as they looked and felt and thought and acted. He exhibits, for example, the growth of the magnificent power of Rome, and its decadence; and shows the all-conquering empire subdued to the manners, the gods, and the institutions of the conquered. And worse: — «They had become enamored of the arts, the letters, and the philosophy of Greece, and dying Greece had avenged itself by transmitting to them the corruption which had dishonored its old age.»

The drift of his argument appears in this paragraph, in which he sums up his story of the Eternal City: — «In the earlier portion of its history may be seen the happy effects of a progressively liberal policy; in the later the baneful consequences of absolute power, governing a servile society through a venal administration.»

THE NATIONAL POLICY

From the 'History of Rome'

THE Roman power, till then confined to the West, was now to penetrate into another universe,—that of the successors of Alexander. The eternal glory of Rome, the immense benefaction by which she effaces the memory of so many unjust wars, is to have reunited those two worlds that in all former ages were divided in interest, and strangers to each other; is to have mingled and fused the brilliant but corrupt civilization of the East with the barbaric energy of the West. The Mediterranean became a Roman lake,—*mare nostrum*, they said,—and the same life circulated on all its shores, called for the first and the last time to a common existence.

In this work were employed a century and a half of struggles and diplomacy; for Rome, working for a patient aristocracy and not for a man, was not compelled to attain her end at a bound. Instead of rearing suddenly one of those colossal monarchies formed like the statue of gold with feet of clay, she founded slowly an empire which fell only under the weight of years and of the Northern hordes. After Zama she could have attempted the conquest of Africa, but she left Carthage and the Numidians to enfeeble each other. After Cynoscephalæ and Magnesia, Greece and Asia were all ready for the yoke, but she accorded them fifty years more of liberty. This was because, along with the pride of the Roman name and the necessity for dominion, she always retained some of her ancient virtues. The Popiliuses were more numerous than the Verreses. Now she preferred to rule the world; later she will put it to pillage. Thus, wherever Rome saw strength she sent her legions; all power was broken; the ties of States and leagues were shattered; and when her soldiers were recalled they left behind them only weakness and anarchy. But the task of the legions accomplished, that of the Senate began. After force came craft and diplomacy. Those senators, grown old amidst the terrors of the second Punic war, seemed now to have less pleasure in arms than in the game of politics,—the first, in all ages, of Italian arts.

Several other causes dictated this policy of reserve. Against the Gauls, the Samnites, Pyrrhus, and Hannibal,—in other words, for the defense of Latium and of Italy,— Rome had employed all her strength; it was then a question of her existence: whereas, in the wars with Greece and with Asia, her ambition and her pride alone were interested; and wisdom demanded that some relaxation be given to the plebeians and the allies. The Senate had moreover too many affairs on its hands — the wars with Spain, with Corsica, with Cisalpina, and with Istria — to admit of its becoming deeply involved in the East. Therefore two legions only will fight Philip and Antiochus — that will suffice to conquer, but would be too little to despoil them. Furthermore, the Senate believed that in penetrating into this Greek world, where an old glory concealed so much weakness, they could not accord too much to prudence. These pitiless enemies of the Volscians and the Samnites will not proceed in their next wars by exterminating their adversaries and wasting their country. «It was not with such a purpose,» said they, «that they came to pour out their blood; they took in hand the cause of oppressed Greece.» And that language and that policy they will not change after victory. The first act of Flamininus, on the day after Cynoscephalæ, was to proclaim the liberty of the Greeks. All who bore that respected name seemed to have the right to Roman protection; and the little Greek cities of Caria, and of the coasts of Asia and Thrace, received with astonishment their liberty from a people that they hardly knew. All were captivated by this apparent generosity. None perceived that in restoring independence to the cities and States, Rome wished to break up the confederations that sought to reorganize and would perhaps have given new force to Greece. In isolating them and attaching them to herself by grateful ties, she placed them almost insensibly under her influence. She made allies of them; and every one knows what the allies of Rome became. Thus the Senate was so well satisfied with this policy, which created division everywhere and awakened extinct rivalries, that for half a century it followed no other.

RESULTS OF THE ROMAN DOMINION

From the ‹History of Rome›

Although in literature Rome was but the echo of Greece, she civilized all the Western world, for which the Greeks had done nothing. Her language, out of which sprang the various languages of the Romance nations, is in case of need a means of communication among scholars of all countries, and her books will always remain — a wise selection being made — the best for the higher culture of the mind. They have merited above all others the title of *litteræ humaniores*, the literature by which men are made. A cardinal, reading the ‹Thoughts of Marcus Aurelius› (written in Greek, it is true, but written by a Roman), exclaimed, « My soul blushes redder than my scarlet at sight of the virtues of this Gentile.»

Suppose Rome destroyed by Pyrrhus or Hannibal, before Marius and Cæsar had driven the German tribes back from Gaul: their invasion would have been effected five centuries sooner; and since they would have found opposed to them only other barbarians, what a long night would have settled down upon the world!

It is true that when the Roman people had laid hands upon the treasures of Alexander's successors, the scandal of their orgies exceeded for a century anything that the East had ever seen; that their amusements were sanguinary games or licentious plays; that the Roman mind, after receiving a temporary benefit from Greek philosophy, went astray in Oriental mysticism; and that finally, after having loved liberty, Rome accepted despotism, as if willing to astonish the world as much by her great corruption as she did by the greatness of her empire.

But can we say that no other age or nation has known servility of soul, licentiousness in public amusements, and the conspicuous depravity in morals that is always to be seen where indolence and wealth are united?

To the legacies left by Rome which have now been enumerated, we must add another, which ranks among the most precious. Notwithstanding the poetic piety of Virgil, and Livy's official credulity, the dominant note of Latin literature is the indifference of Horace, when it is not the daring skepticism of

Lucretius. To Cicero, Seneca, Tacitus, and the great jurisconsults, the prime necessity was the free possession of themselves, that independence of philosophic thought which they owed to Greece. This spirit, begotten of pure reason, was almost stifled during the Middle Ages. It reappeared when antiquity was recovered. From that day the renascent world set forward again; and in the new path France, heir of Athens and of Rome, was long her guide — for art in its most charming form, and for thought, developed in the light.

Upon a medal of Constantine his son presents to him a globe surmounted by a phœnix, symbol of immortality. For once the courtiers were not in the wrong. The sacred bird which springs from her own ashes is a fitting emblem of this old Rome, dead fifteen centuries ago, yet alive to-day through her genius: *Siamo Romani.*